CONTRACTOR'S BUSINESS REFERENCE MANUAL

Robert Gregory

D1609033

KAPLAN AEC EDUCATION

President: Roy Lipner
Vice President of Product Development and Publishing: Evan M. Butterfield
Editorial Project Manager: Karen Goodfriend
Director of Production: Daniel Frey
Quality Assurance Editor: David Shaw
Typesetter: Janet Schroeder
Creative Director: Lucy Jenkins

Published by Kaplan® AEC Education
30 South Wacker Drive
Chicago, IL 60606-7481
(312) 836-4400
www.kaplanaeccontracting.com

CONTENTS

INTRODUCTION   V
ACKNOWLEDGMENTS   VI

1   BUSINESS ORGANIZATION
Types of Business Organizations   1
Making a Business Organization Decision   9
Sales Tax   11
Tax Deductions   11
Summary   11

2   BUSINESS MANAGEMENT
Getting Started   13
Market Research   13
The Business Plan   17
Marketing the Business   19
Managing the Business   22
Ethics   23
Summary   24

3   ESTIMATING AND BIDDING
The Bidding Process   25
Estimating   28
Estimating Methods   36
The Formal Bid   37
Sample Estimate and Bid   38
Summary   40

4   CONTRACTS
Written Contract   41
Contract Validity   42
Rights and Responsibilities   46
Additional Contract Categories   47
Miscellaneous Contract Considerations   48

Construction Contract Types   52
Contract Payments   54
Claims   56
Liens   56
Summary   58

5   RISK MANAGEMENT
Loss Prevention   59
Types of Insurance   60
Bonds   63
The Miller Act   65
Summary   66

6   PROJECT MANAGEMENT
Planning and Scheduling   67
Project Supervision   72
Summary   78

7   EMPLOYMENT LAW
Equal Employment Opportunity Issues   79
Wage and Work Hour Issues   80
Hiring Issues   84
Contracts with the Federal Government   85
Employee Benefits Issues   86
Summary   87

8   ACCOUNTING
Definitions of Terms   90
Depreciation   93
Record Keeping Systems   93
Accounting Methods   95
Financial Reports (Statements)   98
Financial Ratios   103

Job Cost Analysis   105

Summary   106

9   PAYROLL TAXES

Independent Contractors   107

Employees   108

Payroll Taxes   108

Business Income Taxes   113

Record Keeping   114

Sales and Use Taxes   114

Summary   115

10   OCCUPATIONAL SAFETY AND HEALTH

Personal Protective Equipment   117

Asbestos and Lead Exposure   119

OSHA Record Keeping   122

OSHA Penalties   128

Summary   130

11   ENVIRONMENTAL ISSUES

Asbestos   133

Lead   134

Erosion and Sediment (E&S) Control   135

Hazardous Materials   135

Underground Utilities   135

Wetlands   136

Summary   136

APPENDIXES

A   BUSINESS DEVELOPMENT

Government Web Sites   137

Business Forms and Worksheets   138

Writing a Business Plan   139

B   CONTRACTS

Property Improvement Agreement   170

Subcontractor Agreement   174

Change Order (Contractor)   177

Change Order (Owner/Architect)   178

C   TAX INFORMATION

Calendar of Federal Taxes for Sole Proprietors   180

Calendar of Federal Taxes for Partnerships   181

Calendar of Federal Taxes for Corporations   182

Calendar of Federal Taxes for Subchapter S Corporations   183

IRS Publication 15, Circular E   185

Form W-4   253

D   EMPLOYMENT LAW

Handy Reference Guide to the Fair Labor Standards Act   256

General Information about Form I-9   266

The I-9 Process in a Nutshell   267

Employment Eligibility Verification and Form I-9   274

E   OSHA

29 CFR OSHA 1904   278

GLOSSARY   307
INDEX   312

INTRODUCTION

INTRODUCTION

The *Contractor's Business Reference Manual* is designed to provide a new contractor with the necessary tools for understanding what is initially required of the profession. It is a compilation of the fundamental concepts that must be understood in order to enter the contracting business.

Many decisions must be made before starting a contracting business: choosing a type of business structure, a bank, an accounting system, and employees. The *Contractor's Business Reference Manual* explains in simple terms what it takes to become a contractor and to operate a successful contracting business. This manual provides guidance in making informed decisions about a type of business, insurance, accounting, and other essentials.

The material in this manual was compiled based on nearly 40 years of working with contractors in the field and in the classroom. The contracting profession is populated with individuals who have incredible talent and ability and create marvels of form and beauty. However, a few contractors have demonstrated instances of incredible misjudgment, and they become subjects of study for those who develop training programs. We learn from them all, and it is always interesting.

A manual of this scope is not an individual effort. I would like to thank my editor at Kaplan AEC, Karen Goodfriend, for her continued effort to make this a readable document. Then there is Allison Camacho who conducted extensive research and was always my cheerleader. Thank you, Allison.

My gratitude is extended to the experts who gave their time to return calls, explain minutiae of regulation, and clarify issues. These include: Warren Timmons of Wilson, Timmons, and Wallerstein Insurance who made insurance policy issues understandable; the staff of the Virginia Department of Professional and Occupational Regulation for answering e-mails immediately and in detail; the incredibly patient folk at the State Corporation Commissions; and other federal, state, and local agencies who were contacted during this writing. I am impressed that these dedicated and knowledgeable people took their time to help with inquiries that often went beyond the normal daily routine.

A special thanks to numerous contractors who shared their experiences, along with their disasters, so that we as contractors can learn where to walk and from where we need to run.

It is my hope that the reader of this manual is a success in the contracting business. The job is hard work, never boring, and incredibly rewarding. See you on the job site.

Robert Gregory
Contractors Institute, Inc.
Oilville, Virginia

ACKNOWLEDGMENTS

The publisher would like to thank the following people for their invaluable review of material during development. Their comments are greatly appreciated.

Paul D. Naylor, PhD, Psychometric Consultant
Jayme L. Loy, Examination Administration Specialist

Additionally, the following companies provided permission to reprint their materials:

ABCA Forms, Inc.
www.ABCAForms.com

Dearborn Trade Publishing
www.DearbornTrade.com

CHAPTER **1**

BUSINESS ORGANIZATION

The first step in establishing a contracting business is to decide on the type of business to form. Business types include sole proprietorships, partnerships, and corporations. There are advantages and disadvantages to each type of business. Once the type of business is determined, many additional steps are required to establish the business, including choosing a name, registering with the proper agencies, setting up a record keeping system, choosing an accounting system, developing a business plan, and selecting a bank.

TYPES OF BUSINESS ORGANIZATIONS

The various business types that can be established are: sole proprietorship, partnership, or corporation. There are differences among the types in ease of getting started, liability limits, and tax advantages.

Sole Proprietorships

A **sole proprietorship** is easy to set up and easy to terminate. There are minimum regulations to deal with, but the contractor, as with any business, still must comply with all licensing, labor, and tax laws at the federal, state, and local levels. The business is owned solely by the proprietor, and there are no partners in the business. Because there are no other people to answer to regarding business decisions, the sole proprietor makes all decisions necessary to operate the business.

The benefit of a sole proprietorship is the minimal regulation governing the company. The only registration necessary may be to a local agency to reserve a unique name for the company under which it will operate, usually called "doing business as" (DBA).

The locality may also require contractors to obtain special use permits to operate their businesses from their homes, a common practice for small contracting companies. The permit is usually a formality, but there is a small fee for the advertisement and mailing of letters to notify the neighbors. If there are no neighbor objections and the contractors have agreed to restrictions (such as not parking construction equipment on the front lawn), then the use permit will normally be granted.

Duration is the legal life or existence of the company. Because the sole proprietor is considered to be the business, if the contractor dies, the business ceases to exist. Many contractors operate as sole proprietors and hire family members. If the proprietor dies and the family wishes to continue operating, the business must be reestablished and a new license obtained.

Liability. Even though the business is registered as a DBA, no difference exists under the law between the business and the sole proprietor owner. If there is a lawsuit, all of the assets of the contractor, not just those of the business, are at risk. Good record keeping, excellent work performance, and adequate insurance policies are essential for a sole proprietor.

Some personal property may be protected from lawsuit by making it a "joint entirety." A *joint entirety* gives the spouse ownership in a portion of the property so that it cannot be considered a company asset. There are reasonable exceptions to this protection. For instance, a bulldozer typically is used in construction and not used to take the kids to soccer. But, an SUV can be used for personal activities, not strictly for construction tasks. A bulldozer cannot be made joint entirety property, but an SUV may be titled to both the company owner and spouse. A jointly owned house can be made a joint entirety. In order to clearly establish the property as a company asset, the SUV's title should be in the name of the company and the company name should be clearly painted on the door or hood of the vehicle. Protection of these assets makes insurance critical, and it may be worthwhile to consult with an attorney knowledgeable about liability issues.

Taxes. A sole proprietorship is taxed at the individual income rate. Profits made during the year are reported as income to the sole proprietor. As of this writing, a 15.3 percent self-employment tax on the first $94,200 profits is charged, which basically consists of Social Security and Medicare taxes at the full tax rate.

The sole proprietor, who is also an employer, will pay out of profits Social Security benefits and Medicare tax for each employee. There is also federal unemployment tax charged on a certain percentage of each employee's wages, and there may be a state unemployment tax (this varies by state). The sole proprietor is not responsible for withholding employment taxes for independent contractors. Tax law is covered in Chapter 9, and it is important to note that the law changes every year. Visit the Internal Revenue Service (IRS) Web site, *www.irs.gov,* periodically and keep current on relevant tax laws.

A business loss reduces profit and, subsequently, taxes due. The loss offsets the personal income of the contractor, and filing jointly with a spouse, can also offset the income of the spouse as well. Operations of the company that incur an expense are deducted from profits. And if the company has suffered a loss, the contractor's tax obligation will be less. (See Figure 1.1.)

Partnerships

A **partnership** is a for profit business operated by two or more people. Partners may be equal in investment and ownership, or they be may be unequal, such as in a limited partnership. There are three types of partnership organization: general, limited, and limited liability company (LLC). All partnerships offer considerable freedom in the operation of the business because they are not regulated as heavily as a corporation.

FIGURE 1.1

Advantages and
Disadvantages of a
Sole Proprietorship
LEAST REGULATED

Advantages	■ A sole proprietorship can be easily created.
	■ A sole proprietorship has few regulations to follow and few forms to file.
	■ The sole proprietor (contractor) makes all business decisions.
	■ A sole proprietorship is eligible to establish a deductible Keogh Plan for retirement.
	■ Health care costs are deductible.
Disadvantages	■ The sole proprietor (contractor) has unlimited personal liability.
	■ The sole proprietorship ceases with the proprietor's death. (Family members must reapply for a new license to continue the business.)
	■ All funds to operate the sole proprietorship come from the proprietor's personal assets or credit.
	■ Profits to the sole proprietorship are taxed as the proprietor's ordinary income.
	■ Self-employment taxes are based on net income.

General Partnership.   A **general partnership** can be formed by two or more persons. Partners may share equally in the business or they may invest different amounts, have different responsibilities, and share different percentages of the profits. General partnerships are usually formed by a written agreement called articles of partnership. The articles detail the name of the business, ownership proportions, partners' duties, and distribution of profits. Partnerships may enter into contracts, buy and sell property, hire and fire employees, and sue to enforce contracts and agreements. However, the partners are not employees. They are legally self-employed and pay taxes on their share of any profits.

Partners have the authority to make business decisions and enter into business agreements, and they are legally responsible for their actions. Legal notice, such as a subpoena served to any partner, is considered served to all partners. Decisions to sell or mortgage partnership assets require the consent of all partners.

General partnerships do not protect the partners from legal liability for all partnership obligations. If three partners each have a one-third interest in the partnership, and the partnership has acquired a $250,000 obligation, each partner, regardless of their investment or share of the business, is liable for the entire $250,000.

Any partnership interest can be sold or otherwise transferred only with the consent of all partners. While a new person can purchase a partnership interest, the new person does not become a partner unless the partners elect to make the new person a partner. The new person has only purchased the right to receive the partner's profits.

A partnership ends by the death of any partner, by bankruptcy of either the partnership or any partner, or by agreement in arbitration.

The issues of insurance, taxes, liability, and choosing a name are the same as for a sole proprietorship. Banking options may be different for a partnership because of the pooling of resources, making a partnership more financially attractive to the bank. (See Figure 1.2.)

FIGURE 1.2
Advantages and
Disadvantages of a
General Partnership

Advantages	■ Investment in a general partnership by more than one party provides greater financial resources.
	■ Participation in a general partnership by more than one party provides additional talents for the business.
	■ Daily operational responsibilities of the general partnership can be shared.
	■ Profits of the general partnership are taxed only once.
	■ Business losses may be used as an offset to other taxable income.
Disadvantages	■ Each partner is personally liable for all debts (unlimited liability).
	■ The general partnership ends with the death, bankruptcy, or withdrawal of any partner.
	■ No partnership interest can be transferred without the consent of all partners.
	■ A general partnership must pay self-employment taxes.

All INVESTORS FULLY LIABLE

Limited Partnership.   In a **limited partnership** at least one person is considered a general partner. The general partner has the responsibility and liability for the day-to-day operation and financial decisions. The general partner has unlimited liability for debts of the partnership, even though they may not have contributed financial resources to the partnership.

A limited partner invests money, property, or both, in the partnership but does not work for the business, provide services, or participate in the day-to-day operation of the business. Limited partners receive a portion of the profits proportional to their investment. The only liability is the potential loss of their investment.

An example of a limited partnership is a real estate company forming a partnership with a contractor to fix up old houses or to make alterations to homes for the real estate firm's customers. The general partner (the contractor) makes all decisions about repairs and construction, and the limited partner (the real estate company) provides the resources.

The downside of a limited partnership, aside from liability, is that if the limited partner declares bankruptcy, the assets of the general partner are at risk. The issues of choosing a name, insurance, taxes, and liability are the same for the limited partnership as for a sole proprietor.

Limited Liability Company (LLC).   The name of the organization is chosen using the same requirements as a sole proprietor, but the letters LLC or the words "limited liability company" must be part of the name.

A **limited liability company (LLC)** is neither a strict partnership nor a corporation. The business structure of the LLC is the same as a partnership if the company is set up without a manager; otherwise it will be like a corporation with the partners as shareholders. The default structure is that the partners directly manage the company, unless the articles of organization stipulate that a manager will be employed.

An LLC is a distinct type of business that offers an alternative to partnerships and corporations by combining the corporate advantage of limited liability with the partnership advantage of pass-through taxation. *Pass-through taxation* is a tax advantage that allows no assessment of taxes on the profits of the company but only on the amount of income distributed to the partners. Profits are taxed as individual earnings, even if they are not distributed during the tax year.

Taxes for limited liability corporations can be complicated. In some states, an LLC can elect to be taxed as a partnership, with profits passed along as individual income, or it can be taxed as a corporation. Some states treat an LLC as a partnership and then add on a special tax. The state in which the LLC is registered will determine the tax status. Federal tax is assessed as if the LLC were a partnership.

The LLC is formed by filing articles of organization with the state. Profits are distributed as stipulated in the articles of organization and are not necessarily proportional to investment. Registration with the IRS is required to obtain an employer identification number (EIN).

Publication Requirement. Some states require a notice to be published in a newspaper that an LLC has been formed. This requirement must be confirmed with the state agency processing the LLC papers.

Agent Authority. The LLC is not physically capable of signing contracts because, technically, it exists only on paper. Therefore, an **agent authority** is required to represent the corporation. The agent must sign documents as an agent acting for the LLC and not as an individual person (see Chapter 4, Contracts). Having an agent sign for the LLC will preserve limited liability in the business transaction. (See Figure 1.3.)

Corporations

A **corporation** is legally a unique entity, separate from its partners, who are called shareholders. The main benefit to the shareholders is limited liability. Regardless of the debts and obligations incurred by the corporation, the shareholders have no liability beyond the potential loss of their investment. In exchange for this protection from liability for the shareholders, corporations are highly regulated.

Corporation contracts, properties, legal responsibilities, and finances are not attached to the shareholders' personal assets. Legal fees to create and maintain a corporation are higher than for other forms of businesses. Corporations must provide information about their business activities to state and federal governments. Corporation records are public records open to the media or any member of the public with an interest.

Establishing a Corporation. A corporation doing business in the state where it is chartered is called a "domestic" corporation. A corporation doing business in one state but chartered in another is a "foreign" corporation. A foreign corporation must register with and obey all the laws of the state in which it is working.

Most corporations are incorporated in the home state of the shareholders; however, there are advantages to incorporating in another state. Some states, such as Nevada, have no state tax on corporate profits or personal income and do not list the names of stockholders in the public record. Delaware also has low incorporation fees and no state corporate income tax for businesses operating outside of the state. Incorporating in a different state will require filing a notice and selecting a registered agent in each state in which the company operates.

Number of Persons Required. One or more persons may form a corporation. Some states, however, require that the number of shareholders at least equal

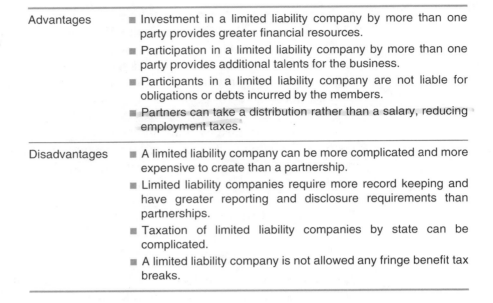

FIGURE 1.3
Advantages and Disadvantages of a Limited Liability Company

Advantages	■ Investment in a limited liability company by more than one party provides greater financial resources.
	■ Participation in a limited liability company by more than one party provides additional talents for the business.
	■ Participants in a limited liability company are not liable for obligations or debts incurred by the members.
	■ Partners can take a distribution rather than a salary, reducing employment taxes.
Disadvantages	■ A limited liability company can be more complicated and more expensive to create than a partnership.
	■ Limited liability companies require more record keeping and have greater reporting and disclosure requirements than partnerships.
	■ Taxation of limited liability companies by state can be complicated.
	■ A limited liability company is not allowed any fringe benefit tax breaks.

the number of directors, that is, even if there are only two shareholders, there must be two directors.

Requirements for Establishing a Corporation. The requirements for establishing a corporation vary between states but have some similar basic conditions that include:

■ the articles of incorporation.

■ a unique corporate name dissimilar from any other to avoid confusion. Most states require inclusion of the word "corporation," "company," or "incorporated."

■ a statement of the purpose of the business.

■ the revelation of how many shares are authorized and whether or not they are issued.

■ the name, address, and signature of each party to the incorporation.

■ a filing fee.

Articles of Incorporation. The **articles of incorporation** and the corporate bylaws control what a corporation does, how it is organized, and its financial activities. The corporation is granted a charter to operate, and annual reports of meetings are required to verify that the corporation is operating within the laws of the state.

Board of Directors. Shareholders may elect a **board of directors** to act as their representatives in overseeing the operation of the corporation. Shareholders must elect corporate officers, usually a president, vice president, secretary, and treasurer to conduct daily business. Corporate officers may be found legally liable for misconduct or neglect, but they are not otherwise personally liable for debts of the corporation. While corporate officers may also be shareholders, their personal liability extends solely to the potential loss of their investment.

The existence of a corporation does not depend on the presence of individual shareholders or officers. Termination of a corporation requires passing of a motion by the shareholders and submission of this approved motion to the state. Upon termination of the corporation, all assets of the corporation must be distributed to the shareholders proportionately to the number of their shares in the corporation.

Constitutional Protections for Corporations. A corporation is a legal entity separate from its shareholders and has constitutional protections that include:

■ The right to due process and equal protection under the Fifth Amendment (protection from double jeopardy) and the Fourteenth Amendment (civil rights and due process) to the U.S. Constitution. However, there is no privilege against self-incrimination (Fifth Amendment). If corporate records are subpoenaed that contain incriminating evidence, the corporation would have to provide them.

■ Freedom of speech and right to counsel. A corporation has a Sixth Amendment right to counsel, but a corporation cannot be imprisoned and does not have the right to appointed counsel if it cannot afford an attorney.

Duration of a Corporation. A corporation's **duration** is indefinite, meaning the corporation may continue in existence indefinitely. Its existence is not affected by death or incapacity of its officers or shareholders, or by the sale of stock.

Taxes. A corporation pays taxes based on a determined income tax rate and files a tax form each year (IRS Form 1120). Corporate taxes range from 15 percent to 39 percent depending on income.

Fringe Benefits. Corporations may offer employees fringe benefits such as a retirement plan and health and life insurance, all of which are deductible as business expenses within certain limits.

Shareholders may increase or decrease their investment by purchasing or selling company stock. Shareholders who are not employees pay taxes only on corporate profits actually paid out as dividends. Those shareholders who work for the corporation must pay normal income taxes on their earnings as well as taxes on the dividends they receive. The corporation also pays taxes on its profits, meaning that corporate profits are taxed twice—once at the corporate level and once at the individual level when profits are paid out as dividends.

Shareholder Liability for Corporate Debts. If the articles of incorporation and the bylaws of the corporation are not followed, shareholders could be held personally liable for corporate debts. A court or the IRS may "pierce the corporate veil" and hold the shareholders personally liable for corporate debts.

Leasing Assets to the Corporation. Personal property, such as a truck or equipment, may be leased to the corporation, which can provide a tax savings to the individual leasing the items. However, the lease terms must be defensible based on acceptable rate levels and terms.

Registered Agent. A registered agent is required of all corporations. A **registered agent** is the person designated by the company and named on papers filed with a state agency. The agent does not have to be an employee of the company

FIGURE 1.4
Advantages and
Disadvantages of a
Corporation

Advantages	■ The corporation limits one's personal liability.
	■ The corporation is a separate legal entity. It has its own tax identification number and is its own legal entity, separate and apart from the members.
	■ Sole proprietorships and partnerships normally end upon death, disability, bankruptcy, or retirement of the proprietor or partner. Corporations, being a separate legal entity, do not cease to exist when one of the founding members leaves.
	■ As the corporation grows, management and ownership can be separated so that the business can continue and the owners can still reap benefits. However, they may choose not to run the business.
	■ Corporations have the ability to consolidate, merge, or buy other corporations.
	■ Corporate stock may be freely transferred by sale or gift.
	■ A corporation has numerous tax advantages, including pension and profit-sharing options, and the election of S corporation status.
Disadvantages	■ It is expensive to create and, depending on the situation, to maintain. Incorporating may cost $1,000 to $10,000, depending on the type and complexity.
	■ Corporations are subject to double taxation. The corporation is taxed on profits; then when profits are distributed, the shareholders are taxed on dividends.
	■ A corporation is subject to greater governmental regulation and control than other types of business entities.

and usually is not. The only duty of the agent is to act as a public contact by receiving legal forms for the corporation sent by public and private agencies. States will require a foreign corporation to name a resident registered agent, and states may also require that the director of the agency regulating contractors be named as an agent.

Agent of the Principal. The corporation, just like the LLC, is not physically capable of signing any contracts and requires an **agent of the principal.** This agent is different from the "registered agent." To maintain liability protection, the person signing for the company must be identified as acting as an agent of the company (agent of the principal) and must be acting solely in the interests of the company. To maintain this protection, the agent must sign all agreements using the word "by" before their signature and writing the name of the company after their signature. (See Figure 1.4.)

Subchapter S or "S" Corporation

Certain small corporations may be registered as **subchapter S corporations.** The "S" corporation is designed for small businesses with less than 75 shareholders and modest revenues. It has the limited liability of a corporation while avoiding the double taxation of profits characteristic of a standard corporation.

Profits and losses of an "S" corporation are passed to individual shareholders and taxed as individual income. Because "S" corporations do not pay taxes on

FIGURE 1.5
Advantages and
Disadvantages of a
Subchapter S
Corporation

Advantages	■ A subchapter S corporation does not pay income taxes (but must pay employment taxes). ■ The corporate status of a subchapter S corporation provides the shareholders protection from liability. ■ The debts of a subchapter S corporation do not accrue to the shareholders. ■ Profits of a subchapter S corporation may be paid to the shareholder and taxed at the individual rate.
Disadvantages	■ The fringe benefits for shareholders of a subchapter S corporation are limited. ■ Shareholders in a subchapter S corporation are taxed on corporate income.

their profits, tax issues do not affect decisions regarding the payout or reinvestment of income. The corporation may elect to pay a dividend rather than a bonus to officer shareholders, saving employment taxes.

In an "S" corporation, only earnings actually paid out to a partner as compensation for services are subject to payroll taxes. Revenue left in the business for reinvestment or distributed to the shareholder as a dividend is not subject to payroll taxes or self-employment tax.

While "S" corporations are more highly regulated than sole proprietorships or partnerships, they can be quite advantageous for small businesses. (See Figure 1.5.)

Joint Ventures

A **joint venture** is a partnership of two or more individual companies joining together to work on a particular project. For example, Contractor A may be too small to finance a project on which it wants to bid. Contractor B is similarly capable of the project, but is also too small to handle the job alone. They can join together as Contractor C to complete this project together.

Licensing laws will require that all participants in the joint venture must be individually licensed to perform any of the work required for the project. Both companies retain their business type (sole proprietorship, partnership, or corporation), while the joint venture may be another type entirely. When the project is completed, the joint venture is disbanded.

MAKING A BUSINESS ORGANIZATION DECISION

The type of business defines ownership and the degree of personal liability applicable to the owners. Businesses with minimum governmental regulation also carry the greatest personal risk. Businesses in which the owners have the maximum protection from personal liability (as in a corporation) are subject to the most regulation.

No matter what type of business structure is selected, there are certain business choices a contractor must make. These choices are evaluating and choosing a bank, choosing a company name, hiring employees, and considering and understanding tax issues.

Banking

When looking for a bank, choose one with the fewest and lowest fees and charges, but one that also offers the services your company will require as it grows. Also, try to find banks that have free business checking accounts and lines of credit. Sometimes banks will offer a line of credit tied to the checking account to prevent insufficient funds and overdraft fees. This line of credit may also qualify the company for free checking because of the amount of "on-paper" money tied to the account.

Banks often work in conjunction with a credit card provider to enable the company to accept credit card payments. Although most companies need to accept credit cards to stay in business in today's economy, there is a downside to this: credit card fees cost the company a percentage (between 2 percent to 5 percent) of each sale. These fees should be considered overhead, especially on large projects. A 5 percent fee on a $25,000 invoice would be $1,250.

Unless the sole proprietor has established outstanding credit and has vast resources, banks typically prefer to extend privileges to corporations. Borrowing money is harder for sole proprietors due to liability issues incurred by this type of company. Sole proprietors can make borrowing money easier by having a well-prepared business plan. A business plan is a road map of the company that details what the company does, how it plans to grow, and what it needs to do to be successful. The development of a business plan is detailed in Chapter 2, Business Management.

Doing Business As

Doing business as (DBA) is a term used to describe a company that uses a name other than the owner's birth name. The DBA is registered with the locality, usually the clerk of the court. The application for business registration and the contractor license application will ask for disclosure of the type of business and the company name. This registration is necessary to make the locality aware that there is a new revenue source for tax purposes. Some jurisdictions also have a business tax on gross proceeds, machinery, or revenue.

The name of the company should reflect the type of work the company performs, such as "Bob the Contractor" or "Beth's Excavating." The state corporation commission and the state contractor licensing board will have records of existing company names so that a unique name can be selected. It is not ethical or legal to choose a name of a company that is deceptively close to an existing company. For example, "Caterpillar" might be selected for an excavating company in the hopes that name recognition will bring in business, but if it is not tagged with words that distinguish it from the manufacturer of earth-moving equipment, then the company currently using the name can sue for infringement.

Some names are more whimsical than descriptive, such as "Astral Contracting" rather than "A1 Contracting." This is acceptable as long as the name is unique to the jurisdiction or state.

Employees

A contractor is responsible for hiring and firing all employees as needed and in accordance with employment laws of the state and local jurisdiction. **At-will employment** describes the procedure of hiring an employee for an indefinite period of time without an employment contract. The employee can usually be released by the employer, or quit, without restriction or cause, and with only minimal notice. The other type of employment is **contractual employment** where a contract is signed for a specified period and the employment can be terminated only for cause. The financial resources of the company are the only limit to the number of employees that a company can employ.

An alternative to hiring employees is to work as a contract manager, where oversight of the project is the contractor's only task and no labor is provided by the contractor. Subcontractors are hired who meet the criteria of "independent contractor" (see Independent Contractor in Chapter 7, Employment Law), and registration is not necessary with the state employment or tax commission.

If the contractor hires employees, state registration with the employment and tax commission is required. Also, a Federal Employment Identification Number (EIN) must be obtained from the Internal Revenue Service. An EIN is easy to obtain via the Internet at *www.irs.gov*. This is the same Web site that provides tax law information.

SALES TAX

Many contractors buy materials retail, use the materials, and pass the cost on to the customer. A retail sale occurs when a person walks into a store, buys a product for personal use, and pays the sales tax. A wholesale purchase occurs when a quantity of material is purchased and no sales tax is paid. Sales tax is collected when the wholesale material is sold to the end user (the customer).

If the contractors buy material from a supplier, pay the sales tax, and install the material, then there is typically no further sales tax due. The tax has been paid by the contractors at the point of retail sale. Contractors recover the costs when billing for the time and materials used.

The state typically does not consider the contractor to be a manufacturer even though the contractor may be buying materials to build a house for resale. The state will collect sales tax on the entire house from the homebuyer when the house is purchased after completion.

Buying goods retail rather than wholesale is much easier from a record keeping standpoint. Not having to track sales tax is a considerable savings of time because reporting of sales tax is either a monthly or quarterly process and is very complicated. However, if the company does need a sales tax number, it can be obtained from the department of taxation at the state level.

TAX DEDUCTIONS

Deductions for reasonable and necessary expenses to operate the company are allowed by the IRS. Tax laws change each year, and keeping up with tax laws and regulations is challenging, but necessary. Some of the tax issues relating to business types are covered in both this chapter and in Chapter 9, Payroll Taxes. However, it is not feasible for this manual to provide a comprehensive guide to business taxes. It is strongly advised that contractors consult professional tax specialists.

SUMMARY

A variety of ways exist to organize a company. Many contractors choose sole proprietorship as a means of doing business because it is easy to set up. Some contractors who wish to form a partnership will select an LLC for the liability protection, and others will form a corporation for the tax benefits. Choosing a business organization type to suit the company needs requires careful study. Expert legal and financial advice is also advised.

CHAPTER 2

BUSINESS MANAGEMENT

S tarting a business is an exciting adventure. There is excitement about working for oneself and the potential for making a lot of money. However, many businesses fail in the first five years because the company does not have a strategic business plan. Many contractors go into business hoping that the business will continue but have no clue about how to make that happen. This chapter will explore the steps in starting a business that include communicating with existing contractors, conducting market research, developing a business plan, and running the business ethically. A successful contractor has the ability to organize projects and to use labor and materials efficiently and profitably.

GETTING STARTED

There are many steps required to create a successful business. While these steps apply to any business, they are vital in establishing a contracting business. When starting a contracting business, the following areas should be addressed:

- Analyze the actual requirements of starting a business and managing operations. Be sure to prepare for and understand what is involved in this big step.

- Assess the risks involved in starting a business and be prepared for financial setbacks.

- Evaluate the credit history of the business principals and whether that history will attract investors and bankers who may be asked to front cash or refinance a loan.

- Choose a business focus that has market opportunity. Experience in performing in the market area is essential to attracting an investor.

- Develop a business plan.

MARKET RESEARCH

Before creating a business plan and establishing a company, examine the market for the same type of services in the proposed area. The number and type of existing contractors for the work available will determine if the market is ready for another contractor. Also, be prepared for variations in market conditions as the company grows.

For example, a contractor who is considering construction as the main focus of the business will need to have an alternative plan to compensate for the loss of business that can occur when interest rates rise and customers find that borrowing money is too expensive to begin new projects. This is particularly an issue for contractors who build houses on speculation (that is, the house is built with the intent that someone will buy it when it is finished). If the economy is good, a potential homeowner will have no problem finding a low interest rate and will be able to obtain a larger loan. If the economy is poor, interest rates will rise and more of the loan amount will be taken up by interest payments, leaving less home-buying value. Either one of these scenarios will affect the contractor's business. A contractor building a speculation house will find that the sale of the house will take longer. This is more expensive for the contracting company because the investment of construction money and interest on the money will affect the contractor's profit.

In order to be a successful contractor, in addition to being knowledgeable in the technical aspects of the field, one must be able to handle the business aspects of the company as well. Be aware of factors that will affect success, such as the ability to find customers, workers, and materials. Also, consider influences such as local and regional business laws and regulations, wage rates, local taxes, weather, and soil types that will have an impact on costs.

Customers differ in their wants and needs. Some may want the highest quality materials and construction no matter the cost, while others may want results at minimum cost. It is unlikely that any single contractor (or company) can satisfy all customers.

Similarly, employees, subcontractors, and suppliers differ in their needs. Some employees want lots of overtime that will increase the size of their paycheck, and for the contractor, this results in fast completion of the project. Other employees will want a specific schedule so they can have a regular *workweek* and plan family activities.

Specialty subcontractors who provide high quality custom work (such as cabinetmaking or stair building) may be available for occasional projects when required, eliminating the need to carry these workers on permanent payroll. Suppliers want prompt payment and will work hard to keep a contractor who pays on time by making sure that deliveries are made when needed.

Another key to success as a contractor is conducting a careful study of existing contractors who will be competitors in order to discover their capabilities, styles, fees, and reputations. These competitors have already built their business, and one can learn from their experience. Compare these contractors to your own interests and abilities. How one goes about interviewing them is left to the contractor's own personal skills, but it is suggested to ask how they started, what worked for them, and what didn't work for them. Additionally, determine the type of customer you would like to serve. You should understand their interests, values, and background. What type of services are they looking for? (See Figure 2.1.)

By determining who your customers are, the task of determining your services and products becomes much simpler. Choose a marketing position that takes advantage of weaknesses in a competitor's market coverage. Alternatively, if resources are available, purchase an existing business, along with its employees, subcontractors, suppliers, and market position. (See Figure 2.2.)

FIGURE 2.1
Determine Your Customer's Interests

Describe your customers in detail. In addition to demographic data, consider psychographic issues:

_____

- Hobbies _____

- Disposable income _____

- Leisure activities _____

- Memberships _____

- Vacations _____

- Family status _____

- Other lifestyle information _____

What additional information should you obtain about your customers? _____

_____

_____

_____

_____

_____

How does this information have an impact on your marketing strategy? _____

- Marketing _____

- Sales _____

- Advertising _____

- Public relations _____

- Networking _____

FIGURE 2.2
Determine Your Services and Products

Describe precisely the attributes of your services and products: _____

_____

■ Service/Product A: _____

_____

_____

■ Service/Product B: _____

_____

_____

■ Service/Product C: _____

_____

_____

How can you make your services and products come alive for your prospective customers/clients?

_____

_____

_____

For one of your services or products, write a brief pitch that grabs attention. Focus on the *needs* of your customers and the service/product *benefits*.

_____

_____

_____

_____

_____

_____

Anatomy of a Business Plan by Linda Pinson. © 2005 Dearborn Trade Publishing. *www.dearborntrade.com.*

Once the business focus is established, prices must be set for services. Prices must be competitive or market acceptable if the product is unique. Either set prices competitively or make services so attractive that customers are willing to pay more for them. (See Figure 2.3.)

THE BUSINESS PLAN

One of the most important steps to creating and maintaining a successful business is to have a business plan. A **business plan** is an organized summary of a business. It states the kind of business to be established, presents a general outline of goals for the business, and estimates the costs and potential income. The business plan also describes the business and principals, the current and projected financials, and future markets and how to exploit them. Unless the business can be financed entirely from personal assets, establishing credit or borrowing money will be necessary. Creditors and suppliers must be convinced that the bills will be paid. The business plan helps creditors see how the contractor has planned to cover costs.

An essential skill in contracting is the ability to organize projects and use labor and materials efficiently and profitably. This organizational skill will be reflected in the business plan.

Business Plan Basics

The business plan should only be as long as necessary to present essential information. Normally a plan developed to interest investors should not exceed 20 pages. A lengthy plan should also have a stand-alone summary in order to give a busy investor a quick overview of the company and what is requested. A company that is already established should have a business plan that outlines the goals for the coming year and strategies for meeting those goals.

The most fundamental piece of a business plan is the company's mission. The *mission* is the foundation on which the business is built and is the company's primary reason for existing. When developing a mission, answers to the following questions will reveal the goals of the owner:

- What is the company's purpose for being in business?
- What specifically does the business do?
- Where should the company be in the future that is different from where it is today?

The answers to these questions will form the mission statement. The **mission statement** identifies what the company is about. The mission statement is a critical first step in developing a business plan because everything that follows must support it. A business plan should contain at least an executive summary, timetables and goals, a market analysis, and financials for the company.

Executive Summary. An **executive summary** provides a description of the business. It identifies company offerings to potential customers, creditors, and employees. The executive summary should identify the company's mission and include a mission statement.

FIGURE 2.3
Set Prices

How does your present pricing structure compare to your competitors? Equal to, more than, or less than? _____

_____

_____

_____

_____

Have you covered all of the following expenses to produce this product or provide this service?

■ Materials _____

■ Labor _____

■ Overhead expenses _____

■ Handling costs _____

■ Shipping costs _____

■ Storage _____

For services you provide, what are the advantages and disadvantages of the following pricing structures? _____

■ Hourly billing rates _____

■ Project by project estimates _____

■ Monthly retainer structure _____

What is your price floor? Ceiling? _____

_____

_____

_____

_____

Anatomy of a Business Plan by Linda Pinson. © 2005 Dearborn Trade Publishing. *www.dearborntrade.com.*

Timetables and Goals.   Along with a mission statement, a business needs an outline of timetables to accomplish its goals. These goals are the steps necessary to start the company, grow the business, and realize profits. *Goals* are what the company hopes to achieve; *timetables* reflect when the goals are to be achieved. An early goal may be to achieve profitability. The timetable for this goal may be two years. Usually, goals related to profits are stated over a five-year or ten-year period, and then are outlined for annual achievements needed to reach these goals. Monthly and weekly goals allow the company resources. *Strategies* describe how the goal is to be achieved.

Market Analysis.   **Market analysis** includes an evaluation of the market research and describes how the company is going to enter the market through identified goals. The market analysis section is where the plan should detail any unique advantage that the company may have to meet its goals.

Financials.   **Financials** outline the funds that are needed to achieve the goals established in the business plan. A general income and expense estimate is the foundation of the business. A comparison of anticipated income and expenses (including start-up costs and operating costs) is essential to setting prices. New businesses are seldom profitable at start-up, so a reserve operating capital is also essential. (See Figure 2.4.)

The business plan should also show all sources of capital and how it is to be repaid. Investors need to know how their money is going to be used and must be confident that their money will be returned in a timely fashion and with interest.

A business plan is not a static document. If an opportunity arises or the market changes during the year, the plan should also change to reflect new or modified goals and the means to achieve them.

Writing the Business Plan

Excellent resources are available to assist in developing a business plan, and many of them are free. Libraries have books on the topic and the Internet has sites that offer advice on writing a business plan. An Internet word search for business plan will bring up many resources. The U.S. Government Small Business Administration Web site, *http://www.sba.gov/*, is an excellent source of information about business plans and small business requirements. Additionally, a sample business plan and blank forms and worksheets have been provided in Appendix A to assist in developing your plan.

MARKETING THE BUSINESS

An essential activity for the success of the business is marketing. **Marketing** is identifying customers and attracting them to the company's products and services. Many new business owners believe professional marketing assistance is too expensive. However, the cost of a professional service may well be offset by the benefits of a well-planned marketing campaign. (See Figure 2.5.)

Traditional marketing approaches include a professional-quality company brochure, well-designed ads in newspapers and trade journals, and highly visible vehicle and project signs. It outlines how the company will be represented to the community. Simply posting the company's name and phone number in the yellow pages or advertising its existence in the local paper may bring some work, but it

FIGURE 2.4
Financials

EXPENSES WORKSHEET		
Time Period Covered: January 1–December 31, 2005		

1. START-UP COSTS

Business license	$ 30	
Corporation filing	500	
Legal fees	920	
Other start-up costs		
a.		
b.		
c.		
d.		
TOTAL START-UP COSTS		$ 1,450

2. INVENTORY PURCHASES

Cash out for goods intended for resale	32,000

3. VARIABLE EXPENSES (SELLING)

Advertising/marketing	8,000	
Freight	2,500	
Fulfillment of orders	800	
Packaging costs	0	
Sales salaries/commissions	14,000	
Travel	1,550	
Miscellaneous	300	
TOTAL SELLING EXPENSE		27,150

4. FIXED EXPENSES (ADMINISTRATION)

Financial administration	1,800	
Insurance	900	
Licenses and permits	100	
Office salaries	16,300	
Rent expenses	8,600	
Utilities	2,400	
Miscellaneous	400	
TOTAL ADMINISTRATIVE EXPENSE		30,500

5. ASSETS (LONG-TERM PURCHASES)

Cash to be paid out in current period	6,000

6. LIABILITIES

Cash outlay for retiring debts, loans, and/or accounts payable	9,900

7. OWNER EQUITY

Cash to be withdrawn by owner	24,000

TOTAL EXPENSES	$131,000

Anatomy of a Business Plan by Linda Pinson. © 2005 Dearborn Trade Publishing. *www.dearborntrade.com.*

FIGURE 2.4 (continued)
Financials

INCOME WORKSHEET	
Time Period Covered: January 1–December 31, 2005	
1. CASH ON HAND	$20,000
2. SALES (REVENUES)	
Product sales income * * Most of this sales revenue will not be received until Nov. or Dec.	90,000
Services income	22,000
Deposits on sales or services	0
Collections on accounts receivable	3,000
3. MISCELLANEOUS INCOME	
Interest income	1,000
Payments to be received on loans	0
4. SALE OF LONG-TERM ASSETS	0
5. LIABILITIES	40,000
Loan funds (to be received during current period; from banks, through the SBA, or from other lending institutions)	
6. EQUITY	
Owner investments (sole proprietors/partners)	10,000
Contributed capital (corporation)	
Sale of stock (corporation)	
Venture capital	35,000
Total Income	$221,000
Total Expenses	−131,000
Total Profit	$ 90,000

Anatomy of a Business Plan by Linda Pinson. © 2005 Dearborn Trade Publishing. *www.dearborntrade.com.*

FIGURE 2.5
Marketing Strategy

A. General Description	1. Allocation of marketing efforts (percentage of budget dedicated to online versus offline)
	2. Expected return on investment from most significant components
B. Method of Sales and Distribution	1. Stores, offices
	2. Catalogs, direct mail
	3. Web site
C. Packaging	1. Quality consideration
	2. Packaging
D. Pricing	1. Price strategy
	2. Competitive position
E. Branding	
F. Database Marketing (Personalization)	

Anatomy of a Business Plan by Linda Pinson. © 2005 Dearborn Trade Publishing. *www.dearborntrade.com.*

does not differentiate you from your competitors. "Old world brick craftsmanship" or "Homes designed to suit family values" are statements that define the company's specialty and position it in comparison to other firms in the community.

A Web site is quickly becoming an essential marketing tool for many businesses. Many companies use a Web site as an inexpensive and efficient tool for reaching customers.

MANAGING THE BUSINESS

The business owner is responsible for planning, organizing, and managing the resources and activities of the business. Management includes looking ahead for business opportunities and determining how to take advantage of them, setting goals, and identifying the resources necessary to achieve them.

A good manager creates a structured plan of ways to do work. This plan is used to determine the investment, employees, equipment, and time needed to accomplish each task. Tasks and projects are delegated to other members of the organization, who are then held responsible and accountable for the results.

Customer Relations

Customers keep contractors in business. A good customer is one who pays bills on time, communicates with the contractor about what needs to be done, and has reasonable expectations for the job. A good contractor is one who is able to communicate with the customer and does the job according to the contract.

It is important to remember that when doing a job for a customer, all relationships should be kept on a professional level. Be friendly with customers but do not make friends until the job is completed and paid for. Some customers may try to take advantage of a friendship and start asking for free work or extra discounts. Most contractors will accommodate a customer when they ask a "favor," but this could cause problems, such as undocumented change orders.

Problems can also arise when the contractor simply does not do what was agreed upon or performs it in such a fashion that it does not meet standards of practice.

Sometimes communication between the customer and the contractor fails, provoking an argument. The contractor may feel that it is impossible to complete the job under the circumstances and may walk off the job. This can be a disaster to the career of the contractor because it not only places the contractor in breach of contract, but it also subjects the contractor to discipline by a licensing board. Many contractors who have been disciplined by the state said that it would have been much easier to have just completed the job, as difficult as it may have been, rather than face the legal consequences.

ETHICS

Ethics is practicing a standard of honesty in all business dealings. Ethics in contracting should encompass every aspect of the business on a daily basis. This means incorporating ethical standards in the day-to-day transactions with the customer, suppliers, and the competition. It should start with advertising, include the bid, a professional attitude, and end with a finished product. The results of meeting this standard will be long-term business growth and a positive, professional standing in the community. The consequences of not meeting this standard may mean short-term profits and a dismal reputation. A contractor should make every effort to avoid objectionable behavior.

An ethical contractor is honest in advertising, assembles fair bids, has a professional attitude, and produces a quality product. An example of ethical behavior is in advertising. Ethical advertising means advertising that accurately reflects the company's experience, product, and delivery.

If a company advertises 20 years of experience, it could be interpreted that the contractor, as an individual, has been in business for 20 years, or it may mean that two of the staff each have ten years of experience. A customer may look differently at a company with a generation of continuous business than one that began business the previous year. If a contractor states that siding is a specialty, then there should be a history of direct experience with siding. The customer will have an expectation that the installation will be completed in a professional manner and will not be a learning experience for the contractor. Accurately reflecting the experience and longevity of the company will help increase the overall reputation of the company.

Examples of objectionable behavior are bid rigging and bid shopping. **Bid rigging** is the practice where a contractor conspires with other bidders to ensure the award of a bid, with the result of a certain bid. Bid rigging is a felony. **Bid shopping** is the practice of revealing a subcontractor's bid information to a competitor. While bid shopping is not a crime, it is an unethical business practice. The short-term result of bid rigging or bid shopping is getting a low price, but eventually the action will be disclosed and the contractor may find the purchasing market is much smaller and costs will rise.

Aside from bidding infractions, another area of concern regarding ethics is the deliberate concealment of errors or of shoddy work, which may be a crime, depending on the severity. An example of this can be either poor construction practices or code violations. For example, the use of a shim to bring a structurally sound beam to level is acceptable, but shimming a built-up beam with a cracked member is not acceptable. The cracked beam may be discovered in the inspection process and will be much more expensive to tear out and replace than it would have been to select sound timber at the start. It also casts a shadow of doubt over the quality of all of the contractor's work when the cover-up is discovered. The most common ethical mistakes that contractors make are the following:

- **Choosing not to work to the specifications of the contract.** If the contract stipulates ceramic tile on the floor of the foyer, then vinyl that looks like tile does not meet the contract.

- **Intentionally violating the building code.** The code may require hurricane straps installed on each rafter, and it would be a violation to not install them, hoping that the insulator will bury the connections under fiberglass.

- **Misusing customer's funds.** The acceptance of a payment is a contract to perform. Any money received from the customer must be used on that customer's job. Starting a new job using money that was intended for materials delivered to a customer's job site is illegal in many states.

- **Creating improper contracts.** Most states mandate that times, dates, and terms be incorporated into a contract.

- **Not cooperating with investigative agencies.** If an enforcement agency requests records in the course of an investigation, it is required that the documents be produced unless the company's attorney advises otherwise.

- **Working in a field or area in which the contractor lacks expertise.** If a company has no experience in a certain construction area, it is not a good idea to attempt to practice in that area without adequate preparation.

- **Abandoning the job.** Quitting the job due to an argument between the contractor and the customer is a breach of contract by the contractor.

- **Gross negligence.** If a contractor is working on a roof and there is a likelihood of rain, it would be gross negligence to not protect the roof from heavy rain entering the building.

The best business practice is to operate in an ethical manner. This will certainly assist in staying out of trouble and avoiding fines, and will enhance the company's reputation. One way to determine if the proposed action could be construed as unethical is to consider whether it would cause embarrassment if disclosed. If there are doubts, then consult with a trusted friend, mentor, or attorney. Contracting is a great profession and a rewarding business. Operating ethically will certainly enhance the chance of success over time.

SUMMARY

The ability to manage the company by conducting market research into the needs of the area that the business will be serving, having a detailed business plan, and managing the business properly and ethically will increase the likelihood of continued success in the contracting business.

CHAPTER 3

ESTIMATING AND BIDDING

Accurate estimating and bidding are crucial to a contractor's success. Identifying job costs and unit costs are essential for creating accurate estimates and bids. This chapter will explore the tasks of deciding to bid, developing an estimate, and submitting a formal bid.

THE BIDDING PROCESS

A **bid** is an offer to furnish labor, equipment, and materials in a specified manner and time for a certain price. An **estimate** is a projection of job costs. A bid is a formal proposal, whereas an estimate is an informed guess. In construction, though the words "bid" and "estimate" have different meanings in a legal sense, they are often used interchangeably. All bids that are submitted by a contractor must be as accurate as possible.

A decision about whether to bid on a job should be made after considering the following factors: the bid request, scope of work, cost, capability to perform the work, schedule, location, site visit, and making a decision.

Invitation to Bid

Contractors begin the decision-making process when they receive an invitation to bid. An **invitation to bid** is a document that describes the proposed project and states the manner in which the bid must be prepared. Instructions for obtaining the project documents will be included. The invitation to bid specifies the rules for bidding, ensuring that all bids can be compared and reliably evaluated against each other.

An invitation to bid typically includes a bid sheet. A **bid sheet** is a form that must be used to submit a formal bid proposal. Information required on the bid sheet includes the name (and number, if applicable) of the project, the name of the contractor (bidder), the bid amount (in words and numbers), any allowances, and the contractor's signature. Certain owners and agencies will also require a bid bond. Government agencies may require affidavits concerning minority participation, ownership (including gender), capability to finance the project, or other special requirements.

In addition to invitations to bid, subscription services are available that have a project reporting service to advise contractors of new projects in a particular area. Contractors may also subscribe to a national service (e.g., Dodge Reports). Private builders and property owners may simply invite a few known contractors to bid. Membership in a local builders' association or service club can often lead to opportunities to bid on local projects.

Sometimes a pre-bid meeting is held, with mandatory attendance required for those who wish to submit a bid. At the pre-bid meeting, the issuing authorities will go over the project requirements with all contractors. The issuing authority answers questions and clarifies any confusion relating to the bid documents. If no pre-bid meeting is mandatory, a meeting with the owner or agency should be requested by the contractor if there is any question about the project, the bid documents, or any specification modifications.

Contractors are familiar with customers who call and ask for a bid or estimate and then do not follow through with a contract. This happens for a number of reasons: the estimate submitted may have been too high or the customer realizes that they cannot afford the job. To compensate, some contractors will charge for an estimate and then deduct the cost of the estimate from the job price if a contract is awarded. This practice ensures that the contractor's time is compensated, but it may entail fewer invitations to bid when other contractors will provide a bid as a free service.

Public projects must be advertised for bids. The invitation to bid (incorporated in the advertisement) will outline the project and its location, and will identify the authorizing agency. Items included in the advertisement include where and when to apply for project documents, a cost estimate (range), and any fees or deposits required.

Federal project advertisements (pre-solicitation notices) are often posted in public places, such as a post office. Some agencies will send copies of these announcements to contractors they know are capable of the work. Prequalification may be required prior to submitting a bid on public projects to ensure that the contractor is capable of completing the project.

While bidding for public projects must be open to all parties, agencies may be required to set aside certain projects or a certain number of projects for minority-owned businesses or small companies. All application and bidding policies must be spelled out in the Instructions to Bidders. Bidders must abide by these rules, complete the proper forms, and submit their bid by the proper date to avoid having the bid rejected.

Scope of Work

One question a contractor must have answered is what specifically does the customer want done? Understanding what the customer wants is necessary to determine the scope of work. A customer wanting a deck built may have in mind one that is attached to the house at the second level with a winding staircase to ground level, but the contractor is picturing a deck on grade with one or two steps. The on-site visit will resolve any final questions, but getting to know what is needed up front will help the contractor determine whether they can provide the required service.

Cost

Once the scope of the work is understood, the customer should be given an idea of what the project will cost so they can determine whether the job is affordable. Some customers may not have any idea of what a construction job costs, and it is a service to disclose probable costs up front. This can be done by providing a non-binding, ballpark figure. A contractor who has a working relationship with a financial institution can offer the customer a way to make the project happen by providing financing.

Capability

Another factor that must be considered is whether the proposed project is within the capability, and license limitations, of the contractor. It is not good practice to work outside one's experience level because this usually results in an expensive learning process for the contractor. Additionally, it is not legal to perform work that is beyond the scope of the license.

Schedule

A contractor should look carefully at their current work schedule and determine whether taking on another job is feasible. While a contractor must always have work lined up to keep the crews working, it is not ethical to consider a project that will conflict with existing contracts.

Location

The location of the work is another factor to consider in deciding whether to take a job. Excessive travel time will be expensive and tiring for a crew. Jobs located a distance from the contractors home location may also require using suppliers with whom the contractor has not established a working relationship. The supplier's loyalty may be to other companies even when the contractor is scrambling to complete a project on time and within budget. The location will also affect whether suppliers are able to deliver materials when needed.

Site Visit

Unless the proposed project is very small, a site visit is required. The site itself, or unusual site conditions, may make it difficult to complete the job or to comply with local ordinances. Some job site conditions that must be taken into consideration include the following:

- Erosion and sediment control, especially when the job is close to a body of water, must be factored into the project cost.
- Local tree ordinances may prohibit removal of certain trees.
- Burning may be prohibited, requiring all cleared brush and trees to be hauled away.
- The site may have been used for dumping or have buried tanks or other contamination that must be removed, with approval by environmental agencies, before construction begins.

- The presence of any archeological remains or a cemetery may hold up the project, or there may be special property covenants such as a historical district or subdivision restrictions.

- Limitations may exist regarding site access and security that need to be overcome.

- Utilities such as electricity, water, and telephone may not be readily available, requiring extension of these services to the site.

- Utility services may be inadequate for the new load added to an existing building.

- Special care may be required due to the condition or closeness of existing buildings, especially if the project adds on to an existing structure.

A job site inspection should be conducted by an individual experienced in the type of work to be performed. A record of the site and any visible problems can be made by camcorder, digital camera, or drawings, and notes can be dictated to a tape recorder. A compass should be used during the site inspection to orient the job site to a specific direction. This will provide a basis for developing site plans if necessary. A thorough written description (with pictures) will help prevent over-looking any items when preparing the estimate.

Decision Making

Once all of these factors are considered, a decision about whether to bid can be made. If the decision is to decline the work, it would be a nice gesture to recommend to the customer another contractor who may be able to do the work. This ends the conversation on a positive note. If the decision is to accept the project, then an estimate is prepared.

ESTIMATING

In order to produce an estimate, the contractor must understand exactly what the bid entails, including the actual project needs, proposal forms, building codes and regulations applicable to the job, and any quality control or material testing requirements. The biggest part of the estimating process is crunching the numbers.

When preparing an estimate, the contractor works from the quantity takeoff, comparing it with the job specifications to ensure that every item is addressed. A **quantity takeoff** is an analysis and detail of all components of a project. A complete and accurate listing of all materials to be used and all work to be done is prepared in the detailed survey estimate.

Developing an estimate using computer software greatly simplifies the estimating process. Software programs are available that use national estimating guides and Construction Specifications Institute (CSI) documents (*www.csinet.org*). The contractor inputs the dimensions, selects the materials, and a detailed quantity take off is prepared with unit costs. The programs are compatible with accounting software programs so everything is integrated regarding billing and time sheets.

If the specifications call for new technology or unfamiliar materials, the architect or engineer must be contacted for sources of information about the technology and supply of these materials.

Project Documents

Every job requires project documents. **Project documents** are the plans and specifications prepared for the owner by an architect and/or engineer. There may be a fee to obtain these documents, but a bid cannot be prepared without them. Some projects are more complex than others. However, the project documents must always be thoroughly reviewed because they provide the basis for preparing an estimate and then the bid. Project documents include general conditions, supplementary conditions, plans and drawings, and specifications.

General Conditions. The *general conditions* outline the roles of the owner, contractor, architect, and engineer. Additional owner representatives may also be specified.

Supplementary Conditions. *Supplementary conditions* are additions or modifications to the "boilerplate" general conditions that apply to the specific project.

Plans and Drawings. Plans and drawings detail the project and show dimensions, size, and location of each item in the project. The **plans (blueprints)** are the drawings that detail the job. The plans may be as informal as a hand drawn layout on a legal pad that has notes describing the job with dimensions, or it may be a full set of blueprints drawn by an architect. The plans are used as a reference when preparing the quantity takeoff. *Drawings* detail the architectural, electrical, mechanical, and plumbing portions of the project.

Specifications. *Specifications* describe the materials to be used and the quality of the construction required. They may specify the manufacturers or suppliers to be used for various materials. The Construction Specifications Institute has developed a system of codes for every material and activity that could be part of a project. Most architects use the CSI MasterFormat® Division codes for organizing the specification booklet that goes with the project plans. (See Table 3.1.)

Determining Job Costs

Job costs from previous projects should provide unit costs, including overhead, to apply to each new estimate. These costs are reviewed and adjusted as necessary for price increases on labor, materials, equipment, and for special conditions at the new job site. Job costs aid in monitoring the project as it proceeds and assist the accountant in preparing progress payment requests. Job costs that must be determined include labor, materials and equipment, overhead, allowances, contingencies, and profit.

Labor Costs. Labor costs can be estimated in several ways. One method is to assign labor hours to each work item. Nonproductive tasks performed by workers at the job site must be included. Paid rest breaks and time spent on tool maintenance and at various meetings are all part of the labor cost.

If a good cost analysis method has been developed, labor can be determined based on the material costs. Some estimators may average all labor costs (direct, indirect, regular hours, and overtime) into a single labor factor for each unit. For example, if material for a siding job is $10,000, and the records show that this job is standard and similar to other completed projects, and the standard is to charge 100 percent of materials for labor, then the labor charge will be $10,000 for a total

TABLE 3.1
CSI MasterFormat® Divisions

DIVISION 1 **GENERAL** **REQUIREMENTS**	01100 SUMMARY 01200 PRICE AND PAYMENT PROCEDURES 01300 ADMINISTRATIVE REQUIREMENTS 01400 QUALITY REQUIREMENTS 01500 TEMPORARY FACILITIES AND CONTROLS 01600 PRODUCT REQUIREMENTS 01700 EXECUTION REQUIREMENTS 01800 FACILITY OPERATION 01900 FACILITY DECOMMISSIONING
DIVISION 2 **SITE** **CONSTRUCTION**	02050 BASIC SITE MATERIALS AND METHODS 02100 SITE REMEDIATION 02200 SITE PREPARATION 02300 EARTHWORK 02400 TUNNELING, BORING, AND JACKING 02450 FOUNDATION AND LOAD-BEARING ELEMENTS 02500 UTILITY SERVICES 02600 DRAINAGE AND CONTAINMENT 02700 BASES, BALLASTS, PAVEMENTS, AND APPURTENANCES 02800 SITE IMPROVEMENTS AND AMENITIES 02900 PLANTING 02950 SITE RESTORATION AND REHABILITATION
DIVISION 3 **CONCRETE**	03050 BASIC CONCRETE MATERIALS AND METHODS 03100 CONCRETE FORMS AND ACCESSORIES 03200 CONCRETE REINFORCEMENT 03300 CAST-IN-PLACE CONCRETE 03400 PRECAST CONCRETE 03500 CEMENTITIOUS DECKS AND UNDERLAYMENT 03600 GROUTS 03700 MASS CONCRETE 03900 CONCRETE RESTORATION AND CLEANING
DIVISION 4 **MASONRY**	04050 BASIC MASONRY MATERIALS AND METHODS 04200 MASONRY UNITS 04400 STONE

	04500 REFRACTORIES 04600 CORROSION-RESISTANT MASONRY 04700 SIMULATED MASONRY 04800 MASONRY ASSEMBLIES 04900 MASONRY RESTORATION AND CLEANING
DIVISION 5 **METALS**	05050 BASIC METALS AND METHODS 05100 STRUCTURAL METAL FRAMING 05200 METAL JOISTS 05300 METAL DECK 05400 COLD-FORMED METAL FRAMING 05500 METAL FABRICATIONS 05600 HYDRAULIC FABRICATIONS 05650 RAILROAD TRACK AND ACCESSORIES 05700 ORNAMENTAL METAL 05800 EXPANSION CONTROL 05900 METAL RESTORATION AND CLEANING
DIVISION 6 **WOOD AND** **PLASTICS**	06050 BASIC WOOD AND PLASTIC MATERIALS AND METHODS 06100 ROUGH CARPENTRY 06200 FINISH CARPENTRY 06400 ARCHITECTURAL WOODWORK 06500 STRUCTURAL PLASTICS 06600 PLASTIC FABRICATIONS 06900 WOOD AND PLASTIC RESTORATION AND CLEANING
DIVISION 7 **THERMAL AND** **MOISTURE** **PROTECTION**	07050 BASIC THERMAL AND MOISTURE PROTECTION MATERIALS AND METHODS 07100 DAMPPROOFING AND WATERPROOFING 07200 THERMAL PROTECTION 07300 SHINGLES, ROOF TILES, AND ROOF COVERINGS 07400 ROOFING AND SIDING PANELS 07500 MEMBRANE ROOFING 07600 FLASHING AND SHEET METAL 07700 ROOF SPECIALTIES AND ACCESSORIES 07800 FIRE AND SMOKE PROTECTION 07900 JOINT SEALERS

TABLE 3.1 (continued)
CSI MasterFormat® Divisions

DIVISION 8 **DOORS AND** **WINDOWS**	08050 BASIC DOOR AND WINDOW MATERIALS AND METHODS 08100 METAL DOORS AND FRAMES 08200 WOOD AND PLASTIC DOORS 08300 SPECIALTY DOORS 08400 ENTRANCES AND STOREFRONTS 08500 WINDOWS 08600 SKYLIGHTS 08700 HARDWARE 08800 GLAZING 08900 GLAZED CURTAIN WALL
DIVISION 9 **FINISHES**	09050 BASIC FINISH MATERIALS AND METHODS 09100 METAL SUPPORT ASSEMBLIES 09200 PLASTER AND GYPSUM BOARD 09300 TILE 09400 TERRAZZO 09500 CEILINGS 09600 FLOORING 09700 WALL FINISHES 09800 ACOUSTICAL TREATMENT 09900 PAINTS AND COATINGS
DIVISION 10 **SPECIALTIES**	10100 VISUAL DISPLAY BOARDS 10150 COMPARTMENTS AND CUBICLES 10200 LOUVERS AND VENTS 10240 GRILLES AND SCREENS 10250 SERVICE WALLS 10260 WALL AND CORNER GUARDS 10270 ACCESS FLOORING 10290 PEST CONTROL 10300 FIREPLACES AND STOVES 10340 MANUFACTURED EXTERIOR SPECIALTIES 10350 FLAGPOLES 10400 IDENTIFICATION DEVICES 10500 LOCKERS 10520 FIRE PROTECTION SPECIALTIES 10530 PROTECTIVE COVERS 10600 PARTITIONS 10670 STORAGE SHELVING 10700 EXTERIOR PROTECTION 10750 TELEPHONE SPECIALTIES 10800 TOILET, BATH, AND LAUNDRY ACCESSORIES 10880 SCALES 10900 WARDROBE AND CLOSET SPECIALTIES
DIVISION 11 **EQUIPMENT**	11010 MAINTENANCE EQUIPMENT 11020 SECURITY AND VAULT EQUIPMENT 11030 TELLER AND SERVICE EQUIPMENT 11040 ECCLESIASTICAL EQUIPMENT 11050 LIBRARY EQUIPMENT 11060 THEATER AND STAGE EQUIPMENT 11070 INSTRUMENTAL EQUIPMENT 11080 REGISTRATION EQUIPMENT 11090 CHECKROOM EQUIPMENT 11100 MERCANTILE EQUIPMENT 11110 COMMERCIAL LAUNDRY AND DRY CLEANING EQUIPMENT 11120 VENDING EQUIPMENT 11130 AUDIO-VISUAL EQUIPMENT 11140 VEHICLE SERVICE EQUIPMENT 11150 PARKING CONTROL EQUIPMENT 11160 LOADING DOCK EQUIPMENT 11170 SOLID WASTE HANDLING EQUIPMENT 11190 DETENTION EQUIPMENT 11200 WATER SUPPLY AND TREATMENT EQUIPMENT 11280 HYDRAULIC GATES AND VALVES 11300 FLUID WASTE TREATMENT AND DISPOSAL EQUIPMENT 11400 FOOD SERVCIE EQUIPMENT 11450 RESIDENTIAL EQUIPMENT 11460 UNIT KITCHENS 11470 DARKROOM EQUIPMENT 11480 ATHLETIC, RECREATIONAL, AND THERAPEUTIC EQUIPMENT 11500 INDUSTRIAL AND PROCESS EQUIPMENT 11600 LABORATORY EQUIPMENT 11650 PLANETARIUM EQUIPMENT 11660 OBSERVATORY EQUIPMENT 11680 OFFICE EQUIPMENT 11700 MEDICAL EQUIPMENT 11780 MORTUARY EQUIPMENT 11850 NAVIGATION EQUIPMENT 11870 AGRICULTURAL EQUIPMENT 11900 EXHIBIT EQUIPMENT
DIVISION 12 **FURNISHINGS**	12050 FABRICS 12100 ART 12300 MANUFACTURED CASEWORK

CHAPTER 3
Estimating and Bidding

TABLE 3.1 (continued)
CSI MasterFormat® Divisions

DIVISION 12 FURNISHINGS (continued)	12400 FURNISHINGS AND ACCESSORIES 12500 FURNITURE 12600 MULTIPLE SEATING 12700 SYSTEMS FURNITURE 12800 INTERIOR PLANTS AND PLANTERS 12900 FURNISHINGS RESTORATON AND REPAIR	**DIVISION 14 CONVEYING SYSTEMS**	14100 DUMBWAITERS 14200 ELEVATORS 14300 ESCALATORS AND MOVING WALKS 14400 LIFTS 14500 MATERIAL HANDLING 14600 HOISTS AND CRANES 14700 TURNTABLES 14800 SCAFFOLDING 14900 TRANSPORTATION
DIVISION 13 SPECIAL CONSTRUCTIONS	13010 AIR-SUPPORTED STRUCTURES 13020 BUILDING MODULES 13030 SPECIAL PURPOSE ROOMS 13080 SOUND, VIBRATION, AND SEISMIC CONTROL 13090 RADIATION PROTECTION 13100 LIGHTNING PROTECTION 13110 CATHODIC PROTECTION 13120 PRE-ENGINEERED STRUCTURES 13150 SWIMMING POOLS 13160 AQUARIUMS 13165 AQUATIC PARK FACILITIES 13170 TUBS AND POOLS 13175 ICE RINKS 13185 KENNELS AND ANIMAL SHELTERS 13190 SITE-CONSTRUCTED INCINERATORS 13200 STORAGE TANKS 13220 FILTER UNDERDRAINS AND MEDIA 13230 DIGESTER COVERS AND APPURTENANCES 13240 OXYGENATIONS SYSTEMS 13260 SLUDGE CONDITIONING SYSTEMS 13282 HAZARDOUS MATERIAL CONTAINMENT 13400 MEASUREMENT AND CONTROL INSTRUMENTATION 13500 RECORDING INSTRUMENTATION 13550 TRANSTATION CONTROL INSTRUMENTATION 13600 SOLAR AND WIND ENERGY EQUIPMENT 13700 SECURITY ACCESS AND SURVEILLANCE 13800 BUILDING AUTOMATION AND CONTROL 13850 DETECTION AND ALARM 13900 FIRE SUPPRESSION	**DIVISION 15 MECHANICAL** **DIVISION 16 ELECTRICAL**	15050 BASIC MECHANICAL MATERIALS AND METHODS 15100 BULDING SERVICES PIPING 15200 PROCESS PIPING 15300 FIRE PROTECTION PIPING 15400 PLUMBING FIXTURES AND EQUIPMENT 15500 HEAT-GENERATION EQUIPMENT 15600 REFRIGERATION EQUIPMENT 15700 HEATING, VENTILATING, AND AIR CONDITIONING EQUIPMENT 15800 AIR DISTRIBUTION 15900 HVAC INSTRUMENTATION AND CONTROLS 15950 TESTING, ADJUSTING, AND BALANCING 16050 BASIC ELECTRICAL MATERIALS AND METHODS 16100 WIRING METHODS 16200 ELECTRICAL POWER 16300 TRANSMISSION AND DISTRIBUTION 16400 LOW-VOLTAGE DISTRIBUTION 16500 LIGHTING 16700 COMMUNICATIONS 16800 SOUND AND VIDEO

bid of $20,000 for the job. Another way to estimate labor costs is to use a published cost schedule, available from construction book stores.

Direct labor cost is the basic hourly rate for building, installing, or modifying a work item (unit). *Indirect labor costs* are unemployment insurance, workers' compensation insurance, health insurance, etc., that are not a part of the hourly wage. To determine indirect labor costs, the contractor develops an average indirect labor charge as a percentage (usually from 20 percent to 50 percent) of hourly wages. This percentage is then multiplied by the estimated direct labor costs. Subcontractors will already have included indirect labor costs when submitting an estimate to the prime contractor.

Subcontractors.   Subcontractors represent another form of labor, or labor and equipment. When developing an estimate, the prime contractor will solicit bids from several subcontractors. The subcontractor develops a bid in the same way as the prime contractor, calculating costs based on information received about the contract proposal and past experience.

Subcontractors and suppliers must be contacted with requests for bids as soon as possible after beginning the estimating process to allow them time to develop their own bid. Preliminary bids can be based on the specifications outlined in the project documents, with the understanding that final costs will be based on the quantity takeoff. Several subcontractors and suppliers should be invited to bid to provide a competitive comparison. Only qualified and licensed subcontractors can be considered.

Material and Equipment.   Material and equipment costs are based on the quantity takeoff plus an allowance for waste. Once a materials list has been completed, costs can be calculated. **Material costs** are the total of all costs for materials used by the contractor, including the price of the materials, the cost of delivery, and any storage charges. If a software program is used to track material costs, it is important that it be kept up to date as costs change.

In order to minimize costs, the contractor should try to have materials delivered (preferably at no charge) on an as-needed basis. A written commitment from each supplier to furnish the materials required at a quoted price will help avoid surprises in costs. Having materials delivered as-needed will also reduce storage costs and potential theft.

Equipment costs are all expenses associated with any equipment used for the job. Everything from hand tools to front-end loaders and cranes must be included. The cost of any equipment or tools purchased solely for a particular project are totally charged to that project, whereas equipment and tools used for more than one project are charged to each project in proportion to their use.

The cost of equipment owned by the contractor, including purchase cost, delivery, maintenance, and fuel, should be amortized (written off over a fixed period of time) in order to calculate an hourly or daily cost for the equipment. This cost will be charged to the project based upon the hours or days it will be needed for that project. If the contractor owns the equipment, the equipment cost when it is not in use becomes a part of overhead.

Specialized or expensive equipment that is used only occasionally or is too expensive to own should be rented or leased for the time it is needed. Renting usually applies to short-term needs, while equipment for long-term use (over one year) is normally leased. In either case, the rental or lease cost is applied to the project on which the equipment is used. Lease costs for equipment not in service on a project are charged to overhead.

Bids should be obtained from at least three suppliers for all materials where possible. Daily, weekly, and monthly costs for equipment rental or leases must be confirmed, preferably in writing. In some cases, purchasing equipment will prove more economical than rental or leasing; prorated costs for this equipment and its maintenance must be calculated.

Overhead

Overhead costs are the costs incurred from each project and in running the business. They are the costs associated with furniture, offices, salaries, insurance, and other line items. Overhead is generally separated into general overhead and project overhead.

General overhead represents all the operating costs of the company that are not related to any project. For example, office rent and secretarial salaries, utilities, office supplies, and taxes are general overhead expenses. Monthly or annual overhead costs are estimated and then reduced to daily charges. These charges are applied to current projects as a percentage of the projected project revenues.

General overhead costs are included in a bid as a percentage that has been determined using historical data. General overhead costs must be reviewed regularly, at least annually, and with computer tracking, overhead costs can easily be recalculated for each project. General overhead includes the following:

- Accounting and legal fees
- Advertising and public relations
- Equipment costs not assigned to any project
- General liability insurance
- All business expenses not specific to any project(s), such as office furniture and equipment (computers, copiers, and telephones), office rent /mortgage and taxes, office staff, including managers, secretaries, and maintenance personnel, and office utilities
- Travel expenses, including costs of company vehicles and business trips

A portion of general overhead must be incorporated into every bid. If the contractor is working on only one job at a time, all overhead must be applied to that job. If several jobs are under way simultaneously, the overhead should be portioned to each job based on the cost or complexity of the job.

Project overhead is the cost, except labor, associated with a particular project. Project overhead may be a percentage. As with general overhead, these charges are applied to current projects as a percentage of the projected project revenues. Project overhead includes the following:

- Barricades, signs, and fences
- Financing costs (construction loans, etc.)
- Insurance and bonds
- Legal fees related to the project
- Salaries and fees for surveying, security, safety personnel, etc.
- Salaries for project management (foremen, superintendents)
- Site cleanup before and after the project
- Utilities for the project (telephone, electricity, water, portable toilets)

Calculating General Overhead and Project Overhead.   Example: In 2004, revenues were $3,150,000, general overhead was $472,500, and project overhead was $115,000.

$$\frac{\text{General}}{\text{Overhead}} = \frac{\$472,500}{\$3,150,000} = 0.15 = 15\%$$

$$\frac{\text{Project}}{\text{Overhead}} = \frac{\$315,000}{\$3,150,000} = 0.10 = 10\%$$

These percentages are then used for all new bids in the fiscal year.

Direct Costs are expenses for the materials going into the project. For example, costs for subcontractors, concrete, carpeting, or shingles are direct costs.

Scheduling.   Scheduling of the project can influence project cost. Many components of the estimate are measured in hours, days, or months to completion. Any task that increases the time required to complete the job increases scheduling costs. Any task that decreases the time required to complete the job decreases scheduling costs. Any difference between the time allotted in the estimate and the actual time to complete the tasks will contribute to cost overruns or underruns.

Just as costs must be estimated, a preliminary schedule must be considered. Both the order and duration of tasks must be considered because certain tasks must be completed before others begin. Some tasks may overlap. Whenever tasks can be performed simultaneously, overhead for those tasks is reduced. If overtime will be needed to complete the project (or a portion of it) on time, it must be included in the cost estimate.

Allowances.   *Allowances* are funds for unique items or skilled work in the project. Handmade cabinetry or tile floor inlays are examples of skilled labor. A suggested cost for these allowances must be included in the bid. An allowance may be a line item in the estimate for appliances that the customer will select later. It is an estimate and may be adjusted either up or down when the items are purchased and installed. If the amount is higher than the allowance, a change order will be issued. Using allowances gives the customer a good picture of what the project will cost when there are unknown elements to consider.

Contingency.   A *contingency* is a percentage added to an estimate to cover any unexpected costs. Contingencies include items such as special delivery of mail or materials, unplanned overtime, or equipment breakdowns. The contingency is usually inserted as a percentage of estimated cost before markup. Percentages vary between 5 percent and 20 percent depending on the estimator's confidence in their work. Contingency monies not used become profit and sometimes ensure that there will be a profit.

Profit.   **Profit (markup)** represents the money left over after all expenses are paid. Profit is normally calculated as a percentage of total project costs. It may vary according to several factors, but should be a minimum of 5 percent and a maximum of 20 percent, with an average of 10 percent. When determining the profit percentage to use, the following should be considered:

- Competition
- Difficulty of working with a particular owner or agency
- How much time the contractor has available for new projects
- Size of the project
- The type of expertise required and complexity of the project
- Location of the project

Addenda

Addenda are changes, additions, or clarifications developed after the project has been released for bid. The changes often result from questions that bidders have asked during the pre-bid meeting.

ESTIMATING METHODS

There are many approaches to estimating. Every qualified contractor must decide what estimating method to use to develop a bid. The choice may depend on the type of project, the contractor's preferences, or the owners or agency's requirements. Small projects may be estimated by simple, less time-consuming methods such as adding up the cost to the contractor and doubling that to arrive at a bid price. As the complexity of the project increases, so must the accuracy of the estimate. Common estimating methods include the detailed survey estimate, components (unit-price) method, the cubic-foot method, the square-foot method, and the architect's estimate.

Detailed Survey Estimate

The detailed survey estimate, also called takeoff or quantity survey method, is a very accurate estimating method. A **detailed survey estimate** is based on a takeoff from the drawings and specifications and applies unit costs to all required materials and labor. While the bid documents may provide an estimate of the supplies needed, this list may be incomplete. Contractors should do their own quantity takeoff to be sure all materials are considered.

Materials and labor for each work item or unit is estimated. Pricing units are applied to each item on the takeoff sheet, the costs calculated, and the calculations checked. The sum of all the materials and labor are added to the costs for equipment, overhead, contingencies, and the desired profit margin. This total becomes the bid. Errors in the detailed survey method can cause a bid to be too high, making it non-competitive, or the bid can be too low, resulting in no profit or a loss on the project. A number of aids are available, such as those from the Construction Specifications Institute (CSI) and various computer programs, to track and verify the costs.

Components (Unit-Price) Method

The **unit-price method** relies on job costs from previous projects, with labor, materials, and overhead for similar items or subassemblies combined into unit costs for those items. It can include cost per cubic foot of poured concrete, cost per square foot of completed interior or exterior walls, or cost per square of roofing material. The unit-price method allows for calculation of costs with a minimum of time and information. However, it provides no protection from cost increases in labor or materials since the last job cost update.

A unit-price estimate may be required for construction projects where the owner needs to know the cost of each step in the construction process or where quantities of materials or labor are hard to determine. As in the detailed survey method, a quantity survey is required in order to know what materials will be needed. Rather than summarizing the costs of these materials, the job is divided into units and the costs of all materials, labor, and overhead for each unit are summarized.

A homebuilding contract for a subdivision may ask for unit costs for grading and landscaping, paving streets, constructing basements, erecting framing, and so forth. Earthmoving costs can vary widely depending on the type of soil, presence of rocks, and drainage requirements. The contractor must estimate the cost of moving one cubic yard of dirt, including equipment rental and/or maintenance, labor, overhead, and profit. The estimator can then calculate the cost of any earth-moving job by multiplying the unit cost by the number of cubic yards to be moved. For best results, these unit costs are developed based on job costing from prior projects. Increased accuracy in estimating may be possible with the use of specialized computer programs designed for this purpose. Estimating manuals and computer software are available that can be used in preparing estimates.

Square-Foot Method

The square foot method can be used where projects involve similar size and type structures, such as a series of single-story homes. It is based on job costs from similar projects. While quick and easy, the square-foot method does not compensate for material or labor cost increases, abnormal site conditions, or other unusual requirements.

Cubic-Foot Method

The cubic-foot method is similar to the square-foot method, but it adds height to the cost calculations. An excavating company may use the cubic-foot method and charge for each cubic foot or cubic yard of material removed. The cubic-foot method has the same deficiencies as the square-foot method in that it is very general and not job specific.

Architect's Estimate

The architect's estimate or conceptual estimate is usually based on published cost guides or prior experience with similar projects. It may not reflect unusual site conditions or cost increases since publication of the guides.

THE FORMAL BID   GUARANTEE

The **formal bid** is a statement that the contractor agrees to build the project in accordance with the bid documents for the stated price. It cannot be emphasized too strongly that bids must be based on accurate takeoff and careful estimating. Once the bid is accepted and the contract signed, the contractor must complete the project as specified or suffer serious legal consequences.

The bid must respond directly to the specifications without the contractor imposing special provisions. If the bid does not respond exactly to the owner's or agency's needs, it may be rejected. Municipal, state, and federal agencies are especially careful when reviewing a bid to ensure that all the elements of the bid are included and the procedures for developing the bid have been followed.

If there are any discrepancies, the bid may be declared unresponsive and rejected. A typical unresponsive element is the failure to state how a certain item will be provided when the issuing agency has identified the item as a matter of concern. The item may simply have been overlooked by the contractor during the estimating process; nonetheless, the bid will still be rejected. Owners may overlook discrepancies in the bid if they choose.

Bids are normally accepted or rejected within 30 days to 90 days from the closing date. In some cases, the owner or agency may state in the invitation to bid when the project will be awarded.

SAMPLE ESTIMATE AND BID

A contractor wants to hire a subcontractor to perform site preparation for a building project. The job will entail tree removal, grading, silt fence installation, and seeding to stabilize the site until construction is started.

The site visit shows that the underground utilities have been marked and will have to be moved. The local jurisdiction requires filing a land disturbance plan as well as a permit to remove trees.

The bid may be assembled as seen in Table 3.2.

Direct costs for the project have been estimated at $3,000.

The bid is calculated in two steps. First, combine the desired overhead and profit percentages and subtract from 100 percent. This yields the percent of the bid equal to the actual direct costs. (See Table 3.3.)

Another way to develop an estimate is to determine the direct costs and then multiply by 100 percent. This will result in a bid price of $6,000, will provide for contingencies, and will also allow room for negotiations in price.

Avoiding Common Errors

It is essential that estimates be numerically accurate and meet all of the requirements of the bid documents. If an estimate is too high, the bid will not be competitive. If errors result in low estimates, project costs may exceed projected profit—resulting in a loss. Any loss is paid by the contractor.

TABLE 3.2
Direct Cost Estimate

Permits	$75
Tree Removal	$800
Stump Grinding	$325
Grading	$500
Silt Fencing	$800
Labor	$500
Direct Cost Total	$3,000

TABLE 3.3
Bid Calculation

Description	Percent
Project Overhead	10
General Overhead	15
Profit (before taxes)	20
Combined Overhead and Profit	45
Bid price	100
Less Combined Overhead and Profit	(45)
Allowable Direct Costs	55

Convert 55% to a decimal = 0.55

The bid price is calculated as: $\dfrac{\$3{,}000}{0.55} = \$5{,}454$

The bid can be summarized as follows:

Bid Amount		$5,454
Direct Costs	5,454 × 0.55	(3,000)
Project Overhead	5,454 × 0.10	(545)
Gross Profit	5,454 − 3,545	$1,909
Company Overhead	5,454 × 0.15	(818)
Before Tax Profit	1,901 − 818	$1,100

CHAPTER 3 Estimating and Bidding

A common and potentially expensive error is to leave an item out of the bid. The complexity of quantity takeoff and specifications may generate lengthy lists of materials. To ensure that no item is overlooked, each item should be checked off as it is added to the summary. A second person should always double-check the bid, preferably using a different color checkmark or highlighter. Calculations are best done on a computer or, at a minimum, using a calculator with a register tape so that calculations can be checked against each item. Results should be crosschecked against similar projects to determine if they are reasonable.

Another troublesome error is transposing (reversing) numbers. If the cost of the item is $4,100 but the amount is entered as $1,400, the severity of the error is obvious. In another case, if the estimator has 300 units at $65 but has entered $56 as the cost per unit, an inaccurate bid price will result.

$$300 \times \$65 = \$19{,}500$$

$$300 \times \$56 = \$16{,}800$$

$$\$19{,}500 - \$16{,}800 = \$2{,}700.$$

The error has cost the contractor $2,700.

Bidding Competitively

Whenever an invitation to bid is issued, the contractor should try to determine who else is bidding. No one wants to compete with a contractor who routinely underbids. Every bid should be competitive and realistic with numbers that will ensure that costs are recovered and a profit realized.

When local contractors bid against each other, the material costs should be nearly the same. They will be purchasing from the same or competing suppliers. They will (usually) be offered the same discounts. They should be quoting the same quality materials, as detailed in the specifications.

Subcontractor bids may vary and the quality of the work may be the cause. Some subcontractors will provide better quality, but charge a higher price. The prime contractor must determine which subcontractors offer the best value. One contractor may have mostly skilled employees while another uses more apprentices. This will influence the labor rates, which are often 25 percent to 33 percent of the total project cost.

A thorough knowledge of the competition will aid in pricing the bid competitively. Underbidding the job may help win the contract, but it may not be profitable for the company. A contractor risks losing the contract by overpricing the work. An occasional low bid designed to maintain basic operations (keep key employees, pay utilities, etc.) may be acceptable, but a company will not last long with many low-bid contracts.

Bid Rigging

Bid rigging occurs when a contractor conspires with other bidders to ensure the award of a bid, with the result of winning the bid. Bid rigging (also called "price fixing") is a crime. Contractors who conspire together to rig bids are subject to criminal prosecution and fines.

SUMMARY

Selecting the job that is right for the company and clearly understanding what the customer wants are critical elements that need to be in place before the estimating and bidding process begins. The job must fit the profile of the contracting company's ability and experience. Once it is assured that the customer and the contractor are on the same page, the estimate and bid can be prepared. The use of a particular estimating method will be determined by the scope of the job. No matter what method is selected, it must be done accurately and the figures checked by another person because once the bid is submitted the contractor must abide by the document.

CHAPTER 4

CONTRACTS

The title "contractor" clearly states what is done in this profession. A contractor signs contracts and performs according to the terms of a legal document, the contract. It is important that the contract be a written document because it is then a record of what has been agreed to by both parties. Even though a conversation and a handshake may suffice in some informal settings, a written contract provides binding, legal proof of what was agreed upon and will be useful in contract disputes. This chapter will review the elements and obligations of a contract.

WRITTEN CONTRACT

A **contract** is a binding agreement between two or more persons. It is a formal summary of what has been agreed upon and provides a legal obligation to perform in a certain manner.

A contract begins with a negotiation. A **negotiation** is when both parties discuss or bargain to reach an agreement. The negotiation process is started when a bid is requested by a customer. A *bid* is an offer to furnish labor, equipment, and materials in a specified manner and time and for a certain price. There is a difference between an offer and a negotiation: a negotiation occurs when a contractor offers to perform a service but neither the price nor the project start date is fixed. For the negotiation to become an offer, the service must be defined, the time in which the service will be performed is set, and the cost is determined.

Offers are usually time-constrained, that is, the customer must accept the offer within a certain time frame. This is done because the price of goods may change or the contractor will need to make other work commitments. An offer made in writing by the contractor must be accepted in writing by the customer.

A written contract details the formal acceptance of negotiations or a bid by both parties. All information listed in the bid documents is also referenced in the contract. These documents then become a binding part of the contract. Additional requirements that have been agreed to by both the owner and the contractor may also be added to the contract. The final contract can be quite lengthy and very detailed. A contract should always be reviewed, preferably by an attorney, before signing.

CONTRACT VALIDITY

For the courts to consider a contract valid, it must include the following essential elements:

- Competent parties. The parties signing the contract have the authority to do so and have reached the age of majority (they are adults).

- Offer or subject matter. The details of what is going to be performed in a certain manner, in a certain time frame, and at a certain price.

- Consideration. This is the value of the contract; normally an exchange of money. The contractor will perform the work and will be paid by the owner.

- Acceptance. The mutual agreement of the parties to the obligation of the terms of the contract.

A thorough understanding of the contract and agreement with its terms prior to signing (accepting) is essential. The contract represents a legally binding mutual agreement between the parties. If disagreements over contract terms and conditions arise, the courts will interpret strictly by what is written, not what may have been said or was thought to be understood.

A contract does not need to be in writing to be valid. However, oral agreements or contracts can lead to many disputes based on different memories or interpretations of what was said. Many states require that any contracts involving real property must be in writing. Required or not, common sense dictates that a contractor always have a written contract. The contract must include the full legal name of the signatories, along with the registered name of their business. Anyone signing the contract should disclose their title.

Legal Guidelines

Court decisions over many years have established several legal guidelines regarding contracts, as follows:

- Written agreements take precedence over oral agreements.
- Later agreements supersede earlier agreements.
- Special clauses prevail over general clauses.
- Handwritten agreements override printed agreements.
- Specifications prevail over drawings.
- Words prevail over numbers; all dollar amounts in a contract should be written out.
- Ambiguous, misleading, or confusing statements are always interpreted against the party preparing the contract.

Standard Form of Agreement

The primary contract document is the standard form of agreement. A *standard form of agreement* is a summary of all the documents related to the contract agreement that confirms the scope of the project, assigns responsibility for the project, lists bonding and insurance requirements, and sets the price and payment details. The following are minimum standards for residential construction or building contracts:

- The owner's name and address
- A description of the property and its location
- A description of the work
- When the work is to begin and the estimated completion date
- A listing of specific materials that have been requested by the owner
- A statement of the total cost of the contract and the amounts and schedule for progress payments, including a specific statement on the amount of the down payment
- An identification of drawings and specifications applicable to the project
- A "plain-language" exculpatory clause concerning events beyond the control of the contractor
- A statement that delays caused by events beyond the control of the contractor do not constitute abandonment and are not included in calculating time frames for payment or performance
- A statement of assurance that the contractor will comply with all local requirements for building permits, inspection, and zoning
- A disclosure of the cancellation rights of all parties
- For contracts resulting from door-to-door solicitation, a signed acknowledgment by the consumer (owner) that said consumer has been provided with, has read, and understands the right to cancel the contract (required in some states)
- A statement that any modification to the contract that changes the cost, materials, work to be performed, or estimated completion date must be in writing and signed by all parties
- The contractor's name, address, license number, phone number, expiration date, and the classifications or services authorized under the license
- Signature of the owner and contractor and the date
- Any required state and locality documents

Typically, the standard form of agreement is the only document actually signed by both parties, although some owners or contractors require both party's initials on every included document. Project documents used in the estimating and bidding process may be included by reference or may be attached as part of the contract.

Signing the Contract

The contract must be signed by both the owner (customer) and the contractor. In order to avoid personal liability, it is critical that the contractor sign the contract as an agent for the company, otherwise, the liability exemption of an LLC or a corporation would be null and void. If the contractor signs a contract personally, then the contractor is personally responsible for all liability. It is very simple to avoid this problem through the use of the word "by." The procedure is to insert the word "by" before the contractor's name on the signature line. The contractor's position or title, such as president or manager, should appear after the contractor's name. This signifies that the contractor is acting as the agent of the company and is not signing the contract personally, maintaining the shift of liability from the contractor to the corporation.

The use of this one word indicates to all parties that the person signing the contract is doing so as an agent of the company and not as an individual. The difference is that a salesman signing a contract "Ace Fuentes, Sales Manager, Bob the Builder Co." means that Ace is obligating himself personally to the contract as opposed to signing "by Ace Fuentes, Sales Manager, Bob the Builder Co.," which indicates that Ace is accepting the contract on behalf of the company. One little word is very important and makes a huge difference.

Standard Contract Forms

Most contractors, builders, architects, engineers, attorneys, and owners prefer standard contract forms. Standard contract forms use legally tested wording, provide for all necessary information, and remind all parties of what information is required in the contract. Because all parties are familiar with standard contract forms, fewer disagreements arise. A standard contract is convenient, but may not contain provisions required by the state. The contract must be reviewed, and amended if necessary, by a person competent in the specific requirements of the state. The most common contract forms used (except for government projects) are available from construction bookstores and via the Internet. Some standard contracts have a clause that requires arbitration should there be a disagreement between the contract parties. This may preclude using the court system to resolve the issue. Government agencies may develop their own contract forms and bid requirements.

A sample offer, when signed, is the contract. (See Figure 4.1.) Note that this document is provided for information purposes only and is not offered as a standard to be used for all contracts.

Surety Bonds

Contracts may require that contractors provide a surety bond to ensure compliance or performance. A **surety bond** is a legal document under which one party agrees to answer to another party for the debt, default, or failure to perform for a third party. Surety bonds are issued by insurance companies. Surety bonds include performance bonds, payment bonds, and lien bonds, and should be included as part of the contract. The performance bond (frequently called a contract bond in the bid process) and lien bond protect the owner from the contractor's failure to complete the project and failure to pay project debts. The payment bond guarantees payment to the contractor for work performed.

Proof of public liability, workers' compensation, and unemployment insurance carried by the contractor may also be required.

General Conditions.   Any contract may have general conditions. The general conditions specify the rights and responsibilities of the owner and contractor, and their official representatives under the contract. For example, the general conditions may allow an owner to give the architect, engineer, or construction manager the owner's responsibility for approving specification changes or modifications. Construction bookstores offer standard forms of general conditions designed to incorporate typical federal and state requirements.

Special or Supplementary Conditions

Special conditions modify the general conditions to suit situations unique to the project. These conditions must be completely understood, since they add to or override any related general conditions.

FIGURE 4.1
Sample Offer

January 1, 2005

This offer is provided:

To the Owner:

    Mary Customer

    5858 Somestreet Dr

    Richmond, VA 12345

    804-555-0001

By the Contractor:

    Bob the Builder

    PO BOX 001

    Oilville, VA 23219

    804-555-1234

    State Contractor A Building License #A121212, expires September 30, 2007

For the following proposed services:

1. Construct at the residence of Mrs. Customer at 5858 Somestreet Drive consisting of an 8' (eight foot) by 10' (ten foot) deck consisting of composite 5/4 thick decking boards secured by stainless steel screws supported on 6" × 6" wood posts supported on concrete pedestals. The pedestals will rest on concrete footings, 24" × 24" × 12" consisting of 3,500 lb. psf air-entrained concrete. The deck will be one platform and will rise no more than 8" (eight inches) from the ground level plane. A drawing of this deck is submitted as Attachment A and is incorporated by reference into this offer. All work will be performed in a workmanlike manner in accordance with all applicable regulations. The contractor will obtain all permits.

2. The work will begin February 1, 2005, and will be completed by March 1, 2005. The work schedule and completion date may be amended due to incidents beyond the control of the contractor such as acts of God, weather, delays caused by public agencies, labor delays not caused by the contractor, or start date delays caused by the owner. A delay based on any of these circumstances does not constitute the abandonment of the job by the contractor.

3. The cost for all services outlined in this offer will be a total of $5,000.00 (five thousand dollars) payable according to the following schedule:

    $1,000 due upon signing

    $2,000 due upon completion of footings

    $2,000 due upon completion and acceptance of the project

4. This offer is valid for 30 (thirty) days from January 1, 2005.

5. Any changes or additions to this offer must be in writing and signed by both the owner and the contractor.

6. The owner acknowledges receipt of the document "Right to Cancel" the contract and has read and understands the right to cancel the contract.

Accepted

_____

Owner

_____

Date

Accepted by

_____

Sales Manager, Bob the Builder

_____

Date

Drawings and Specifications

The drawings and specifications provide the actual physical description of the project and the materials to be used. Any substantial project will have these documents prepared by a qualified and licensed architect, designer, or engineer. The drawings detail the location, quantity, size, and type of every item needed to complete the project. The specifications provide detailed requirements for performance characteristics of materials and the completed assembly. Large projects may have separate sets of drawings and specifications for several construction disciplines including the following:

- Architectural
- Civil
- Electrical
- Mechanical (Plumbing, HVAC)
- Structural

Addenda

Addenda are changes made to the project or contract documents before the date that bids are accepted because they contain information that could affect bid prices. They are part of the project documents, and are therefore incorporated into the standard form of agreement or contract.

Modifications

Modifications are changes made to the project after the agreement is signed. It is critical that each modification is signed or initialed by both the owner, or owner's representative, and the contractor. Because modifications will most likely affect the project costs, provisions should be made to adjust the contract price as part of the modification agreement.

RIGHTS AND RESPONSIBILITIES

The contract establishes a legal and binding relationship between the owner, the contractor, and their representatives. The prime contractor is independent; the owner may not interfere with the contractor's work. If the contractor is not permitted to direct the work, the owner risks becoming an employer, with all the legal and tax liabilities.

Standard construction contracts detail the legal requirements and procedures for resolving disputes, seeking remedies for breach of contract and the termination of the contract. Payment of legal costs in cases of contract disputes will be borne by the losing party and may include arbitration and administrative and legal costs.

Owner Rights

The owner has the right, based on the terms of the contract, to

- begin occupancy and use of completed portions of the project that have been approved and authorized by the locality;
- inspect project work;

- request additions, deletions, or modifications to the project;
- offer other contracts related to the project;
- perform or contract to a third party any work not done by the contractor;
- require contract bonds and insurance;
- request different completion schedules; and
- withhold or deduct payments for incomplete work or work not done according to specifications.

Owner Responsibilities

The owner is responsible for providing

- access to the job site;
- complete plans and specifications;
- legally unencumbered property (site) for the project; and
- timely payments to the prime contractor.

Contractor Rights

The contractor's basic right is prompt payment for the work done. Procedures for progress payments, retainage, and adjustments for modifications are detailed in the contract. Bonuses may be available for completing all or part of the project prior to the scheduled completion date, and penalties for late or incomplete work are specified when appropriate. There may be an escalation clause on longer-term projects to reimburse the contractor for wage increases or unanticipated rises in the cost of materials or equipment. An example would be an adjustment for the steadily increasing cost of fuel.

Contractor Responsibilities

The contractor's basic responsibility is to complete the project on time in accordance with the contract. This includes but is not limited to

- advising the owner of any delays, errors, or other problems;
- complying with all state and federal regulations (employment, payroll, tax, safety, etc.);
- ensuring completion of the project as specified;
- hiring and subcontracting in accordance with contract guidelines on government projects;
- maintaining all required or agreed-upon insurance coverage; and
- paying attention to the project at all times.

ADDITIONAL CONTRACT CATEGORIES

The basic type of contract is an agreement between an owner or agency and a single prime contractor. There are several different special contract relationships to meet specific needs. Contract categories include design/build, turnkey, phased or fast track, multiple prime contractors, and partnering.

Design/Build

A design/build contract is one where a prime (or general) contractor takes responsibility for the architectural, engineering, bidding, contracting, construction (building) inspection, and final approval of the project. The prime contractor may or may not manage the actual construction but may elect to simply manage the project, hiring another contractor to do the work. With a single person in charge of the entire project, the owner or agency does not need to be involved in conflicts between parties or groups responsible for design, engineering, and construction.

Turnkey

A turnkey contract gives the prime contractor responsibility for developing the entire project. The contractor's responsibilities include finding or providing financing, purchasing the land, and obtaining any necessary rezoning of the property, in addition to all the responsibilities of a design/build contract. Turnkey construction should increase the income and profit potential to the contractor.

Phased or Fast Track

The fast track contract provides for starting construction before all the plans and drawings are complete. In a fast track approach, each phase of the project is bid and contracted separately to a single prime contractor.

Multiple Prime Contractors

In instances when the project is extremely demanding and requires more expertise than is available from a single contractor, the owner or agency may assume the responsibility to coordinate and manage the project. The owner or owner's representative will call for separate bids for each part of the project. Each contract must specify the relationships between the prime contractors and their responsibility for any interference with each other.

Partnering

Partnering contracts are used to help the owner, architect, engineer, and contractor work smoothly together. They enter a cooperative agreement (partnership) on all aspects of the project in order to successfully complete the project.

MISCELLANEOUS CONTRACT CONSIDERATIONS

There are additional issues that must be considered when developing a contract. Some of these issues are the indemnification clause, the time schedule, time extensions or delays, accelerated schedules, change orders, and field orders. Additionally, aesthetic changes, Brand X considerations, site conditions, necessary permits and fees, and code compliance issues must be considered before the contract is signed.

Indemnification or Hold Harmless Clauses

An *indemnification clause* is a contractual obligation in which one person agrees to secure another person as not responsible in cases of loss or damage from certain liabilities. Indemnification is used to protect one party (usually the owner) from liability for events caused by mutual activities. The contract may state that the contractor will hold the owner harmless for property damage or personal injury regardless of who is responsible. This protection should be provided by an appropriate insurance policy.

Time Schedules

Time schedules are very important considerations in most construction contracts. The contract will specify when the project should commence and when it is considered completed. The contractor is responsible for starting and completing the project on time. Starting the project late, finishing late, or disregarding the schedule is a breach of contract.

Penalties (damages) for late completion (damages) or bonuses for early completion may be a part of the contract. These penalties (called liquidated damages) are usually in the form of a specific dollar amount for each day after the scheduled completion date. Liquidated damages are specified; there is no relationship to actual damages. Conversely, a bonus may be offered for early completion, again usually a fixed dollar amount for each day between the actual date of completion and the scheduled date.

Time Extensions

Time extensions are permitted in response to unavoidable delays in the project. The contract should require the owner/agency to adjust time schedules when the project is delayed through no fault of the contractor. Typical conditions that permit time extensions are the following:

- Acts of God
- Additions to the project
- Changes to the scope of the project
- Delays caused by public agencies or utilities
- Design errors
- Environmental delays
- Extreme weather (not normal to the area)
- Labor strike, riot, and war
- Legal delays not caused by the contractor
- Owner's failure to provide access to the property
- Start date delays due to actions of the owner, architect, or engineer

Delays

Whenever a contractor discovers a significant delay, the owner must be notified as soon as possible of the nature of the delay and how long it will last. The notification should indicate what time extension is requested. Provision should be made on the notification for the owner's signature or initials indicating acceptance of the proposed extension. Time extensions are not granted for conditions that were present when the contract was signed or which should have been anticipated.

Part of the contractor's role is expecting reasonably foreseeable delays and planning to work around them without delaying the job schedule.

Accelerated Completion

Accelerated completion permits the owner to request the contractor to complete the project before the contracted completion date. All expenses incurred by accelerating the project are the responsibility of the owner.

If the contractor is at fault in delaying a project, the owner may demand an accelerated schedule to meet the target completion date. In this case, the added expenses accrue to the contractor.

Change Orders

Changes or modifications to the project are anticipated in virtually all contracts. Provision is made for issuing written change orders, signed by the owner and contractor, for alterations to the project. The change order includes a description of the work to be done, an estimate of the time required, its impact on the completion date, and any additional compensation. While a change order may be issued orally by the owner, it is imperative that this be followed up with a written order. All change orders become a part of the contract. Some changes may be so major that a new contract will be necessary.

Field Orders

Field orders are changes that are not likely to cost time or money. They are informal orders that are usually not reduced to writing. Be aware that changes to the project that are not signed by the owner may result in a contract dispute.

Aesthetic Changes

Aesthetic changes may be permitted under an "aesthetic intent" clause in the contract. This clause allows the architect to make in-progress changes to ensure the finished construction reflects the original intent of the project. Such changes may delay the project, increase (or decrease) the cost, or make supplies already purchased obsolete. The aesthetic intent clause should contain provisions for time extensions and additional consideration resulting from these changes.

Brand X

A Brand X allowance in the specifications allows the contractor to substitute equivalent materials to those specified. Brand X materials may be less expensive or more readily available than the products specified. Any variance from specifications requires approval by the owner or architect.

Site Conditions

The conditions of the job site can have a major impact on the project. The contract should contain provisions for adjustment in the event of unforeseen conditions that affect the project costs and time schedules. In order to be considered unforeseen, the site conditions must differ appreciably from anticipated conditions, substantially increase costs or delay the project, and be difficult for a reasonably skilled contractor or estimator to discover.

The owner or agency is obligated to disclose all available information about the site during the bidding process. The contractor has a responsibility to perform a thorough site inspection and compare it to the information provided. Discrepancies must be brought to the attention of the owner and resolved prior to bidding. Most contracts will hold the owner and architect harmless for variances in the information on site conditions they supply. The owner is liable for added costs only if the project documents contain inaccurate or misleading information about the site.

Site Access.   Providing access to the site is the owner's responsibility. Timely, ready access to the site is necessary for the contractor to start and complete the project on time.

Cleanup.   Providing a safe environment for employees on site is required by OSHA and includes cleanup of materials and debris during and following construction. Site cleanup is the contractor's responsibility. Some contracts will assign the final cleanup to the owner, with the contractor billed for the cleanup costs.

Permits and Fees

Acquiring the necessary permits required prior to awarding the contract is the responsibility of the owner. Once the contract is signed, the contractor must pay for any necessary permits, fees, licenses, and inspections.

Code Compliance

All plans, specifications, and contract documents must comply with applicable codes. Code compliance for the design is primarily the responsibility of the architect or designer. The contractor must advise the owner if any violations or variations to code are discovered, either during plan review or at the job site. The contractor cannot perform any construction in a manner that is inconsistent with the code.

Subcontracts

When a prime contractor needs help with a project, other contractors are employed to perform some of the work. The prime contractor selects, directs, and pays the subcontractors, much like an owner. The actual owner of the project may insist on approving all subcontractors. If so, this is stipulated in the contract. The subcontractor must accept and follow all conditions of the general contract and the project documents.

It is suggested that a contract with a subcontractor contain a provision that 20 percent of the value of the contract will be retained by the contractor if the subcontractor cannot provide proof of workers compensation insurance in those states where it is required.

A written contract with all subcontractors protects both the subcontractor and the prime contractor. While an oral agreement (contract) may be valid, it will be very difficult to enforce. The general contract should be included by reference, and the subcontractor should receive copies of all project documents pertinent to the subcontract. A subcontractor should inquire and make it a contract requirement that any "flowdown" clauses are disclosed. A *flowdown clause* is a statement in the general contract that any subcontractors must comply with certain conditions of the general contract. Unless the subcontractor is advised of these conditions, they will remain a mystery and a potential minefield. The subcontractor may violate a condition in the general contract and be unaware of the issue. The subcontract will contain essentially all of the same information and documents as contained in a general contract. A sample subcontractor agreement is provided in Appendix B.

When the contractor signs a subcontract, it is considered acceptance of the subcontractor's bid. The written acceptance of the bid must include a reference to the offer (bid), an acceptance of that offer, the date of acceptance, and signatures of all parties.

A payment schedule is part of the subcontract. The payment schedule may be a lump sum, unit price, or cost plus agreement. There may also be statements about retainage, progress payments, insurance, and bonding in the schedule. Customarily, subcontracts will specify payment of the subcontractor promptly after receiving payment from the owner. Federal contracts usually specify this payment must be made within 14 days.

Value Engineering

Value engineering is a term applied to a contractor discovering and disclosing to the owner ways to save money on a project. Contracts will often contain a value engineering clause, under which the contractor receives a portion of the savings resulting from cost-saving suggestions.

Warranties

A warranty gives the owner the right to require the contractor to correct deficiencies in the work performed. Where components are covered by manufacturers' warranties, the contract may require the contractor to cover the labor cost for the warranty period. Some states have specific laws requiring warranties.

Certificate of Substantial Completion

A certificate of substantial completion is issued, usually by the architect, when the project is sufficiently complete so that the owner can use at least a portion for its intended purpose. Once the certificate is issued, the contractor will usually issue a request for payment. The regulating agency, usually the building inspection department, must approve the use.

Certificate of Occupancy

A certificate of occupancy (CO) is issued by the building inspector certifying that the structure conforms to all relevant codes and is safe to use. A certificate of occupancy is required before a building can be occupied. Some jurisdictions may issue a certificate of partial occupancy when the structure is such that portions may be occupied safely while the balance of the construction is completed.

CONSTRUCTION CONTRACT TYPES

The type of construction contract used is determined by contract negotiations and financing. Some contract types assign more risk to the contractor, some to the owner. If a contractor is willing to accept more risk, there is also the opportunity for more reward.

Lump Sum or Fixed Price Contracts

A lump sum contract is a very commonly used contract. A lump sum contract, sometimes called a detailed survey or fixed price contract, reflects the contractor's guarantee to the owner that the project will be completed for a fixed (contract) price. If unforeseen expenses occur, the contractor must pay them. The project must be completed, even if the contractor suffers a loss. If the contract is completed for less than the agreed price, the balance accrues to the contractor as additional profit. The contract may contain provisions for sharing unexpected costs under specific situations.

A lump sum contract requires a very detailed survey and a careful estimate. A contractor with a good record of accurately estimating project costs may prefer a lump sum contract. The extra risk in a lump sum contract is offset by the contractor's opportunity for increased profit. Owner's usually like the lump sum contract because the cost of the project is fixed, with no extra charges for unanticipated costs.

Unit Price Contracts

A unit price contract is used when the total number of units is unknown. The owner will not know the total cost of the contract until it is completed; however, they will know the cost of each unit. The contractor must complete the project whether the total number of units is more or less than the estimate. The owner must pay for all units used or constructed. Both the contractor and the owner will want as accurate an estimate as possible to avoid surprises during construction.

Cost Plus Contracts

Cost plus contracts guarantee that the owner will pay for all materials, labor, equipment, etc., used on the project plus a fee for the contractor's administration and supervision. Be aware that some states do not permit an open ended contract regarding costs. Provisions must be made to give the owner an estimate of the cost.

Cost Plus Fee Contract.   In a cost plus fee contract, a fixed dollar amount is paid to the contractor for their services.

Cost Plus Percentage Contract. A cost plus percentage contract is similar to a cost plus fee contract, except that the fee is a percentage of the costs. The percentage may be a fixed or variable amount. The fee or the percentage is always prescribed in the contract. Fee limits, bonuses for completing ahead of schedule, penalties for late completion, and a cost ceiling may also be included in the contract.

When the contractor can provide a good estimate of the project costs, the contract will usually include a fixed fee. When an accurate cost estimate is not possible—rebuilding after a fire, hurricane, or tornado, for example—a cost plus percentage contract is more desirable to both parties.

CONTRACT PAYMENTS

Contracts may extend for months or years. Meanwhile, the contractor must pay for labor, materials, equipment rental, and subcontractors. In order to cover these expenses, the contract usually calls for progress payments as the project proceeds. These payments may be due at regular intervals (i.e., monthly) during the construction or they may be based on completion of specific steps. Typically, the contractor will submit a payment request. The owner or owner's representative will inspect the work completed and authorize payment.

Retainage

Retainage is a certain percentage of the payment retained by the customer to ensure satisfactory completion of the project. Retainage is commonly a percentage, such as 10 percent, of the amount due. This money is held until the project is completed; it is a part, or may be all, of the final payment. The contractor will also withhold retainage from subcontractors and suppliers. This helps offset the retainage withheld from the contractor by the owner. The final payment is not made until the owner has occupied the project and is satisfied with all aspects of the project. Recovery of the retainage may take a long time, which can be a problem for contractors who bid low, because the retainage may be more than the expected profit.

Sample Progress Payments

A contract is issued for a project that will cost $2,970,000 and take 24 months to complete. Progress payments will be made monthly. Retainage will be withheld at 10 percent. Each invoice (payment request) is equal to the project cost divided by the time to complete the project (24 months). (See Figure 4.2.)

Final Payment

The final payment is the unpaid balance, which will be the retainage: $297,000. This will be withheld until all inspections have been completed, and any punch-list work is done. A **punch-list** is a list developed by the owner and/or the contractor that identifies corrections that are required. For example, a piece of trim may be missing, or a drywall nail needs more mudding. All documents are provided to the owner. If there is no retainage, the last progress payment is the final payment. Typical documents required for final payment include the following:

- Affidavits confirming payment of all labor, materials, equipment, and subcontractors' costs
- A certificate of completion from the architect or design person certifying the work has been completed satisfactorily in accordance with the contract
- An occupancy permit issued by the local building official
- As-built drawings
- Maintenance bonds
- Operating instructions for all equipment
- Releases or waivers of all liens

FIGURE 4.2
Sample Progress
Payments

1st Payment Request	Contract Amount	$2,970,000
	Payment Amount (2,970,000 ÷ 24)	123,750
	Less 10% Retainage	(12,375)
	Prior Payments	0
	Payment Due	$111,375
2nd Payment Request	Contract Amount	$2,970,000
	Payment Amount 2 × (2,970,000 ÷ 24)	247,500
	Less 10% Retainage	(24,750)
	Prior Payments	(111,375)
	Payment Due	$111,375
5th Payment Request	Contract Amount	$2,970,000
	Payment Amount 5 × (2,970,000 ÷ 24)	618,750
	Less 10% Retainage	(61,875)
	Prior Payments	(445,500)
	Payment Due	$111,375
24th Payment Request	Contract Amount	$2,970,000
	Payment Amount 24 × (2,970,000 ÷ 24)	2,970,000
	Less 10% Retainage	(297,000)
	Prior Payments	2,561,625
	Payment Due	$111,375

- Warranties for labor and materials used
- Written descriptions of any unresolved disputes or claims

As evident from the sample, the retainage can be a substantial amount. Contractors must be financially sound in order to operate while awaiting their money. This is a good incentive to complete the punch-out work and submit the documentation as quickly as possible.

CLAIMS

A **claim** is a written statement of disagreement with the purpose of putting a disagreement in writing. A claim arises when a contractor feels the owner owes an additional amount or the instructions under the contract are wrong, but the owner disagrees. A claim is not a request for payment in accordance with the contract.

A claim may arise when changes are made in the project but include no clear indication of who is responsible for any increased costs. It may be caused by local officials requiring changes during construction or before final approval and issuance of the certificate of occupancy.

If the claim cannot be resolved between the owner and contractor, then most contracts will have a provision to take the claim to arbitration. Meanwhile, the work must continue unless the disagreement is over a safety issue or the work is not a part of the contract.

Breach of Contract

A contract breach is a failure to perform to the contract. In the profession of contracting, there may be two levels of contract breach: material and immaterial.

Material Breach. A **material breach** is a significant violation of the contract and gives the other party a right to stop further performance and sue for damages. Some examples of this type of breach are: the owner locking the contractor out of the job site, resulting in the contractor not able to perform the work agreed upon; the owner refusing to pay for work done; or the contractor refusing to build in accordance with the specifications of the contract.

Immaterial Breach. An **immaterial breach,** although technically a violation of the contract, is a minor or inconsequential violation. It does not allow the other party to stop further performance. For example, the painter using the wrong trim color is not a serious enough offense for the owner to kick the painter off the job. A payment check lost in the mail is not a breach and would not entitle the contractor to walk off the job. The offending party must be given an opportunity to resolve the problem and make things right. If the offending party does not correct the situation, the immaterial breach may become a material breach and can become grounds for a lawsuit.

There must be a legal excuse (reason) for the actions of either the owner or the contractor, not an emotional one. If no legal reason is given for the action, the immaterial breach will likely result in damages awarded by a court to the other party. Should a contractor become involved in what is perceived as a breach, resolution with the owner must be attempted and documented, and advice sought from an attorney. The guiding principle is to work to the contract and resolve the differences as work proceeds.

LIENS

A **lien** is a claim on the property of another as security against the payment of a just debt. It is a legal action taken to force payment for labor or materials used to improve another's property. The lien threshold value, that is, the minimum amounts of material or labor that must be surpassed before a lien can be filed, is set by state law.

Lien laws allow material or equipment suppliers, subcontractors, and laborers to bind the property that has gained value from their materials or services. Liens take precedence over other debts related to the property. Liens can be relieved by foreclosure proceedings, under which the property can be sold to repay the lien holder.

A lien is a very serious threat to the property. Creditors will not accept property with a lien as collateral for a loan. Payments to the prime contractor are halted until the lien is cleared. Suppliers who are aware of the lien usually will not sell or ship materials to the contractor. The property owner is left with a property that cannot be improved and cannot be sold until the lien is cleared.

Any person who provided labor or materials used in the construction, alteration, remodeling, repair, or demolition of any building, land, or other structure can file a lien. The lien is always filed against the property, regardless of who is at fault. Thus, if a subcontractor fails to pay laborers assigned to the project, the laborers can obtain a lien against the property—and thereby penalize the property owner. The property includes the land on which the project is built as long as the owner of the construction contract was owner of record when the project was commissioned.

If sufficient lien claims are presented to cause court action, the court will sell the property and use the proceeds to satisfy the liens. If sale of the property yields less money than is required to satisfy all liens, payments are normally made in the following sequence:

- Laborers
- Material suppliers
- Subcontractors
- Prime contractors

Note that the prime contractor is last on this list. If an owner goes bankrupt, for example, it is quite possible that there will not be enough money from the forced sale of the property to satisfy all liens. The prime contractor is then out everything put into the project, with no recourse.

Contract Assignment

Selling the contract agreement, although it is common among mortgages and loan institutions, is prohibited under most contracts. The owner has a right to expect the contractor who won the bid to do the work. Similarly, the owner cannot sell the contract prior to completion without the contractor's agreement.

Contract Termination

Contract termination is permitted only under very specific conditions. A contract can be terminated if one party to the contract violates the terms so badly that the contract (or even the project) is no longer salvageable. Such failures are considered a breach of contract under contract law. Termination of the contract must include significant evidence of breach of contract. An invalid termination can lead to litigation and punitive damages. Both parties should be represented by competent legal counsel.

SUMMARY

A contract, whether purchased from a vendor or created on a computer, should be carefully reviewed to ensure that it contains all state specific requirements. Once the contract is signed, it legally binds the parties to the terms of the document. Any changes or additions must be in writing and signed by both parties.

CHAPTER **5**

RISK MANAGEMENT

The contracting profession is one where there is the risk of damage to customer's property or injury to an employee. A contractor must take necessary precautions to control the working environment and minimize the risk of injury to employees and damage to property. Events may occur that are beyond the ability to control such as fire or theft. A contractor must identify potential risks and take steps to minimize them or provide for compensation by others should they occur. **Risk management** is the process of identifying potential risks and taking action to protect the contracting company from those risks. When risks are identified, possible courses of action are to provide safety training to staff, provide more supervision, or have others (such as an insurance company) assume liability.

It is important to understand that an insurance company is in business, and it does not benefit the business to pay out money. The policy terms will outline what is covered as well as all exclusions. These terms limit the liability of the insurance company. This is why reading the coverage of a policy carefully prior to purchasing insurance is important. Coverage for an incident must be in place before it occurs. If no coverage is in place when an incident occurs, the incident will not be covered and damages will have to be paid by the contractor.

This chapter will discuss the minimum types of insurance that a contractor should carry; liability that protects personal injuries or property damage caused to others; and property insurance to cover the contractor's equipment and materials. It will also explore the importance of reading the policy carefully before purchasing and will conclude with a discussion of bonds that may be required on some projects.

LOSS PREVENTION

Preventing loss is the least expensive form of risk management. The contractor must be familiar with all aspects of the project to evaluate potential hazards and to take necessary steps to minimize them. For example, the site should be surveyed to determine the presence of electric wires that may be contacted by tall equipment. Underground utilities must be marked before excavating so that a gas line or electric line will not be cut during excavation. In addition, safety training programs will reduce the potential for accidents and prepare employees for a quick response when needed.

CHAPTER 5
Risk Management

Evaluation of the potential risks in the project is important. Estimates must be made of the likely frequency and severity of each hazard. The effects of uncontrollable events, such as severe weather, must be considered. A good construction insurance agent can help with this evaluation. Many insurance companies also have loss prevention experts available to train clients' personnel. They may also specify standard safety procedures that must be followed to keep the policies in force.

Protection against loss is available in the form of insurance or bonding. Once all the risks have been identified and the probability and severity of their occurrence has been determined, the contractor must obtain protection against financial liability for these risks. The cost of a single major accident or natural disaster can wipe out a company that does not have sufficient insurance coverage. An insurance agent experienced in construction services will help select the appropriate insurance or bonding approach for each project.

TYPES OF INSURANCE

The contractor should carry at least two types of insurance: liability insurance and property insurance. The state may require additional types of insurance.

Subcontractors should carry their own insurance coverage for themselves and their employees. The required insurance coverage for subcontractors is similar to what is required for prime contractors. Failure of the subcontractor to provide adequate coverage, as prescribed in the subcontract, is a breach of contract.

The prime contractor is responsible for any damages not covered by the subcontractor's insurance and so may require the subcontractor to obtain additional insurance, at the subcontractor's expense, to ensure coverage for any damages caused by the subcontractor. The prime contractor may purchase the necessary coverage and bill it to the subcontractor or terminate the subcontract. Contractors should require that they be indemnified by the subcontractor. Indemnification, a hold harmless clause, states that one person will not be held responsible for actions committed by another person that caused the loss or damage. This protection should be provided by an insurance policy.

Comprehensive General Liability

Comprehensive general liability (CGL) is a blanket insurance policy that provides broad coverage for personal injuries or property damage caused to others who are not employed by the contractor. There are a number of exclusions to the policy, and it is important to evaluate the policy carefully and obtain protection for the company against these exclusions through additional specific policies.

CGL coverage provides

- damage of property owned by other persons,
- injuries to those who are not the contractor's employees, and
- separate limits and provisions for property damage and injuries.

CGL coverage does not protect

- property owned by the contractor,
- injuries to the contractor's employees,
- environmental damage,
- defects in workmanship,

- breaches of warranty, and

- motor vehicle or water craft operation.

It is important to read the policy to determine what is covered and the extent of any deductions for payment. It is in the best interests of the insurance company to pay as little as possible under the terms of the policy, and the insurance company is typically required to pay for actual cash value, not replacement cost. A TV set that cost $500 new and is five years old will be replaced by paying the value of a five year old set.

A CGL policy allows the insurer to deduct a portion of the reimbursement based on the actual cash value, which is a depreciated value of the property, and payment will be for less than it will cost to replace the items with brand new ones. This will create a significant loss of good will between the owner, who wants new items to replace the old ones, and the contractor is in a terrible position. For example, a contractor is replacing a roof, and rain enters the building, destroying interior items. The CGL policy will pay for damage to items, but only at actual cash value, not what it will cost to go out and buy new items. A $3,000 desk purchased five years ago may be determined to have depreciated a percentage of its value and the insurance company will pay much less than the replacement cost. If the insurance company pays $750 for the desk, the remainder of $2,250 will be sought by the owner from the contractor. The owner will want a new desk, and who wouldn't? It is recommended that a contractor have a fund set aside to cover instances such as these, or buy a better policy.

Specific forms of liability insurance (or endorsements) are necessary to cover exclusions from a standard comprehensive general liability policy. In some cases, the small business owner may be compelled to purchase certain specialized liability insurance (e.g., errors and omissions liability insurance) depending on the particular circumstances.

The actual language in the policy will define the scope of the coverage and exclusions from coverage. In fact, what many contractors do not understand is that denial of a claim begins well before a claim is made. The denial began with the carefully selected wording in an insurance policy as to what is or is not covered.

Professional Liability Insurance

Professional liability insurance, also know as errors and omissions insurance, covers errors or negligence in performing the normal duties of a contractor. This insurance can be written to cover contingent liabilities due to actions or omissions by contract professionals and employees who are under the direction of the contractor. Professional liability insurance is particularly important when the contractor provides design, architectural, or engineering services.

Director's and Officer's Liability. *Director's and officer's (D&O) liability insurance* is a type of professional liability insurance that protects the company's senior management for reasonable, proper, and legal acts that occur in carrying out their role as officers of the company. Director's and officer's insurance will protect against a decision by the management to open a new office that goes bankrupt a year later. It will not protect against liabilities due to deliberate acts, such as embezzlement or failure to file required tax or labor notices.

Property Insurance

Property insurance is insurance that covers fire, smoke, theft, vandalism, etc., and provides coverage on structures and their contents. Property insurance is the business equivalent of a homeowner's policy, and covers structures, office equipment, and personal property. A rider to the policy (or a separate policy) may cover business interruption losses or temporary rental of quarters and equipment. In order to recover all losses, the property must be insured to its full value.

Builder's Risk Insurance

Builder's risk insurance is insurance that protects the contractor against any loss or damage to the project structure and materials or equipment purchased for the project while it is under construction. One form of builder's risk insurance is project property insurance, which covers all of the property owned by the contractor (e.g., tools or rental equipment).

Claims are usually valued at replacement cost rather than original cost. The policy may also include coverage for work interruption, loss of income, and any increased expenses due to the situation that resulted in a claim.

Equipment or Installation Floater Policy

An equipment or *installation floater policy* is an insurance policy purchased to protect against loss or damage to equipment or goods, whether owned or rented at the building site. This type of coverage is important if there are expensive fixtures or equipment involved.

Automobile (Vehicle) Insurance

Automobile (vehicle) insurance is insurance that covers cars, trucks, trailers, or other self-propelled or towed vehicles used for the business. Automobile coverage will protect against claims for property damage and personal injury as a result of the vehicle operation. Most states require that a person have automobile insurance before they are allowed to register the vehicle.

Burglary Insurance

Burglary insurance is insurance against burglary, robbery, and theft by persons other than employees.

Key Man Insurance

Key man insurance is a type of life insurance that provides monetary assistance to the company in the event of the death of essential staff. Key man insurance is particularly valuable to small companies.

Buying an Insurance Policy

When buying an insurance policy, the following principles should be kept in mind:

- Get quotes from several companies.
- Compare the premiums.
- Compare the policies.
- Pay the premium and make sure they are paid as required.
- Consider including a "duty to defend clause" wherein the insurance company supplies an attorney at their cost to defend a lawsuit against the insured.

The terms of a policy are normally standard for every company, and it is not expected that an agent will change them. It is best to read the entire policy, including terms of coverage and exclusions before purchasing a policy. The policy has to provide the protection needed. With insurance, as with many other purchases, one gets what one pays for. Just as in contracting, a low bid may offer something that in the long run will prove to be more expensive than the higher bid, and a cheap insurance policy may prove to be very expensive.

Making a Claim

When it is necessary to make a claim on the insurance policy, all insurance company policies should be followed closely to ensure payment of the claim. A few guidelines are as follows:

- Reread the policy.
- Call the insurance agent and follow up with a letter.
- Prepare to defend the claim by taking pictures and documenting the incident.
- Attempt to have another insurance company be responsible for the claim, such as a subcontractor's insurance company, if the subcontractor is at fault.

"Bad faith" is a term used when the insurance company does not act in accordance with the policy. Insurance companies do not stay in business by paying large claims and will try to pay as little as possible. A final measure, if an insurance agency has refused to pay a reasonable claim, is to file suit that the agency has acted in bad faith. For example, a claim is submitted that exceeds the policy limits and the insurance company refuses to pay and is willing to go to court. The insurance company is taking a chance that the court settlement will be less than the policy limit, and if greater, the policy holder will have to pay the difference. The risk for the insurance company is that if the claim can be shown to be reasonable, then the insurance company can be held as acting in bad faith and can be made to pay the policy limits as well as any amount over the limit in accordance with the judgment. Sometimes the mere mention of the term bad faith will cause the insurance company to take another look at their decision.

BONDS

A **bond** is a surety that guarantees completion of a project or recovery of a loss. Bonds are considered third party security. Fidelity bonds, for example, guarantee against losses suffered due to illegal or fraudulent activity by an employee. The bonding company pays the damages and is free to recover payment and legal costs from the person causing the loss. The bonding company may even seek criminal prosecution, all in the name of the bondholder.

Bonds are issued by surety companies. They are regulated by the state much like insurance companies, with state regulators controlling their rates. The U.S. Treasury Department must approve any surety company bonding for federal projects. A contractor may purchase all bonds and insurance from the same company.

Some bonds may be required by the contract. The bid and contract bonds are usually submitted with the bid. The lien bond and proof of liability insurance are not required until the bid is accepted.

The return or cancellation of a bond at the appropriate time is good project management. The contractor should note when the bond has been satisfied and take action to cancel the bond in order to reduce overhead costs.

Bid Bonds

A **bid bond** is a guarantee that the successful bidder will enter into a project contract for the agreed-upon price. Bid bonds are used to avoid tying up capital, as the owner may require a certified check as bid security without the bond. Bid bonds from unsuccessful bidders are returned to them shortly after the bid opening. The bid bond from the successful bidder is returned when the contract is signed.

Contract Bonds

A *contract bond (performance bond)* is a guarantee that the successful bidder will complete the project in accordance with the plans and specifications and in a timely manner. Contract bonds are returned upon completion of the project once the owner has released the contractor from obligation.

Payment Bonds

A *payment bond (lien bond)* is a bond that protects the owner against liens from suppliers and/or subcontractors for unpaid labor, materials bills, or labor. Lien bonds are returned upon completion of the project once the owner has been provided with documentation that all payments that would subject the property to a lien have been made.

Statutory Bonds

A *statutory bond* is a bond, usually required for public projects, that has been required by law. They incorporate all the requirements of the statute that applies to the project under consideration by reference, without spelling them out. Claims may be made for any requirement listed under the statute. State agencies responsible for public projects will normally furnish the necessary bond format for the state. The bonding company will have bonding agreements designed to comply with statute requirements. Federal agencies require use of a standard bond based on the Miller Act. The Miller Act is presented later in this chapter.

Bonding Rating and Capacity

A **bond rating** is the measure of risk of a bond going into default. The bond rating is based on the insurance company's evaluation of the contractor and probability of that contractor defaulting. The contractor must furnish financial statements, an affidavit of current bank credit, a list of property owned by the contractor, and performance references. The insurance company will investigate the reputations of the owner(s) and key personnel. They will review the company's bookkeeping and accounting, as well as their management style. Based on this information, the surety company assigns a rating to the contractor. The bonding premiums (costs) are based on this rating.

Capacity is the bonding agency's statement of the maximum amount of bonds they will carry for the contractor. Capacity is usually limited to 10 times the contractor's working capital. It is their estimate of the contractor's capabilities. This effectively limits the size and/or number of the contractor's projects. Capacity is determined using the following formula:

$$\text{Current assets} - \text{Current liabilities} = \text{Working capital} \times 10 = \text{Capacity}$$

For example, if a contractor had $500,000 in current assets and $300,000 in current liabilities, then $500,000 – $300,000 = $200,000 in working capital × 10 = $2,000,000 capacity.

A claim for a bond may be filed with the bonding company only after reasonable effort has been made to obtain payment. The bonding company will specify the procedure required in the bond document. On public projects, the claim process is defined by statute. A written notice of the claim must be filed within a given time frame. Usually, notice to the contractor and the owner is required under the bonding agreement. If the contractor disputes the claim, legal resolution is required for payment. No claim should be filed without the advice and assistance of an attorney familiar with construction law.

The bonding company is only responsible for activities or situations listed in the bonding document. Project changes made after the bond has been issued are not covered. Where significant changes in the project are desired, the bond(s) affected by those changes should be revised or replaced before proceeding with the changes.

THE MILLER ACT

The Miller Act, originally passed in 1935, requires bonding on all federal projects valued in excess of $100,000. The act applies to contracts for construction, alteration, remodeling, or repair of any public building or public work. Two bonds are required: a performance bond to protect the government and a payment bond to protect the contractor's employees, subcontractors, and suppliers.

Performance Bonds

Performance bonds guarantee project completion. The Miller Act requires a 100 percent performance bond, meaning a bond to cover 100 percent of the contract amount.

Payment Bonds

Payment bonds guarantee payment to laborers, subcontractors, and suppliers. The Miller Act requires a payment bond of 50 percent of the contract price for all project amounts up to $1,000,000 and 40 percent of the contract price for all project amounts between $1,000,000 and $5,000,000. Projects costing over $5,000,000 require a $2,500,000 bond.

To recover against a bond, a subcontractor (or other injured party) on a government project must sue in the name of the United States in the U.S. District Court for the district where the contract was to be performed. No matter when the subcontractor performed their portion of the work, suit cannot be brought prior to 90 days before project completion nor after one year after completion. If the subcontractor was hired by the prime contractor, there is no requirement for the subcontractor to give notice of the suit to the prime contractor. It is assumed that the subcontractor has already investigated all other remedies.

SUMMARY

A contractor should have at least two insurance policies: one to cover liability for damage to property and injury to others, and one to cover the contractor's property. Policies are written to limit the liability of the insurance company based on the terms of the policy and this is related to the premium paid. A contractor can limit claims by enforcing safe work practice on the job site.

CHAPTER 6

PROJECT MANAGEMENT

This chapter will present suggested methods that a contractor should take in planning a project. Project planning is similar to installing a building foundation. The strength of a house depends on how well the foundation is laid. Similarly, project success depends on how well the project is planned.

Once a contract is signed, the contractor takes full responsibility for managing the project. For relatively small firms, the contractor may manage the entire project personally. Large firms with multiple projects require that responsibilities be delegated to an experienced project manager, site superintendents, and foremen.

PLANNING AND SCHEDULING

All aspects of a project require careful attention—planning, scheduling, purchasing, and supervising—so that the requirements of the contract are met at the lowest possible cost. Many contractors use project management software to plan, schedule, and manage their projects. Many of these programs are customizable to fit the needs of a particular project.

The profit to be made from a project can be increased or lost depending on how well the project is planned and scheduled. Some benefits of good planning and scheduling are the following:

- Improved cash flow
- Increased attention paid to the time required for each task or work unit
- Minimized need for overtime
- Consistent use of resources (labor, equipment, and materials)
- Reduced time to complete the project

Project Planning

Project planning is the process of carefully looking at a project to determine the time sequence of the work schedule and the relationship of job tasks to each other. The work is planned so that the trades do not conflict with each other. For example, the plumbing fixtures are scheduled after the ceramic tile is in place. Finish electrical work should not be scheduled at the same time as painting or laying carpet.

The project manager first divides the project into major operations and develops a critical task analysis. A **critical task analysis** is the process of looking at an entire project, identifying each task, and determining how long each task will take.

Critical Path Method

Planning and scheduling are commonly based on the critical path method (CPM) of project analysis. For each major operation, every step of the work is analyzed, including the following:

- Determining how long each step will take (duration), including any residual time required. For example, the concrete has been poured, but it must cure prior to installing sill plates and applying torque to the anchor bolts.

- Identifying the sequence in which the steps (tasks) must be performed (clearing the site) before installation of utilities. This sequencing is often called "job logic."

- Determining which tasks from other major operations may conflict with or impact these tasks. Is painting done before installation of carpeting?

- Identifying where the work is located in the structure.

Critical Tasks. A critical task is a task that depends on one task before another is started. For example, when taking a shower, the critical tasks can be identified as turn on the water, wash hair, wash face, wash body, turn off water, dry off, apply deodorant, comb hair, put on shirt. A subtask is to make sure that needed supplies are present for each task. Some subtasks can occur concurrently, that is, shave while showering. The CPM is prepared as follows:

- Prepare a list of individual critical (vacant shower) and noncritical activities (use wash cloth).

- Identify where the activity fits into the project schedule.

- Draw a diagram of the activity.

- Determine the estimated duration of each activity. This can be done by using time and material manuals available from construction bookstores or through practical experience.

- Identify the critical path through the project.

- Update the CPM diagram as the work progresses.

The CPM drawing in Figure 6.1 is a simple illustration of a project with five tasks, Tasks A though E, and their interrelationship regarding starting, finishing, and sequencing. Note that the longest the project will take is six weeks.

The chart in Table 6.1 is a bid sheet developed from an estimate. This type of chart can be used to identify the critical tasks: tree removal, stump grinding, silt fence installation, and seed and straw. Labor is included on the estimate but, because it is an expense and not a task, it is not included in the CPM. The critical path is seen in Figure 6.2.

FIGURE 6.1
Five-Task CPM

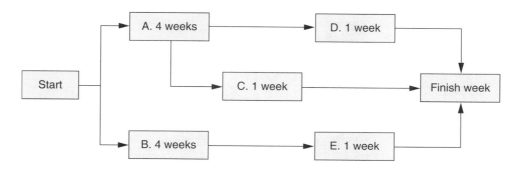

Notice that on the critical path, tree removal and stump grinding are grouped together. These tasks will be completed by one subcontractor, and no other work will be scheduled until that part of the project is completed. The critical path through this project is 5 weeks and 1 day (3 weeks + 1 week + 1 week + 1 day = 5 weeks and 1 day). There are no other tasks concurrent so the path is straight. Most projects will have other tasks occurring at the same time.

Cash Flow Schedule. The cash flow schedule is developed based on the critical path. The *cash flow schedule* reflects the costs of each portion of the project and the anticipated revenues from each progress payment. The timing of the anticipated receipts and disbursements indicates what additional working capital will be required to support the project. If additional funds are required, the cost of the loans or other supplements can be incorporated into the estimate and bid. (See Figure 6.3.)

Other than a down payment, there may not be income from the project for the first several weeks. A contractor must have enough working capital available to cover costs for this period. Also, some customers may delay payments well beyond the due date. A computer accounting program will prove very useful and cost-effective in this situation. The program will track costs, identify bills and payments due, and reveal the financial condition of the company. The program will identify late payments, and the contractor can take appropriate action such as contacting the customer for payment, or filing a lien, if appropriate.

TABLE 6.1
CPM Bid Sheet

	Customer Mr. Gates	Estimate ($)
	Project 404	4,500
Site Preparation		
Tree removal		
Grind stumps		
Install silt fence		
Seed and straw		
Labor		
Obtain permits		

FIGURE 6.2
Critical Path

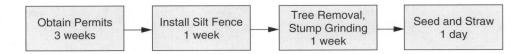

If progress payments are made as equal payments each month, there may be times when cash receipts exceed expenses. In this case (a front-loaded contract), the contractor has invoiced the owner for more than actual costs. Front-loaded contracts will almost always provide cash in excess of expenses during the early stages of the project. If progress payments are based on percentage of completion, it is likely that cash receipts will be less than project costs through most of the project's duration. The contractor must plan invoices and payments to ensure that financial obligations are met throughout the project.

Project Scheduling

Project scheduling is the process of designating where each task or work unit fits into the project plan and when it will be completed. The tasks that depend on completion of another task are identified from the CPM and scheduled accordingly. Tasks that might be done simultaneously, but are performed in the same space, are scheduled separately to avoid conflict. Materials, labor, and equipment are scheduled to be available as needed. Some flexibility and contingency time should be built into the schedule to allow for individual trade schedule changes and unforeseen problems.

Major Activity Schedules.   On most projects, several schedules will be developed to serve different levels of responsibility. The owner and contractor need an overview of the project, with major activity timetables indicating how the project can be completed within the contract time frame. The project manager and site superintendent's schedule should also show how work units fit into the major activity schedules and when material and equipment deliveries are expected. Foremen, expediters, and subcontractors will each have detailed daily schedules of work to be performed, and materials and equipment to be used.

Duration.   Several time management factors are key to effective scheduling. **Duration** is the time required to complete each task. Duration is expressed in hours, shifts, or days. When measuring the time required for all tasks, the same unit should be used. Accurate time standards for most typical construction tasks are available from several sources such as construction books or software. Even with these standards, the contractor should base all calculations on time standards developed through experience and history of job costing.

The time required for each task is first estimated independent of all other work. Allowances or adjustments are made based on the impact of other tasks that are performed simultaneously. If the estimate is made from historical job cost records, changes in labor or equipment availability must be evaluated and taken into consideration when determining equipment costs.

FIGURE 6.3
Partial Cash Flow Schedule

Partial Cash Flow Statement

	Jan	Feb
BEGINNING CASH BALANCE	20,000	58,606
CASH RECEIPTS		
A. Sales and revenues	4,000	2,000
B. Receivables		0
C. Interest income	100	120
D. Sale of long-term assets		0
TOTAL CASH AVAILABLE	24,100	60,726
CASH PAYMENTS		
A. Cost of goods to be sold		
1. Purchases	0	30,000
2. Material		0
3. Labor	5,000	400
Total Cost of Goods	5,000	30,400
B. Variable Expenses (Selling)		
1. Advertising	300	
2. Freight	120	
3. Fulfillment of order	0	
4. Packaging costs	270	
5. Sales and salaries	0	
6. Travel	285	
7. Miscellaneous selling expense	165	
Total Variable Expenses	1,140	
C. Fixed Expenses (Administrative)		
1. Financial administration	0	
2. Insurance	125	
3. Licenses and permits	200	
4. Office salaries	500	
5. Rent expenses	110	
6. Utilities	200	
7. Miscellaneous administrative expense	0	
Total Fixed Expenses	1,215	
D. Interest expense	0	
E. Federal income tax	0	
F. Other uses	0	
G. Long-term asset payments	1,139	
H. Loan payment	0	
I. Owner draws	2,000	
TOTAL CASH PAID OUT	10,494	
CASH BALANCE/DEFICIENCY	13,606	
Loans to be received	40,000	
Equity deposits	5,000	
ENDING CASH BALANCE	58,606	

CONTINUE as in JANUARY

Anatomy of a Business Plan by Linda Pinson. © 2005 Dearborn Trade Publishing. *www.dearborntrade.com.*

The schedule should be based on a normal five-day workweek without overtime. Once the duration of every task is determined and built into a preliminary schedule, the total time required is compared with the contracted time for completion of the project. Overtime schedules can then be developed or additional equipment resources assigned as needed.

Time Contingencies.   A **time contingency** is a buffer incorporated into the schedule to provide allowances for unexpected delays. Time contingencies are estimated based on the likelihood of delay for a particular task. For example, concrete work will likely take longer during winter than summer, or a newly installed complex computerized climate control system may not work the first time.

Adding contingency times to each task permits some flexibility in the schedule. Whenever the contingency time for a specific task is not needed, other tasks may be started ahead of schedule.

Float Time.   **Float time** results when a task is completed in less than the scheduled time. Float time is not deliberately scheduled. It may be due to performance above standard, it may be unused contingency time, or it may be both. When it occurs, it is an opportunity to prepare for the next task, clean or maintain equipment, prepare reports, or accelerate the project.

Gantt Chart

A Gantt chart (bar chart) is the chart most often used for project scheduling. A *Gantt chart* is a greatly simplified schedule chart, usually derived from the CPM chart on larger projects. Small projects may need nothing more than the bar chart, which can be prepared by the project manager.

One shortcoming of a Gantt chart is that it does not show the dependency of one activity on other activities, and it does not indicate when cash is needed. To address the weakness of the Gantt chart regarding interdependency of tasks, an activity schedule can be prepared that specifies the start time of one activity as it relates to another. (See Figure 6.4.)

Subcontractors should review and sign off on the Gantt chart or the CPM chart. They should be especially aware of those parts of the schedule that apply to them and how their work will impact everyone else. A separate detailed bar chart is often presented to each subcontractor.

PROJECT SUPERVISION

All projects require supervision. The owners/contractors of small firms may supervise their projects directly. Large firms with multiple and/or large projects require more complex supervision, including a project manager, site superintendent, foreman, expediter, and owner's representative.

Some of these roles may be combined, depending on the project. Small projects or small contracting firms may find the contractor fulfilling all these roles and working at the site.

Project Manager

The *project manager* is responsible for everything relating to the project. This individual deals with architects, equipment dealers, government agencies, home and site office personnel, subcontractors, suppliers, and union representatives.

FIGURE 6.4
Modified Gantt Chart for Building a Home

	Description	April				May				June				July				August			
C	Site preparation	█																			
D	Excavate foundation	█																			
E	Pour footings	█																			
F	Pour foundation		█																		
G	Frame			█	█	█															
H	Build chimney		█																		
I	Install site utilities		█																		
J	Install rough plumbing					█															
K	Install rough wiring					█	█														
L	Pour basement floor					█															
M	Install siding					█	█														
N	Install subfloor			█	█																
O	Install water lines						█														
P	Install heating ducts						█														
Q	Install insulation								█												
R	Install sheet rock, etc.									█	█										
S	Install finish plumbing										█	█									
T	Install floor and wall tile											█									
U	Paint walls and trim													█							
V	Install kitchen equipment												█								
W	Install cabinets												█								
X	Install electric fixtures														█						
Y	Install carpet														█						
Z	Apply roofing					█	█														
AA	Install downspouts						█														
BB	Pour driveway					█															
CC	Finish grade lot															█					
DD	Landscape															█					
EE	Site cleanup																█				
FF	Inspection*																█				

*Note that inspections are required as certain tasks are completed.

The project manager is responsible for completing the project on time and at or under budget. Project manager tasks include developing budgets and schedules, keeping records, paying invoices, and receiving and applying change orders. The project manager has the same authority as the contractor.

Site Superintendent (Project Superintendent)

The *site superintendent* is responsible for all the activities at the job site. This includes directing workers and subcontractors, coordinating with various code officials and inspectors, scheduling material deliveries, and preparing daily reports. The site supervisor is responsible for safety on the job through safety meetings, correcting unsafe conditions, and monitoring employees and their work practices.

Foreman

The *foreman* provides support to the site superintendent. The foreman manages the project area in which they specialize, such as carpentry, plumbing, electrical, or HVAC. The foreman is responsible for the quality of work done by workers, assignment of workers to various tasks, and writing reports to the site superintendent.

Expediter

The *expediter* orders materials and sets delivery schedules, monitors the ordering process, and reports the delivery status to the site superintendent. While the expediter may work on site for very large projects, more often a single expediter handles several projects simultaneously from the contractor's office.

Owner's Representative

The representative may be the owner, the project architect, the project engineer, or any other designated party. The *owner's representative* acts on the owner's behalf when any questions or issues arise about the project. The architect or engineer may assist in interpreting the drawings and specifications or give field approval to minor changes. The owner's representative will be identified in the contract, along with their rights and responsibilities. These rights and responsibilities usually include access to the site and the production records. The owner's representative may also inspect material quality and project progress and may approve progress payment requests, indicating the work covered has been satisfactorily completed.

The owner's representative has no direct authority over the contractor's employees or subcontractors. All comments, complaints, and directions must be given to the project manager or contractor for any needed action. The owner's representative has no responsibility for the work done or not done by the contractor's employees or subcontractors.

Monitoring

Monitoring refers to the process of overseeing the work and overcoming any obstacles to timely completion. It provides for adjusting the schedule or portions thereof for more advantageous use of workers, or to overcome delays due to weather or accident. Monitoring allows the project manager to compare the work done to the schedule, thereby identifying schedule problems so the manager can seek solutions.

Inspections and Quality Control. Inspections and quality control may be the responsibility of the owner, owner's representative, the prime contractor, or the project manager. There may be any number of inspections and tests required throughout a project. For example, slump tests are used to measure the consistency of concrete, or samples of concrete may be taken to a laboratory and tested to ensure it meets specifications. Inspections may be performed by a third party (private inspector) who will make sure that unique items are in compliance, such as ensuring that the bolts of steel framing are torqued (tightened) to specifications. Local governmental agencies may also inspect for code compliance of the structure, maintenance of silt fences, water quality, and job site safety.

Quality control inspections and monitoring information are recorded and reports are given to the owner or contractor on a daily or weekly basis, depending on the contract. The reports detail progress on the project, any problems encountered, and what corrective measures were taken.

The quality of the finished project is important both from a visual standpoint and to ensure the safety of building occupants. Deficiencies are normally recognized and fixed, but many times owners complain that cosmetic defects are not fixed. Although cosmetic defects do not affect the integrity of the project, they can be seen by all and set the standard by which the rest of the project and the contractor's reputation are measured. At the end of a project the contractor and the owner, or the owner's representative, should walk through the project and develop a punch list. A **punch list** is a list of deficiencies, usually minor, that need to be corrected. A contractor may feel that a project seems to be endless with these types of corrections, but satisfactory completion is a matter of ethics, and a contractual requirement.

Work Records. Work records are all the documents generated in the course of the project. Daily records of everything related to the project should be kept as part of the permanent record of the project. Typical work records include the following:

- Change orders
- Contractor correspondence
- Cost reports
- Daily log
- Original project documents
- Original time schedules and all modifications or adjustments
- Periodic progress reports, including any photographs or permit inspections
- Purchase orders issued
- Shop drawings
- Subcontractor correspondence
- Surveys
- Test reports

Shop Drawings. *Shop drawings* are additional drawings prepared to clarify the architect's drawings and specifications. They may be prepared by a material or equipment supplier, by the contractor, or by a specialist subcontractor. For example, an electrical contractor working as a subcontractor might prepare as-built drawings of switching boxes and related electrical connections for installed equipment. These drawings are compared to the project plans and specifications, and then approved by the contractor and the owner or owner's representative. Exact copies of the approved shop drawings are supplied to the owner's representative, the prime contractor, and the subcontractor or employee doing the work.

Daily Log. The *daily log* is a complete record of everything that happens at the construction site. It is also called the daily journal. The daily log should be a bound book so that no pages can be removed without damaging the book. The log is written in ink, every day, and signed by the site superintendent. No scheduled workday may be omitted, even if the weather or other unanticipated event prevents any work from being done. The daily log includes a record of the following:

- All deliveries
- All equipment used
- All visitors, including owners, inspectors, union representatives, or utility workers
- All work performed
- Any accidents, how seriously anyone was hurt, and who was notified
- Any problems that arose and how they were resolved
- Any scheduled deliveries that did not arrive
- Weather conditions
- Subcontractors on site

Schedule Adjustments. Schedule adjustments result from delays and changes that are to be expected in any significant project. If the contractor bases the schedule on the critical path method, adjustments can be made relatively easily. Some tasks will fit within float time. Other adjustments can be offset with the addition of scheduled overtime. Extensive adjustments may require changing start or finish dates, assigning new critical tasks, or extending the project completion date. All changes affecting the cost or the completion date must be approved by the owner or owner's representative.

Cost Control. *Cost control* is monitoring costs as the project progresses. The accounting system must be able to compare estimated costs with actual costs. Any deviation from expected costs is examined and the cause determined. If corrective action can be taken, it should be done as soon as possible after it is discovered. If no correction is possible, consideration must be given as to whether the contractor must absorb any cost increase or whether there are contract provisions that call for cost sharing by the owner.

One cost control method is to request materials to be delivered free of charge, more commonly referred to as free on board (FOB). A contractor who frequently purchases large amounts of materials from a supplier can expect delivery charges to be absorbed by the supplier as a means of keeping a good customer. Another method of cost control is to have the expediter arrange for delivery of materials to the job site when they are needed. Stockpiled materials are subject to damage, pilferage, and obsolescence.

Cost control can also be achieved by providing prompt payment for delivered materials. If an invoice is marked 2/10 net 30, this means that the contractor can subtract 2 percent of the invoice if the bill is paid within 10 days, otherwise the full amount is due in 30 days.

Construction Equipment. One of the most expensive elements of a project, other than materials and labor, is the cost of construction equipment. Equipment can be purchased, rented, or leased. The choice of how the equipment is obtained depends on the following factors:

- How long the equipment is needed
- If the equipment will be needed for another job
- Finances of the company

Equipment rental is rental of equipment to meet short-term equipment needs. Equipment rentals can be expensive when considered on a day-to-day basis; however, renting equipment is useful for equipment that is needed on a short-term basis or is a unique piece of equipment needed only for one job. The equipment can be used on one job and returned, removing its cost of maintenance from job expenses. Renting is an advantage if the equipment is needed for a short time on a distant job. The cost and aggravation of transporting owned equipment may more than offset the cost of rental of equipment closer to the job site. Renting is also an option if a required piece of equipment breaks down and a replacement is needed immediately. Equipment rental is considered job overhead and is a recognized tax deduction.

Equipment leasing is the rental of equipment using long-term contracts lasting one year or more. One advantage of leasing is that the equipment will be turned in at the end of a lease and a new, possibly better piece of equipment, can be leased. Sometimes dealers will offer very attractive terms for leased equipment. Leasing is an attractive option for company vehicles because a contractor can drive a new truck every other year. A new vehicle is a material indication to customers that the contractor is solvent. Leasing is considered an operating expense, which can be tax deductible. Leased equipment must be insured and meticulously cared for, otherwise the leasing company will charge for damages (wear and tear).

Purchased equipment is equipment bought as a long-term investment. Equipment purchasing should be considered when there will be a continued need for the equipment for several years. An advantage of purchasing is that the equipment is a capital investment and can be depreciated for tax purposes. Because purchased equipment belongs to the company, it is free of the worry associated with the care of leased equipment.

Daily Reports. Daily reports are collected and a summary prepared. Daily reports permit the contractor to review the project costs as a whole. An analysis may show that spending more than originally budgeted on one task may result in completion of the project sooner. For example, if cost analysis shows that a task on the critical path can be shortened five days by adding overtime to the schedule, project completion is shortened by the same amount, perhaps even earning a bonus.

Time Cards. *Time cards* record hours worked and are customary in construction. Either the worker or a supervisor records the work unit to which the worker's time is assigned. The supervisor then totals the time for all the workers assigned to that work unit each day and records it in the daily log. A report is forwarded at least weekly to payroll and to the job cost department. Regular entries in the job cost program help to keep it up to date. All time cards must be signed by the employee and the foreman.

Inventory Control. *Inventory control* is the art of keeping inventory costs as low as possible. The best way to do this is to order materials delivered directly to the job site just before they are needed. Ordering materials "on time" and "as needed" also reduces loss through theft of materials from the job site.

Project Closeout

Upon completion of the project and approval of the finished product, project closeout takes place. Project closeout should include the following:

- Return any rental equipment and receive deposits from suppliers.
- Clean up site and remove all construction materials.
- Resolve any outstanding code violations and any other issues relating to government agencies. Make sure certificates are completed.
- Make sure that all subcontractors and material suppliers have been paid and obtain a release or waiver of any liens that may be outstanding.
- Walk through the project with owner or representative to develop a punch list.
- Arrange for completion of the punch list with subcontractors or contractor staff.
- Upon completion of the punch list, schedule another walk through.
- Obtain a signed and dated release of the contract obligation. This completion date is important because the warranty begins on that day. Many states require retention of contracts for a specified number of years from the completion date.
- Collect any retainage from the owner.
- Settle any outstanding bonding issues with insurers.
- Take digital pictures of the project for use in a catalog of company projects, or as defense if a dispute arises.
- Give owner drawings, warranties, keys, certificate of occupancy, equipment operating, and maintenance instructions.
- Get a letter of recommendation from the owner to use in the next project.
- Complete the accounting of the project by updating the job cost records and evaluating the original cost estimate. Prepare a profit and loss statement for the project.
- Compare the original cost estimate with the actual job costs and determine where changes can be made.
- Make a digital copy of most paper documents (using a computer scanner to reduce the amount of paper and to expedite recall of data).
- Label and file hard copy of remaining documents.

SUMMARY

Examining the profit and loss statement for the project and the factors that raised or lowered costs will provide guidance for the next project. It is important to evaluate where things went right and fix those that went wrong. Again, a computer accounting program is worth its weight in gold. In seconds it can generate a list of outstanding bills or money owed to the company. It can also prepare a profit and loss statement (income statement) that details the actual net income from the project and provides data for the next project.

CHAPTER 7

EMPLOYMENT LAW

E mployers must be aware of the numerous federal employment laws that ensure employees are paid correctly, treated fairly, and are not discriminated against. This chapter contains summaries or excerpts of many of these federal employment laws and safety regulations. Understanding and implementing these laws will ensure that the company is in compliance with applicable federal laws. The government has enacted legislation to protect employees on the job, to standardize hiring and firing procedures, and to require human resource management. Internet searches should be performed periodically to keep up to date on changes to regulations. A list of Web sites for additional information on each of these topics is provided at the end of this chapter. (See Table 7.1 on page 88.)

EQUAL EMPLOYMENT OPPORTUNITY ISSUES

Employers must understand the specific laws governing equal employment opportunities to ensure that all employees, even prospective employees, are treated fairly. The Department of Equal Employment Opportunity enforces the federal laws prohibiting discrimination in the workplace. Current law requires employers to post notices about the federal laws regarding discrimination, equal pay, and disability. At the very minimum, employers should be familiar with the Americans with Disabilities Act (ADA), Employee Polygraph Protection Act, and the Immigration and Nationality Act. Additionally, there are certain pre-employment actions from which employers must refrain, and rules covering exempt and nonexempt employees.

Americans with Disabilities Act

The **Americans with Disabilities Act (ADA)** is regulated by the Equal Employment Opportunity Commission of the U.S. Department of Labor. The ADA prohibits job discrimination based on disability. The Americans with Disabilities Act applies to all employers with 15 or more employees.

An individual is considered to have a disability if there is a physical or mental impairment that substantially limits one or more major life activities or a record of such impairment, or is regarded as having such impairment. For example, an individual who has epilepsy, HIV infection, or AIDS is covered under the ADA. An individual who has a minor, nonchronic condition such as a sprain, broken limb, or drug or alcohol addiction, is not covered.

A qualified individual with a disability is a person who meets the skill, experience, education, or other legitimate requirements of a position. The inability to perform marginal or incidental job functions is not considered a disqualification for employment.

A written job description, prepared in advance of advertising or interviewing applicants for a job, is considered evidence of the essential functions of the job.

The employer must make reasonable accommodation to permit employment of disabled workers. A reasonable accommodation is a modification that will enable a qualified employee to perform essential job functions.

Employee Polygraph Protection Act

The *Employee Polygraph Protection Act* prohibits most private employers from using any type of lie detector test either for pre-employment screening of job applicants or for testing current employees during the course of employment.

Immigration and Nationality Act

The *Immigration and Nationality Act* requires every employer to verify the nationality and employability of every candidate for employment. Employers must complete Form I-9 at the time of hire no later than three business days after commencement of employment. The List of Acceptable Documents is the form that details the identification documents that can be used to prove one's identity for employment purposes. (See Figure 7.1.)

Equal Pay Act

The **Equal Pay Act** requires that men and women be paid equal pay for equal work in an establishment. This requires employers to pay employees based on skill, work, and responsibility levels but only within the same establishment. If two employees have similar jobs, within the same office, one employee may not be paid less because of gender.

Title 7 of the Civil Rights Act of 1964

The **Civil Rights Act of 1964** prohibits employment discrimination based on race, color, religion, sex, or national origin. It also is illegal for employers to fail or refuse to hire or fire anyone based on sex, race, color, or national origin, or to segregate these employees at the workplace. The Civil Rights Act applies to employers with 15 or more employees.

WAGE AND WORK HOUR ISSUES

Wage and work hour issues are governed by the Wage and Hour Division of the U.S. Department of Labor. The Wage and Hour Division is also responsible for administering child labor laws, and the Fair Labor Standards Act, as well as minimum wage and overtime pay provisions. The following acts and laws are important to the employer, particularly the contractor or subcontractor, because they provide information on the minimum wage, important definitions used within employment

FIGURE 7.1
Immigration and Nationality Act Acceptable Documents List

LISTS OF ACCEPTABLE DOCUMENTS

LIST A	LIST B	LIST C
Documents that Establish Both Identity and Employment Eligibility	**OR** — **Documents that Establish Identity**	**AND** — **Documents that Establish Employment Eligibility**

LIST A — Documents that Establish Both Identity and Employment Eligibility

1. U.S. Passport (unexpired or expired)
2. Certificate of U.S. Citizenship (INS Form N-560 or N-561)
3. Certificate of Naturalization (INS Form N-550 or N-570)
4. Unexpired foreign passport, with *I-551 stamp* or attached INS Form I-94 indicating unexpired employment authorization
5. Permanent Resident Card or Alien Registration Receipt Card with photograph (INS Form I-151 or I-551)
6. Unexpired Temporary Resident Card (INS Form I-688)
7. Unexpired Employment Authorization Card (INS Form I-688A)
8. Unexpired Reentry Permit (INS Form I-327)
9. Unexpired Refugee Travel Document (INS Form I-571)
10. Unexpired Employment Authorization Document issued by the INS which contains a photograph (INS Form I-688B)

LIST B — Documents that Establish Identity

1. Driver's license or ID card issued by a state or outlying possession of the United States provided it contains a photograph or information such as name, date of birth, gender, height, eye color and address
2. ID card issued by federal, state or local government agencies or entities, provided it contains a photograph or information such as name, date of birth, gender, height, eye color and address
3. School ID card with a photograph
4. Voter's registration card
5. U.S. Military card or draft record
6. Military dependent's ID card
7. U.S. Coast Guard Merchant Mariner Card
8. Native American tribal document
9. Driver's license issued by a Canadian government authority

For persons under age 18 who are unable to present a document listed above:

10. School record or report card
11. Clinic, doctor or hospital record
12. Day-care or nursery school record

LIST C — Documents that Establish Employment Eligibility

1. U.S. social security card issued by the Social Security Administration *(other than a card stating it is not valid for employment)*
2. Certification of Birth Abroad issued by the Department of State *(Form FS-545 or Form DS-1350)*
3. Original or certified copy of a birth certificate issued by a state, county, municipal authority or outlying possession of the United States bearing an official seal
4. Native American tribal document
5. U.S. Citizen ID Card (INS Form I-197)
6. ID Card for use of Resident Citizen in the United States (INS Form I-179)
7. Unexpired employment authorization document issued by the INS *(other than those listed under List A)*

Illustrations of many of these documents appear in Part 8 of the Handbook for Employers (M-274)

Form I-9 (Rev. 10/4/00)Y Page 3

law, and the acts governing work on federal projects. Some of the wage and work hour acts that employers are governed by include the Fair Labor Standards Act (FLSA), the Walsh-Healey Public Contracts Act, the Davis-Bacon Act, the Service Contract Act, and the Contract Work Hours and Safety Standards Act.

Fair Labor Standards Act

The **Fair Labor Standards Act (FLSA)** sets minimum wage and overtime requirements, including child labor standards.

Definitions of Terms used in FLSA

> **hours worked** Includes all time an employee must be on duty or at the place of business.

> **overtime pay** Wages due an employee for hours over 40 worked in a workweek.

> **workweek** A period of 168 hours during 7 consecutive 24-hour periods. It can begin on any day of the week and at any hour of the day.

The Fair Labor Standards Act requires the following:

- Minimum wage of $5.15 per hour, with a few exceptions.
- Overtime pay for all work over 40 hours within that period regardless of the wage payment schedule.
- Overtime pay for all work over 40 hours in a workweek must equal 1½ times the employee's hourly rate (not 1½ times the minimum wage).
- The employer must establish a workweek of seven 24-hour days (128 hours).
- Employers may not use comp time in lieu of overtime pay.
- Detailed employment and pay records must be kept for every employee.

The FLSA allows an employer to make deductions from the employee's wages for items such as cash or merchandise shortages that are the fault of the employee, required uniform fees, and tools of the trade, as long as the deductions do not bring the wages of the employee below minimum wage.

For example, an employee of Joe's Wood Working Corporation is required to have three sets of uniforms ($230), a tool belt ($70), and one hammer ($20) for a total of $320—all of which is deducted from the employee's wages. If the employee works for minimum wage, $5.15, and works 60 hours in a two week period, the total amount of wages for that period before taxes is $309. It would be illegal to deduct the full amount for the company equipment, $320, from this employee's paycheck. The deductions would have to be spread over a greater length of time. Note that some states do not allow any deductions from an employee's wages other than those required by law or agreed to by the employee.

While FLSA does set basic minimum wage and overtime pay standards and regulates the employment of minors, there are a number of employment practices that FLSA does not regulate. For example, FLSA does not require the following:

- Vacation, holiday, severance, or sick pay
- Meal or rest periods, holidays off, or vacations
- Premium pay for weekend or holiday work
- Pay raises or fringe benefits
- A discharge notice, reason for discharge, or immediate payment of final wages to terminated employees

Exempt and Nonexempt Employees

Some employees, administrators, and professionals are exempt from the overtime pay requirement and minimum wage provisions. Typically, there are very few exempt employees on a construction site. *Exempt employees* are usually salaried employees; however, there are exceptions. Because exemptions are narrowly defined under FLSA, an employer should carefully check the exact terms and conditions for each. Detailed information is available from local wage-hour offices.

Nonexempt employees are employees who are typically paid hourly. Under the new Fair Pay rules, overtime pay must be paid to exempt employees who earned less than $455 per week or $23,660 per year.

Employees under 20 years of age or who are family members of the owner(s) may be exempt from basic minimum wage requirements. Employees under 20 years of age may be paid $4.25 per hour during their first 90 consecutive calendar days of employment with an employer. Employers facing this situation should examine the laws carefully.

Equal pay provisions of FLSA prohibit gender-based wage differentials between men and women employed in the same establishment who perform jobs that require equal skill, effort, and responsibility and that are performed under similar working conditions.

Youth Employment

Child Labor laws, governed by the Fair Labor Standards Act, require that an employee be at least 16 years old to work in most nonfarm jobs and at least 18 to work in nonfarm jobs declared hazardous by the Secretary of Labor. OSHA has determined that construction work is hazardous. The Department of Labor has revised the regulation to prohibit all work on or about roofs for minors (16- and 17-year-olds).

Youths 14- and 15-years-old may work outside school hours in various non-manufacturing, nonmining, nonhazardous jobs under the following conditions:

- No more than 3 hours on a school day or 18 hours in a school week.
- 8 hours on a nonschool day or 40 hours in a nonschool week.
- Work may not begin before 7 A.M. or end after 7 P.M., except from June 1 through Labor Day, when evening hours are extended to 9 P.M. Different rules apply in agricultural employment.

Enforcement of Employment Laws

Enforcement of the Fair Labor Standards Act is through the Department of Labor. The Department of Labor may recover back wages, either administratively or through court action, for employees who have been underpaid in violation of the law. Violations may result in civil or criminal action.

Fines of up to $10,000 per violation may be assessed against employers who violate the child labor provisions of the law and up to $1,000 per violation against employers who willfully or repeatedly violate the minimum wage or overtime pay provisions. The FLSA prohibits discriminating against or discharging workers who file a complaint or participate in any proceedings under the act.

HIRING ISSUES

An employer is allowed to ask questions about the ability of the applicant to perform specific job functions and may, with certain limitations, ask an individual with a disability to describe or demonstrate how the work would be performed.

A post-offer medical examination may disqualify an individual if the employer can demonstrate that the individual would pose a "direct threat" to the health or safety of the individual or others in the workplace. "Direct threat" means a significant threat of substantial harm that cannot be eliminated or reduced below the direct threat level through a reasonable accommodation. Such a disqualification is job-related and consistent with business necessity.

Information from all medical examinations and inquiries must be kept apart from general personnel files as a separate, confidential medical record, available only under limited conditions.

Employer Pre-Employment Actions

Before a prospective employee has been offered a job, an employer is restricted from the following actions:

- May not ask or require a job applicant to take a medical examination before making a job offer
- Cannot make any pre-employment inquiry about a disability or the nature or severity of a disability
- May not use a test for illegal drug use as a medical examination

FLSA Record Keeping Requirements

Every employer who is governed by the FLSA must keep certain records on wages, hours worked, and other items as specified in the Department of Labor record keeping regulations. Time clocks do not have to be used to track hours worked, but the time must be noted on a form and employees must be paid for all hours worked (see hours worked definition). There is not a specific format for the record, but it must contain the following information:

- Employee's full name and Social Security number
- Address including zip code
- Birth date if younger than 19
- Sex and occupation
- Time and day of week when employee's workweek begins
- Hours worked each day
- Total hours worked each workweek

- Basis on which employee's wages are paid (e.g., "$6 an hour," "$220 a week," "0.25¢ per piece")
- Regular hourly pay rate
- Total daily or weekly straight-time earnings
- Total overtime earnings for the workweek
- All additions to or deductions from the employee's wages
- Total wages paid each pay period
- Date of payment and the pay period covered by the payment

Employers need to retain payroll records for at least three years. Records on which wage computations are based should be retained for two years (e.g., time cards and piecework tickets, wage rate tables, work and time schedules, and records of additions to or deductions from wages). These records must be open for inspection by the Division's representatives, who may ask the employer to make extensions, computations, or transcriptions. The records may be kept at the place of employment or in a central records office. Employee tax records must be maintained for four years.

CONTRACTS WITH THE FEDERAL GOVERNMENT

When entering into a contract to perform work for the federal government, employers, and particularly contractors and subcontractors, are governed by specific federal acts. Each act sets wage standards and fringe benefits (such as sick leave) required to be paid to employees for different federal contract types and amounts. These acts include the Walsh-Healey Public Contracts Act, the Davis-Bacon Act, the Service Contract Act, and the Contract Work Hours and Safety Standards Act.

Walsh-Healey Public Contracts Act

The *Walsh-Healey Public Contracts Act* requires payment of minimum wage rates and overtime pay on contracts in excess of $10,000 that provide materials, supplies, or equipment to the federal government.

Davis-Bacon Act

The *Davis-Bacon Act* requires that prevailing wage rates and fringe benefits be paid to all employees involved with federal construction projects valued in excess of $2,000. Simply put, this act requires contractors and subcontractors to pay employees working on a federal project no less than what other employees were paid on similar projects. Federal projects include such activities as construction, alteration, or repair of public buildings or public works facilities.

Service Contract Act

The *Service Contract Act* requires payment of prevailing wage rates and fringe benefits. However, this act refers specifically to contracts over $2,500 that will be using service personnel to provide services to the federal government and does not cover construction of buildings. (A service contract would be for something like providing a cleaning crew for the Library of Congress.) If the contract amount is less than $2,500, the wage requirement is minimum wage ($5.15). Any employer performing work who falls under this act must post the Notice to Employees Working on Government Contracts.

The Service Contract Act also limits the amount of an individual's income that may be legally garnished and prohibits firing an employee whose pay is garnished for payment of a single debt.

Contract Work Hours and Safety Standards Act

The *Contract Work Hours and Safety Standards Act* applies to contractors or subcontractors who have service or construction contracts with the federal government over $100,000. This act states that employees must be paid overtime for all hours worked over 40 hours per week at a rate of 1½ times the employees basic wage rate.

EMPLOYEE BENEFITS ISSUES

The federal law not only offers basic wage standards and protection from discrimination, but provides for employee benefits and pre-employment help for people who have lost their jobs. Employers should have a basic knowledge of the following acts: the Employee Retirement Income Security Act (ERISA), the Family and Medical Leave Act (FMLA), and the Trade Adjustment Assistance (TAA) Program.

Employee Retirement Income Security Act

The **Employee Retirement Income Security Act (ERISA)** regulates the minimum standards for employers who maintain pension plans; however, ERISA does not require that employers have pension plans. If the employer has a pension plan, ERISA sets guidelines for who must be allowed to participate in the plan, how long an employee must work at the company to earn a nonforfeitable interest in the plan, whether spouses may participate, and how long an employee may be away from their job and still retain benefits.

Family and Medical Leave Act

The **Family and Medical Leave Act (FMLA)** entitles eligible employees to take up to 12 weeks of unpaid job-protected leave each year, with maintenance of group health insurance, for the birth and care of a child; for the placement of a child for adoption or foster care; for the care of a child, spouse, or parent with a serious health condition; or for the employee's serious health condition. The employee is responsible for providing up to 30 days of advanced notice if the leave is foreseeable. To qualify for FMLA, the employee must work for an employer who is covered by this law. Employers of 50 or more people for each workday for 20 or more calendar workweeks are covered by this law.

Consolidated Omnibus Reconciliation Act

Federal law does not require employers to maintain health insurance for its employees; however, the *Consolidated Omnibus Reconciliation Act (COBRA)* provides for continuing health care benefits for individuals who have lost coverage because of termination of employment or death or divorce of a spouse who had the coverage. COBRA provides for a continuation of benefits for up to 18 months. This law normally applies to businesses that have 20 or more employees. Coverage under this act is dependent on several factors and should be researched carefully.

Trade Adjustment Assistance Program

The purpose of the Trade Adjustment Assistance (TAA) Program (Job Service) is to help individuals, who have lost their job because of increased imports or shifts in production to foreign countries, find employment. To qualify for assistance from this program, individuals must first fill out a petition with the U.S. Department of Labor's Division of Trade Adjustment.

Workers Compensation Insurance

Workers compensation insurance offers income to employees who have become injured through an on-the-job accident or illness. Each state has developed different laws and regulations governing workers compensation. For more information regarding the necessity of this insurance and the laws governing compliance, refer to the U.S. Department of Labor's Office of Worker's Compensation Program at *www.dol.gov/esa/owcp_org.htm*. Also, each state maintains a state government Web page that lists workers compensation insurance information.

Unemployment Insurance

Unemployment insurance is offered for individuals who have lost their job for reasons other than poor performance. Unemployment insurance laws vary from state to state and should be researched using the state's government Web page.

Wage Garnishment and the Consumer Protection Act

Wage garnishment is the act of withholding money from an employee's paycheck when required by a court order. Wage garnishment commonly occurs for child support payments or alimony.

Title III of the Consumer Protection Act prohibits an employer from dismissing an employee whose earnings are being garnished for one debt; however, it does not protect an employee from being fired if more than one debt is being withheld. The Consumer Protection Act also limits the amount of money that can be withheld per week.

SUMMARY

Contractors working with the federal government will have more laws to consider and more compliance requirements than those working for private citizens. No matter what involvement, all contractor employees must act in accordance with employment laws. It is advised to adopt a policy handbook, which can be purchased from bookstores, that outline the hiring and employment procedures. This will ensure compliance with the laws and will make the hiring process easier by providing suggested legal interview topics as well as post-employment policies.

TABLE 7.1
Employment Law
Web Sites

Information regarding employment laws or discriminatory practices can be found at the following Web sites:

	U.S. Department of Labor (DOL)	*www.dol.gov/index.htm*
	U.S. Equal Employment Opportunity (EEOC)	*www.eeoc.gov/*
Equal Employment Opportunity	U.S. Equal Employment Opportunity	*www.eeoc.gov/* or *www.eeoc.gov/types/ ada.html*
	U.S. Department of Labor	*www.dol.gov/dol/compliance/comp-eppa.htm*
Wage and Work Hour Issues	Wage and Work Hour Division	*www.dol.gov/esa/whd/*
	Fair Labor Standards Act	*www.dol.gov/esa/whd/flsa/index.htm*
	Exempt and Non-Exempt Employees	*www.dol.gov/esa/regs/compliance/whd/fairpay/ main.htm*
Contracts with the Federal Government	Walsh-Healy Public Contracts Act Information	*www.dol.gov/asp/programs/guide/walshh.htm*
	Service Contract Act	*www.dol.gov/esa/regs/compliance/posters/ sca.htm*
	Contract Work Hours and Safety Standards Act	*www.dol.gov/asp/programs/guide/cwhssa.htm*
Employee Benefits Issues	Employee Retirement Income Security Act (ERISA)	*www.dol.gov/ebsa/compliance_assistance.html*
	Family and Medical Leave Act (FMLA)	*www.dol.gov/esa/whd/fmla/*
	Consolidated Omnibus Reconciliation Act (COBRA)	*www.dol.gov/dol/topic/health-plans/cobra.htm*
	Trade Adjustment Assistance (TAA) Program (Job Service)	*www.doleta.gov/tradeact/*
	Workers Compensation Insurance	*www.dol.gov/esa/owcp_org.htm*

CHAPTER 8

ACCOUNTING

This chapter will present elements of basic accounting terms, methods, and statements. Contractors must be sufficiently familiar with accounting processes in order to understand their bookkeeper or accountant, and to understand the financial condition of their company. Contractors need to understand not only what income and expenses to expect but also when to expect them. Contractors must also make financial decisions, such as how and when to bill, as work progresses. Billing can be done on a percentage completed basis, where the owner is billed according to a formal schedule, or on a completed contract basis, where the owner makes a lump sum payment. The payment schedule will determine the composition of the company's financial picture because revenue (income) will vary depending on the method selected. It will also vary according to how prompt customers are in paying their bills.

There are several excellent software accounting programs, such as Quick-Books or Peachtree Accounting, to handle basic bookkeeping needs. These programs can handle virtually all aspects of financial activities, including payroll, job costing, taxes, and budgeting. They can generate almost any financial report needed for any period, and because they are already preloaded with all of the accounts that a contractor will need, there is minimal start-up effort. While the contractor (or the bookkeeper) may be able to set these accounts up manually, part of a competitor's success is due to using these modern computer-based methods.

A contractor needs to have some grasp of basic accounting in order to understand what the accountant and the financial statements are revealing about the business. This information is crucial to recognizing when or if the business is financially sound. Understanding the financial statements of the company will help with developing estimates and bids. These statements will help find which customers pay on time and which are slow, which jobs are truly profitable and which just skim by or lose money. If a contractor is considering doing the accounting in-house, they must consider factors such as the time involved in completing the reports and whether they have an adequate level of professionalism and expertise in order to accurately complete all necessary forms. For contractors who choose to do their own accounting, help is available through local community colleges. Community colleges offer excellent one-day training classes on most of the popular computer software accounting programs.

DEFINITIONS OF TERMS

Accounting has a language of its own. The following terms are used in the profession and are provided as a resource to assist the contractor in understanding the concepts presented in the chapter.

accelerated depreciation Depreciation method in which a greater amount of depreciation or expense is taken in the early years and less in the later years.

accounts payable Money owed by the business.

accounts receivable Money owed to the business.

accumulated depreciation The total amount of depreciation accumulated over several years and charged against appropriate fixed assets.

asset Anything of value belonging to the business. Assets include accounts receivable, cash, land, prepaid bills, equipment, buildings, furniture, and fixtures.

cash budget A comparison of expected receipts and planned expenses, disregarding all noncash assets. A cash budget is intended to ensure that there is enough money for payroll, accounts payable, and other short-term obligations.

cash discount A discount in the purchase price of supplies or a deduction off the invoice in exchange for prompt payment.

cash flow Money that has been received and spent. Cash flow is based on cash receipts minus cash disbursements from a given operation over a given period. A positive cash flow is essential to successful operation of the company, and that is why the amount of money owed to the company by customers must be monitored. Payments are usually based on work substantially completed minus retainage.

completed contract method Accounting method that recognizes profit only when the job is completed.

completion-capitalized cost method Accounting method in which a certain percentage of the project cost and revenue is identified and income and expenses are calculated by that percentage in the current year. The balance is deferred until the project is completed in the next year.

current asset Cash or any asset that can be converted to cash within one year or one operating cycle. Such assets may include accounts receivable, inventory, and prepaid expenses.

current liability Any money owed by the contracting company that must be paid within one year. Current liabilities may include loan payments due, accounts payable, wages, and taxes.

depreciation A method of spreading out the cost of equipment or property (asset) over its life span rather than entering the full cost in the first year. Depreciation is entered in the financial records as an expense each year. The two methods of depreciation are straight-line depreciation and accelerated depreciation.

direct costs The costs that relate to the actual productive activities of the business. In construction, these include labor, payroll taxes, insurance, employee benefits, equipment costs or equipment leases, materials, subcontracts, permits, and bonds. Direct costs may be recognized as specific project costs.

fixed asset Property owned by the business that will not be converted to cash within one year. Fixed assets include land, buildings, equipment, furniture, and fixtures.

general and administrative (G&A) costs Costs incurred in the daily operation of a business. General and administrative costs include salaries of office staff, all office operating expenses, furniture and supplies, legal and accounting expenses, and advertising.

gross profit The amount remaining after deducting direct and indirect costs from revenues.

indirect costs Costs that are not related to any specific job, such as the cost of company vehicles and their operation.

job costs All costs related to any single project.

liability Any claim against the business' assets. Liabilities can be short-term (current) or long-term.

long-term liability Any debt or obligation normally due over a period longer than one year and that is not a current liability.

net income The amount resulting after taxes are deducted from net income before taxes.

net income before taxes (NIBT) The amount left after subtracting general and administrative costs from gross profit. NIBT is shown on the bottom of the income statement.

net worth The value of all assets after deducting all liabilities.

overhead Expenses that are not related to any project. These include building rent, utilities, office equipment, and salaries for management, supervisors, and full-time staff.

percentage of completion Accounting method that recognizes and records expenses and revenues as the project progresses.

prepaid expenses An expense that is paid before the material is actually used. These are the opposite of unpaid expenses. For example, a company buys insurance for the year but the expense is for the actual period benefited, or office supplies are purchased in bulk and then expensed when used.

revenue The operating income or income due to the normal activities of the business.

retainage A certain percentage of the payment retained by the customer to ensure satisfactory completion of the project. Percentage of completion payments follow a schedule and the contract will be specific regarding when payment is expected and the amount that may be retained. There is usually an upper limit of 50 percent total retention on projects.

source documents All documents relating to income or expenses. Source documents may include check stubs, invoices received and sent, cash receipts, and time cards.

straight-line depreciation The cost of the asset is divided by a certain number of years, and each year this cost is charged as an expense.

working capital Cash or equivalent assets available to pay bills. Working capital is figured as a ratio, and should be no less than one dollar of debt to one-and-a-half dollars in assets (ratio of 1:1.5). In accounting terms, working capital is the difference between current assets and current liabilities. Working capital is the number that an insurance company will look at when deciding whether to issue a bond. Contractors must have a good cash flow to pay laborers and material suppliers. Inadequate working capital will also have an impact of taking on new projects because there will be no money for the upfront costs involved in future projects.

zero profit method Accounting method used when the project is such that the profit is difficult to estimate, so it is determined to be zero until such time that the project has progressed sufficiently to make a determination.

DEPRECIATION

Before entering the discussion of accounting methods, it is important to understand depreciation and its impact on the financial picture of the company. Some assets lose their ability to perform over time due to basic wear and tear that lowers the value of the equipment. Depreciation allows for deducting the amount of value a fixed asset loses over a specified time. Fixed assets are such things as buildings, office equipment, machinery, trucks, cars, computers, and other hard items. Those items that are rented or leased are not depreciated. Instead, the rent is charged off as an expense. Depreciation is calculated annually for tax (and other) purposes.

Straight-Line Depreciation

Straight-line depreciation assumes that equipment loses a fixed portion of its value each year. For example, if a contractor buys a truck, it may be depreciated over a period of five years, that is, a $50,000 truck loses $10,000 value each year. There will always be a residual value because a truck is worth at least salvage. Buildings are always depreciated using straight-line depreciation.

Accelerated Depreciation

Accelerated depreciation is a more realistic approach to asset depreciation. It assumes a greater cost in the first year and less in the remaining years; therefore, it is a more accurate assessment of the loss of value over time. For example, as soon as a contractor drives the truck off the dealer's lot, it loses quite a bit of value. The first year may be calculated as double the straight-line depreciation, possibly $20,000, and then the remaining years are calculated at a lesser amount. Accelerated depreciation is an attractive option for contractors who have made a large profit in one year and need to reduce that amount, which would in turn reduce the income tax due.

RECORD KEEPING SYSTEMS

Accurate record keeping is essential for business operation in accordance with state and federal tax laws and is also a good business practice. When preparing estimates, a job cost history will save time and provide an accurate basis for determining costs for future projects. There are three categories of accounting records for tracking the receipt and use of business finances: source documents, journals, and the general ledger. The bookkeeping method using journals and ledgers is a traditional pen and paper method of "keeping books." This method has generally been replaced by computerized accounting programs. However, it is necessary to understand bookkeeping concepts, similar to knowing how to add and subtract, even though there are calculators available.

Source Documents

Source documents are all documents relating to income or expenses. These documents are created when money is paid or received, a debt is incurred, or a receivable is created. They are part of the first transaction in the bookkeeping process and consist of contracts, invoices, purchase orders, receipts, deposits, payments, time cards, and check stubs. The source documents are entered daily in the journal. (See Figure 8.1.)

FIGURE 8.1
Source Documents Entered Daily in Journal

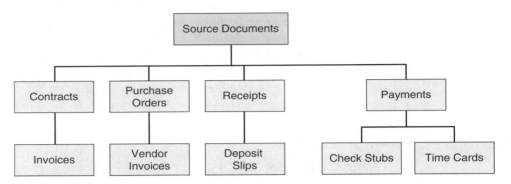

Journals

The **journal** is basically a blank book with lines and columns in which all the source documents are recorded by type. This is the first formal recognition of the source documents. Each day, all invoices, receipts, cash received, time cards, and other source documents are entered in the journal. There are several types of journals used: payroll journal, disbursements journal, sales and cash receipts journal, and the general journal. (See Figure 8.2.)

Payroll Journal. The *payroll journal* is a logbook that tracks employee wages and provides the records necessary for state and federal reports. The payroll journal also keeps track of some types of insurances, such as workers compensation, and contains a classification of employee wages for job costing.

Disbursements Journal. The *disbursements journal* is a journal that tracks how monies are paid out and in what amounts. In a small company, the payroll and disbursements journals may be combined.

Sales and Cash Receipts Journal. The *sales and cash receipts journal* is a record of all income. This journal can be used as the basis for preparing sales tax returns and job costing.

General Journal. The *general journal* is a record of noncash transactions, such as depreciation of assets and corrections. The general journal also tracks installment purchases of equipment.

FIGURE 8.2
Types of Journals

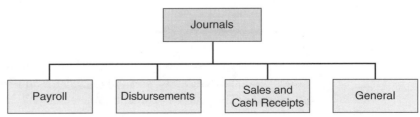

TABLE 8.1
Typical General Ledger
Postings by Number

		General Ledger
Balance Sheet Accounts	100s	Assets
	200s	Liabilities
	300s	Stockholders/Owners' Equity
Income Statement Accounts	400s	Revenue (Income)
	500s	Direct Costs
	600s	Indirect Costs
	700s	General and Administrative Costs
	800s	Other Income/Expense
	900s	Taxes

General Ledger

The **general ledger** contains a monthly summary of information from the journal and recorded in the appropriate balance account. After the posting process, financial statements can be prepared. The accounts are usually set up in a prescribed order. (See Table 8.1.)

ACCOUNTING METHODS

The profit or loss of a contracting company is revealed by the accounting and reporting process. The processes or methods by which the numbers are assembled are selected through a deliberate choice by the contractor. Because choices are involved as to which accounting methods to use, the numbers, and the bottom line, can vary.

For example, because most contractors will purchase new equipment sometime during the year, they must decide whether to use the accelerated or the straight-line method of depreciation. Whichever method is used, the company's bottom line and taxes due will be affected. If the company is likely to make a large profit in the current year, then accelerated depreciation would be a good choice because the larger depreciation amounts will reduce taxes owed. A company that is likely to make more profit in the next year may want to consider straight-line depreciation, which will carry the deduction to later years and offset future profits. Both of these methods will affect the financial report of the company.

A contractor must also decide which method of recording sales revenue to use. It may be advantageous to record project revenue later rather than earlier to make the cash flow of the company more balanced. However, on long-term contracts it is not a good idea to tempt fate with the IRS and avoid posting revenue to avoid taxes that normally would be due earlier.

Another choice that must be made is how to deal with bad debts. A contracting company operates on the premise that payment for services will be made, while the reality is that not all customers are inclined to pay. This creates a "bad debt" for the contracting company. The bad debt can be offset in the books if the company uses the accrual method and has made a good faith effort to collect the debt. The customer has to have been repeatedly contacted for payment, with a record of each time an attempted collection is made. Only after repeated attempts at collection can the debt finally be determined to be uncollectable. This bad debt can then be recorded as an expense for tax purposes.

Because the price of materials changes rapidly, materials bought and stored at the start of the year will have a different value or cost than materials purchased at the end of the year. The *cost of goods sold* is the sum of the costs of materials sold to a customer. Figuring the cost of goods sold can get complicated because there may be materials in the project that cost $1.50 each at one point in the project and cost $2.00 each later.

When the contractor prepares the customer's invoice, the costs will be recovered through the customer's payment, but the contractor must decide how to report those costs for financial reporting purposes. How costs are reported is determined by how the materials are used. There are several methods to choose from. One method is "FIFO," which means first in first out. Material that was purchased first goes out first, which is a good practice because it prevents materials being damaged during lengthy storage. The final inventory is made up of the most recent purchases. This method will show the lowest amount for the cost of goods and the highest amount for gross profit. Periods of inflation will show a higher gross profit. Another method to use is "LIFO," which means last in first out. This method depletes the expensive inventory.

Whichever method is used, it should be used consistently throughout the project. Talk with successful contractors about their accounting program and the methods they use and an accountant experienced with contracting companies.

Cash and Accrual Methods

Income and expenses must be accurately recorded to reflect the financial stability of the company. Without a clear understanding of where the company is financially, the contractor does not have the necessary information required to make sound financial decisions, which could lead to failure of the company. There are two primary methods of recording income and expenses, the cash method and the accrual method.

Cash Method. The **cash method** of accounting records transactions only when money exchanges hands, that is, when a check is written or a deposit is made. It is similar to a mom and pop grocery. When a loaf of bread is purchased, the money is placed in the cash drawer and rung up on the register tape. When a delivery is made to the store, the cash is taken out of the cash drawer and recorded on the register tape. The cash method of accounting is the easiest method of accounting because the amount in the drawer is cash on hand. However, the cash method cannot record bad debts. If a customer wants to take groceries and pay for them the next week, nothing is recorded on the tape. If the customer does not pay, then no deduction can be taken from taxes owed because no transaction occurred, even though money was earned when the customer left with the unpaid groceries. The only items the cash method will show are monies that have been collected or that have been paid out, not what has been earned.

Accrual Method. The **accrual method** of accounting records income and expenses when they are earned or incurred, even though no payment is made. For example, when a customer calls and orders groceries, an invoice is prepared, an entry is made in accounts receivable, and money is shown as earned. When a business owner calls a distributor and orders a case of bread, an invoice is prepared by the baker and sent to the grocer who records the amount in accounts payable. This transaction is then listed as an expense. Even though no money has changed hands at this point, an accurate financial picture of the company is created. In this case, if the errant customer in the situation above left with a basket of groceries, an invoice would have been created and entered in receivables. Then, if there was no payment, the invoice could be deducted as a bad debt. The accrual method is a fair representation of the company's financial position and is accepted as the preferred method of accounting for most businesses.

Contract Accounting

Keeping track of past project costs is important because it not only provides a basis for determining job profit, it also identifies areas where higher than expected costs may have occurred. These areas of high costs must be examined so that modifications can be made to purchasing procedures or the next estimate can be calculated to reflect the higher cost of performing work. This will give the contractor the information necessary to develop estimates that are based on actual costs and will provide a basis for determining an accurate profit. The methods of contract accounting are completed contract method, percentage of completion method, zero profit method, and completion-capitalized cost method.

Completed Contract Method. The completed contract method accumulates costs for the period of the contract (up to two years), but it defers recognition of the project income until the final payment is made on the contract. When the job is complete, the company registers the revenue and deducts costs to calculate the profit of the project. One reason to use the completed contract method is to provide a less fractured financial picture. The company can elect to choose when the profit should be recognized to achieve a more balanced profit report. Be aware that the IRS does not look favorably towards artificially delaying profit reporting in order to postpone or reduce federal income taxes.

Percentage of Completion Method. The percentage of completion method records costs and revenues and provides a profit and loss picture as the project is completed. It provides a means of developing financial data as the project progresses. Because this method relies on calculations (actual costs divided by estimated project costs) the financial reporting is an estimate rather than a definitive or rock solid number.

The completion percentage is determined by dividing the actual costs during the year by the estimated total project cost as illustrated in Figure 8.3.

Zero Profit Method. The zero profit method can be used when it is difficult to estimate the outcome of a project. It is a modification of the percentage of completion method. The contractor bases revenue on zero profit as though the costs and revenues are the same. When the project reaches the point where the outcome can be estimated with reasonable accuracy, the contractor adopts the percentage of completion method for the rest of the project.

FIGURE 8.3
Percentage of Completion Calculations

Project	Contract Amount	Estimated Costs	Cost to Date	Percent Complete	Billed to Date	Earnings to Date	Excess Earnings	Excess Billings
Project 1	$225,000	$180,000	$49,680	27.6%	$56,250	$62,100	$5,850	

Contract Amount: The current amount after change orders and additions ($225,000)

Estimated Cost: The current estimate, including all changes and additions ($180,000)

Cost to Date: The actual job costs to date ($49,680)

Percent Complete: The cost to date divided by the estimated cost (27.6%)

$$\frac{\text{Cost to Date}}{\text{Estimated Cost}} = \frac{\$49,680}{\$180,000} = 27.6\%$$

Billed to Date: The amount that has been billed to the customer ($56,250)

Earnings to Date: The contract amount times the percent completed ($62,100)

$$\text{Contract Amount} \times \% \text{ Completed} = \text{Earnings to Date}$$
$$\$225,000 \quad \times \quad 27.6\% \quad = \quad \$62,100$$

Excess Earnings: Excess earnings represent the amount that Earnings to Date exceed *Billings to Date:* The amount billed to the customer that is above what has been earned ($62,100 – $56,250 = $5,850)

$$\text{Earnings to Date} \quad - \quad \text{Billings to Date} \quad = \quad \text{Excess Earnings}$$
$$\$62,100 \quad - \quad \$56,250 \quad = \quad \$5,850$$

Excess Billings: Excess billings occur when billings are greater than earnings to date. This can occur when the contract calls for progress payments or the contractor has determined that the customer's credit is such that it is best to demand payment in advance for each step of the contract.

Completion-Capitalized Cost Method. Rather than depend on subjective estimates, some contractors prefer the completion-capitalized cost method. In this case, only 90 percent (or some other percentage) of the income and expenses calculated by the percentage completion method are applied in the current year. The balance is deferred until the project is completed, at which time adjustments can be made for possible errors in estimating.

FINANCIAL REPORTS (STATEMENTS)

Financial statements provide information about the financial condition of the company. They are used for planning future business, tracking the status of ongoing projects, and assisting in preparing future bids. They will also be required when applying for a loan or credit and preparing tax returns.

Statements are prepared at least annually, but are usually prepared more often so that changes in the financial condition can be quickly identified. The statements required consist of a balance sheet, income statement, and cash flow statement.

Balance Sheet

The **balance sheet** shows the financial condition of the company on a given day. A balance sheet is sometimes called a "snapshot" because it is a picture of a company at a given point in time. It is a summary of assets, liabilities, and stockholder's equity. The balance sheet consists of two parts:

1. *Assets,* consisting of current assets, other assets, and property and equipment at cost.
2. *Liabilities and Stockholders' Equity,* consisting of current liabilities, long-term debt, and retained earnings and stock.

For a balance sheet to be correct the following must be true:

$$Assets = Liabilities + Stockholder's\ Equity$$

On a typical balance sheet, all assets, liabilities, and net worth are identified. The numbers will be different depending on whether the accrual method or the cash method is used. (See Table 8.2.)

Income Statement

The **income statement** shows the financial position of a company for the year. The income statement is also called a profit and loss statement or P&L. This statement may include the annual budget for the year reported in order to allow comparisons between budgeted amounts and actual income and expenses. In larger companies, especially corporations, a multiyear income statement may be provided to show business growth. The income statement is a report on the financial history for the accounting period.

Typical income statement categories include revenues, direct costs, indirect costs, general and administrative costs, other income/expenses, gross profit, net income before taxes, and net income. The two main points of interest on the income statement are gross profit and net income. (See Table 8.3.)

Revenue. *Revenue* is the operating income or income due to the normal activities of the business.

Direct Costs. *Direct costs* are the costs that relate to the actual productive activities of the business. In construction, these include labor, payroll taxes, insurance, employee benefits, equipment costs or equipment leases, materials, subcontracts, permits, and bonds. Direct costs may be recognized as specific project costs.

Indirect Costs. *Indirect costs* are costs that are not related to any specific job, such as the cost of company vehicles and their operation. Indirect costs are also called project overhead.

Gross Profit. *Gross profit* is the amount remaining after deducting direct and indirect costs from revenues.

General and Administrative Costs. *General and administrative costs (G&A)* are costs incurred in the daily operation of a business. General and administrative costs include salaries of office staff, all office operating expenses, furniture and supplies, legal and accounting expenses, and advertising.

TABLE 8.2
Balance Sheet

Assets	Accrual Basis	Cash Basis
Current assets		
Cash	$10,420	$10,420
Contract receivables	160,080	
Costs and estimated earnings in excess of billings or uncompleted contracts	5,890	
Employee advances	200	200
Inventory	1,400	1,400
Prepaid expenses	800	
Total current assets	**$178,790**	**$12,020**
Other assets		
Deposits	4,000	4,000
Investments in joint ventures	10,000	10,000
Total other assets	**$14,000**	**$14,000**
Property and equipment, at cost		
Building	106,000	106,000
Equipment	18,000	18,000
Vehicles	22,000	22,000
Total property and equipment	**146,000**	**146,000**
Less: Accumulated depreciation	(35,000)	(35,000)
Net fixed assets	**$111,000**	**$111,000**
Total Assets	**$303,790**	**$137,020**

Liabilities and Stockholders' Equity

	Accrual Basis	Cash Basis
Current liabilities		
Current portion, long-term debt	15,000	15,000
Accounts payable	9,000	
Accrued payroll	2,500	
Accrued income taxes	5,000	
Billings in excess of costs and estimated earnings on uncompleted contracts	4,500	
Total current liabilities	**$36,000**	**$15,000**
Long-term debt		
Notes and mortgage payable	101,000	101,000
Deferred income taxes	3,500	
Long-term liabilities	**$104,500**	**$101,000**
Stockholders' Equity		
Common stock, $1 par value	5,000	5,000
Retained earnings	72,790	960
Current earnings	85,500	15,060
Net worth	**163,290**	**21,020**
Total liabilities and equity	**$303,790**	**$137,020**

TABLE 8.3
Income Statement

Item Description	$ Amount	Percent
		December 31, 2004
Sales Revenue	**$1,000,400**	**100.00**
Direct Costs		
Materials	310,000	30.98
Subcontractors	170,000	16.99
Labor	225,000	22.49
Other direct costs	0	0.00
Total direct costs	**$705,000**	**70.46**
Project Overhead		
Superintendent salaries	68,900	7.28
Vehicle expenses	2,100	0.02
Supplies	1,200	0.01
Depreciation—Vehicles	4,800	0.04
Depreciation—Equipment	2,900	0.02
Repairs	0	0.00
Total Project Overhead	**$79,900**	**7.90**
Gross Profit	**$212,500**	**21.54**
General and Administrative Costs		
Office salaries	60,024	6.00
Clerical salaries	40,016	4.00
Professional fees	20,008	2.00
Utilities	5,002	0.50
Insurance	10,004	1.00
Dues and subscriptions	200	0.02
Office supplies	4,001	0.40
Depreciation—office equipment	5,002	0.50
Licenses and fees	1,000	0.10
Taxes	1,000	0.10
Travel and entertainment	1,000	0.10
Miscellaneous	1,000	0.10
Total G&A Expenses	**$148,257**	**14.82**
Income from Operations	**$67,243**	**6.72**
Other Income/Expenses		
Gain on asset sales		
Interest income		0.00
Interest expense	−8,003	−0.08
Total Other Income/Expenses		**−0.00**
Net Income before taxes (NIBT)	**$59,240**	**5.92**
Provisions for income taxes	−4,962	0.49
Net Income	**$54,278**	**5.43**

Other Income/Expenses. The other income/expenses column is used to report all income or expenses not related to the operation of the primary business. Such items include gains or losses on the sale of property or income from sale of stock in the company.

Net Income Before Taxes (NIBT). *Net income before taxes* is the amount left after subtracting general and administrative costs from gross profit. When an income statement is generated for each project, general and administrative costs are apportioned to each project.

Net Income. Net income results when taxes are deducted from NIBT.

Cash Flow Statement

A **cash flow statement** shows revenue receipts and expenses for a particular reporting period. (See Table 8.4.)

TABLE 8.4
Cash Flow Statement

		Year Ended December 31, 2004
Cash flow from operations		
Net income		**$54,278**
Adjustments to reconcile net income to net cash from operations		
Depreciation	12,702	
Change in assets and liabilities		
Increase in contract receivables	(30,000)	
Decrease in inventory	14,000	
Decrease in prepaid expenses	(2,500)	
Decrease in accounts payable	(15,000)	
Increase in accrued expenses	5,000	
Increase in deferred taxes	3,500	
Total Adjustments		**(12,298)**
Net cash from operations		**41,980**
Cash flows from investments		
Payments for investment in joint ventures	(3,800)	
Capital expenditures	(16,500)	
Net cash used for investments		**(20,300)**
Cash flows from financing		
Net borrowings under line of credit	1,500	
Principal payments under capital lease	(3,500)	
Proceeds from issuance of common stock	1,000	
Net cash provided by financing		**(1,000)**
Net increase in cash and equivalents		**20,680**
Cash and equivalents at beginning of year		18,500
Cash and equivalents at end of year		**$39,180**

FINANCIAL RATIOS

Financial statements detail a company's financial position and from this data financial ratios can be calculated. Financial ratios can assist with determining the financial future of the company. They are similar to a report card, summarizing the financial performance of the company by evaluating it as a number rather than a letter grade. Financial ratios, such as the current ratio, are required by some states on a contractor license application to assist staff in determining the solvency of the company.

Liquidity Ratios

The **liquidity ratio** is a measure of the ability of a company to pay its current liabilities. Liquidity ratios are current ratio and acid-test ratio.

Current Ratio.   The **current ratio** is a measure of the ability of a company to pay bills promptly. It simply represents the cash on hand or equivalent assets available to pay bills or meet current liabilities. A ratio of less than 1:1 would indicate that the company is unable to pay its bills. Most companies should have at least a current ratio of at least 1.5:1. See the current ratio equation below.

$$\frac{\text{Current Assets (from Balance Sheet)}}{\text{Current Liabilities (from Balance Sheet)}} = \text{Current Ratio}$$

$$\frac{\$178,790}{\$36,000} = 4.96$$

Current Ratio Formula

Quick or Acid-Test Ratio.   The **acid-test ratio** is similar to the current ratio, but it is a more severe test for businesses that carry a large amount of inventory. If a company is required to sell inventory to pay bills, it may be difficult to sell the inventory at the price paid initially. The acid-test ratio is a more accurate indicator of a company's available resources to pay bills because pulling inventory out of the ratio equation means the ratio will be lower. See the acid-test ratio equation below.

$$\frac{\text{Current Assets} - \text{Inventory (from Balance Sheet)}}{\text{Current Liabilities (from Balance Sheet)}} = \text{Acid-Test Ratio}$$

$$\frac{\$178,790 - \$1,400}{\$36,000} = 4.92$$

Acid-Test Ratio Formula

Asset Management Ratios

The **asset management ratio** is a measure of how well a company is managing its assets. Asset management ratios used are the average collection period (ACP) and total asset utilization (TAU).

Average Collection Period (ACP) or Activity Ratio. The **average collection period (ACP),** or activity period, indicates the average days required to collect receivables. It is a measure of the company's ability to collect debts (receivables). See the ACP calculation below.

$$\frac{\text{Accounts Receivable (from Balance Sheet)}}{\text{Sales Revenue} \div 365 \text{ (from Balance Sheet)}} = \text{ACP}$$

$$\frac{\$160,080}{(\$1,000,400 \div 365) = \$2,740} = 58.42$$

Average Collection Period Formula

Total Asset Utilization. Total asset utilization (TAU) measures how well a company uses or turns over its assets. If a hotel has 100 rooms, total asset utilization will show how those rooms are being booked/used to generate sales. A contractor does not usually carry inventory so the TAU will be low. See an example of calculating TAU below.

$$\frac{\text{Sales Revenues (from Income Statement)}}{\text{Total Assets (from Balance Sheet)}} = \text{TAU}$$

$$\frac{\$1,000,400}{\$303,790} = 3.29$$

Total Asset Utilization Formula

Debt Management Ratios

The debt management ratio measures the company's use of debt and fixed costs to maximize earnings, minimize losses, and control risk. The most commonly used debt management ratio is the debt to equity ratio.

Debt to Equity Ratio. The **debt to equity ratio** measures the investment by creditors and contractors. Debt always involves interest and principal payments, which can be a drag on earnings and, therefore, on business growth. A company with a high debt to equity ratio risks bankruptcy if creditors demand payment. See an example of calculating the debt to equity ratio below.

$$\frac{\text{Current Liabilities + Long-Term Liabilities (from Balance Sheet)}}{\text{Stockholders Equity (from Balance Sheet)}}$$

$$= \text{Debt to Equity Ratio}$$

$$\frac{\$36,000 + \$104,500 = \$140,500}{\$163,290} = 0.86$$

Debt to Equity Ratio Formula

Return on Investment

Earnings of an investment are not usually referred to as earnings but as a **return on investment (ROI).** The return on investment is always reported as a percentage. The return on investment formula determines the return on a project as a percentage based on net income divided by the investment or assets. The following formula uses annual income and investment amounts.

$$\frac{\text{Net Income (from the bottom of the Income Statement)}}{\text{Total Assets (from the middle of the Balance Sheet)}} \times 100 = \text{ROI}$$

$$\frac{\$54,278}{\$303,790} = 0.17 \times 100 = 17\%$$

Return on Investment Formula

$$\frac{\text{Net Income (from the Income Statement)}}{\text{Sales Revenue (from the Income Statement)}} \times 100 = \text{Profit Margin}$$

$$\frac{\$54,278}{\$1,000,400} \quad 0.054 \times 100 = 5.4\%$$

Profit Margin Formula

JOB COST ANALYSIS

A **job cost analysis** facilitates financial management of existing projects and provides information necessary for preparing bids for future projects. This analysis could be called "Did we make any money?" Most contractors will use a computer system to generate these reports. The job cost analysis system tracks costs for an individual project. The costs are obtained from labor, materials, equipment, subcontracts, and other costs (including project overhead costs).

The job cost system tracks costs of a project. It provides a means for the contractor to compare actual costs to estimated costs as the project progresses as well as the opportunity to take necessary action to adjust costs. It also provides financial data for preparing a bid on other projects. This is where a computer accounting package pays off since reports are easily generated.

The job cost analysis procedure is to collect all the costs of the project such as labor, materials, subcontracts, overhead, and others, from the source documents. Typical costs and their sources are shown in Table 8.5.

With the assembled data, a report or phase analysis is prepared by entering the data in a timely and accurate manner into the accounting system, or it is entered into the journal and a compilation prepared on the journal entries. This once again shows the importance of a computer-based program because it eliminates double entry of the data and the computer can prepare a lengthy, accurate, and detailed report in less time than it takes for the contractor to select the needed report. The report will show the amount of work completed, cost to date, and variance from costs. Table 8.6 shows an analysis of a landscaping project.

TABLE 8.5
Job Cost Analysis Sources

Cost	Source
Materials, equipment	Invoices, purchase orders
Labor	Time sheets and invoices
Subcontractors	Invoices, contracts
Overhead based on a percentage	Bid documents or company policy

TABLE 8.6
Job Cost Analysis
Project: 404
Customer: Mr. Gates

		Original Estimate	Cost to Date	Cost to Complete	Updated Estimate	Expected Variance
	Total	4,500	3,950	400	4,350	150
Site Preparation						
	Tree removal	1,500	1,200	0	1,200	300
	Grind stumps	400	400	0	400	0
	Silt fence	400	350	0	350	50
	Seed and straw	600	500	100	600	0
	Labor	1,500	1,400	300	1,700	(200)
	Permit	100	100	0	100	0

The analysis shows that the tree removal estimate was a bit over cost and should result in a profit for the company. However, labor costs are higher than estimated and may offset any profit from the tree removal. The contractor will want to determine the reason for this overage. Maybe the crew reported for work, clocked in, began work, and then had to leave because of rain, meaning work would have had to start over the next day. It may also indicate that the time cards are not accurate. In Chapter 6, Project Management, we discussed the importance of the superintendent keeping accurate job records, which provides information about actual time spent on tasks, weather conditions, etc.

Overall, the estimate was fairly accurate, and the contractor can expect to make a profit based on this phase of the project.

SUMMARY

The practice of accounting is probably the most challenging for contractors due to the terms used and the calculations, but consider that an accountant would be just as challenged understanding fiber stress and calculating the load of a beam. The accounting task for a contracting company is made much easier by purchasing a computerized bookkeeping system or by hiring professional help. The contractor should be aware of tax saving items such as depreciation and make sure that they are tracked and be able to look at the financial statements to get a picture of the financial well being of the company.

CHAPTER 9

PAYROLL TAXES

A contractor must pay taxes for all employees. This chapter will identify the basic payroll taxes that a company must pay to the federal government and the company's reporting requirements. There are certain forms that the company completes, and some that are required from the employee. The payment of payroll taxes can be reduced depending on how the contractor staffs the job because there are differences in tax responsibilities depending on whether independent contractors or employees are used. Tax laws change yearly and reporting requirements are complicated. It may be beneficial to consider hiring a payroll company to track and collect payroll taxes and transmit them to the various state and federal agencies along with the various forms.

INDEPENDENT CONTRACTORS

There are several advantages to hiring an independent contractor rather than an employee. An **independent contractor (IC)** is not considered an employee, and the contractor is not required to pay the IC's payroll taxes and benefits. For example, a new clerical employee, whose pay rate is $10 an hour, encumbers the company as follows.

The taxes owed by company include the following five:

1. FUTA, 6.2 percent of the first $7,000 salary
2. FICA, 6.2 percent of the first $94,200 salary
3. Medicare, 1.45 percent of salary
4. State Unemployment, for this instance is 2.92 percent of first $8,000 salary. Each state will differ.
5. Workers Compensation insurance of at least 2 percent

Total taxes due = 18.35 percent, which raises the hourly rate for the company to $11.84 ($10.00 × 18.35 = $11.84).

An IC would not obligate the company for the above taxes. Instead, the company would call a placement service and request temporary clerical help with a ceiling of $10 per hour. The placement service would be obligated to pay the taxes.

When using an IC rather than hiring an hourly worker, a contract is signed for performance of the work. The IC must be a separate business entity with an employee identification number (EIN). The IC is typically hired for one job, and his or her work is not supervised by the contractor. The key here is that the contractor is not hiring an employee but another company to do a portion of the work.

Another advantage of using an IC is that the general contractor is not liable for a tort, or wrongful act, caused by the IC. This is certainly advantageous to the contractor trying to shift liability. Using an IC will result in a tax advantage and protection from lawsuits.

It is critical that an IC meet the legal guidelines set by the Internal Revenue Service (IRS). Otherwise, back taxes for Social Security and Medicare, plus interest and penalties, can be assessed to the contractor.

Independent Contractor Determination Guidelines

In order to be considered an IC, the following conditions must be met:

- There is a contract between the contractor and the IC that clearly states the status of the IC.
- The contractor does not hire, fire, or train employees of the IC.
- The IC establishes the work schedule.
- The IC usually works for several contractors at the same time.
- The IC has established a business structure.
- The IC establishes the means and methods of performing the job.
- The job is one time and once completed, the IC will contract another job.

If the IC meets the above criteria, then the contractor pays the IC and files a Form 1099, *Miscellaneous Income* for payments of $600 or more. If the IC does not meet any one of the criteria, then the person is an employee and should be treated as such.

EMPLOYEES

A contractor may have thousands of employees or just one, but in any case it is required that income taxes be withheld for each employee. An employer is required to withhold FICA and Medicare taxes from each employee's paycheck and is also required to match these taxes. The contractor is solely responsible for paying Federal Unemployment Tax (FUTA).

Payroll is complicated, requiring reports and monies to be sent to various agencies. Although computer software programs make it easier to calculate the taxes, many businesses choose to hire a professional company to perform their payroll functions.

PAYROLL TAXES

Taxes that are calculated on employees' earnings and deducted directly from the employee's check are called payroll taxes. All taxes to be paid by the contractor are held in escrow (not used for business purposes) until they are forwarded to the state or federal government. Taxes that the employer must withhold from employee's earnings are as follows:

- Federal income tax
- State income tax

- Social Security (FICA) tax (6.2 percent of earnings)
- Medicare tax (1.45 percent of all earnings)

Additional amounts that must be paid based on employees' earnings, but which may not be deducted from the employee's wages, are the following:

- Social Security (FICA) taxes equivalent to those paid by the employee (6.2 percent)
- Medicare taxes equivalent to those paid by the employee (1.45 percent)
- Federal Unemployment Tax (FUTA) (6.2 percent of the first $7,000 of earnings)
- State Unemployment tax

An example of payroll tax handling is seen below.

A carpenter earns $18.00 an hour, is paid weekly, and works 40 hours during the period January 1 to January 7. The carpenter's payroll taxes are as follows:

Wages	Social Security	Medicare	Total withheld and sent to federal government	Paycheck amount
40 × $18 = $720	6.2% × $720 = $44.64	1.45% × $720 = $10.44		
$720	− $44.64	− $10.44	$55.08	$644.92

The above table does not include withholding for federal or state income tax.

Based on the carpenter's wages, the contractor will pay the following to the federal government:

Wages	Social Security	Medicare	FUTA*	Employer pays to federal government
40 × $18 = $720	6.2% × $720 = $44.64	1.45% × $720 = $10.44	6.2% × $720 = $44.64	
	$44.64	$10.44	$44.64	$99.72

*Note: FUTA is only paid on the first $7,000 in wages.

The above example does not include state unemployment tax because that varies by each state. It would normally increase the amount that the employer must pay from the company earnings as an expense.

Depositing Taxes

Deposit of taxes withheld must be made on either a monthly or semiweekly (biweekly) schedule determined by the company's past year quarterly tax liability. The only exception applies if the total accumulated unpaid tax liability is $100,000 or more, in which case the entire amount must be deposited the next business day. Deposits are made electronically or to an authorized financial institution (usually a commercial bank) along with Federal Tax Deposit Form 8109. The IRS will forward a coupon book for use with these deposits shortly after registering and receiving the employer identification number (EIN).

New Employers

For tax purposes, new employers are assigned a monthly deposit schedule. If the accumulated tax liability is less than $2,500 during a quarter, payment is made with Federal Form 941, *Employer's Quarterly Federal Tax Return.*

Social Security (FICA) and Medicare taxes withheld are deposited along with the income tax withheld. Each is reported separately. No FICA is withheld on earnings in excess of $87,000. There is no earnings limit for the Medicare tax.

Form W-4

Each newly hired employee must complete a **Form W-4,** *Employee's Withholding Allowance Certificate.* Form W-4 tells the employer how many withholding allowances to use when deducting federal income tax from the employee's pay. Form W-4 includes instructions and a worksheet for computing the number of withholding allowances. A copy of Form W-4 is included in Appendix C.

After the employee completes and signs the Form W-4, it is kept in the company files. This form serves as verification that federal income tax is being withheld as the employee wishes. Form W-4 is not sent to the IRS.

Form W-2 Wage and Tax Statement

A **Form W-2,** *Wage and Tax Statement,* must be furnished in duplicate to each employee as soon after December 31 as possible, but no later than January 31. An employee leaving the company before year-end may request a Form W-2, and one must be provided within 30 days after the request. Most employers use at least a three-part form to accommodate state and local tax reporting.

It is a responsibility of the company to file Copy A of Form W-2, Wage and Tax Statement, with the Social Security Administration (SSA) for employees showing the wages paid and taxes withheld for the year. Because Form W-2 is the only document used to transmit information on employees' Social Security and Medicare wages for the year, it is very important to prepare the forms correctly and in a timely manner.

Form W-3

Form W-3 is a summary of all W-2s issued to employees. Form W-3 must be filed with the IRS by February 28 of the following year. If the company has independent contractors, a Form 1099 must be sent to the independent contractors by January 31 of the following year.

Federal Unemployment Tax

Federal unemployment taxes are paid by the employer and are not deducted from the employee's paycheck. **Federal unemployment tax (FUTA)** is 6.2 percent of the first $7,000 earned by each employee during the year. It is based on one of the following:

1. Employee earns $1,500 or more in any calendar quarter.
2. The company had one or more employees any part of a day during 20 or more weeks during the last 12 months. Determination is made based on the number of weeks worked, not the wages earned. For example, if an employee worked

part time for the company over 20 or more weeks, then the company is subject to paying FUTA regardless of whether the pay was under $1,500.

If the company also pays state unemployment taxes, a credit may be taken for payments into the state fund up to a maximum of 5.4 percent of taxable wages.

A quarter consists of 12 weeks. To determine the minimum payroll amount an individual could make in a week before the employer must pay unemployment taxes, divide $1,500 by 12 (1,500 ÷ 12 = $125 a week). ($1,500 is the minimum amount at which an employer is required to begin paying taxes.) If we were to consider this a minimum wage employee at $5.15 an hour, and ask how many hours they could work with the company not subjected to FUTA, the following calculation would be used:

Wage in one quarter in one year	Weeks in a quarter	Wages per week at $5.15	Hours per week
$1,500	12	$1,500 ÷ 12 = $125	$125 ÷ $5.15 = 24

The number of hours that can be worked would be less if the employee earned more per hour. Remember, this employee can only work one quarter in a year and earn no more than $1,500 during that period.

Form 940–Federal Unemployment Tax Return. An employer, other than a household or agricultural employer, files a Federal Unemployment Tax Return, Form 940, if either of the following situations applies:

1. The company paid $1,500 or more in wages during any calendar quarter, or

2. The company had at least one employee work for some part of a day in any 20 or more weeks.

Form 940 Deposit Requirements. Form 940 (or Form 940EZ), *Employer's Federal Unemployment (FUTA) Tax Return*, is generally due by January 31. Although Form 940 covers a calendar year, deposits may have to be made before filing the tax return. If the contractor's FUTA tax liability exceeds $100, then FUTA taxes are deposited quarterly. (See Table 9.1.) Tables of typical federal tax deadline dates are included in Appendix C. Tables are arranged by type of company organization and they provide information on the date the tax is due, which tax is due, and the necessary form to file. Check with the IRS for any additional taxes that may be required.

If the FUTA tax liability is over $100 for any calendar quarter, it must be deposited through the Electronic Federal Tax Payment System (EFTPS) or by using Form 8109, *Federal Tax Deposit Coupon.*

If the total tax is more than $100, a Record of Quarterly Federal Unemployment Tax Liability must be completed. This part of the form shows the IRS whether the tax deposit has been made on time. There may be a penalty charged for late deposits, for mailing your payment to the IRS instead of depositing it, or for failing to use EFTPS, when required.

TABLE 9.1
Quarterly FUTA Deposit Dates

Tax Due Dates	
Quarter	Due Date
January – March	April 30
April – June	July 31
July – September	October 31
October – December	January 31

Penalties

Failure to make tax deposits or file required information for either federal or state taxes incurs penalties. Established penalties are shown in Table 9.2.

IRS Circular E

If the contractor prefers to perform their own payroll functions, it will be necessary to consult IRS Circular E. **Circular E** is an IRS publication that explains the federal tax responsibilities of an employer. It details the requirements for withholding, depositing, reporting, and paying employment taxes. It explains the forms that must be given to employees and those that employees must give to the company. Circular E explains what must be sent to the IRS and the Social Security Administration. It has tax tables needed to compute taxes withheld from each employee. The files can be downloaded to a local computer to create hard copies. A copy of Circular E is included in Appendix C. Circular E is updated annually, usually in December or January, and can be downloaded from the IRS Web site at *www.irs.gov.* Also, because tax laws change frequently, the IRS Web site should be checked frequently throughout the year to remain current on relevant tax laws. (See Table 9.3.)

TABLE 9.2
Established Late
Payment Penalties

Federal Tax Late Payment Penalties	
Deposits made 1 to 5 days late	2%
Deposits made 6 to 15 days late	5%
Deposits made 16 or more days late	10%
Amounts paid within 10 days after first delinquent tax notice from the IRS	10%
Deposits made at an unauthorized financial institution, paid directly to the IRS, or paid with your tax return	10%
Amounts subject to EFTPS requirements but not deposited using EFTPS	10%
Amounts unpaid more than 10 days after receiving a first delinquent tax notice OR not paid on the day on which you receive a demand for immediate payment	15%

TABLE 9.3
Tax Law Information
Web Sites

Tax Assistance Web Sites	
Pub. 334, Guide for Small Business	*http://ftp.fedworld.gov/pub/irs-pdf/p334.pdf*
Pub. 533, Self-Employment Tax	*http://ftp.fedworld.gov/pub/irs-pdf/p533.pdf*
Pub. 535, Business Expenses	*http://ftp.fedworld.gov/pub/irs-pdf/p535.pdf*
Pub. 538, Accounting Periods and Methods	*http://ftp.fedworld.gov/pub/irs-pdf/p538.pdf*
Pub. 541, Partnerships	*http://ftp.fedworld.gov/pub/irs-pdf/p541.pdf*
Pub. 542, Corporations	*http://ftp.fedworld.gov/pub/irs-pdf/p542.pdf*

BUSINESS INCOME TAXES

Taxable income is payment for work, and the income earned is taxable. The income earned from all side jobs is also taxable regardless of the method of payment. Typical payment methods for work include the following:

- Paid by cash or check
- Received a credit on a bill
- Received other goods or services in exchange
- Collected the payment later
- Received a Form 1099 or W-2 (or not) showing the amount of income earned

Business income taxes are based on the type of business structure. Following is a brief summary listing common business taxes that must be paid by sole proprietors, partnerships, corporations, and subchapter S corporations.

Sole Proprietor

A sole proprietor must submit Schedule C with the individual federal tax returns, and because it is unlikely that withholding tax has been paid, it is probably necessary to file federal estimated taxes quarterly. These quarterly taxes will include both the employer's and employee's portion of FICA and Medicare taxes.

Partnerships

A partnership must submit IRS Form 1065 by the 15th day of the fourth month after the end of their fiscal year. Each partner must report the prorated share of profits as personal income. Because there is no withholding, partners will need to file quarterly estimated taxes.

There may be an additional filing requirement with the IRS related to a foreign partner(s) on the partnership tax return. If the partnership had taxable income connected with a trade or business within the United States that can be allocated to a foreign partner, the IRS requires the partnership to report and pay a withholding tax. The partnership must pay the withholding tax regardless of the amount of the foreign partner's ultimate U.S. tax liability and regardless of whether the partnership makes any distributions during its tax year.

For information on reporting and paying the Section 1446 withholding tax, as well as the general reporting obligations, see the following: Form 8804, Annual

Return for Partnership Withholding Tax; Form 8805, Foreign Partner's Information Statement of Withholding Tax; and Form 8813, Partnership Withholding Tax Payment Voucher.

Corporations

A corporation must submit IRS Form 1120 by the 15th day of the third month after the end of their fiscal year. A corporation pays taxes based on a determined income tax rate and files a tax form each year (IRS Form 1120). Corporate taxes range from 15 percent to 39 percent depending on income.

Subchapter S Corporations

A subchapter S corporation must submit IRS Form 1120-S by the 15th day of the third month following the end of their fiscal year. No tax payment is due with this filing. Shareholders in an S Corporation are taxed on the business income as part of their personal income, prorated proportionately to their percentage of ownership. This income is taxed whether or not it is distributed. Shareholders must pay estimated taxes on this income even though it may not be reported to them until the following year.

RECORD KEEPING

All federal records pertaining to employment taxes must be kept at least four years. In the event of an audit, these records must be kept at least four years after the resolution of the audit. Records that must be kept include, but are not limited to, the following:

- Amounts and dates of all wages, annuities, sick pay, bonuses, and pension payments
- Copies of all returns filed
- Copies of both state and federal income tax withholding allowance certificates
- Dates and amounts of all tax deposits or payments you made
- Dates of employment of all employees
- Employee copies of Form W-2 returned as undeliverable
- Independent contractor/subcontractor copies of Form 1099 returned as undeliverable
- Name, address, Social Security number, and occupation of all employees
- Records of all fringe benefits provided, including validation
- Records of any other payroll deductions authorized by the employee
- The fair market value of any in-kind wages paid
- Employer identification number (EIN)

SALES AND USE TAXES

Most contractors buy materials retail. Because the contractor is considered the user and consumer of all materials and services purchased, they pay the sales tax at the time of purchase of these materials and services. The building contractor normally will not charge sales taxes on products because the sales taxes have already been paid. Labor to repair, renovate, apply, and/or install tangible personal property is not taxable as long as it is listed as a separate charge on the invoice. States and local jurisdictions may have additional rules. Check the IRS Web site regularly for changes to tax laws.

SUMMARY

The preparation and minimizing of taxes owed will be greatly simplified based on how well the books are kept in the accounting system. Payroll taxes are a bit challenging to setup for a company that does this in-house but a computerized accounting system will make it easier. There are a number of private payroll companies that will perform this function and should be considered by small companies without clerical staff. The timely filing of payroll taxes and forms is mandatory, both at the state and federal levels, and can be performed by the payroll service.

CHAPTER 10

OCCUPATIONAL SAFETY AND HEALTH

Nearly every working person, particularly in the construction field, is under the jurisdiction of the Occupational Safety and Health Administration (OSHA). Workplace inspections are one of OSHA's main activities, and it is important that every employer is in compliance with OSHA regulations. Knowledge of the regulations is critical and there is no acceptable excuse that will get a contractor out of a fine or penalty.

Federal OSHA requirements can be found at *www.osha.gov*. Many states have adopted their own OSHA regulations based on federal regulations, and these should be available at the state's government Web page. This chapter will give an overview of some of the federal OSHA regulations specific to the construction industry.

PERSONAL PROTECTIVE EQUIPMENT

The Occupational Safety and Health Administration requires that personal protective equipment (PPE) be used whenever employees are exposed to hazards that cannot be reduced to acceptable levels through administration or engineering controls. It is the responsibility of the employer to determine what hazards exist and when to use PPE. Personal protective equipment includes a variety of equipment from eye protection to respiratory protection to safety nets. Every contractor should have a full working knowledge of OSHA requirements. The employer is responsible for ensuring that protective equipment used meets these standards, whether the equipment is furnished by the employer or by the employee.

Head Protection

Any employees working in an area where there is a risk of falling or flying objects, or the possibility of a head injury from impact, must wear a hard hat (OSHA 1926.100a). Hard hats must have a hard outer shell that has a shock-absorbing liner with a headband and straps that suspend the shell ¼" to 1" away from the head. Hard hats must meet the requirements of American National Standards Institute, ANSI Z89.1, *Safety Requirements for Industrial Head Protection.*

Eye and Face Protection

Employees who work with chemicals, radiation elements, or with machines that present a potential eye or face injury must be provided with eye and face protection [OSHA 1926.102(a)(1)]. For example, employees who operate welding machines must be provided with eye and face protection. If employees wear glasses to correct their vision, then they must be provided with eye protection that can be worn over their glasses or with goggles that incorporate corrective lenses in the goggles.

Hearing Protection

Hearing protection is one of the most often overlooked and violated protective equipment requirements. Whenever noise levels or durations exceed the levels specified in Table D-2, Permissible Noise Exposures (OSHA 1925.52), hearing protection must be used. It is the employer's responsibility to make sure proper hearing protection equipment is available for every employee and that it is properly fitted and used.

In all cases where the sound levels exceed the values shown in the table, a continuing, effective hearing conservation program must be administered. (See Table 10.1.)

When the daily noise exposure is composed of two or more periods of noise exposure of different levels, their combined effect should be considered, rather than the individual effect of each.

Safety Nets

Safety nets must be provided if the work space is 25 feet or more above the ground or water and using a ladder or scaffold is impractical [OSHA 1926.105(a)].

TABLE 10.1
Hearing Protection

Table D-2 – Permissible Noise Exposures	
Duration per day, hours	Sound level, dBA, slow response
8	90
6	92
4	95
3	97
2	100
1½	102
1	105
½	110
¼ or less	115

Protective Clothing

Employees who will be working with hot substances or corrosive or poisonous materials must be provided foot and leg gear and protective gloves. Footwear should have a protective toe and offer impact and compression protection. Leg gear should be comprised of safety snaps for quick removal. Gloves should be appropriate for the work situation. For example, when working with chemicals, treated rubber gloves should be worn. Refer to OSHA 3151, *Personal Protective Equipment,* for more information.

ASBESTOS AND LEAD EXPOSURE

Employees in the construction industry may face asbestos and lead exposure in the course of their work through the installation, removal, or use of certain materials. Protection must be provided to employees when these materials are handled or encountered. Following is a brief summary of protective actions that must be taken when working with these materials. This discussion is provided as information only and is not intended to be a definitive guide. A contractor working with these materials must be aware of all requirements and be licensed or certified to perform such work.

Asbestos

Asbestos is a fibrous mineral with thin fibers. Asbestos is heat resistant, making it useful for many industrial purposes. Asbestos can be woven or spun. Asbestos was commonly used before 1978 to make many products; contractors should assume that asbestos will be present in buildings built prior to 1978. Some common uses of asbestos include furnace duct insulation, fire stopping, textured paints, siding, and flooring.

Permissible Exposure Limit (PEL). Construction workplace exposure must be limited to 0.2 fibers per cubic centimeter of air (0.2 f/cc), averaged over an 8-hour work shift. The short-term limit is one fiber per cubic centimeter of air (1 f/cc) averaged over a sampling period of 30 minutes.

Exposure Monitoring. Employers must do initial monitoring for workers who may be exposed above the action level, the level that requires initiating medical monitoring, of 0.1 f/cc. Subsequent monitoring must be conducted at reasonable intervals, in no case longer than six months for employees exposed above the action level.

In construction, daily monitoring must be continued until exposure drops below the action level (0.1 f/cc). Daily monitoring is not required where employees are using supplied-air respirators operated in the positive pressure mode.

Respirators. In general industry and construction, the level of exposure determines the type of respirator required; OSHA standards specify the respirator to be used for each exposure level.

Regulated Areas. In general industry and construction, regulated areas must be established where the 8-hour time-weighted average (TWA) or 30-minute excursion values for airborne asbestos exceed the prescribed permissible exposure limits. Only authorized persons wearing appropriate respirators can enter a regulated area. In regulated areas, eating, smoking, drinking, chewing tobacco or gum, and applying cosmetics are prohibited.

Warning signs must be displayed at each regulated area and must be posted at all approaches to regulated areas.

Labels.   Caution labels must be placed on all raw materials, mixtures, scrap, waste, debris, and other products containing asbestos fibers.

Record Keeping.   The employer must keep an accurate record of all measurements taken to monitor employee exposure to asbestos. This record is to include the following:

- The date of measurement
- Operation involving exposure
- Sampling and analytical methods used
- Evidence of the accuracy—number, duration, and results of samples taken
- Type of respiratory protective devices worn
- Name, Social Security number, and the results of all employee exposure measurements

This record must be kept for 30 years.

Protective Clothing.   For any employee exposed to airborne concentrations of asbestos that exceed the PEL, the employer must provide and require the use of protective clothing such as coveralls or similar full-body clothing, head coverings, gloves, and foot covering. Wherever the possibility of eye irritation exists, face shields, vented goggles, or other appropriate protective equipment must be provided and worn.

In construction, there are special regulated-area requirements for asbestos removal, renovation, and demolition operations. These provisions include a negative pressure area, decontamination procedures for workers, and a "competent person" with the authority to identify and control asbestos hazards. The standard includes an exemption from the negative pressure enclosure requirements for certain small-scale, short-duration operations provided special work practices prescribed in an appendix to the standard are followed.

Hygiene Facilities and Practices.   Clean change rooms must be furnished by employers for employees who work in areas where exposure to asbestos is above the TWA and/or excursion limit. Two lockers or storage facilities must be furnished and separated to prevent contamination of the employee's street clothes from protective work clothing and equipment. Showers must be furnished so that employees may shower at the end of the work shift. Employees must enter and exit the regulated area through the decontamination area.

The equipment room must be supplied with impermeable, labeled bags and containers for the containment and disposal of contaminated protective clothing and equipment.

Lunchroom facilities for those employees must have a positive pressure, filtered air supply and be readily accessible to employees. Employees must wash their hands and face prior to eating, drinking, or smoking. The employer must ensure that employees do not enter lunchroom facilities with protective work clothing or equipment unless surface fibers have been removed from the clothing or equipment. Employees may not smoke in work areas where they are occupationally exposed to asbestos.

Medical Exams. In general industry, exposed employees must have a preplacement physical examination before being assigned to an occupation exposed to airborne concentrations of asbestos at or above the action level or the excursion level. The physical examination must include chest X-ray, medical and work history, and pulmonary function tests. Subsequent exams must be given annually and upon termination of employment, though chest X-rays are required annually only for older workers whose first asbestos exposure occurred more than 10 years ago.

In construction, examinations must be made available annually for workers exposed above the action level or excursion limit for 30 or more days per year or who are required to wear negative pressure respirators. Chest X-rays are at the discretion of the physician.

Lead

Lead is a lustrous metal that is very soft, highly malleable, ductile, and a poor conductor of electricity. Lead materials in industry that are of concern are metallic leads, all inorganic lead compounds, and organic lead soaps. In building construction, lead is frequently used for roofs, cornices, tank linings, and electrical conduits and was a common component of paint in residential construction.

In the construction industry, lead has frequently been a problem for workers in the plumbing, welding, and painting trades. In plumbing, soft solder is an alloy of lead and tin. It is used for soldering copper pipe joints. However, the use of soft solder has been banned for many uses in the United States. The use of lead-based paint in residential construction has been banned by the Consumer Product Safety Commission. Lead-based paint is still used for some applications, such as bridges, railways, ships, and other steel structures because it inhibits the rusting and corrosion of iron and steel.

The Occupational Safety and Health Administration has determined permissible exposure limits action levels for lead exposure. A permissible exposure limit is the limit to the concentration of lead that an employee is exposed to, averaged over an 8-hour period. The maximum lead concentration that employees can be exposed to is 50 micrograms per cubic meter of air (50 $\mu g/m^3$) averaged over an 8-hour period. An action level is the limit of employee exposure, without regard to the use of respirators, to an airborne concentration of lead of 30 micrograms per cubic meter of air (30 $\mu g/m^3$) calculated as an 8-hour time-weighted average.

Employers must determine if employees may be exposed to lead at or above the action level and must monitor employee exposure. Construction operations that may expose employees to lead dust or fumes include the following:

- Flame-torch cutting, welding, using heat guns, sanding, scraping, and grinding of lead-painted surfaces
- Abrasive blasting of bridges and other structures containing lead-based paints

Respiratory Protection. Respirators used when working with lead-based materials must comply with OSHA respirator standards. Employers are responsible for training their employees regarding the proper use of respirators and safety requirements for working around lead.

Protective Clothing and Equipment. The employer shall provide, at no cost to the employee, and assure that the employee uses appropriate protective work clothing and equipment that prevents contamination of the employee and the employee's garments. Protective clothing includes but is not limited to the following:

- Coveralls or similar full-body work clothing
- Gloves, hats, and shoes or disposable shoe coverlets
- Face shields, vented goggles, or other appropriate protective equipment

Hygiene Facilities and Practices. The employer must assure that food, beverages, and tobacco products are not present or used, and cosmetics are not applied in areas where employees are exposed to lead. Additionally, change areas and hand washing facilities must be provided for employees to change from work clothes to street clothes and to wash after exposure to lead to prevent the transmission of lead dust to others. If employees were to wear their work clothes containing lead dust home, they and their families would be exposed.

Biological monitoring systems, consisting of blood sampling and analysis for lead and zinc, can be used by employers to monitor employees' exposure to lead. A sign must be posted in work areas that states:

WARNING:
LEAD WORK AREA
POISON
NO SMOKING OR EATING

OSHA RECORD KEEPING

Occupational Safety and Health Administration regulations provide for record keeping and reporting of accidents, illnesses, and deaths; prevention of accidents and illnesses; and safety poster requirements. Record keeping of injuries and illnesses is important to help identify problem areas so that future injuries can be prevented and training programs for safety and health issues can be implemented or updated.

Definitions

> **medical treatment** Treatment administered by a physician or by registered professional personnel under the standing orders of a physician. Medical treatment does not include first aid treatment even though it may be provided by a physician or a registered professional personnel.

> **first aid** Any one-time treatment and any follow-up visit for the purpose of observation of minor scratches, cuts, burns, splinters, and so forth, that do not ordinarily require medical care.

> **lost workdays** The number of days including the day of injury or illness during which the employee would have worked but could not do so because of the occupational injury or illness.

Occupational Injury and Illness Log

An occupational injury and illness log must be kept at every job site for businesses that have more than 10 employees. Businesses that have 10 or fewer employees during one calendar year are exempted from keeping this log. However, OSHA may instruct, in writing, that an exempt business maintain the log regardless of exempt status or number of employees. Refer to OSHA 3169, *Record Keeping,* or CFR 29 1904.1 and 1904.2, for more information on exempt employers.

In instances of multiple worksites for one company, injury and illness logs must be kept for worksites that will be operational longer than one year (29 CFR 1904.30(a)). One log may be kept for multiple short-term establishments, but information must be inputted into the log within 7 calendar days of receiving notice of the injury or illness.

Records of every job-related illness, on-the-job injury, or work-related fatality must be maintained in a log, preferably using OSHA Form 300, *Log of Work-Related Injuries and Illnesses.* (See Figure 10.1.) The log must be filled out in a timely and thorough manner. Rules for maintaining the log include the following:

- Record incidents not later than 6 days after the illness or injury occurs.

- In the event of a fatality, the initial report must be made within 8 hours, by telephone or in person.

- The fatality must be reported in writing in the log.

- Report in-patient hospitalization of three or more employees.

- The log must be maintained on a calendar year basis regardless of the company's fiscal year.

- Employers with 10 or more employees must submit an annual summary based on the log and post a copy annually by February 1. It must remain posted for at least 1 month.

- Records are kept on a calendar basis for a period of 5 years.

- Access to records must be available to any employee, former employee, and representative of the employee or OSHA in a reasonable manner and time.

Reporting of Fatality or Multiple Hospitalization Incidents. The employer, as a result of a work-related incident, must report orally to OSHA within 8 hours after the death of any employee from a work-related incident. The report must include the establishment name, location of incident, time of the incident, number of fatalities or hospitalized employees, contact person, phone number, and a brief description of the incident. The employer must also fill out Form 301, *Injury and Illness Incident Report.* This report helps OSHA identify the extent and severity of work-related incidents. (See Figure 10.2.)

OSHA Injury Decision-Making Tree. Recordable occupational injuries or illnesses are any occupational injuries or illnesses that result in

- fatalities, regardless of the time between the injury and death, or the length of the illness;

- lost workdays;

- nonfatal cases without lost workdays that result in a transfer to another job or termination of employment, or require medical treatment beyond basic first aid; or

- loss of consciousness or restriction of work [29 CFR 1904.7(a)].

FIGURE 10.1
OSHA Injury and Illness Log

OSHA's Form 300 (Rev. 01/2004)

Log of Work-Related Injuries and Illnesses

U.S. Department of Labor
Occupational Safety and Health Administration

Form approved OMB no. 1218-0176

Year 20____

Attention: This form contains information relating to employee health and must be used in a manner that protects the confidentiality of employees to the extent possible while the information is being used for occupational safety and health purposes.

You must record information about every work-related death and about every work-related injury or illness that involves loss of consciousness, restricted work activity or job transfer, days away from work, or medical treatment beyond first aid. You must also record significant work-related injuries and illnesses that are diagnosed by a physician or licensed health care professional. You must also record work-related injuries and illnesses that meet any of the specific recording criteria listed in 29 CFR Part 1904.8 through 1904.12. Feel free to use two lines for a single case if you need to. You must complete an Injury and Illness Incident Report (OSHA Form 301) or equivalent form for each injury or illness recorded on this form. If you're not sure whether a case is recordable, call your local OSHA office for help.

Establishment name _____

City _____ State _____

Identify the person

(A) Case no.	(B) Employee's name

Describe the case

(C) Job title (e.g., Welder)	(D) Date of injury or onset of illness	(E) Where the event occurred (e.g., Loading dock north end)	(F) Describe injury or illness, parts of body affected, and object/substance that directly injured or made person ill (e.g., Second degree burns on right forearm from acetylene torch)

Classify the case

CHECK ONLY ONE box for each case based on the most serious outcome for that case:

Death (G)	Days away from work (H)	Remained at Work Job transfer or restriction (I)	Other recordable cases (J)

Enter the number of days the injured or ill worker was:

Away from work (K) days	On job transfer or restriction (L) days

Check the "Injury" column or choose one type of illness:
(M) Injury (1) | Skin disorder (2) | Respiratory condition (3) | Poisoning (4) | Hearing loss (5) | All other illnesses (6)

Page totals ▶

Be sure to transfer these totals to the Summary page (Form 300A) before you post it.

Page ____ of ____

Public reporting burden for this collection of information is estimated to average 14 minutes per response, including time to review the instructions, search and gather the data needed, and complete and review the collection of information. Persons are not required to respond to the collection of information unless it displays a currently valid OMB control number. If you have any comments about these estimates or any other aspects of this data collection, contact: US Department of Labor, OSHA Office of Statistical Analysis, Room N-3644, 200 Constitution Avenue, NW, Washington, DC 20210. Do not send the completed forms to this office.

FIGURE 10.1 (continued)
OSHA Injury and Illness Log

OSHA's Form 300A (Rev. 01/2004)

Summary of Work-Related Injuries and Illnesses

Year 20___

U.S. Department of Labor
Occupational Safety and Health Administration

Form approved OMB no. 1218-0176

All establishments covered by Part 1904 must complete this Summary page, even if no work-related injuries or illnesses occurred during the year. Remember to review the Log to verify that the entries are complete and accurate before completing this summary.

Using the Log, count the individual entries you made for each category. Then write the totals below, making sure you've added the entries from every page of the Log. If you had no cases, write "0."

Employees, former employees, and their representatives have the right to review the OSHA Form 300 in its entirety. They also have limited access to the OSHA Form 301 or its equivalent. See 29 CFR Part 1904.35, in OSHA's recordkeeping rule, for further details on the access provisions for these forms.

Number of Cases

Total number of deaths	Total number of cases with days away from work	Total number of cases with job transfer or restriction	Total number of other recordable cases
___ (G)	___ (H)	___ (I)	___ (J)

Number of Days

Total number of days away from work	Total number of days of job transfer or restriction
___ (K)	___ (L)

Injury and Illness Types

Total number of... (M)
(1) Injuries ___
(2) Skin disorders ___
(3) Respiratory conditions ___
(4) Poisonings ___
(5) Hearing loss ___
(6) All other illnesses ___

Establishment information

Your establishment name ___
Street ___
City ___ State ___ ZIP ___

Industry description (e.g., Manufacture of motor truck trailers) ___

Standard Industrial Classification (SIC), if known (e.g., 3715) ___ ___ ___ ___
OR
North American Industrial Classification (NAICS), if known (e.g., 336212) ___ ___ ___ ___ ___ ___

Employment information *(If you don't have these figures, see the Worksheet on the back of this page to estimate.)*

Annual average number of employees ___
Total hours worked by all employees last year ___

Sign here

Knowingly falsifying this document may result in a fine.

I certify that I have examined this document and that to the best of my knowledge the entries are true, accurate, and complete.

Company executive ___ Title ___
Phone ___ Date ___/___/___

Post this Summary page from February 1 to April 30 of the year following the year covered by the form.

Public reporting burden for this collection of information is estimated to average 50 minutes per response, including time to review the instructions, search and gather the data needed, and complete and review the collection of information. Persons are not required to respond to the collection of information unless it displays a currently valid OMB control number. If you have any comments about these estimates or any other aspects of this data collection, contact: US Department of Labor, OSHA Office of Statistical Analysis, Room N-3644, 200 Constitution Avenue, NW, Washington, DC 20210. Do not send the completed forms to this office.

CHAPTER 10
Occupational Safety and Health

FIGURE 10.2
OSHA Injury and Illness Report Form

U.S. Department of Labor
Occupational Safety and Health Administration

Form approved OMB no. 1218-0176

OSHA's Form 301
Injury and Illness Incident Report

This *Injury and Illness Incident Report* is one of the first forms you must fill out when a recordable work-related injury or illness has occurred. Together with the *Log of Work-Related Injuries and Illnesses* and the accompanying *Summary*, these forms help the employer and OSHA develop a picture of the extent and severity of work-related incidents.

Within 7 calendar days after you receive information that a recordable work-related injury or illness has occurred, you must fill out this form or an equivalent. Some state workers' compensation, insurance, or other reports may be acceptable substitutes. To be considered an equivalent form, any substitute must contain all the information asked for on this form.

According to Public Law 91-596 and 29 CFR 1904, OSHA's recordkeeping rule, you must keep this form on file for 5 years following the year to which it pertains.

If you need additional copies of this form, you may photocopy and use as many as you need.

Completed by _____

Title _____

Phone (_____) _____ - _____   Date ___ / ___ / ___

Attention: This form contains information relating to employee health and must be used in a manner that protects the confidentiality of employees to the extent possible while the information is being used for occupational safety and health purposes.

Information about the employee

1) Full name _____

2) Street _____
   City _____ State _____ ZIP _____

3) Date of birth ___ / ___ / ___

4) Date hired ___ / ___ / ___

5) ☐ Male   ☐ Female

Information about the physician or other health care professional

6) Name of physician or other health care professional _____

7) If treatment was given away from the worksite, where was it given?
   Facility _____
   Street _____
   City _____ State _____ ZIP _____

8) Was employee treated in an emergency room?
   ☐ Yes
   ☐ No

9) Was employee hospitalized overnight as an in-patient?
   ☐ Yes
   ☐ No

Information about the case

10) Case number from the *Log* _____ *(Transfer the case number from the Log after you record the case.)*

11) Date of injury or illness ___ / ___ / ___

12) Time employee began work _____ AM / PM

13) Time of event _____ AM / PM   ☐ Check if time cannot be determined

14) *What was the employee doing just before the incident occurred?* Describe the activity, as well as the tools, equipment, or material the employee was using. Be specific. *Examples:* "climbing a ladder while carrying roofing materials"; "spraying chlorine from hand sprayer"; "daily computer key-entry."

15) *What happened?* Tell us how the injury occurred. *Examples:* "When ladder slipped on wet floor, worker fell 20 feet"; "Worker was sprayed with chlorine when gasket broke during replacement"; "Worker developed soreness in wrist over time."

16) *What was the injury or illness?* Tell us the part of the body that was affected and how it was affected; be more specific than "hurt," "pain," or sore." *Examples:* "strained back"; "chemical burn, hand"; "carpal tunnel syndrome."

17) *What object or substance directly harmed the employee? Examples:* "concrete floor"; "chlorine"; "radial arm saw." *If this question does not apply to the incident, leave it blank.*

18) *If the employee died, when did death occur?* Date of death ___ / ___ / ___

Public reporting burden for this collection of information is estimated to average 22 minutes per response, including time for reviewing instructions, searching existing data sources, gathering and maintaining the data needed, and completing and reviewing the collection of information. Persons are not required to respond to the collection of information unless it displays a current valid OMB control number. If you have any comments about this estimate or any other aspects of this data collection, including suggestions for reducing this burden, contact: US Department of Labor, OSHA Office of Statistical Analysis, Room N-3644, 200 Constitution Avenue, NW, Washington, DC 20210. Do not send the completed forms to this office.

FIGURE 10.3
Injury Decision-Making Tree

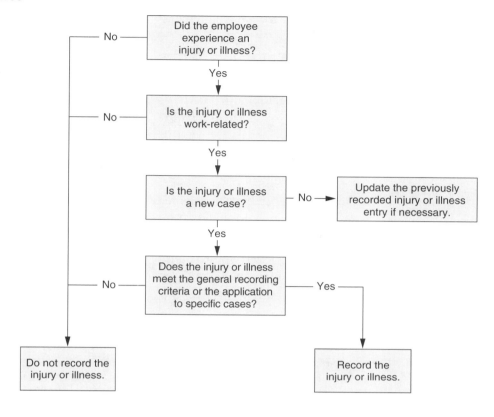

To help determine whether an injury or illness must be recorded, an injury decision-making tree can be used. (See Figure 10.3.)

Access to Records

Employees, former employees, their personal representatives, and their authorized employee representatives have the right to access the OSHA injury and illness records, with some limitations. A *personal representative* is a person that an employee has designated in writing as representing the employee's interests. When a request to see Form 300 is submitted to the employer, the employer must provide the record by the end of the next business day. Be aware that state requirements may differ from federal regulations.

Falsification of Report

Knowingly making a false statement in an injury log is punishable by a fine of not more than $10,000 or by imprisonment for not more than 6 months, or both.

Change of Ownership

When an establishment changes ownership, the employer is responsible for maintaining records and filing reports only for that period of the year during which the establishment is owned.

Record Retention

Records of OSHA 300 and 301 must be kept at least 5 years [29 CFR 1904.33(a)]. Be aware that state requirements may differ from federal regulations.

Employees Not in Fixed Establishments

Employers of employees engaged in construction who do not report to any fixed establishment on a regular basis but are subject to common supervision may satisfy the provisions of OSHA by

- maintaining the required records in an established central place;

- having the address and telephone number of the central place available at each worksite; or

- having personnel available at the central place during normal business hours to provide information from the records maintained there by telephone and by mail.

An employer who has ten or fewer employees need not comply with maintaining the injury and illness records.

OSHA PENALTIES

The construction industry was the recipient of half of all federal and state OSHA inspections during the year 2000. All employers are expected to adhere to the regulations and to any recommendations provided by the OSHA inspector. Violating OSHA regulations, whether intentionally or not, can be very costly.

The maximum allowable penalty is $70,000 for each willful or repeated violation and $7,000 for each serious or other-than-serious violation, as well as $7,000 for each day beyond a stated abatement date for failure to correct a violation.

The penalty amounts are maximums, not minimums. However, in order to ensure that the most flagrant violators are in fact fined at an effective level, OSHA has adopted a minimum penalty of $5,000 for a willful violation of OSHA regulations. OSHA has determined base penalties for violations. The base penalties for violations are assessed by looking at the probability that the event will occur and the severity of the situation. (See Figure 10.4.)

FIGURE 10.4
Base OSHA Penalties

Severity	Probability	Penalty
High	Greater	$5,000
Medium	Greater	$3,500
Low	Greater	$2,500
High	Lesser	$2,500
Medium	Lesser	$2,000
Low	Lesser	$1,500

TABLE 10.2
Typical Violation Penalties

Violation	Penalty
Willful—Maximum	$70,000
Willful—Minimum	$5,000
Repeated violation	$70,000
Other than serious violation	$1,000
OSHA notice	$1,000
Annual summary	$1,000
Failure to post citation	$3,000
Failure to maintain forms	$1,000
Failure to report fatality within 48 hours	$5,000
Denying access to records	$1,000
Not informing employees of inspection	$2,000

Adjustment Factors

The penalty may be reduced or adjusted by OSHA. Penalty amounts are proposed penalties issued with the citation. The employer may contest the penalty amount in a number of ways. First, there is a 15-day contest period in which the employer may contest the citation or the penalty. Second, the penalty may be adjudicated by the independent Occupational Safety and Health Review Commission. Finally, OSHA may negotiate with the employer to settle for a reduced penalty amount if this will lead to speedy abatement of the hazard.

The size adjustment factor is as follows:

- For an employer with 1 to 25 workers, the penalty reduction is 60 percent.
- With 6 to 100 workers, the reduction is 40 percent.
- With 101 to 250 workers, the reduction is 20 percent.
- With more than 250 workers, there is no reduction.

There may be up to an additional 25 percent reduction if the employer has a written and implemented safety and health program and is making a good faith effort to provide good workplace safety and health, and an additional 10 percent reduction if the employer has not been cited by OSHA for any serious, willful, or repeat violations in the past three years. Typical violation penalties are shown in Table 10.2.

Emergency Action Plan

An emergency action plan is a plan that details what to do in case of an emergency, such as a fire, and what the responsibilities of employees and the employer are (e.g., who is responsible for calling 911). A written emergency action plan is required for employers with 11 or more employees. Employers with 10 or fewer employees may communicate the plan orally and do not need to maintain a written plan [29 CFR 1910.38(b)(4)(ii)].

Posting Requirements

All employers are required to post, in a conspicuous place where employees can easily view it, the You Have a Right to a Safe and Healthful Workplace poster (OSHA 3165). This poster may be downloaded from the OSHA Web site, *www.osha.gov/Publications/poster.html.* (See Figure 10.5.)

Complaints

Complaints may be filed orally or in writing. An oral complaint is considered informal, while written complaints are considered formal. Any formal complaint requires an inspection. Informal complaints may be handled by letter. Complaints may be filed by an employee or employee's representative. Representatives considered authorized by statute are

■ a lawyer or physician retained by the employee or the employee's family;

■ an official of an employee bargaining unit (union); and

■ any member of the employee's immediate family acting on behalf of the employee.

No employer may discriminate against or discharge an employee for filing a complaint.

SUMMARY

The safety of employees is required by law and is required as a matter of common sense. An injury on the job is expensive due to the loss of time, medical expense, possible legal action, fines, and employee morale. Employers must supply employees with as safe a working environment as possible and ensure that work practices are conducted in a safe manner. This includes requiring employees to wear supplied protective equipment and follow established procedures. OSHA requires reporting of injury and illness and retention of the records for five years.

FIGURE 10.5
OSHA Poster

You Have a Right to a Safe and Healthful Workplace.

IT'S THE LAW!

- You have the right to notify your employer or OSHA about workplace hazards. You may ask OSHA to keep your name confidential.

- You have the right to request an OSHA inspection if you believe that there are unsafe and unhealthful conditions in your workplace. You or your representative may participate in the inspection.

- You can file a complaint with OSHA within 30 days of discrimination by your employer for making safety and health complaints or for exercising your rights under the *OSH Act.*

- You have a right to see OSHA citations issued to your employer. Your employer must post the citations at or near the place of the alleged violation.

- Your employer must correct workplace hazards by the date indicated on the citation and must certify that these hazards have been reduced or eliminated.

- You have the right to copies of your medical records or records of your exposure to toxic and harmful substances or conditions.

- Your employer must post this notice in your workplace.

The *Occupational Safety and Health Act of 1970 (OSH Act),* P.L. 91-596, assures safe and healthful working conditions for working men and women throughout the Nation. The Occupational Safety and Health Administration, in the U.S. Department of Labor, has the primary responsibility for administering the *OSH Act.* The rights listed here may vary depending on the particular circumstances. To file a complaint, report an emergency, or seek OSHA advice, assistance, or products, call 1-800-321-OSHA or your nearest OSHA office: • Atlanta (404) 562-2300 • Boston (617) 565-9860 • Chicago (312) 353-2220 • Dallas (214) 767-4731 • Denver (303) 844-1600 • Kansas City (816) 426-5861 • New York (212) 337-2378 • Philadelphia (215) 861-4900 • San Francisco (415) 975-4310 • Seattle (206) 553-5930. Teletypewriter (TTY) number is 1-877-889-5627. To file a complaint online or obtain more information on OSHA federal and state programs, visit OSHA's website at **www.osha.gov.** If your workplace is in a state operating under an OSHA-approved plan, your employer must post the required state equivalent of this poster.

1-800-321-OSHA
www.osha.gov

U.S. Department of Labor • **Occupational Safety and Health Administration** • **OSHA 3165**

CHAPTER 10
Occupational Safety
and Health

CHAPTER 11

ENVIRONMENTAL ISSUES

Environmental issues such as energy conservation, recycling, and pollution control are increasingly important issues for contractors. Contractors must be aware of how their businesses affect the environment because they operate heavy equipment that can cause great harm. If a backhoe strikes a gas line and burns or a bulldozer destroys a wetland, the environment is seriously impacted, as is the contractor who will be investigated by state officials and likely fined.

When working on environmentally delicate job sites, precautions must be taken to prevent injury or illness to workers and residents. For example, when removing asbestos from a building, a negative pressure environment must be provided so that air will flow into the building and not out of the building. If air is allowed to flow out of the building, asbestos fibers may enter the atmosphere and possibly be inhaled by residents. Disposal of hazardous materials such as lead and asbestos is regulated, but everyday construction items such as paints and thinners must also be disposed of properly. Most municipalities provide special containers at landfills for paint disposal.

Construction must be performed to prevent negatively impacting the environment, or to lessen any negative impact, such as through the creation of new wetlands to replace those removed. To help limit the impact of construction on the environment, some municipalities have instituted arboreal regulations that require a permit before any tree can be removed.

The penalties for violating a regulation are extreme. Not only is there a monetary penalty, but the reputation of the company may be affected as well. This chapter will summarize some of the environmental issues of which a contractor must be aware. The more common environmental issues that contractors and contracting companies need to be aware of include asbestos, lead, erosion, hazardous materials, waste disposal, underground utilities, and wetlands.

ASBESTOS

Asbestos was a commonly used building material in the early 1970s and before. Asbestos material that can be easily crushed is considered to be friable. A *friable* material is a material that can be easily crumbled or pulverized. This state allows the small fibers to be released into the atmosphere. If the surface to which asbestos is applied is stable, the asbestos does not pose a health risk. As long as the surface is not disturbed by sanding, drilling, cutting, or removal, the asbestos fibers will not become friable and cannot be released into the air.

Asbestos can only be identified through microscopic analysis. Not all material in an older building will contain asbestos, but it will be a huge problem for a contractor if the product is intentionally misidentified and removed improperly. Removal and disposal must only be performed by a trained and licensed professional. A contractor working on an older building that may contain asbestos provides an excellent example of an instance where a contract should contain a provision about what steps are to be taken when hazardous materials are encountered during a renovation.

Sources of information on asbestos are available from the U.S. Environmental Protection Agency, including *Guidance for Controlling Asbestos-Containing Materials in Buildings,* Washington, D.C., Office of Toxic Substances—USEPA EPA 580/5-05-084 (also known as the "Purple Book"). Information is also available by writing to the United States Environmental Protection Agency, Air, Pesticides & Toxics Management Division, 61 Forsyth Street SW, Atlanta, GA 30303.

LEAD

Lead is another element that has had many uses in the construction industry. It was commonly added to paint, window blinds, and other products. Lead is an especially vicious hazard for young children who ingest the element by chewing on window sills or eating paint chips. Lead paint is dangerous to children because it can cause damage to the brain and nervous system, behavior and learning problems, slowed growth, hearing problems, and headaches. In adults, lead can cause difficulties during pregnancy, reproductive problems for both men and women, high blood pressure, nerve disorders, memory and concentration problems, and muscle and joint pain. Lead can be dangerous to both workers and their families if the worker brings home equipment or clothing that has picked up lead material on the job.

The Lead Pre-Renovation Education Rule

The lead pre-renovation education rule affects construction contractors, property managers, and others who perform renovations for compensation in residential housing that may contain lead-based paint. It applies to residential houses and apartments built before 1978. The **lead pre-renovation education rule** requires distribution of the EPA pamphlet *Protect Your Family from Lead in Your Home* before starting renovation work. Renovation work includes most repairs, remodeling, and maintenance activities that disturb painted surfaces.

The pamphlet must be distributed to the housing owner and occupants by mail seven days prior to beginning work or may be hand-delivered anytime before the renovation begins. The renovation then must start within 60 days of the delivery. A record of delivery must be kept for three years.

Excluded from this rule is housing built in 1978 or later, housing for the elderly or disabled persons (unless children will reside there), zero-bedroom dwellings (studio apartments, dormitories, etc.), emergency renovations and repairs, minor repairs, and maintenance that disturbs not more than two square feet of paint.

A civil penalty up to $25,000 per day may be assessed for each violation, whether intentional or accidental. Criminal fines up to $25,000 per day and imprisonment up to one year may be imposed for deliberately violating the rule. Both penalties may be assessed at the discretion of the court.

EROSION AND SEDIMENT (E&S) CONTROL

Soil erosion is the removal of material from a site by water, wind, or gravity. Construction site erosion is not the biggest cause of sediment pollution, but it is the most noticeable and damaging because of the rate at which it occurs. Erosion from construction activities are many times greater than agricultural activity and vastly greater than natural processes.

Most states and local jurisdictions have enacted erosion and sediment control regulations that require submitting control plans indicating the steps taken to prevent erosion. The regulations are specific to limiting driving through streams with construction vehicles, the placement of excavated materials, site management of vehicles, and other items. The best place to obtain information about erosion and sediment control requirements is by contacting the local building department of the jurisdiction in which the construction will occur.

HAZARDOUS MATERIALS

All construction sites and storage facilities contain hazardous materials, such as cleaning agents, fuels, greases, paints, and paint thinners. OSHA regulations require that a material safety data sheet (MSDS) be available for every hazardous material on-site or in storage. All personnel must be trained about the meaning of the MSDS and the potential hazards posed by each material they may handle. The supplier of each hazardous material is required to furnish the MSDS and label the containers in accordance with OSHA requirements.

Waste Disposal

The *Resource Conservation and Recovery Act (RCRA) of 1976* is intended to protect people and the environment from potential hazards due to waste disposal and to conserve energy and natural resources. The RCRA is enforced by the Environmental Protection Administration (EPA). Any waste that can burn, is corrosive or reactive, or contains toxic chemicals, is controlled under the RCRA and EPA regulations.

All wastes generated by construction activities should be considered hazardous. This includes waste lumber, plaster, drywall, roofing materials, fuels, greases, paints, thinners, etc. All such materials must be disposed of in accordance with EPA regulations under RCRA. Enforcement is usually the responsibility of the local building authority, although the EPA may become involved if there are serious violations of the act and the regulations.

UNDERGROUND UTILITIES

An **underground utility** is a public service or utility that is buried below ground. Underground utilities include telephone lines, gas lines, electrical lines, and petroleum transmission lines. Many of these utilities were installed years ago and may be difficult to find after the ground cover has been re-established. The landscape can change over time and what had been buried several feet underground with marking tape above it may now be only several inches down and the tape has long since been scraped away. This is especially true for utilities near roads, where ditches and shoulders are regularly reconfigured. If an excavation is to be made, the contractor must know where these utilities are located.

Utility companies will mark the location of underground utilities free of charge. Most localities have set up toll-free numbers to call to have the local locator service come to the site and mark the approximate location of the underground utility. Note that "approximate" is used here because the utility may be several feet to either side of the mark.

After the marking of the utilities is complete, excavation in the marked area is done carefully. Otherwise, the utility line can be damaged. Excavating machinery cannot be used in these areas as the exact location of the utility is still unknown. Once excavation is dug to a few feet from the locator mark, hand-operated tools must finish the digging near the markings.

There are severe consequences, both financial and environmental, for cutting a utility, even if it was done unintentionally. Cutting a fiber optic cable will result in costs for fines and damages; cutting an underground commercial oil supply line will cause major environmental damage.

WETLANDS

Wetlands generally include swamps, marshes, bogs, and similar areas. These areas are protected by federal law and enforced by the EPA. Wetlands serve an environmental function in that they act as a filter, breaking down dead leaves and providing food for insects, shellfish, and fish.

Wetlands in the middle of a construction project cannot be filled, dredged, or disturbed without a permit. Provisions for wetlands, and required permits, are usually specified in the job specifications. The permit will require

- avoiding impacting wetlands, where practical;
- minimizing any potential impact to the wetlands; and
- providing compensation for any remaining, unavoidable impact by restoring or creating new wetlands.

SUMMARY

Environmental issues are so much more important since the time this author started contracting. A wetland was seen just as a swamp and not as part of the ecological system. Asbestos was in daily use for insulation and flooring. Changing our awareness takes time such as the great resistance from some in the plumbing industry when 50/50 solder was banned from water supply systems. Possibly the awareness of our environment and hazardous materials is one of the reasons why we are living longer. Environmental issues are an aspect of contracting that fortunately does not create an insurmountable problem for compliance. The procedure for complying with programs relating to hazardous materials is specific and the information is readily available.

APPENDIX A

BUSINESS DEVELOPMENT

GOVERNMENT WEB SITES

Pub. 334, Guide for Small Business
http://ftp.fedworld.gov/pub/irs-pdf/p334.pdf

Pub. 533, Self-Employment Tax
http://ftp.fedworld.gov/pub/irs-pdf/p533.pdf

Pub. 535, Business Expenses
http://ftp.fedworld.gov/pub/irs-pdf/p535.pdf

Pub. 538, Accounting Periods and Methods
http://ftp.fedworld.gov/pub/irs-pdf/p538.pdf

Pub. 541, Partnerships
http://ftp.fedworld.gov/pub/irs-pdf/p541.pdf

Pub. 542, Corporations
http://ftp.fedworld.gov/pub/irs-pdf/p542.pdf

Information regarding employment laws or discriminatory practices can be found at the following Web sites:

Equal Employment Opportunity

U.S. Department of Labor (DOL)
www.dol.gov/index.htm

U.S. Equal Employment Opportunity (EEOC)
www.eeoc.gov/

Wage and Work Hour Issues

Wage and Work Hour Division
www.dol.gov/esa/whd/

Fair Labor Standards Act (FLSA)
www.dol.gov/esa/whd/flsa/index.htm

Exempt and Nonexempt Employees
www.dol.gov/esa/regs/compliance/whd/fairpay/main.htm

Contracts with the Federal Government

Walsh-Healy Public Contracts Act Information
www.dol.gov/asp/programs/guide/walshh.htm

Service Contract Act
www.dol.gov/esa/regs/compliance/posters/sca.htm

Contract Work Hours and Safety Standards Act
www.dol.gov/asp/programs/guide/cwhssa.htm

Employee Benefits Issues

Employee Retirement Income Security Act (ERISA)
www.dol.gov/ebsa/compliance_assistance.html

Family and Medical Leave Act (FMLA)
www.dol.gov/esa/whd/fmla/

Consolidated Omnibus Reconciliation Act (COBRA)
www.dol.gov/dol/topic/health-plans/cobra.htm

Trade Adjustment Assistance (TAA) Program (Job Service)
www.doleta.gov/tradeact/

Workers Compensation Insurance
www.dol.gov/esa/owcp_org.htm

BUSINESS FORMS AND WORKSHEETS

The forms on the following pages have been provided for your use in writing a business plan.

The forms that contain "Variable Expenses" and "Fixed Expenses" have spaces to fill in categories. They should be customized to your particular business. This will require a decision on category headings when beginning the financial section of the business plan, and follow-through with the same headings throughout all financial sections.

The categories are developed by looking at different accounts in the ledger or by using the categories from the revenue and expense journal. Expenses that are frequent and sizable will have a heading of their own (e.g., advertising, rent, salaries, etc.). Expenses that are very small and infrequent will be included under the heading "miscellaneous" in either the variable or fixed expenses section of each of your financial statements.

Note: Some testing agencies do not allow any handwriting in the manual when taking the exam. It is recommended that the exam be taken and passed before filling in the following forms. Check the Candidate Information Bulletin or with your local testing agency for specific rules regarding allowable test materials.

Writing a Business Plan

What goes in a business plan? The body can be divided into four distinct sections:

1) Description of the business
2) Marketing
3) Finances
4) Management

Addenda should include an executive summary, supporting documents, and financial projections.

Although there is no single formula for developing a business plan, some elements are common to all business plans. They are summarized in the following outline:

Elements of a Business Plan

   I. Cover sheet
  II. Statement of purpose
 III. Table of contents
     A. The business
        1. Description of business
        2. Marketing
        3. Competition
        4. Operating procedures
        5. Personnel
        6. Business insurance
     B. Financial data
        1. Loan applications
        2. Capital equipment and supply list
        3. Balance sheet
        4. Breakeven analysis
        5. Pro-forma income projections (profit and loss statements)
           a. Three-year summary
             i. Detail by month, first year
             ii. Detail by quarters, second and third years
           b. Assumptions upon which projections were based
        6. Pro-forma cash flow
     C. Supporting documents
        1. Tax returns of principals for last three years
        2. Personal financial statement (all banks have these forms)
        3. For franchised businesses, a copy of franchise contract and all supporting documents provided by the franchisor
        4. Copy of proposed lease or purchase agreement for building space
        5. Copies of licenses and other legal documents
        6. Copies of resumes of all principals
        7. Copies of letters of intent from suppliers, etc.

Writing a Business Plan (continued)

Following is a sample abbreviated business plan, containing the first several pages outlining what the company does, what is needed in regard to capital, and what the company will do with the capital.

1.0 Executive Summary

Stairways to Heaven will provide custom stair building for contractors in the eastern United States. The company officers have found that there is a need for a stair builder that can combine craftsmanship and economy. Currently there are few companies able to provide this product and at great expense. Stairways to Heaven has access to extremely accurate woodworking machinery, talented designers, and sources of fine woods.

The objectives for Stairways to Heaven for the next three years are to

- achieve sales revenues of $500,000 in the first year and $1,000,000 by year three.
- achieve a customer mix of 90 percent residential, 10 percent commercial.
- expand operations to include all the states east of the Mississippi by the third year.

The company is committed to providing a quality product delivered on time. This is identified as critical to success. The company officers will only accept an order that is within the experience of the design team and fabricators. This will establish a reputation of reliability and growth through referrals and repeat business.

Stairways to Heaven will institute the following key procedures to reach its goals:

- Create an Internet site with a catalogue of available stairways.
- Create a design program so that potential customers can have a visual representation of the stair in a setting similar to their needs.

Stairways to Heaven is a start-up limited liability company consisting of four principal officers with construction and cabinet-making experience. The officers have leased a building that is suitable for current needs as well as exponential growth. The excess space is going to be leased to contractors and cabinet builders who are willing to participate in this enterprise. The officers have invested significant amounts of their own capital into the company and will also be seeking a loan of $100,000 to cover start-up costs and future growth.

Initially the company will focus on opportunities in the Washington, D.C./Baltimore corridor as this is a source of high-end residential and commercial customers. The expectation is to expand operations into the North/South Carolina seashore development by the beginning of the second year. The company has rigorously examined its financial projections and concluded that they are both conservative in profits and generous in expenditures. This was done deliberately to provide for unforeseeable events. The company's principals believe that cash flow projections are realistic.

1.1 Objectives

The objectives for Stairways to Heaven over the next three years are to

- achieve sales revenues of $500,000 in the first year and $1,000,000 by year three.
- achieve a customer mix of 90 percent residential, 10 percent commercial.
- expand operations to include all the states east of the Mississippi by the third year.

Writing a Business Plan (continued)

1.2 Mission

The mission of Stairways to Heaven is to build quality custom stairs at reasonable cost and provide a profit to company investors. The company will provide this product in a consistent manner. The company recognized the time demands of the construction industry and the quality expectations of customers.

1.3 Keys to Success

The officers of Stairways to Heaven have years of experience in the contracting business. They understand the needs of contractors regarding costs and delivery. The officers have established working relationships with wood and steel suppliers who will ensure that raw materials will be available when needed at a reasonable price. The employees of the company are experienced in design and fabrication.

The main problem that contractors experience with stair construction is that there is very little creativity in the design. A stair should be either a centerpiece or a compliment to setting. The second problem is delivery of the stair when it is needed. This is due to fabricators accepting a contract for which they are unfamiliar with the construction or it is beyond their capability.

Stairways to Heaven will institute the following key procedures:

- Creation of a Web site that clearly shows what the customer will be getting
- Development of software that facilitates Web site creation and presentation of a custom stair

1.4 Use of Proceeds

Stairways to Heaven will need $100,000 start-up capital to contract with a software engineering firm to modify an existing proprietary stairway design program. The requirements are to make it user-friendly, interactive, and attractive. A software company has been identified and has negotiated a prospective contract to complete this work in six months for $25,000.

The development of a Web site that will have a catalogue, design program, and a shopping basket is necessary. This development has been estimated to cost $5,000 and can be completed in one month.

A catalogue of past products can be assembled from digital photos that are kept on disk. A graphic designer with an impressive history of this type of project has been contacted and has agreed to develop the catalogue for $3,000 in two months.

A steel framing fabrication machine will need to be purchased at a cost of $10,000.

The rest of the capital will be used for purchases necessary to the implementation of this business plan as well as to provide resources to accommodate unexpected costs.

Insurance Update Form

Company Name: **Updated as of**

Company	Contact Person	Coverage	Cost Per Year
			$
			$
			$
			$
			$
			$
			$
1. TOTAL ANNUAL INSURANCE COST			$
2. AVERAGE MONTHLY INSURANCE COST			$

Notes:

1.
2.

Anatomy of a Business Plan by Linda Pinson. © 2005 Dearborn Trade Publishing. *www.dearborntrade.com.*

Location Analysis Worksheet

Address: _____

Name, address, phone number of REALTOR®/contact person: _____

Square footage/cost:_____

History of location: _____

Location in relation to your target market:_____

Traffic patterns for customers: _____

Traffic patterns for suppliers:_____

Availability of parking (include diagram): _____

Crime rate for the area:_____

Quality of public services (e.g., police, fire protection):_____

Notes on walking tour of the area: _____

_____

Neighboring shops and local business climate: _____

Zoning regulations: _____

Adequacy of utilities (information from utility company representatives): _____

Availability of raw materials/supplies: _____

Availability of labor force: _____

Labor rate of pay for the area: _____

Housing availability for employees: _____

Tax rates (state, county, income, payroll, special assessments): _____

Evaluation of site in relation to competition: _____

_____

_____

Competition Evaluation Worksheet

1. COMPETITOR: _____

   _____

2. LOCATION: _____

   _____

3. PRODUCTS OR SERVICES OFFERED: _____

   _____

4. METHODS OF DISTRIBUTION: _____

   _____

5. IMAGE: _____

   a. Packaging: _____

   b. Promotional materials: _____

   c. Methods of advertising: _____

   d. Quality of product or service: _____

6. PRICING STRUCTURE: _____

   _____

7. BUSINESS HISTORY AND CURRENT PERFORMANCE: _____

   _____

8. MARKET SHARE (number, types, and location of customers): _____

   _____

9. STRENGTHS (the strengths of the competition can become your strengths): _____

   _____

10. WEAKNESSES (looking at the weaknesses of the competition can help you find ways of being unique and of benefiting the customer):

   _____

   _____

Note: A Competition Evaluation Worksheet should be made for each competitor. Keep these records and update them. It pays to continue to rate your competition throughout the lifetime of your business.

Cash to Be Paid Out Worksheet

Business Name: _____   Time Period: _____ to _____

1. START-UP COSTS
Business license   _____
Accounting fees   _____
Legal fees   _____
Other start-up costs:
   a.   _____
   b.   _____
   c.   _____
   d.   _____
TOTAL START-UP COSTS   _____

2. INVENTORY PURCHASES
Cash out for goods intended for resale   _____

3. VARIABLE EXPENSES (SELLING)
   a.   _____
   b.   _____
   c.   _____
   d.   _____
   e.   _____
   f.   _____
   g. Miscellaneous variable expense   _____
TOTAL SELLING EXPENSES   _____

4. FIXED EXPENSES (ADMINISTRATIVE)
   a.   _____
   b.   _____
   c.   _____
   d.   _____
   e.   _____
   f.   _____
   g. Miscellaneous fixed expense   _____
TOTAL ADMINISTRATIVE EXPENSE   _____

5. ASSETS (LONG-TERM PURCHASES)
Cash to be paid out in current period   _____

6. LIABILITIES
Cash outlay for retiring debts, loans,
and/or accounts payable   _____

7. OWNER EQUITY
Cash to be withdrawn by owner   _____

TOTAL CASH TO BE PAID OUT $ _____

Anatomy of a Business Plan by Linda Pinson. © 2005 Dearborn Trade Publishing. *www.dearborntrade.com.*

Sources of Cash Worksheet

Business Name: _____

Time Period Covered: _____ ___, _____ **to** _____ ___, _____

---

1. CASH ON HAND   _____

2. SALES (REVENUES)

   Product sales income   _____

   Services income   _____

   Deposits on sales or services   _____

   Collections on accounts receivable   _____

3. MISCELLANEOUS INCOME

   Interest income   _____

   Payments to be received on loans   _____

4. SALE OF LONG-TERM ASSETS   _____

5. LIABILITIES   _____
   Loan funds (to be received during current period; from banks,
   through the SBA, or from other lending institutions)

6. EQUITY

   Owner investments (sole proprietor/partners)   _____

   Contributed capital (corporation)   _____

   Sale of stock (corporation)   _____

   Venture capital   _____

TOTAL CASH AVAILABLE   *A. Without sales* = $ _____

                                    B. With sales   = $ _____

Anatomy of a Business Plan by Linda Pinson. © 2005 Dearborn Trade Publishing. *www.dearborntrade.com.*

Pro Forma Cash Flow Worksheet

Business Name: _____

Year: _____

	Jan	Feb	Mar	Apr	May	Jun	6-MONTH TOTALS	Jul	Aug	Sep	Oct	Nov	Dec	12-MONTH TOTALS
BEGINNING CASH BALANCE														
CASH RECEIPTS														
A. Sales/revenues														
B. Receivables														
C. Interest income														
D. Sale of long-term assets														
TOTAL CASH AVAILABLE														
CASH PAYMENTS														
A. Cost of goods to be sold														
1. Purchases														
2. Material														
3. Labor														
Total cost of goods														
B. Variable expenses														
1.														
2.														
3.														
4.														
5.														
6.														
7. Misc. variable expense														
Total variable expenses														
C. Fixed expenses														
1.														
2.														
3.														
4.														
5.														
6.														
7. Misc. fixed expense														
Total fixed expenses														
D. Interest expense														
E. Federal income tax														
F. Other uses														
G. Long-term asset payments														
H. Loan payments														
I. Owner draws														
TOTAL CASH PAID OUT														
CASH BALANCE/DEFICIENCY														
LOANS TO BE RECEIVED														
EQUITY DEPOSITS														
ENDING CASH BALANCE														

Quarterly Budget Analysis

Business Name: _____   **For the Quarter Ending:** _____ __, _____

BUDGET ITEM	THIS QUARTER			YEAR-TO-DATE		
	Budget	Actual	Variation	Budget	Actual	Variation
SALES REVENUES						
Less cost of goods						
GROSS PROFITS						
VARIABLE EXPENSES						
1.						
2.						
3.						
4.						
5.						
6.						
7. Miscellaneous variable expense						
FIXED EXPENSES						
1.						
2.						
3.						
4.						
5.						
6.						
7. Miscellaneous fixed expense						
NET INCOME FROM OPERATIONS						
INTEREST INCOME						
INTEREST EXPENSE						
NET PROFIT (Pretax)						
TAXES						
NET PROFIT (After Tax)						

NON-INCOME STATEMENT ITEMS

1. Long-term asset repayments						
2. Loan repayments						
3. Owner draws						

BUDGET DEVIATIONS   This Quarter   Year-to-Date

	This Quarter	Year-to-Date
1. Income statement items:		
2. Non-income statement items:		
3. Total deviation		

Anatomy of a Business Plan by Linda Pinson. © 2005 Dearborn Trade Publishing. *www.dearborntrade.com.*

Three-Year Income Projection

Business Name: Updated: _____ ___, _____

	YEAR 1 20___	YEAR 2 20___	YEAR 3 20___	TOTAL 3 YEARS
INCOME				
1. Sales revenues				
2. Cost of goods sold (c – d)				
a. Beginning inventory				
b. Purchases				
c. C.O.G. avail. sale (a + b)				
d. Less ending iventory (12/31)				
3. Gross profit on sales (1 – 2)				
EXPENSES				
1. Variable (selling) (a thru h)				
a.				
b.				
c.				
d.				
e.				
f.				
g. Miscellaneous selling expense				
h. Depreciation (prod/serv assets)				
2. Fixed (administrative) (a thru h)				
a.				
b.				
c.				
d.				
e.				
f.				
g. Miscellaneous fixed expense				
h. Depreciation (office equipment)				
TOTAL OPERATING EXPENSES (1 + 2)				
NET INCOME OPERATIONS (GPr – Exp)				
OTHER INCOME (interest income)				
OTHER EXPENSE (interest expense)				
NET PROFIT (LOSS) BEFORE TAXES				
TAXES 1. Federal, self-employment				
2. State				
3. Local				
NET PROFIT (LOSS) AFTER TAXES				

Breakeven Analysis Graph

Business Name: _____   Analysis Date: _____ __, _____

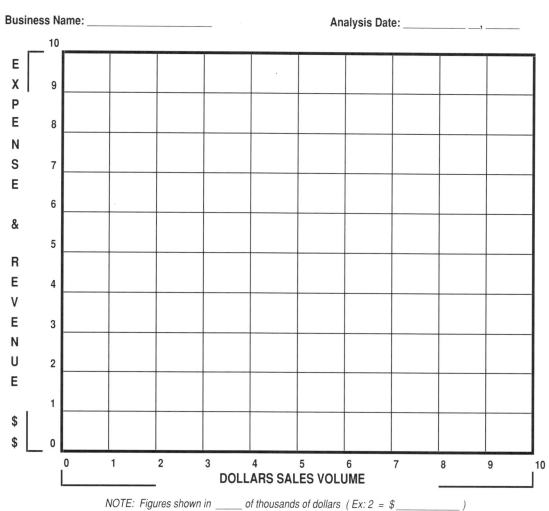

NOTE: *Figures shown in* _____ *of thousands of dollars (Ex: 2 = $_____)*

Breakeven Point Calculation

B-E Point (Sales) = Fixed Costs + [(Variable Costs/Estimated Revenues) × Sales]

1. B-E Point (Sales) = $_____ + [($_____ / $_____) × Sales]

2. B-E Point (Sales) = $_____ + (_____ × Sales)

3. Sales = $_____ + _____Sales

4. Sales   **-** _____Sales = $_____

5. _____Sales = $_____

6. Sales (S) = $_____ / _____

Breakeven Point
S = $

Balance Sheet

Business Name: Date: _____ ___, _____

ASSETS

Current assets

Cash $ _____
Petty cash $ _____
Accounts receivable $ _____
Inventory $ _____
Short-term investments $ _____
Prepaid expenses $ _____

Long-term investments $ _____

Fixed assets

Land (valued at cost) $ _____

Buildings $ _____
1. Cost _____
2. Less acc. depr. _____

Improvements $ _____
1. Cost _____
2. Less acc. depr. _____

Equipment $ _____
1. Cost _____
2. Less acc. depr. _____

Furniture $ _____
1. Cost _____
2. Less acc. depr. _____

Autos/vehicles $ _____
1. Cost _____
2. Less acc. depr. _____

Other assets
1. $ _____
2. $ _____

TOTAL ASSETS $ _____

LIABILITIES

Current liabilities

Accounts payable $ _____
Notes payable $ _____
Interest payable $ _____

Taxes payable
Federal income tax $ _____
Self-employment tax $ _____
State income tax $ _____
Sales tax accrual $ _____
Property tax $ _____

Payroll accrual $ _____

Long-term liabilities
Notes payable $ _____

TOTAL LIABILITIES $ _____

NET WORTH (EQUITY)

Proprietorship $ _____
or
Partnership
(name)_____, ___% equity $ _____
(name)_____, ___% equity $ _____
or
Corporation
Capital stock $ _____
Surplus paid in $ _____
Retained earnings $ _____

TOTAL NET WORTH $ _____

Assets – Liabilities = Net Worth
and
Liabilities + Equity = Total Assets

Anatomy of a Business Plan by Linda Pinson. © 2005 Dearborn Trade Publishing. www.dearborntrade.com.

Monthly Profit & Loss (Income) Statement

Business Name: _____

Beginning: _____ ___, _____   **Ending:** _____ ___, _____

INCOME		
1. Sales revenues		$
2. Cost of goods sold (c – d)		
a. Beginning inventory (1/01)		
b. Purchases		
c. C.O.G. avail. sale (a + b)		
d. Less ending inventory (12/31)		
3. Gross profit on sales (1 – 2)		$
EXPENSES		
1. Variable (selling) (a thru h)		
a.		
b.		
c.		
d.		
e.		
f.		
g. Misc. variable (selling) expense		
h. Depreciation (prod/serv. assets)		
2. Fixed (administrative) (a thru h)		
a.		
b.		
c.		
d.		
e.		
f.		
g. Misc. fixed (administrative) expense		
h. Depreciation (office equipment)		
Total operating expenses (1 + 2)		
Net income from operations (GP – Exp)		$
Other income (interest income)		
Other expense (interest expense)		
Net profit (loss) before taxes		$
Taxes		
a. Federal		
b. State		
c. Local		
NET PROFIT (LOSS) AFTER TAXES		$

Profit & Loss (Income) Statement Yearly Summary

Business Name:

For the Year:

	Jan	Feb	Mar	Apr	May	Jun	6-MONTH TOTALS	Jul	Aug	Sep	Oct	Nov	Dec	12-MONTH TOTALS
INCOME														
1. Net sales (Gr – R&A)														
2. Cost of goods to be sold														
a. Beginning inventory														
b. Purchases														
c. C.O.G. available for sale														
d. Less ending inventory														
3. Gross profit														
EXPENSES														
1. Variable (selling) expenses														
a.														
b.														
c.														
d.														
e.														
f.														
g. Misc. variable expense														
h. Depreciation														
Total variable expenses														
1. Fixed (admin) expenses														
a.														
b.														
c.														
d.														
e.														
f.														
g. Misc. fixed expense														
h. Depreciation														
Total fixed expenses														
Total operating expense														
Net Income from Operations														
Other Income (Interest)														
Other Expense (Interest)														
Net Profit (Loss) before Taxes														
Taxes: a. Federal														
b. State														
c. Local														
NET PROFIT (LOSS) AFTER TAXES														

Financial Statement Analysis

Ratio Table

Business Name:

For the Year: _____

Type of Analysis	Formula	Projected: Year 1	Historical: Year 1
1. Liquidity analysis a. Net working capita	**Balance Sheet** Current Assets − Current Liabilities	Current Assets _____ Current Liabilities _____ **Net Working Capital** $ _____	Current Assets _____ Current Liabilities _____ **Net Working Capital** $ _____
b. Current ratio	**Balance Sheet** Current Assets Current Liabilities	Current Assets _____ Current Liabilities _____ **Current Ratio** _____ .	Current Assets _____ Current Liabilities _____ **Current Ratio** _____ .
c. Quick ratio	**Balance Sheet** Current Assets minus Inventory Current Liabilities	Current Assets _____ Inventory _____ Current Liabilities _____ **Quick Ratio** _____ .	Current Assets _____ Inventory _____ Current Liabilities _____ **Quick Ratio** _____ .
2. Profitability analysis a. Gross profit margin	**Income Statement** Gross Profits Sales	Gross Profits _____ Sales _____ **Gross Profit Margin** _____ %	Gross Profits _____ Sales _____ **Gross Profit Margin** _____ %
b. Operating profit margin	Income from Operations Sales	Income from Ops. _____ Sales _____ **Operating Profit Margin** _____ %	Income from Ops. _____ Sales _____ **Operating Profit Margin** _____ %
c. Net profit margin	Net Profits Sales	Net Profits _____ Sales _____ **Net Profit Margin** _____ %	Net Profits _____ Sales _____ **Net Profit Margin** _____ %
3. Debt ratios a. Debt to assets	**Balance Sheet** Total Liabilities Total Assets	Total Liabilities _____ Total Assets _____ **Debt to Assets Ratio** _____ %	Total Liabilities _____ Total Assets _____ **Debt to Assets Ratio** _____ %
b. Debt to equity	Total Liabilities Total Owners' Equity	Total Liabilities _____ Total Owners' Equity _____ **Debt to Equity Ratio** _____ %	Total Liabilities _____ Total Owners' Equity _____ **Debt to Equity Ratio** _____ %
4. Measures of investment a. ROI *(Return on Investment)*	**Balance Sheet** Net Profits Total Assets	Net Profits _____ Total Assets _____ **ROI (Return on Invest.)** _____ %	Net Profits _____ Total Assets _____ **ROI (Return on Invest.)** _____ %
5. Vertical financial statement analysis	**Balance Sheet** 1. Each asset % of Total Assets 2. Liability & Equity % of Total L&E **Income Statement** 3. All items % of Total Revenues	**NOTE:** *See Attached* **Balance Sheet &** **Income Statement**	**NOTE:** *See Attached* **Balance Sheet &** **Income Statement**
6. Horizontal financial statement analysis	**Balance Sheet** 1. Assets, Liab & Equity measured against 2nd year. Increases and decreases stated as amount & % **Income Statement** 2. Revenues & Expenses measured against 2nd year. Increases and decreases stated as amount & %	**NOTE:** *See Attached* **Balance Sheet** **&** **Income Statement**	**NOTE:** *See Attached* **Balance Sheet** **&** **Income Statement**

Anatomy of a Business Plan by Linda Pinson. © 2005 Dearborn Trade Publishing. *www.dearborntrade.com.*

APPENDIX B

CONTRACTS

Property Improvement Agreement

PROPERTY IMPROVEMENT AGREEMENT

This form complies with professional standards in effect
January 1-December 31, 2005

THIS DOCUMENT CONSISTING OF THIS AGREEMENT, PLANS AND SPECIFICATIONS, IF ANY, AND NOTICE OF CANCELLATION, ALL ATTACHED HERETO AND MADE A PART HEREOF, SHALL CONSTITUTE THE AGREEMENT.

THIS AGREEMENT IS BETWEEN

CONTRACTOR/ SELLER/ BENEFICIARY	NAME				DATE /05
	ADDRESS	CITY	STATE/ZIP	PHONE	LICENSE NO

BUYER/ OWNER	NAME				
	RESIDENCE ADDRESS	CITY	STATE/ZIP		RESIDENCE PHONE
	PLACE OF BUSINESS (IF ANY)	CITY	STATE/ZIP		BUSINESS PHONE

Hereinafter called "Buyer", "Owner" and/or "Trustor" agrees to pay therefore the price hereinafter set forth upon the following terms and conditions.

CONSTRUCTION PROJECT

PROJECT ADDRESS - STREET	CITY	STATE - PROVINCE	ZIP CODE

Also Known as Legal Description; Lot # _____ Tract # _____ Block # _____
Recorded in Book # _____ Page # _____ in the office of the County Recorder of _____ State of _____ .

DESCRIPTION OF PROJECT: CONTRACTOR WILL CONSTRUCT THE IMPROVEMENTS IN THIS AGREEMENT AND DESCRIBED GENERALLY AS FOLLOWS.

☐ Check here if this space insufficient for complete specifications (staple additions to original and each copy).

☐ Check here if there are plans (staple plans to original and each copy).

If checked, additional specifications or plans are attached to and incorporated in this Agreement.

Property Improvement Agreement (continued)

NOT INCLUDED: THE FOLLOWING ITEMS ARE SPECIFICALLY EXCLUDED FROM THIS CONTRACT AND ARE TO BE PROVIDED BY THE OWNER:.

ALLOWANCES: The following items, where specific prices are indicated, are included in the Contract Price as allowances for the purchase price of those items to be selected by Owner. Owner and Contractor agree to adjust the Contract Price after verification of actual cost difference (if any) of said items selected by Owner.

APPLIANCES	$	LIGHT FIXTURES	$	BATH ACCESSORIES	$
FLOOR COVERING	$	HARDWARE FINISH	$	AND "OTHER"	$

Finish hardware is interpreted to include all knobs, pulls, hinges, catches, locks, drawer slide accessories or other items that are normally installed subsequent to final painting. Light fixtures are interpreted to include only those fixtures that are surface mounted. Bath accessories are interpreted to include medicine cabinets, towel bars, paper holders, soap dishes, etc.

TIME FOR STARTING AND COMPLETING PROJECT: Work shall commence within ten days after the last to occur of the following: (1) Receipt by the Contractor of all necessary building permits; (2) Owner has complied with all Terms and Conditions of the Agreement to date; (3) Receipt of all construction funds by Escrow or Funding Control (if any). Subject to adjustment for the above conditions, work shall begin approximately on _____ and be substantially completed approximately on _____ with additional time to be allowed as detailed in paragraph entitled "Delays" of the Terms and Conditions. Commencement of work shall be defined as

(BRIEFLY DESCRIBE TYPE OF WORK REPRESENTING COMMENCEMENT)

CONTRACT PRICE

PAYMENT: Owner agrees to pay Contractor a total cash price of $. OWNER represents that this agreement is a cash transaction wherein no financing is contemplated and contractor acts in reliance on said representation. The payment schedule will be (1) Down payment of $, (2) Payment schedule as follows:

All payments will be made within five (5) days after billing. Overdue payments will bear interest at the maximum legal permissible rate. If any payment is not made when due, Contractor may keep the job idle until such time as all payments due have been made. A failure of payment for a period in excess of said five (5) days shall be considered a major breach.

Contractor or Owner prior to commencement of construction and subject to lending institution (if any) approval, may request funds to be placed in an Escrow or Funding Voucher Control Service prior to commencement of work with funds to be disbursed to Contractor in accordance with the escrow instructions or voucher orders signed by the Contractor. In the absence of an Escrow or Funding Control Service, funds will be paid directly to the Contractor in accordance with the progress payments schedule referred to above.

NOTICE TO THE BUYER: (1) Do not sign this Agreement before you read it or if it contains any blank spaces. (2) You are entitled to a completely filled in copy of this Agreement. Owner acknowledges that he/she has read and received a legible copy of this Agreement signed by Contractor, including all terms and conditions herein included, before any work was done, and that he/she has read and received a legible copy of every document that owner has signed during the negotiation. If owner cancels this Agreement after the right of recession has expired, and before commencement of construction, owner shall pay Contractor the amount of expenses incurred to that date plus loss of profits.

TERMS AND CONDITIONS

The terms and conditions on the following are expressly incorporated into this Agreement. This Agreement constitutes the entire understanding of the parties. No other understanding or representations, verbal or otherwise, shall be binding unless in writing and signed by both parties. This Agreement shall not become effective or binding upon Contractor until signed by Contractor or a principal of Contractor. By Owner's signature below, Owner acknowledges receipt of a fully completed copy of the Agreement.

NOTICE

You, the buyer, may cancel this transaction at any time prior to midnight of the third business day after the date of this transaction. See the attached notice of cancellation form for an explanation of this right.

SALESMAN (If Any)	OWNER - BUYER SIGNATURE	DATE
	X	/05
ACCEPTED BY CONTRACTOR - SELLER SIGNATURE	OWNER - BUYER SIGNATURE	DATE
X	X	/05

Property Improvement Agreement (continued)

TERMS AND CONDITIONS

ASBESTOS / HAZARDOUS MATERIALS

1.   Owner represents that the property being remodeled does not contain asbestos and / or other hazardous materials. This contract does not contemplate the removal of, testing for appropriate corrective work and any other additional expenses incurred by the corrective work.

CONTRACTOR'S RIGHTS AND RESPONSIBILITIES

1.   SUBCONTRACTORS. Contractor may subcontract all or any portion of the work.

2.   Contractor shall have right to stop work and keep the job idle if payments are not made when due. Failure to make payment within five (5) days of the date that payment is due will be considered a material breach of this Agreement. If the work shall be stopped for any reason, for a period of sixty (60) days, then Contractor may, at Contractor's option, upon five (5) days written notice, demand and receive payment for all work executed and material ordered or supplied and any other loss sustained including Contractor's usual fee for overhead and profit based upon the contract price. Thereafter, Contractor is relieved from any further liability. In the event of work stoppage for any reason, Owner shall provide for protection of and be responsible for, any damage, warpage, racking, or loss of material on the premises.

3.   Contractor, at Contractor's option, may alter specifications only so as to comply with requirements of governmental agencies having jurisdiction over same. Any alterations or work undertaken to further this end shall be treated as an Extra Work.

CONTRACTOR'S RESPONSIBILITIES AND LIMITED WARRANTY

1.   Contractor agrees to furnish the materials for the project and complete the work in a professional manner. All materials furnished under this Agreement shall be construction grade and meet industry standards. Where brand names have been specified, Contractor may select substitutes when such substitutions are due to unavailability or other circumstances beyond Contractor's control. All substitutions shall be consistent in quality and character to the selections previously specified. THE LIABILITY OF THE CONTRACTOR FOR DEFECTIVE MATERIALS OR INSTALLATION IS HEREBY LIMITED TO THE REPLACEMENT OR CORRECTION OF SAID DEFECTIVE MATERIAL AND / OR INSTALLATION, AND NO OTHER CLAIMS, OR DEMANDS WHATSOEVER SHALL BE MADE UPON OR ALLOWED AGAINST THE CONTRACTOR. THIS LIMITED WARRANTY EXTENDS ONLY TO OWNER AND IS NOT TRANSFERABLE. THERE IS NO IMPLIED WARRANTY OR MERCHANTABILITY NOR ANY IMPLIED WARRANTY OF FITNESS FOR ANY PARTICULAR PURPOSE. THERE ARE NO WARRANTIES EITHER EXPRESSED OR IMPLIED WHICH EXTEND BEYOND THE DESCRIPTION WITHIN THIS PARAGRAPH #1. THIS WARRANTY SHALL TERMINATE ONE YEAR FROM FINAL BUILDING INSPECTION OR THE DATE OF THE COMPLETION, WHICHEVER IS FIRST.

NOTE THAT EQUIPMENT, ASSEMBLIES, OR UNITS PURCHASED BY CONTRACTOR, INCLUDED IN THIS CONTRACT ARE SOLD AND INSTALLED SUBJECT TO THE MANUFACTURER'S OR PROCESSOR'S GUARANTEE OR WARRANTIES, AND NOT CONTRACTOR'S. TO THE EXTENT PERMITTED BY APPLICABLE LAW, ALL WARRANTIES GIVEN BY MANUFACTURERS PERTAINING TO MATERALS USED BY CONTRACTOR IN CONNECTION WITH THE PROJECT WILL BE PASSED THROUGH AND INURE TO THE BENEFIT OF OWNER.

2.   Contractor shall pay all subcontractors, laborers and material suppliers. Contractor shall, to the best of Contractor's ability, keep Owner's property free of valid labor or material suppliers liens.

ITEMS NOT RESPONSIBILITY OF CONTRACTOR

1.   EXISTING VIOLATIONS AND CONDITIONS. Contractor shall not be held responsible for any existing violations of applicable building regulations or ordinances, whether cited by the appropriate authority or not.   Contractor is not responsible for any abnormal or unusual preexisting conditions or any unusual or abnormal concrete footings, foundations, retaining walls, or piers required, or any unusual depth required for same, such as, but not limited to that condition caused by poor soil, lack of compaction, hillside, or other slope

conditions. Correction of such violations or abnormal conditions by Contractor shall be considered additional work and shall be dealt with as herein provided for under "Extra Work".

2.   DELAYS. Contractor agrees to start and diligently pursue work through to completion, but shall not be responsible for delays for any of the following reasons: failure of the issuance of all necessary building permits within a reasonable length of time, funding of loans, disbursement of funds into funding control or escrow, acts of neglect or omission of Owner or Owner's employees or Owner's agent, acts of God, stormy or inclement weather, strikes, lockouts, boycotts, or other labor union activities, extra work ordered by Owner, acts of public enemy, riots or civil commotion, inability to secure material through regular recognized channels, imposition of government priority or allocation of materials, failure of Owner to make payments when due, or delays caused by inspection or changes ordered by the inspectors of authorized governmental bodies, or for acts of independent contractors, or holidays, or other causes beyond Contractor's reasonable control.

3.   Contractor is not responsible for matching existing paint or texture and further, there is no guarantee against hairline cracks or discolorization in stucco or concrete.

OWNER'S RESPONSIBILITIES
UTILITIES

1.   The Owner is responsible for water, gas, sewer and electric utilities, from the appropriate agency to the metering device, unless otherwise agreed to in writing.   It is the Owner's responsibility, at Owner's expense, to provide toilet facilities, electricity and water to the site as needed by the Contractor.

ACCESS TO PROPERTY

2.   Owner agrees to keep driveway clear and available for movement and parking of trucks and other equipment during normal working hours. If Owner denies access to any worker or material supplier during the scheduled working hours, the Owner will be held in breach of the Agreement and will be liable for such breach.

FINANCING

3.   The Owner is responsible for having sufficient funds to comply with this Agreement. This is a cash transaction.

INSURANCE

4.   Owner will purchase insurance, at Owner's expense, before any work begins.   Such insurance will have course of construction, fire, vandalism, malicious mischief and other perils, clauses attached. The insurance must be in an amount at least equal to the contract price and provide that any loss be payable to the Contractor.   The insurance is to cover the Owner, Contractor, Subcontractor and Construction Lender in the amount of their respective interests.

   If the Owner does not purchase such insurance, the Contractor, as agent for the Owner may purchase it and charge such cost to the Owner.

DAMAGE OR DESTRUCTION

5.   If the project, or any portion of it, is destroyed or damaged by fire, storm, flood, landslide, earthquake, theft, or other disaster or accidents, any work done by the Contractor to rebuild, etc., shall be paid for by Owner as an Extra and dealt with as herein provided for under "Extra Work".

   In the event of any of the above occurrences, If the cost of replacement work, for work already done by the Contractor, exceeds twenty (20) percent of the contract price, the Owner has the option to cancel the contract but, if the Owner cancels, the Contractor shall be paid for all costs incurred plus Contractor's usual fee for overhead and profit for all work performed by Contractor to date of cancellation.

OWNER'S PROPERTY

6.   It is the Owner's responsibility to remove or protect any personal property including, but not limited to, carpets, drapes, furniture, driveways, lawns, and shrubs, and Contractor will not be held responsible for damages of loss of said items.

NOTICE OF COMPLETION

7.   Owner agrees to sign & record a Notice of Completion within five (5) days after the project is substantially completed and ready for occupancy. Failure by the Owner to do so authorizes the Contractor to act as the Owner's agent to sign and record a Notice of Completion. This agency is irrevocable and is an agency coupled with an interest. The Contractor has the right to bar occupancy of the project of Owner or anyone else until Contractor has

3

Property Improvement Agreement (continued)

received all payments due under the Contract and the Notice of Completion is recorded. When the Owner or another authorized by the Owner uses and / or occupies the premises then the project is considered completed. If a funding or joint control is used it is agreed that the control shall act as the Owner's agent and sign and record a Notice of Completion.

BOUNDRY LINES

8. The Owner represents ownership of the property where construction is to occur. It is the Owner's duty to point out boundary lines of the property and Owner is responsible for the accuracy of such lines and how they are represented on drawings. If required, the Owner will pay for a survey to chart boundary lines.

EASEMENTS, ETC.

9. Prior to construction, the Owner is to give the Contractor a copy of any easements, restrictions or rights of way relating to the property. If Owner does not do so, Contractor will assume that none exist.

ENGINEERING AND GEOLOGY

10. Unless specifically agreed upon in writing between Owner and Contractor, and made a part of this Agreement under "Description of Materials", "Specifications" or "Plans", this Agreement does not include any engineering or geology surveys, drawings, studies, reports or calculations as may be required by a public body or building authority as a condition for issuance of a building permit or as a condition to securing final building inspection. The cost of any such required professional services shall be paid by Owner.

OTHER

DRAWINGS AND SPECIFICATIONS

1. The project will be constructed according to drawings and specifications that have been examined by Owner and that have been or may be signed by the parties to this contract. Unless otherwise specifically provided, Contractor will obtain and pay for all required building permits. Owner will pay any assessments and charges required by public bodies and utilities for financing or repaying the cost of sewers, storm drains, water service, other utilities including sewer and storm drain reimbursement charges, use fees, revolving fund charges, hookup charges and the like.

ITEMS EXCLUDED

2. Unless specifically agreed upon in writing between Owner and Contractor and made part of this Agreement, under "Description of Work", "Description of Material", "Specifications", or "Plans", this contract does not include:

a. Plumbing, gas, waste and water lines outside foundations of existing buildings or any required relocation or replacement of any such existing lines that may be discovered within the boundaries of any new ground floor addition;

b. Electrical service, other than addition of circuit breakers or fuse blocks to distribute electric current to new outlets;

c. Any work which may be required regarding cesspools or septic tanks.

d. Rerouting, relocating or replacing vents, pipes, ducts or conduits not shown or those encountered during construction or changes required to existing wiring, vents, pipes, ducts or conduits in areas undisturbed by construction. Unless specified elsewhere, existing wiring and electrical systems are represented by the Owner as adequate to carry load for existing structure and work to be performed herein.

e. Any additional work required for excavation or foundations due to inadequate bearing capacity or rock or any other material not removable by ordinary hand tools;

f. Any work to correct damage caused by termites or dry rot;

g. Changes or alterations from the specifications which may be required by any public body, utility or inspector.

h. Painting, preparation, filing, finishing, grading, retaining walls, new or relocating gutters and downspouts, screen doors, weather stripping, staining, seeding, landscaping, or decorating. Any work necessary to correct, change, alter or add the above items will be considered additional work and shall be dealt with as herein provided for under "Extra Work".

MEASUREMENTS

3. Measurements, sizes and shapes in plans and specifications are approximate and subject to field verification. Unless otherwise specified, all dimensions are exterior dimensions. In the event of a conflict between the plans, specifications, etc., and the Agreement, this Agreement is controlling. Contractor is not responsible for any existing illegal conditions.

MATERIAL REMOVED AND DEBRIS

4. Unless specifically designated by Owner in writing, prior to commencement of construction, Contractor may dispose of all material removed from structures in course of alteration. Contractor is to remove construction debris at end of project and leave premises in a neat broom-clean condition.

FLOOR COVERING

5. Unless specifically agreed upon in writing, floor covering is not covered under this Agreement.

ADDITIONAL REQUIREMENTS FOR COMPLETION

6. Contractor shall promptly notify Owner of any additional requirements necessary to facilitate the project's completion. Any subsequent amendment, modification or agreement, which operates to alter this contract, and which is signed or initialed by Contractor and Owner, shall be deemed a part of this contract and shall be controlling in case of conflict, to the extent that it alters this contract.

EXTRA WORK

7. The Owner and Contractor must agree in writing to any modification or addition to the work covered by this contract. The Contractor shall do no extra work without the written authorization of the Owner. Any written agreement shall list the agreed price and any changes in terms and be signed by both parties. Failure to have written authorization shall not be deemed fatal to the collection of the extra work.

For any extra work performed, Contractor shall be compensated in an amount to be determined before the extra work is performed and such amount including Contractor's usual fee for overhead and profit shall be made as the extra work progresses, concurrently with payments, made under payments scheduled.

Any change-order forms for changes or extra work shall be incorporated in, and become part of the contract.

STANDARDS FOR SPECIFICATIONS

8. If all or any part of the following is included in this Agreement under specifications, the following will apply: All cabinets to be paint grade, or if same is noted to be other than paint grade, to be of veneer construction. All cabinet doors to be lipped construction. All inside portions such as shelves, bulkheads and partitions may be of other species than exposed portions, but not limited to solid stock plywood, or particle board with fixed shelve without backs. All plumbing fixtures to be white in color and selected by Contractor. All appliances and fixtures to be Builders models. Medicine cabinets to be single, recessed, and metal. Tile, if ceramic, to be domestic, non-decorator, 4¼" x 4¼" . All fireplaces to be prefab with a metal flue. All extra materials remain the property of the Contractor. If any of the materials used vary from the above, such variation must be agreed upon between Contractor and Owner, in writing and listed in this Agreement under "Specifications", "Description of Materials" or attached to this Agreement and initialed by Owner and Contractor.

CORRECTIVE WORK

9. If minor corrective or repair work remains to be finished after the project is ready for occupancy, Contractor shall perform work expeditiously and Owner shall not withhold any payment pending completion of such work. If major corrective or repair work remains to be finished after the building is ready for occupancy, and the cost exceeds one (1) percent of the gross contract price, the Owner may withhold payment sufficient to pay for completion of the work, pending completion of the work, but may not withhold an amount which is greater.

GENERAL

10. This contract, including incorporated documents, constitutes the entire agreement of the parties. No other oral or written agreements between Contractor and Owner, regarding construction to be performed exist.

11. This agreement shall be construed in accordance with, and governed by, the laws of the state in which the work is performed.

NOTICE

12. Any notice required or permitted under this contract may be given by ordinary mail sent to the address of either the Owner or Contractor as listed in this contract, but the address may be changed by written notice from one party to the other. Notice is considered received five (5) days after deposited in the mail, postage paid.

ATTORNEY FEES

13. In the event legal action or arbitration is instituted for the enforcement of any term or condition of this Agreement, the prevailing party shall be entitled to an award of reasonable attorney fees in said action or arbitration, in addition to costs and reasonable expenses incurred in the prosecution or defense of said action or arbitration.

By initialing and dating below, you are indicating receipt of both pages of these Terms and Conditions:

| _____ | _____ | _____ | _____ |
| Initial | Date | Initial | Date |

4

Subcontractor Agreement

SUBCONTRACT AGREEMENT
(Between Subcontractor and General /Prime Contractor)
This form complies with professional standards in effect January 1-December 31, 2005

This Subcontract Agreement is entered into this _____ day of, _____, 2005 at _____.

Subcontractor, _____, hereinafter called "Subcontractor" agrees to provide the following described labor, materials and construction in accordance with plans and specifications as may be referred to herein by reference, upon the following described property:

Owner: _____   Lender: _____
(Owner)   (If There is No Lender, Put None)

_____   _____
(Business Address)   (Address)

_____   _____
(Residence Address)   (City, State, Zip)

LEGAL AND COMMON DESCRIPTION OF JOBSITE:

Prime Contractor, _____, hereinafter called the "Contractor," agrees to pay to the Subcontractor for the satisfactory performance of the Subcontractor's work the sum of _____ dollars ($ _____) in accordance with the following terms and conditions:

DESCRIPTION OF WORK (Labor, Materials, Equipment):

SCOPE OF WORK: All work necessary or incidental to complete work for the project in strict accordance with this subcontract and all terms and conditions hereof and as more particularly specified as (in):

with the following additions or deletions:

OTHER SPECIAL PROVISIONS:

SCHEDULE OF PAYMENT(S):

and for extra work, if any, as follows:

This schedule of payment(s) is strictly construed and is not conditioned upon Contractor(s) first being paid by owner. Contractor's obligation to pay Subcontractor when payments are due is independent of Contractor receiving payment from owner.

TIME AND SCHEDULING WORK: Subcontractor shall not deliver any materials to the jobsite or commence work until notified to do so by Contractor. Subcontractor shall commence work within _____ days after written notice from Contractor. After Subcontractor commences work, he will then complete the work within approximately _____ working days thereafter, subject to excusable delays. Working days are defined as Monday through Friday, inclusive, holidays excluded. Scheduling of work, as provided for in this subcontract, is based on acceptable industry standards.

The subcontract provision for price and time included herein shall be void at the option of the subcontractor, if subcontractor is not called upon to commence work within six (6) months from the date of the signing of this contract. Should this situation arise, subcontractor is relieved of any responsibility to perform under this subcontract agreement and shall be held harmless by contractor of any liability associated with his refusal to perform. Any amounts that are not paid when due shall bear interest at a rate of 1½% per month until paid or the maximum rate permitted by law, whichever is higher. The Contractor's supervisor of this project shall be the designated agent for the Contractor.

SOLE AGREEMENT: This Agreement, including all terms and conditions hereof, is expressly agreed to and constitutes the entire Agreement as of this date. No other Agreement or understandings, verbal or written, expressed or implied, are a part of this Agreement unless specified herein.

IN WITNESS HEREOF the parties have accepted this Agreement the day and year first above written.

Subcontractor: _____   Contractor _____
(Subcontractor)   (Contractor)

_____   _____
(Address)   (Address)

_____   _____
(City, State, Zip)   (City, State, Zip)

By: _____   By: _____
(Signature/Title)   (Signature/Title)
License Number: _____   License Number: _____

Subcontractor Agreement (continued)

TERMS AND CONDITIONS

1. Permits and Licenses

Subcontractor shall obtain and pay for all permits and licenses governing the Subcontractor's specific work in sufficient time to allow uninterrupted progress of this work and that of others.

2. Extra Work

Subcontractor shall provide in a good and workmanlike manner only that labor and materials specified herein. Additional work not specified in this agreement will be provided only upon written authorization of Contractor. Payment for such additional work shall be provided in accordance with the Terms of Payment specified herein. In the event that there are unit prices for the original scope of work or the extra work, then the extra work shall be at an identical unit price to the original scope of work.

In the event of an emergency condition, the General Contractor's job supervisor may authorize the extra work. In any event, a signed change order covering the emergency work shall be executed by the parties within 48 hours after the extra work is completed.

3. Labor and Material Releases

Subcontractor shall provide satisfactory proof of payment in the form of labor and material releases covering work for each payment applied for and received from Contractor. Such releases provided by Subcontractor are only valid and conditioned upon receipt by Subcontractor of lawful U.S. currency for full amount of said payment.

4. Extra Time

Time is of the essence of this agreement. Subcontractor agrees to start work within 72 hours of proper notification by the Contractor and to diligently pursue work through to completion. Subcontractor shall not be responsible for delays incurred as a result of acts of neglect or omission of Owner, Owner's employees or agent, Contractor, Contractor's employees or agents, other subcontractors, acts of God, stormy or inclement whether, strikes, lockouts, boycotts, or other union activities, extra work ordered by Contractor, acts of public enemy, riots or civil commotion, inability to secure material through regular recognized channels, imposition of government priority or allocation of materials, failure of Contractor to provide payments when due, or delays caused by inspections, or changes ordered by the inspectors of governmental bodies concerned, or other causes beyond control of Subcontractor.

5. Indemnity

All of the work performed at the site of construction or in preparing or delivering materials or equipment to the site shall be at the risk of Subcontractor exclusively. Subcontractor shall indemnify and hold Contractor harmless from any claim, liability, loss, damage, cost, expense, including reasonable attorney's fees, award, fine or judgment with respect to or arising out of the work, including without limitation, any such claims, liability, loss, damage, cost, expense, award, fine or judgment arising by reason of death or bodily injury to persons, injury to property, defects in workmanship or materials, or design defects (if the design originated with Subcontractor), or arising by reason of Contractor's alleged or actual negligent act or omission, regardless of whether such act or omission is active or passive. Subcontractor shall not be obligated to indemnify Contractor with respect to the sole negligence or willful misconduct of Contractor, its agents or servants or other subcontractors who are directly responsible to Contractor.

6. Insurance

Subcontractor shall carry, at Subcontractor's expense, Workers Compensation insurance covering all Subcontractor's employees and public liability and property damage insurance covering Subcontractor's liability in the minimum amount of $300,000 unless specified otherwise.

Subcontractor shall also carry automobile public liability and property damage insurance in an amount agreeable to Contractor.

Prior to commencement of work, Subcontractor agrees to provide to Contractor certificates of such coverage upon request of Contractor. Subcontractor agrees to maintain said insurance in full force and effect during the construction herein. In the event that Subcontractor does not provide said insurance, or said insurance shall for any reason lapse, then General Contractor may purchase said insurance and charge Subcontractor therefor.

7. Bonding of Subcontractor.

Concurrently with the execution of this agreement or any time during its performance, Subcontractor shall, if required by Contractor, execute a Labor Material Bond and Faithful Performance Bond in an amount equal to one-hundred percent (100%) of the contract price. Said bonds shall be executed by a corporate surety acceptable to Contractor and shall be in a form satisfactory to Contractor.

8. Work Stoppage

Subcontractor shall have the right to stop work if payments are not made when due. If the work shall be stopped under an order of any court or other authority, or by Owner, or Contractor for a period of sixty (60) days, without the fault of the Subcontractor, then Subcontractor may, at Subcontractor's option, upon five (5) days written notice, demand and receive payment for all work executed and materials supplied including an amount for overhead and profit, proportionate to the work completed.

9. Guarantee

Unless otherwise specified, Subcontractor guarantees that all materials fabricated or furnished by Subcontractor will be a standard quality, free from defects, and will be installed or applied in a good and workmanlike manner. Such labor and materials guaranteed for a period of one-year when subject to normal use and care, and provided Contractor has complied in full with payments and all terms and conditions of this contract. Specified assemblies or units purchased by Subcontractor which are included in this agreement are provided subject to the manufacturer's or distributor's guarantee or warranty and not that of Subcontractor. THIS IS IN LIEU OF ALL GUARANTEES EXPRESSED OR IMPLIED.

10. Clean-up

Subcontractor agrees to keep the premises in a neat and safe condition and at the end of Subcontractor's performance (or each day), Subcontractor shall leave the premises in neat broom-clean condition.

11. Arbitration

If at any time any controversy shall arise between Subcontractor and Contractor with respect to any matter in question arising out of, or related to, this agreement or the breach thereof, which the parties do not properly adjust and determine, said controversy shall be decided by arbitration administered by and in accordance with the Construction Industry Arbitration Rules of the American Arbitration Association then obtaining unless the parties mutually agree otherwise. This agreement so to arbitrate shall be specifically enforceable under the prevailing arbitration law. The award rendered by the arbitrators shall be final, and judgment may be entered upon it in any court having jurisdiction thereof. Administrative fees as described by the American Arbitration Association shall be advanced one half by each party. However, in the event that the dispute between the parties is less than $5000, then either party may choose to litigate the matter in the Small Claims Courts and the agreement to arbitrate shall not be binding.

The prevailing party in any dispute shall be entitled to its reasonable costs including attorney's fees.

Subcontractor Agreement (continued)

TERMS AND CONDITIONS:

1. Asbestos and Hazardous Materials. Asbestos or other hazardous materials disturbance, removal or abatement is not provided for by the terms of this subcontract and in the event that asbestos or other hazardous material is encountered or disturbed in order to complete this project, it will be treated as extra work under Paragraph 11 of this Agreement. Subcontractor may stop work upon discovering asbestos or other hazardous material, until the terms of the "extra" are negotiated. Subcontractor, at Subcontractor's sole option, can require Owner or Contractor to be responsible for the removal or abatement of asbestos or any other hazardous materials found on the job site.

2. Arbitration, Validity and Damages. Any controversy or claim arising out of or related to this contract, or the breach thereof, shall be settled by arbitration in accordance with the Construction Industry Arbitration Rules of the American Arbitration Association, and judgment upon the award rendered by the Arbitrator(s) may be entered in any court having jurisdiction thereof. Claims within the monetary limit of the Small Claims Court shall be litigated in such court at the request of either party. Any claim filed in Small Claims Court shall not be deemed to be a waiver of the right to arbitrate, and if a counter claim in excess of the jurisdiction of the Small Claims Court may be filed in Municipal or Superior Court, then the party filing in the Small Claims Court may demand arbitration pursuant to this paragraph.

In case one or more of the provisions of this Agreement or any application thereof shall be invalid, unenforceable or illegal, the validity, enforceability and legality of the remaining provisions and other application shall not in any way be impaired thereby.

ANY DAMAGES FOR WHICH SUBCONTRACTOR MAY BE LIABLE TO OWNER OR CONTRACTOR SHALL NOT, IN ANY EVENT EXCEED THE CASH PRICE OF THIS AGREEMENT.

3. Reservation of Rights of Dispute. In the event that the Subcontractor is required to, or deems it appropriate, to proceed with and complete any work which is the subject of a dispute between the Contractor and the Subcontractor as to whether such work should be classified as a "change" or as an "extra," Subcontractor may, if it deems it appropriate, but is not required to, proceed with such work, and thereafter or contemporaneously, file for arbitration in accordance with the Construction Industry Rules of the American Arbitration Association, to determine whether such work is in fact a "change" or an "extra" without waiving any said rights, as well as determining the effect of the extra.

4. Attorney Fees. In the event legal action or arbitration is instituted for the enforcement of any term or condition of this subcontract, the prevailing party shall be entitled to an award of reasonable attorney fees in said action or arbitration, in addition to costs and reasonable expenses incurred in the prosecution or defense of said action or arbitration.

5. Removal of Debris. Upon completion of the work, the Subcontractor agrees to remove all of its own debris and surplus materials from Owner's property and leave said property in a neat and broom-clean condition. Subcontractor will not accept any charges for any pro-rated proportion of general clean-up of the premises, nor will be responsible for the disposal of central scrap piles.

6. Failure to Make Payments. If Contractor fails to make the scheduled progress payments as defined in "Schedule of Payments," then Subcontractor has the absolute option to cease the performance of any further work until such time said payment is made. If said payment is more than ten (10) working days late, Subcontractor may treat said lateness as a material breach of this Subcontract Agreement and justifiably refuse to complete the balance of this subcontract. Subcontractor may then institute arbitration proceeding as described herein for any and all damage incurred including but not limited to lost profits.

7. Retention. Contractor is authorized to withhold retention from Subcontractor only to the extent that Owner withholds funds from Contractor for the work performed by Subcontractor. In no event shall Contractor withhold more than ten (10) percent of payments due Subcontractor. All retentions must be paid to Subcontractor within thirty-five (35) days of the date the Subcontractor substantially completes all work.

8. Items Not Responsibility of Subcontractor. Unless specifically included in the Agreement, Subcontractor shall not be held responsible for any existing violations of applicable building regulations or ordinances, whether cited by the appropriate authority or not. Subcontractor is not responsible for any abnormal or unusual pre-existing conditions. Correction of any such violations or abnormal conditions by Subcontractor shall be considered additional work and shall be dealt with as herein provided under Paragraph 11 for extra work.

9. Excusable Delays. If the Subcontractor is delayed in the performance of the work by conditions that could not be reasonably foreseen by Subcontractor or out of the reasonable control of Subcontractor, which include, but are not limited to actions taken by Owner; acts of God; fire; explosions or other casualty losses; strikes, boycotts or other labor disputes; lockouts; hazardous material disturbance, abatement, or removal; and acts of government body, then Contractor shall grant Subcontractor a reasonable extension of time. If additional work or cost is required of, or incurred by, Subcontractor as a result of the delay, then Subcontractor shall be entitled to compensation as called for in Paragraph 11.

10. Contractor's Responsibilities and OSHA Requirements. Water, sewer, gas, and electric utilities from the serving agency to the point of entry at Owner's property line, or the metering devices are required and are the responsibility of the Contractor.

In compliance with Federal and State law, Contractor agrees to make drinking water and toilet facilities available to all workers, or compensate Subcontractor for cost of rental units.

Contractor agrees to provide electricity at the job site to effect the work herein.

Contractor shall provide adequate job site storage and work area as required for the convenience and use of Subcontractor for work under this Agreement. -

Contractor agrees to comply with all local, state, and national laws, including without limitation the provisions of the Accident and Safety Health Act of 1970 and the Construction Safety Act of 1969, and Subcontractor is not responsible for any liability caused by the Contractor's noncompliance.

11. Extra Work. Subcontractor shall provide in a good and workmanlike manner only that labor and materials specified therein. Additional work not specified in this subcontract will be provided only upon written authorization of Contractor. However, in the event that the parties cannot agree on the sum necessary to compensate Subcontractor for the extra work, then Subcontractor shall be paid his actual costs for the additional labor and material as well as his normal overhead and profit.

For any extra work performed, Contractor shall be compensated in an amount to be determined before the extra work is performed and such amount, including Contractor's usual fee for overhead and profit shall be made as the extra work progresses, concurrently with payments made under payments scheduled. However, in the event that an emergency exists, then Subcontractor may proceed upon the verbal authorization of the Contractor or the Contractor's job superintendent and request written confirmation of the verbal authorization within seventy-two (72) hours.

12. Assignment and Subcontracting. Subcontractor shall be allowed to assign any work under this subcontract or subcontract any portion of it without the written consent of the Contractor.

13. Protection of Work. To the extent noted herein, Subcontractor will protect its own work until completion and acceptance of his work. To allow Subcontractor to protect the work, Contractor shall provide to Subcontractor adequate storage space and security on the construction site. Once Subcontractor's work is completed, then Contractor shall be responsible for the protection of the work as well as the entire project.

If Subcontractor's work is damaged or destroyed during the course of Subcontractor's work and said damage or destruction is a result of the negligence of Subcontractor, then Subcontractor shall agree to repair or replace said damaged work. If the work is damaged or destroyed as a result of actions beyond the reasonable control of the Subcontractor or through the negligence of persons other than Subcontractor, then Subcontractor shall repair or replace said damaged or destroyed work but will do so only upon being compensated for same. Compensation shall be treated as extra work and the compensation shall be determined as provided in Paragraph 11.

14. Concealed Conditions. In the event that Subcontractor encounters rock, ground-water, underground structures, utilities or other conditions unknown to Subcontractor and not reasonably foreseeable by Subcontractor, then Subcontractor shall immediately stop work and call Contractor's attention to such concealed conditions in writing. The subcontract time and price will be equitably adjusted in writing.

15. Insurance. Contractor will procure at Contractor's expense and before commencement of any work under this contract, fire insurance , with course of construction, vandalism and malicious mischief clauses attached. The insurance is to name Contractor and Subcontractors as additional insured, and to protect Owner Contractor and Subcontractors, and construction lender as their interests may appear. Should Contractor fail to do so, Subcontractor may procure to do so. If the project is destroyed or damaged by any accident, disaster, or calamity such as fire, storm flood, landslide, subsidence, or earthquake, or by theft or vandalism, any work done by Subcontractor in rebuilding or restoring the project shall be paid for by the Contractor as an extra and shall be dealt with under the provisions of Paragraph 11 above. If, however, the estimated cost of replacement of work already accomplished by Subcontractor exceeds twenty (20) percent of the contract price, Contractor shall have the option to cancel this contract and, in that event, shall pay Subcontractors usual overhead and a net profit to Subcontractor the amount of _____ percent, of all work performed by Subcontractor before cancellation.

Subcontractor will carry Worker's Compensation Insurance to protect Subcontractor's employees during the progress of the work. Contractor shall obtain and pay for insurance against injury to his own employees and persons not under the control of Subcontractor.

16. Indemnification. Contractor shall indemnify and hold harmless Subcontractor from and against any and all claims arising from Contractor's use of the job site, or from the conduct of Contractor's business or from any activity, work or things done, permitted or suffered by Contractor or others in or about the job site or elsewhere, and shall further indemnify and hold harmless Subcontractor from and against any and all claims arising from any breach or default in the performance of any obligation on the Contractor's part to be performed under the terms of the Subcontract Agreement, or arising from any breach or default in the performance of any obligation on the Contractor's part to be performed under the terms of the Subcontract Agreement, or arising from any negligence of the Contractor or any of Contractor's agents, Contractors, subcontractors, or employees, and from and against all costs, attorney's fees, expenses and liabilities incurred in the defense of any such claims or any action or proceeding brought thereon; and in case any action or proceeding be brought against Subcontractor by reason of any such claim. Contractor, upon notice from Subcontractor shall defend same at Contractor's expense by counsel satisfactory to Subcontractor.

Consult a lawyer if you doubt the form's fitness for your purpose and use.

Change Order (Contractor)

CHANGE ORDER

No. _____

This form complies with professional standards in effect January 1-December 31, 2005

Contractor: _____

_____

_____

License No: _____

OWNER			PHONE		DATE /05		
STREET			JOB NAME			JOB NUMBER	
CITY	STATE	ZIP CODE	STREET				
EXISTING CONTRACT NUMBER		DATE OF EXISTING CONTRACT	CITY		STATE		ZIP CODE

Add ___ calendar days to contract completion date.

ADDITIONAL CHARGE FOR ABOVE WORK IS: $ _____

Payment will be made as follows:
Above additional work to be performed under same conditions as specified in original contract unless otherwise stipulated.

Date _____ 2005 Authorizing Signature **X**_____

(OWNER SIGNS HERE)

We hereby agree to furnish labor and materials - complete in accordance with the above specifications, at above stated price.

Authorized Signature _____ Date ___/___/05

NOTE: This Revision becomes part of, and in conformance with, the existing contract.

Change Order (Owner/Architect)

CHANGE ORDER
This form complies with professional standards in effect January 1-December 31, 2005

☐OWNER ☐ARCHITECT xwe25
CONTRACTOR ☐FIELD ☐OTHER

PROJECT:

_____
(Name)

_____
(Address)

_____
(City, State, Zip)

_____
(Phone)   (Fax)

CONTRACTOR:

_____
(Name)

_____
(Address)

_____
(City, State, Zip)

_____
(Phone)   (Fax)

The Contract is hereby modified and amended as follows:
It is mutually agreed that the contract price is: ☐ increased ☐ decreased by $ _____ ☐ payable ☐ deductible immediately upon completion of the work called for in this Change Order.

As a result of this Change Order, the time for completion of the above-mentioned contract is hereby extended by an additional _____ days.

This Change Order is incorporated into and governed by the above mentioned contract and is incorporated therein.

X
/05 _____
(Contractor/Owner)   Date

X
/05 _____
(Owner/Contractor)

Consult a lawyer if you doubt the form's fitness for your purpose and use.

© ABCAForms.com 2005.

APPENDIX C

TAX INFORMATION

Calendar of Federal Taxes for Sole Proprietors

Sole Proprietor
Calendar of Federal Taxes for Which You May Be Liable

January	15	Estimated tax	Form 1040ES
	31	Social Security (FICA) tax and the withholding of income tax Note: See IRS rulings for deposit—Pub. 334	Forms 941, 941E, 942, and 943.
	31	Providing information on Social Security (FICA) tax and the withholding of income tax	Form W-2 (to employee)
	31	Federal unemployment (FUTA) tax	Form 940-EZ or 940
	31	Federal unemployment (FUTA) tax (only if liability for unpaid taxes exceeds $100)	Form 8109 (to make deposits)
	31	Information returns to nonemployees and transactions with other persons	Form 1099 (to recipients)
February	28	Information returns to nonemployees and transactions with other persons	Form 1099 (to IRS)
	28	Providing information on Social Security (FICA) tax and the withholding income tax	Forms W-2 and W-3 (to Social Security Admin.)
April	15	Income tax	Schedule C (Form 1040)
	15	Self-employment tax	Schedule SE (Form 1040)
	15	Estimated tax	Form 1040ES
	30	Social Security (FICA) tax and the withholding of income tax Note: See IRS rulings for deposit—Pub. 334	Forms 941, 941E, 942, and 943
	30	Federal unemployment (FUTA) tax (only if liability for unpaid taxes exceeds $100)	Form 8109 (to make deposits)
June	15	Estimated tax	Form 1040ES
July	31	Social Security (FICA) tax and the withholding of income tax Note: See IRS rulings for deposit—Pub. 334	Forms 941, 941E, 942, and 943
	31	Federal unemployment (FUTA) tax (only if liability for unpaid taxes exceeds $100)	Form 8109 (to make deposits)
September	15	Estimated tax	Form 1040ES
October	31	Social Security (FICA) tax and the withholding of income tax Note: See IRS rulings for deposit—Pub. 334	Forms 941, 941E, 942, and 943
	31	Federal unemployment (FUTA) tax (only if liability for unpaid taxes exceeds $100)	Form 8109 (to make deposits)

If your tax year is not January 1st through December 31st:

- Schedule C (Form 1040) is due the 15th day of the 4th month after end of the tax year. Schedule SE is due same day as Form 1040.

- Estimated tax (1040ES) is due the 15th day of 4th, 6th, and 9th months of tax year, and the 15th day of 1st month after the end of tax year.

Anatomy of a Business Plan by Linda Pinson. © 2005 Dearborn Trade Publishing. *www.dearborntrade.com.*

Calendar of Federal Taxes for Partnerships

Partnership
Calendar of Federal Taxes for Which You May Be Liable

Month	Day	Description	Form
January	15	Estimated tax (individual who is a partner)	Form 1040ES
	31	Social Security (FICA) tax and the withholding of income tax Note: See IRS rulings for deposit—Pub. 334	Forms 941, 941E, 942, and 943
	31	Providing information on Social Security (FICA) tax and the withholding of income tax	Form W-2 (to employee)
	31	Federal unemployment (FUTA) tax	Form 940-EZ or 940
	31	Federal unemployment (FUTA) tax (only if liability for unpaid taxes exceeds $100)	Form 8109 (to make deposits)
	31	Information returns to nonemployees and transactions with other persons	Form 1099 (to recipients)
February	28	Information returns to nonemployees and transactions with other persons	Form 1099 (to IRS)
	28	Providing information on Social Security (FICA) tax and on withholding income tax	Forms W-2 and W-3 (to Social Security Admin.)
April	15	Income tax (individual who is a partner)	Schedule C (Form 1040)
	15	Annual return of income	Form 1065
	15	Self-employment tax (individual who is partner)	Schedule SE (Form 1040)
	15	Estimated tax (individual who is partner)	Form 1040ES
	30	Social Security (FICA) tax and the withholding of income tax Note: See IRS rulings for deposit—Pub. 334	Forms 941, 941E, 942, and 943
	30	Federal unemployment (FUTA) tax (only if liability for unpaid taxes exceeds $100)	Form 8109 (to make deposits)
June	15	Estimated tax (individual who is a partner)	Form 1040ES
July	31	Social Security (FICA) tax and the withholding of income tax Note: See IRS rulings for deposit—Pub. 334	Forms 941, 941E, 942, and 943
	31	Federal unemployment (FUTA) tax (only if liability for unpaid taxes exceeds $100)	Form 8109 (to make deposits)
September	15	Estimated tax (individual who is a partner)	Form 1040ES
October	31	Social Security (FICA) tax and the withholding of income tax Note: See IRS rulings for deposit—Pub. 334	Forms 941, 941E, 942, and 943
	31	Federal unemployment (FUTA) tax (only if liability for unpaid taxes exceeds $100)	Form 8109 (to make deposits)

If your Tax Year is not January 1st through December 31st:

- Income tax is due the 15th day of the 4th month after end of tax year.
- Self-employment tax is due the same day as income tax (Form 1040).
- Estimated tax (1040ES) is due the 15th day of the 4th, 6th, and 9th month of the tax year and the 15th day of 1st month after end of the tax year.

Calendar of Federal Taxes for Corporations

Corporation
Calendar of Federal Taxes for Which You May Be Liable

January	31	Social Security (FICA) tax and the withholding of income tax Note: See IRS rulings for deposit—Pub. 334	Forms 941, 941E, 942, and 943
	31	Providing information on Social Security (FICA) tax and the withholding of income tax	Form W-2 (to employee)
	31	Federal unemployment (FUTA) tax	Form 940-EZ or 940
	31	Federal unemployment (FUTA) tax (only if liability for unpaid taxes exceeds $100)	Form 8109 (to make deposits)
	31	Information returns to nonemployees and transactions with other persons	Form 1099 (to recipients)
February	28	Information returns to nonemployees and transactions with other persons	Form 1099 (to IRS)
	28	Providing information on Social Security (FICA) tax and the withholding of income tax	Forms W-2 and W-3 (to Social Security Admin.)
March	15	Income tax	Form 1120 or 1120-A
April	15	Estimated tax	Form 1120-W
	30	Social Security (FICA) tax and the withholding of income tax Note: See IRS rulings for deposit—Pub. 334	Forms 941, 941E, 942, and 943
	30	Federal unemployment (FUTA) tax (only if liability for unpaid taxes exceeds $100)	Form 8109 (to make deposits)
June	15	Estimated tax	Form 1120-W
July	31	Social Security (FICA) tax and the withholding of income tax Note: See IRS rulings for deposit—Pub. 334	Forms 941, 941E, 942, and 943
	31	Federal unemployment (FUTA) tax (only if liability for unpaid taxes exceeds $100)	Form 8109 (to make deposits)
September	15	Estimated tax	Form 1120-W
October	31	Social Security (FICA) tax and the withholding of income tax Note: See IRS rulings for deposit—Pub. 334	Forms 941, 941E, 942, and 943
	31	Federal unemployment (FUTA) tax (only if liability for unpaid taxes exceeds $100)	Form 8109 (to make deposits)
December	15	Estimated tax	Form 1120-W

If your tax year is not January 1st through December 31st:

- Income tax (Form 1120 or 1120-A) is due on the 15th day of the 3rd month after the end of the tax year.
- Estimated tax (1120-W) is due the 5th day of the 4th, 6th, 9th, and 12th months of the tax year.

Anatomy of a Business Plan by Linda Pinson. © 2005 Dearborn Trade Publishing. *www.dearborntrade.com.*

Calendar of Federal Taxes for Subchapter S Corporations

<table>
<tr><td colspan="4" align="center">**S Corporation**
Calendar of Federal Taxes for Which You May Be Liable</td></tr>
<tr><td>**January**</td><td>15</td><td>Estimated tax (individual S corp. shareholder)</td><td>Form 1040ES</td></tr>
<tr><td></td><td>31</td><td>Social Security (FICA) tax and the withholding of income tax
Note: See IRS rulings for deposit—Pub. 334</td><td>Forms 941, 941E, 942, and 943</td></tr>
<tr><td></td><td>31</td><td>Providing information on Social Security (FICA) tax and the withholding of income tax</td><td>Form W-2 (to employee)</td></tr>
<tr><td></td><td>31</td><td>Federal unemployment (FUTA) tax</td><td>Form 940-EZ or 940</td></tr>
<tr><td></td><td>31</td><td>Federal unemployment (FUTA) tax (only if liability for unpaid taxes exceeds $100)</td><td>Form 8109 (to make deposits)</td></tr>
<tr><td></td><td>31</td><td>Information returns to nonemployees and transactions with other persons</td><td>Form 1099 (to recipients)</td></tr>
<tr><td>**February**</td><td>28</td><td>Information returns to nonemployees and transactions with other persons</td><td>Form 1099 (to IRS)</td></tr>
<tr><td></td><td>28</td><td>Providing information on Social Security (FICA) tax and the withholding of income tax</td><td>Forms W-2 and W-3 (to Social Security Admin.)</td></tr>
<tr><td>**March**</td><td>15</td><td>Income tax</td><td>Form 1120S</td></tr>
<tr><td>**April**</td><td>15</td><td>Income tax (individual S corp. shareholder)</td><td>Form 1040</td></tr>
<tr><td></td><td>15</td><td>Estimated tax (individual S corp. shareholder)</td><td>Form 1040ES</td></tr>
<tr><td></td><td>30</td><td>Social Security (FICA) tax and the withholding of income tax
Note: See IRS rulings for deposit—Pub. 334</td><td>Forms 941, 941E, 942, and 943</td></tr>
<tr><td></td><td>30</td><td>Federal unemployment (FUTA) tax (only if liability for unpaid taxes exceeds $100)</td><td>Form 8109 (to make deposits)</td></tr>
<tr><td>**June**</td><td>15</td><td>Estimated tax (individual S corp. shareholder)</td><td>Form 1040ES</td></tr>
<tr><td>**July**</td><td>31</td><td>Social Security (FICA) tax and the withholding of income tax
Note: See IRS rulings for deposit—Pub. 334</td><td>Forms 941, 941E, 942, and 943</td></tr>
<tr><td></td><td>31</td><td>Federal unemployment (FUTA) tax (only if liability for unpaid taxes exceeds $100)</td><td>Form 8109 (to make deposits)</td></tr>
<tr><td>**September**</td><td>15</td><td>Estimated tax (individual S corp. shareholder)</td><td>Form 1040ES</td></tr>
<tr><td>**October**</td><td>31</td><td>Social Security (FICA) tax and the withholding of income tax
Note: See IRS rulings for deposit—Pub. 334</td><td>Forms 941, 941E, 942, and 943</td></tr>
<tr><td></td><td>31</td><td>Federal unemployment (FUTA) tax (only if liability for unpaid taxes exceeds $100)</td><td>Form 8109 (to make deposits)</td></tr>
</table>

If your tax year is not January 1st through December 31st:

- S corporation income tax (1120S) and individual S corporation shareholder income tax (Form 1040) are due the 15th day of the 4th month after end of tax year.
- Estimated tax of individual shareholder (1040ES) is due 15th day of 4th, 6th, and 9th months of tax year, and 15th day of 1st month after end of tax year.

IRS Publication 15, Circular E

Department of the Treasury
Internal Revenue Service

Publication 15
(Rev. January 2005)
Cat. No. 10000W

(Circular E), Employer's Tax Guide

(Including 2005 Wage Withholding and Advance Earned Income Credit Payment Tables)

Get forms and other information faster and easier by:

Internet • www.irs.gov
FAX • 703–368–9694 (from your fax machine)

for Business

www.irs.gov/efile

Contents

What's New 1

Calendar................................ 2

Reminders 4

Introduction 6

1. Employer Identification Number (EIN) 7

2. Who Are Employees? 7

3. Family Employees 8

4. Employee's Social Security Number (SSN) 8

5. Wages and Other Compensation 9

6. Tips 12

7. Supplemental Wages 13

8. Payroll Period 14

9. Withholding From Employees' Wages 14

10. Advance Earned Income Credit (EIC) Payment 16

11. Depositing Taxes 18

12. Filing Form 941 23

13. Reporting Adjustments on Form 941 25

14. Federal Unemployment (FUTA) Tax 28

15. Special Rules for Various Types of Services and Payments 30

16. How To Use the Income Tax Withholding and Advance Earned Income Credit (EIC) Payment Tables 34

Tables:
  2005 Income Tax Withholding Tables:
    Percentage Method 36–37
    Wage Bracket Method 38–57
  2005 Advance EIC Payment Tables:
    Percentage Method 58–59
    Wage Bracket Method 60–65

Index 66

Form 7018-A (order blank) 67

Quick and Easy Access to Tax Help and Forms 68

What's New

Additional federal holiday. January 20, 2005, is Inauguration Day and has been designated as a federal holiday for tax purposes. Tax returns due on that day may be filed on the next business day. Also, January 20, 2005, is not a banking day under federal tax deposit rules.

IRS Publication 15, Circular E (continued)

Redesigned Form 941. Form 941, Employer's Quarterly Federal Tax Return, was completely redesigned for tax periods beginning after December 31, 2004. Many of the reporting lines on the redesigned Form 941 have changed from those shown on the January 2004 revision. Form 941 line references in this publication relate to the January 2005 revision of Form 941. Use only the redesigned version of Form 941 (revision date of January 2005 or later) to report employment taxes for tax periods beginning after December 31, 2004. Use the January 2004 revision of this publication for Form 941 line references relating to tax periods ending before 2005, including the fourth quarter 2004 Form 941 that is due January 31, 2005.

Increase to FUTA tax deposit threshold. The Treasury Department recently amended Regulations section 31.6302(c)-3 to increase the accumulated FUTA tax deposit threshold from $100 to $500. The $500 threshold applies to FUTA tax deposits required for taxes reported on Forms 940, 940-EZ, and 940-PR, Employer's Annual Federal Unemployment (FUTA) Tax Return for tax periods beginning after December 31, 2004. For more information about this and other important tax changes, see Publication 553, Highlights of 2004 Tax Changes.

Changes to nonqualified deferred compensation plans. New section 409A added by the American Jobs Creation Act of 2004 provides that all amounts deferred under a nonqualified deferred compensation (NQDC) plan for all taxable years are currently includible in gross income unless certain requirements are satisfied. If section 409A requires an amount to be included in gross income, the statute imposes a substantial additional tax. Section 409A generally is effective with respect to amounts deferred in taxable years beginning after December 31, 2004, but deferrals made prior to that year may be subject to the statute under certain circumstances. The Act also provides significant withholding and reporting requirements for the NQDC. See section 5 of Publication 15-A, Employer's Supplemental Tax Guide, for more information.

New form for reporting discrepancies between Forms 941 and Forms W-2. We recently developed Schedule D (Form 941), Report of Discrepancies Caused by Acquisitions, Statutory Mergers, or Consolidations. You may use Schedule D (Form 941) to explain certain wage, tax, and payment discrepancies between Forms 941 and Forms W-2 that were caused by acquisitions, statutory mergers, or consolidations.

Social security and Medicare tax for 2005. Do not withhold social security tax after an employee reaches $90,000 in social security wages. (There is no limit on the amount of wages subject to Medicare tax.)

Increase to withholding on supplemental wage payments exceeding $1,000,000. Section 904 of the American jobs Creation Act of 2004 increased the flat withholding rate on supplemental wage payments that exceed $1,000,000 during the year to 35%. See section 7 for more information.

Employment contract signing and cancellation payments. Amounts an employer pays as a bonus for signing or ratifying a contract in connection with the establishment of an employer-employee relationship and an amount paid to an employee for cancellation of an employment contract and relinquishment of contract rights are wages subject to social security, Medicare, and federal unemployment taxes and income tax withholding. The IRS will not apply this rule to certain signing bonuses or similar amounts paid in connection with an employee's initial employment with the employer pursuant to a contract entered into before January 12, 2005, or to certain payments made by an employer to an employee or former employee before that date to cancel an employment contract and relinquish contract rights. For more information, see Rev. Ruls. 2004-109 and 2004-110 in Internal Revenue Bulletin 2004-50.

Calendar

The following is a list of important dates. Also see Publication 509, Tax Calendars for 2005.

Note. If any date shown below falls on a Saturday, Sunday, or federal holiday, use the next business day. A statewide legal holiday delays a filing due date only if the IRS office where you are required to file is located in that state. For any due date, you will meet the "file" or "furnish" requirement if the form is properly addressed and mailed First-Class or sent by an IRS-designated private delivery service on or before the due date. See *Private Delivery Services* on page 5 for more information on IRS-designated private delivery services.

By January 31

Furnish Forms 1099 and W-2. Furnish each employee a completed Form W-2, Wage and Tax Statement. Furnish each other payee a completed Form 1099 (for example, Form 1099-R, Distributions From Pensions, Annuities, Retirement or Profit-Sharing Plans, IRAs, Insurance Contracts, etc., and Form 1099-MISC, Miscellaneous Income).

File Form 940 or 940-EZ. File Form 940 or Form 940-EZ, Employer's Annual Federal Unemployment (FUTA) Tax Return. However, if you deposited all of the FUTA tax when due, you have ten additional days to file.

File Form 945. File Form 945, Annual Return of Withheld Federal Income Tax, to report any nonpayroll income tax withheld in 2004. See *Nonpayroll Income Tax Withholding* on page 4 for more information.

By February 15

Request a new Form W-4 from exempt employees. Ask for a new Form W-4, Employee's Withholding Allowance Certificate, from each employee who claimed exemption from income tax withholding last year.

On February 16

Exempt Forms W-4 expire. Any Form W-4 previously given to you claiming exemption from withholding has expired. Begin withholding for any employee who previously claimed exemption from withholding, but has not given you a new Form W-4 for the current year. If the

IRS Publication 15, Circular E (continued)

Employer Responsibilities: The following list provides a brief summary of your basic responsibilities. Because the individual circumstances for each employer can vary greatly, their responsibilities for withholding, depositing, and reporting employment taxes can differ. Each item in this list has a page reference to a more detailed discussion in this publication.

New Employees:
Page

☐ Verify work eligibility of employees 4
☐ Record employees' names and SSNs from social security cards 8
☐ Ask employees for 2005 Form W-4 14

Each Payday:

☐ Withhold federal income tax based on each employee's Form W-4 14
☐ Withhold employee's share of social security and Medicare taxes 16
☐ Include advance earned income credit payment in paycheck if employee requested it on Form W-5 17
☐ Deposit:
  • Withheld income tax
  • Withheld and employer social security taxes
  • Withheld and employer Medicare taxes . . . 18
  Note: *Due date of deposit generally depends on your deposit schedule (monthly or semiweekly).*

Quarterly (By April 30, July 31, October 31, and January 31):
Page

☐ Deposit FUTA tax in an authorized financial institution if undeposited amount is over $500 . 29
☐ File Form 941 (pay tax with return if not required to deposit) 23

Annually (See Calendar for due dates):

☐ Remind employees to submit a new Form W-4 if they need to change their withholding . . . 14
☐ Ask for a new Form W-4 from employees claiming exemption from income tax withholding 14
☐ Reconcile Forms 941 with Forms W-2 and W-3 25
☐ Furnish each employee a Form W-2 2
☐ File Copy A of Forms W-2 and the transmittal Form W-3 with the SSA 3
☐ Furnish each other payee a Form 1099 (for example, Forms 1099-R and 1099-MISC) . . 2
☐ File Forms 1099 and the transmittal Form 1096 3
☐ File Form 940 or Form 940-EZ 29
☐ File Form 945 for any nonpayroll income tax withholding 4

---

employee does not give you a new Form W-4, withhold tax as if he or she is single, with zero withholding allowances. See section 9. However, if you have an earlier Form W-4 for this employee that is valid, withhold based on the earlier Form W-4.

By February 28

File Forms 1099 and 1096. File Copy A of all Forms 1099 with Form 1096, Annual Summary and Transmittal of U.S. Information Returns, with the IRS. For electronically filed returns, see *By March 31* below.

File Forms W-2 and W-3. File Copy A of all Forms W-2 with Form W-3, Transmittal of Wage and Tax Statements, with the Social Security Administration (SSA). For electronically filed returns, see *By March 31* below.

File Form 8027. File Form 8027, Employer's Annual Information Return of Tip Income and Allocated Tips, with the Internal Revenue Service. See section 6. For electronically filed returns, see *By March 31* below.

By March 31

File electronic (not magnetic media) Forms 1099, W-2, and 8027. File electronic (not magnetic media) Forms 1099 and 8027 with the IRS. File electronic (not magnetic media) Forms W-2 with the Social Security Administration. For information on reporting Form W-2 and Form W-2c information to the SSA electronically, visit the Social Se-

curity Administration's Employer Reporting Instructions and Information web page at *www.socialsecurity.gov/employer*

By April 30, July 31, October 31, and January 31

Deposit FUTA taxes. Deposit federal unemployment (FUTA) tax due if it is more than $500.

File Form 941. File Form 941, Employer's Quarterly Federal Tax Return, and deposit any undeposited income, social security, and Medicare taxes. You may pay these taxes with Form 941 if your total tax liability for the quarter is less than $2,500 and the taxes are paid in full with a timely filed return. If you deposited all taxes when due, you have 10 additional days from the due dates above to file the return.

Before December 1

New Forms W-4. Remind employees to submit a new Form W-4 if their withholding allowances have changed or will change for the next year.

On December 31

Form W-5 expires. Form W-5, Earned Income Credit Advance Payment Certificate, expires. Eligible employees

IRS Publication 15, Circular E (continued)

who want to receive advance payments of the earned income credit next year must give you a new Form W-5.

Reminders

Electronic Filing and Payment

Now, more than ever before, businesses can enjoy the benefits of filing and paying their federal taxes electronically. Whether you rely on a tax professional or handle your own taxes, IRS offers you convenient programs to make it easier.

Spend less time and worry on taxes and more time running your business. Use *e-file* and Electronic Federal Tax Payment System (EFTPS) to your benefit.

- For *e-file*, visit *www.irs.gov* for additional information.

- For EFTPS, visit *www.eftps.gov* or call EFPTS Customer Service at 1-800-555-4477.

Use the electronic options available from IRS and make filing and paying taxes easier.

Hiring New Employees

Eligibility for employment. You must verify that each new employee is legally eligible to work in the United States. This will include completing the U.S. Citizenship and Immigration Services (USCIS) Form I-9, Employment Eligibility Verification. You can get the form from USCIS offices or by calling 1-800-870-3676. Contact the USCIS at 1-800-375-5283, or visit the USCIS website at *www.uscis.gov* for further information.

New hire reporting. You are required to report any new employee to a designated state new hire registry. Many states accept a copy of Form W-4 with employer information added. Call the Office of Child Support Enforcement at 202-401-9267 or access its website at *www.acf.hhs.gov/ programs/cse/newhire* for more information.

Income tax withholding. Ask each new employee to complete the 2005 Form W-4. See section 9.

Name and social security number. Record each new employee's name and number from his or her social security card. Any employee without a social security card should apply for one. See section 4.

Paying Wages, Pensions, or Annuities

Income tax withholding. Withhold federal income tax from each wage payment or supplemental unemployment compensation plan benefit payment according to the employee's Form W-4 and the correct withholding rate. If you have nonresident alien employees, see section 9. Withhold from periodic pension and annuity payments as if the recipient is married claiming three withholding allowances, unless he or she has provided Form W-4P, Withholding Certificate for Pension or Annuity Payments, either electing no withholding or giving a different number of allowances, marital status, or an additional amount to be withheld. Do not withhold on direct rollovers from qualified plans or governmental section 457(b) plans. See section 9 and Publication 15-A, Employer's Supplemental Tax Guide. Publication 15-A includes information about withholding on pensions and annuities.

Zero Wage return. All U.S.-based (domestic) taxpayers may file their "Zero Wage" Forms 941 by telephone using the 941TeleFile system. See Publication 3950 for details. Eligible filers must have had (a) no withholding, (b) no federal tax deposits, and (c) no taxes to report for the quarter. Dial 1-800-583-5345 (toll free) to use 941TeleFile.

Information Returns

You may be required to file information returns to report certain types of payments made during the year. For example, you must file Form 1099-MISC, Miscellaneous Income, to report payments of $600 or more to persons not treated as employees (for example, independent contractors) for services performed for your trade or business. For details about filing Forms 1099 and for information about required electronic or magnetic media filing, see the 2005 General Instructions for Forms 1099, 1098, 5498, and W-2G for general information and the separate, specific instructions for each information return that you file (for example, 2005 Instructions for Forms 1099-MISC). Do not use Forms 1099 to report wages and other compensation that you paid to employees; report these on Form W-2. See the separate Instructions for Forms W-2 and W-3 for details about filing Form W-2 and for information about required magnetic media or electronic filing. If you file 250 or more Forms W-2 or 1099, you must file them on magnetic media or electronically. Beginning with tax year 2005 forms (due to SSA in calendar year 2006), SSA will no longer accept Forms W-2 and W-3 filed on tape and cartridge.

Information reporting call site. The IRS operates a centralized call site to answer questions about reporting on Forms W-2, W-3, 1099, and other information returns. If you have questions related to reporting on information returns, call 1-866-455-7438 (toll free) or 304-263-8700 (not toll free). The call site can also be reached by email at *mccirp@irs.gov*.

Nonpayroll Income Tax Withholding

Nonpayroll federal income tax withholding must be reported on Form 945, Annual Return of Withheld Federal Income Tax. Form 945 is an annual tax return and the return for 2004 is due January 31, 2005. Separate deposits are required for payroll (Form 941) and nonpayroll (Form 945) withholding. Nonpayroll items include:

- Pensions, annuities, and IRAs.

- Military retirement.

- Gambling winnings.

- Indian gaming profits.

- Voluntary withholding on certain government payments.

- Backup withholding.

Page 4

IRS Publication 15, Circular E (continued)

For details on depositing and reporting nonpayroll income tax withholding, see the Instructions for Form 945.

All income tax withholding reported on Forms 1099 or W-2G must also be reported on Form 945. All income tax withholding reported on Form W-2 must be reported on Form 941, Form 943, or Schedule H (Form 1040).

Note. Because distributions to participants from some nonqualified pension plans and deferred compensation plans are treated as wages and are reported on Form W-2, income tax withheld must be reported on Form 941, not on Form 945. However, distributions from such plans to a beneficiary or estate of a deceased employee are not wages and are reported on Forms 1099-R, income tax withheld must be reported on Form 945.

Backup withholding. You generally must withhold 28% of certain taxable payments if the payee fails to furnish you with his or her correct taxpayer identification number (TIN). This withholding is referred to as "backup withholding."

Payments subject to backup withholding include interest, dividends, patronage dividends, rents, royalties, commissions, nonemployee compensation, and certain other payments that you make in the course of your trade or business. In addition, transactions by brokers and barter exchanges and certain payments made by fishing boat operators are subject to backup withholding.

Note. Backup withholding does not apply to wages, pensions, annuities, IRAs (including simplified employee pension (SEP) and SIMPLE retirement plans), section 404(k) distributions from an employee stock ownership plan (ESOP), medical savings accounts, health savings accounts, long-term-care benefits, or real estate transactions.

You can use Form W-9, Request for Taxpayer Identification Number and Certification, to request that payees furnish a TIN and to certify that the number furnished is correct. You can also use Form W-9 to get certifications from payees that they are not subject to backup withholding or that they are exempt from backup withholding. The Instructions for the Requester of Form W-9 includes a list of types of payees who are exempt from backup withholding. For more information, see Publication 1679, A Guide to Backup Withholding For Missing and Incorrect Name/TIN(s).

Recordkeeping

Keep all records of employment taxes for at least four years. These should be available for IRS review. Your records should include:

- Your employer identification number (EIN),
- Amounts and dates of all wage, annuity, and pension payments,
- Amounts of tips reported to you by your employees,
- Records of allocated tips,
- The fair market value of in-kind wages paid,
- Names, addresses, social security numbers, and occupations of employees and recipients,

- Any employee copies of Forms W-2 and W-2c that were returned to you as undeliverable,
- Dates of employment for each employee,
- Periods for which employees and recipients were paid while absent due to sickness or injury and the amount and weekly rate of payments you or third-party payers made to them,
- Copies of employees' and recipients' income tax withholding allowance certificates (Forms W-4, W-4P, W-4S, and W-4V),
- Dates and amounts of tax deposits that you made and acknowledgment numbers for deposits made by EFTPS,
- Copies of returns filed, including 941TeleFile Tax Records and confirmation numbers, and
- Records of fringe benefits and expense reimbursements provided to your employees, including substantiation.

Change of Address

To notify the IRS of a new business mailing address or business location, file Form 8822, Change of Address. For information on how to change your address for deposit coupons, see *Making deposits with FTD coupons* in section 11.

Private Delivery Services

You can use certain private delivery services designated by the IRS to mail tax returns and payments. The list includes only the following:

- DHL Express (DHL): DHL Same Day Service; DHL Next Day 10:30 am; DHL Next Day 12:00 pm; DHL Next Day 3:00 pm; and DHL 2nd Day Service.
- Federal Express (FedEx): FedEx Priority Overnight, FedEx Standard Overnight, FedEx 2 Day, FedEx International Priority, and FedEx International First.
- United Parcel Service (UPS): UPS Next Day Air, UPS Next Day Air Saver, UPS 2nd Day Air, UPS 2nd Day Air A.M., UPS Worldwide Express Plus, and UPS Worldwide Express.

Your private delivery service can tell you how to get written proof of the mailing date.

 Private delivery services cannot deliver items to P.O. boxes. You must use the U.S. Postal Service to mail any item to an IRS P.O. box address.

Telephone Help

Tax questions. You can call the IRS with your employment tax questions at 1-800-829-4933.

Help for people with disabilities. Telephone help is available using TTY/TDD equipment. You may call 1-800-829-4059 with any tax question or to order forms

IRS Publication 15, Circular E (continued)

and publications. You may also use this number for assistance with unresolved tax problems.

Recorded tax information (TeleTax). The IRS TeleTax service provides recorded tax information on topics that answer many individual and business federal tax questions. You can listen to up to three topics on each call that you make. Touch-Tone service is available 24 hours a day, 7 days a week. TeleTax topics are also available using a personal computer. Connect to *www.irs.gov/taxtopics*.

A list of employment tax topics is provided below. Select, by number, the topic you want to hear and call 1-800-829-4477. For the directory of all topics, select Topic 123.

TeleTax Topics

Topic No.	Subject
752	Form W-2—Where, When, and How to File
753	Form W-4—Employee's Withholding Allowance Certificate
754	Form W-5—Advance Earned Income Credit
755	Employer identification number (EIN)—How to Apply
756	Employment Taxes for Household Employees
757	Form 941—Deposit Requirements
758	Form 941—Employer's Quarterly Federal Tax Return
759	Form 940 and 940-EZ—Deposit Requirements
760	Form 940 and 940-EZ—Employer's Annual Federal Unemployment Tax Return
761	Tips—Withholding and Reporting
762	Independent contractor vs. Employee

Unresolved Tax Issues

If you have attempted to deal with an IRS problem unsuccessfully, you should contact the Taxpayer Advocate. The Taxpayer Advocate independently represents your interests and concerns within the IRS by protecting your rights and resolving problems that have not been fixed through normal channels.

While Taxpayer Advocates cannot change the tax law or make a technical tax decision, they can clear up problems that resulted from previous contacts and ensure that your case is given a complete and impartial review.

Your assigned personal advocate will listen to your point of view and will work with you to address your concerns. You can expect the advocate to provide:

- A "fresh look" at a new or ongoing problem,
- Timely acknowledgement,
- The name and phone number of the individual assigned to your case,
- Updates on progress,
- Timeframes for action,
- Speedy resolution, and

- Courteous service.

When contacting the Taxpayer Advocate, you should provide the following information.

- Your name, address, and employer identification number (EIN).
- The name and telephone number of an authorized contact person and the hours when he or she can be reached.
- The type of tax return and year(s) involved.
- A detailed description of the problem.
- Previous attempts to solve the problem and the office that had been contacted.
- A description of the hardship that you are facing (if applicable).

You may contact a Taxpayer Advocate online at *www.irs.gov/advocate* or by calling a toll-free number, 1-877-777-4778. Persons who have access to TTY/TDD equipment may call 1-800-829-4059 and ask for Taxpayer Advocate assistance. If you prefer, you may call, write, or fax the Taxpayer Advocate office in your area. See Publication 1546, The Taxpayer Advocate Service of the IRS, for a list of addresses and fax numbers.

Filing Addresses. Generally, your filing address for Forms 940, 940-EZ, 941, 943, and 945 depends on the location of your residence or principal place of business and whether or not you included a payment with your return. There are separate filing addresses for these returns if you are an exempt organization or government entity. If you are located in the United States and do not include a payment with your return, you should file at either the Cincinnati or Ogden Service Centers. File Form CT-1 (for railroad retirement taxes) at the Cincinnati Service Center. See Form CT-1 for details on where to file.

Photographs of Missing Children The Internal Revenue Service is a proud partner with the National Center for Missing and Exploited Children. Photographs of missing children selected by the Center may appear in this booklet on pages that would otherwise be blank. You can help bring these children home by looking at the photographs and calling 1-800-THE-LOST (1-800-843-5678) if you recognize a child.

Introduction

This publication explains your tax responsibilities as an employer. It explains the requirements for withholding, depositing, reporting, and paying employment taxes. It explains the forms that you must give to your employees, those that your employees must give to you, and those that you must send to the IRS and SSA. This guide also has tax tables that you need to figure the taxes to withhold from each employee for 2005. References to "income tax" in this guide apply only to "federal" income tax. Contact your state or local tax department to determine if their rules are different.

Additional employment tax information is available in Publication 15-A, Employer's Supplemental Tax Guide.

IRS Publication 15, Circular E (continued)

Publication 15-A includes specialized information supplementing the basic employment tax information provided in this publication. Publication 15-B, Employer's Tax Guide to Fringe Benefits, contains information about the employment tax treatment and valuation of various types of non-cash compensation.

Most employers must withhold (except FUTA), deposit, report, and pay the following employment taxes.

- Income tax.

- Social security and Medicare taxes.

- Federal unemployment tax (FUTA).

There are exceptions to these requirements. See section 15, *Special Rules for Various Types of Services and Payments*. Railroad retirement taxes are explained in the Instructions for Form CT-1.

Federal Government employers. The information in this guide applies to federal agencies except for the rules requiring deposit of federal taxes only at Federal Reserve banks or through the FedTax option of the Government On-Line Accounting Link Systems (GOALS). See the Treasury Financial Manual (I TFM 3-4000) for more information.

State and local government employers. Payments to employees for services in the employ of state and local government employers are generally subject to federal income tax withholding but not federal unemployment (FUTA) tax. Most elected and appointed public officials of state or local governments are employees under common law rules. See chapter 3 of Publication 963, Federal-State Reference Guide. In addition, wages, with certain exceptions, are subject to social security and Medicare taxes. See section 15 of this guide for more information on the exceptions.

You can get information on reporting and social security coverage from your local IRS office. If you have any questions about coverage under a section 218 (Social Security Act) agreement, contact the appropriate state official. To find your State Social Security Administrator, contact the National Conference of State Social Security Administrators website at *www.ncsssa.org*.

Comments and Suggestions. We welcome your comments about this publication and your suggestions for future editions. You can email us at *taxforms@irs.gov*. Please put "Publications Comment" on the subject line.

You can write to us at the following address:

Internal Revenue Service
TE-GE Forms and Publications Branch
SE:W:CAR:MP:T:T
1111 Constitution Ave. NW, IR-6406
Washington, DC 20224

We respond to many letters by telephone. Therefore, it would be helpful if you would include your daytime phone number, including the area code, in your correspondence.

1. Employer Identification Number (EIN)

If you are required to report employment taxes or give tax statements to employees or annuitants, you need an employer identification number (EIN).

The EIN is a 9-digit number that the IRS issues. The digits are arranged as follows: 00-0000000. It is used to identify the tax accounts of employers and certain others who have no employees. Use your EIN on all of the items that you send to the IRS and SSA. For more information, get Publication 1635, Understanding Your EIN.

If you do not have an EIN, request one on Form SS-4, Application for Employer Identification Number. Form SS-4 has information on how to apply for an EIN by mail, fax, or by telephone. You may also apply for an EIN online by visiting the IRS website at *www.irs.gov/smallbiz.* Do not use a social security number (SSN) in place of an EIN.

You should have only one EIN. If you have more than one and are not sure which one to use, please check with the IRS office where you file your return. Give the numbers that you have, the name and address to which each was assigned, and the address of your main place of business. The IRS will tell you which number to use.

If you took over another employer's business (see *Sucessor employer* in section 9), do not use that employer's EIN. If you do not have your own EIN by the time a return is due, write "Applied For" and the date that you applied for it in the space shown for the number.

See *Depositing without an EIN* in section 11 if you must make a tax deposit and you do not have an EIN.

2. Who Are Employees?

Generally, employees are defined either under common law or under statutes for certain situations.

Employee status under common law. Generally, a worker who performs services for you is your employee if you have the right to control what will be done and how it will be done. This is so even when you give the employee freedom of action. What matters is that you have the right to control the details of how the services are performed. See Publication 15-A, Employer's Supplemental Tax Guide, for more information on how to determine whether an individual providing services is an independent contractor or an employee.

Generally, people in business for themselves are not employees. For example, doctors, lawyers, veterinarians, construction contractors, and others in an independent trade in which they offer their services to the public are usually not employees. However, if the business is incorporated, corporate officers who work in the business are employees.

If an employer-employee relationship exists, it does not matter what it is called. The employee may be called an agent or independent contractor. It also does not matter how payments are measured or paid, what they are called, or if the employee works full or part time.

Statutory employees. If someone who works for you is not an employee under the common law rules discussed

IRS Publication 15, Circular E (continued)

above, do not withhold federal income tax from his or her pay. Although the following persons may not be common law employees, they may be considered employees by statute for social security, Medicare, and FUTA tax purposes under certain conditions.

- An agent (or commission) driver who delivers food, beverages (other than milk), laundry, or dry cleaning for someone else.

- A full-time life insurance salesperson who sells primarily for one company.

- A homeworker who works by guidelines of the person for whom the work is done, with materials furnished by and returned to that person or to someone that person designates.

- A traveling or city salesperson (other than an agent-driver or commission-driver) who works full time (except for sideline sales activities) for one firm or person getting orders from customers. The orders must be for items for resale or use as supplies in the customer's business. The customers must be retailers, wholesalers, contractors, or operators of hotels, restaurants, or other businesses dealing with food or lodging.

See Publication 15-A for details on statutory employees.

Statutory nonemployees. Direct sellers and qualified real estate agents are by law considered nonemployees. They are instead treated as self-employed for all federal tax purposes, including income and employment taxes. See Publication 15-A for details.

Treating employees as nonemployees. You will generally be liable for social security and Medicare taxes and withheld income tax if you do not deduct and withhold them because you treat an employee as a nonemployee. See Internal Revenue Code section 3509 for details. Also see *Special additions to tax liability* in section 13.

Relief provisions. If you have a reasonable basis for not treating a worker as an employee, you may be relieved from having to pay employment taxes for that worker. To get this relief, you must file all required information returns (Form 1099-MISC) on a basis consistent with your treatment of the worker. You (or your predecessor) must not have treated any worker holding a substantially similar position as an employee for any periods beginning after 1977.

IRS help. If you want the IRS to determine whether a worker is an employee, file Form SS-8, Determination of Worker Status for Purposes of Federal Employment Taxes and Income Tax Withholding.

3. Family Employees

Child employed by parents. Payments for the services of a child under age 18 who works for his or her parent in a trade or business are not subject to social security and Medicare taxes if the trade or business is a sole proprietorship or a partnership in which each partner is a parent of the child. If these services are for work other than in a trade or business, such as domestic work in the parent's private home, they are not subject to social security and Medicare taxes until the child reaches age 21. However, see *Covered services of a child or spouse* later. Payments for the services of a child under age 21 who works for his or her parent whether or not in a trade or business are not subject to federal unemployment (FUTA) tax. Although not subject to FUTA tax, the wages of a child may be subject to income tax withholding.

One spouse employed by another. The wages for the services of an individual who works for his or her spouse in a trade or business are subject to income tax withholding and social security and Medicare taxes, but not to FUTA tax. However, the services of one spouse employed by another in other than a trade or business, such as domestic service in a private home, are not subject to social security, Medicare, and FUTA taxes.

Covered services of a child or spouse. The wages for the services of a child or spouse are subject to income tax withholding as well as social security, Medicare, and FUTA taxes if he or she works for:

- A corporation, even if it is controlled by the child's parent or the individual's spouse,

- A partnership, even if the child's parent is a partner, unless each partner is a parent of the child,

- A partnership, even if the individual's spouse is a partner, or

- An estate, even if it is the estate of a deceased parent.

Parent employed by child. The wages for the services of a parent employed by his or her child in a trade or business are subject to income tax withholding and social security and Medicare taxes. Social security and Medicare taxes do not apply to wages paid to a parent for services not in a trade or business, but they do apply to domestic services if:

- The parent cares for a child who lives with a son or daughter and who is under age 18 or requires adult supervision for at least 4 continuous weeks in a calendar quarter due to a mental or physical condition and

- The son or daughter is a widow or widower, divorced, or married to a person who, because of a physical or mental condition, cannot care for the child during such period.

Wages paid to a parent employed by his or her child are not subject to FUTA tax, regardless of the type of services provided.

4. Employee's Social Security Number (SSN)

You are required to get each employee's name and SSN and to enter them on Form W-2. This requirement also applies to resident and nonresident alien employees. You should ask your employee to show you his or her social security card. The employee may show the card if it is available. You may, but are not required to, photocopy the

IRS Publication 15, Circular E (continued)

social security card if the employee provides it. If you do not provide the correct employee name and SSN on Form W-2, you may owe a penalty unless you have reasonable cause. See Publication 1586, Reasonable Cause Regulations and Requirements for Missing and Incorrect Name/TINs.

Any employee who is legally eligible to work in the United States and does not have a social security card can get one by completing Form SS-5, Application for a Social Security Card, and submitting the necessary documentation. You can get this form at SSA offices, by calling 1-800-772-1213, or from the SSA website at *www.socialsecurity.gov/online/ss-5.html*. The employee must complete and sign Form SS-5; it cannot be filed by the employer. If you file Form W-2 on paper and your employee applied for an SSN but does not have one when you must file Form W-2, enter "Applied For" on the form. If you are filing on magnetic media or electronically, enter all zeros (000-00-0000) in the social security number field. When the employee receives the SSN, file Copy A of Form W-2c, Corrected Wage and Tax Statement, with the SSA to show the employee's SSN. Furnish copies B, C, and 2 of Form W-2c to the employee. Up to five Forms W-2c per Form W-3c may now be filed over the Internet. For more information, visit the Social Security Administration's Employer Reporting Instructions and Information page at *www.socialsecurity.gov/employer*. Advise your employee to correct the SSN on his or her original Form W-2.

Note. Record the name and number of each employee exactly as they are shown on the employee's social security card. If the employee's name is not correct as shown on the card (for example, because of marriage or divorce), the employee should request a corrected card from the SSA. Continue to report the employee's wages under the old name until the employee shows you an updated social security card with the new name.

If your employee is given a new social security card following an adjustment to his or her resident status that shows a different name or SSN, file a Form W-2c for the most current year only.

IRS individual taxpayer identification numbers (ITINs) for aliens. Do not accept an ITIN in place of an SSN for employee identification or for work. An ITIN is only available to resident and nonresident aliens who are not eligible for U.S. employment and need identification for other tax purposes. You can identify an ITIN because it is a 9-digit number, beginning with the number "9" with either a "7" or "8" as the fourth digit and is formatted like an SSN (for example, 9NN-7N-NNNN).

 An individual with an ITIN who later becomes eligible to work in the United States must obtain an SSN.

Verification of social security numbers. The Social Security Administration (SSA) offers employers and authorized reporting agents two methods for verifying employee SSNs. Both methods match employee names and SSNs.

- **Telephone verification.** To verify up to five names and numbers, call 1-800-772-6270. To verify up to 50 names and numbers, contact your local Social Security office.

- **Large volume verification.** The **Employee Verification Service (EVS)** may be used to verify more than 50 employee names and SSNs. Paper listings are limited to 300 verifications. Preregistration is required for EVS or for requests made on magnetic media. For more information, call the EVS information line at 410-965-7140 or visit SSA's Employer Reporting Instructions and Information website at *www.socialsecurity.gov/employer*.

5. Wages and Other Compensation

Wages subject to federal employment taxes generally include all pay that you give to an employee for services performed. The pay may be in cash or in other forms. It includes salaries, nonqualified deferred compensation recognized under section 409A, vacation allowances, bonuses, commissions, and fringe benefits. It does not matter how you measure or make the payments. Amounts an employer pays as a bonus for signing or ratifying a contract in connection with the establishment of an employer-employee relationship and an amount paid to an employee for cancellation of an employment contract and relinquishment of contract rights are wages subject to social security, Medicare, and federal unemployment taxes and income tax withholding. Also, compensation paid to a former employee for services performed while still employed is wages subject to employment taxes. See section 6 for a discussion of tips and section 7 for a discussion of supplemental wages. Also, see section 15 for exceptions to the general rules for wages. Publication 15-A, Employer's Supplemental Tax Guide, provides additional information on wages and other compensation. Publication 15-B, Employer's Tax Guide to Fringe Benefits, provides information on other forms of compensation, including:

- Accident and health benefits,
- Achievement awards,
- Adoption assistance,
- Athletic facilities,
- De minimis (minimal) benefits,
- Dependent care assistance,
- Educational assistance,
- Employee discounts,
- Employee stock options,
- Group-term life insurance coverage,
- Lodging on your business premises,
- Meals,
- Moving expense reimbursements,
- No-additional-cost services,
- Retirement planning services,
- Transportation (commuting) benefits,
- Tuition reduction, and

IRS Publication 15, Circular E (continued)

- Working condition benefits.

Employee business expense reimbursements. A reimbursement or allowance arrangement is a system by which you pay the advances, reimbursements, and charges for your employees' substantiated business expenses. How you report a reimbursement or allowance amount depends on whether you have an accountable or a nonaccountable plan. If a single payment includes both wages and an expense reimbursement, you must specify the amount of the reimbursement.

These rules apply to all ordinary and necessary employee business expenses that would otherwise qualify for a deduction by the employee.

Accountable plan. To be an accountable plan, your reimbursement or allowance arrangement must require your employees to meet all three of the following rules.

1. They must have paid or incurred deductible expenses while performing services as your employees.

2. They must adequately account to you for these expenses within a reasonable period of time.

3. They must return any amounts in excess of expenses within a reasonable period of time.

Amounts paid under an accountable plan are not wages and are not subject to income tax withholding and payment of social security, Medicare, and federal unemployment (FUTA) taxes.

If the expenses covered by this arrangement are not substantiated (or amounts in excess of expenses are not returned within a reasonable period of time), the amount paid under the arrangement in excess of the substantiated expenses is treated as paid under a nonaccountable plan. This amount is subject to income tax withholding and payment of social security, Medicare, and FUTA taxes for the first payroll period following the end of the reasonable period.

A reasonable period of time depends on the facts and circumstances. Generally, it is considered reasonable if your employees receive their advance within 30 days of the time that they incur the expenses, adequately account for the expenses within 60 days after the expenses were paid or incurred, and return any amounts in excess of expenses within 120 days after the expenses were paid or incurred. Also, it is considered reasonable if you give your employees a periodic statement (at least quarterly) that asks them to either return or adequately account for outstanding amounts and they do so within 120 days.

Nonaccountable plan. Payments to your employee for travel and other necessary expenses of your business under a nonaccountable plan are wages and are treated as supplemental wages and subject to income tax withholding and payment of social security, Medicare, and FUTA taxes. Your payments are treated as paid under a nonaccountable plan if:

- Your employee is not required to or does not substantiate timely those expenses to you with receipts or other documentation,

- You advance an amount to your employee for business expenses and your employee is not required to or does not return timely any amount he or she does not use for business expenses, or

- You advance or pay an amount to your employee without regard for anticipated or incurred business expenses.

See section 7 for more information on supplemental wages.

Per diem or other fixed allowance. You may reimburse your employees by travel days, miles, or some other fixed allowance. In these cases, your employee is considered to have accounted to you if your reimbursement does not exceed rates established by the Federal Government. The 2004 standard mileage rate for auto expenses was 37.5 cents per mile. The rate for 2005 is 40.5 cents per mile. The government per diem rates for meals and lodging in the continental United States are listed in Publication 1542, Per Diem Rates. Other than the amount of these expenses, your employees' business expenses must be substantiated (for example, the business purpose of the travel or the number of business miles driven).

If the per diem or allowance paid exceeds the amounts specified, you must report the excess amount as wages. This excess amount is subject to income tax withholding and payment of social security, Medicare, and FUTA taxes. Show the amount equal to the specified amount (for example, the nontaxable portion) in box 12 of Form W-2 using code L.

Wages not paid in money. If in the course of your trade or business you pay your employees in a medium that is neither cash nor a readily negotiable instrument, such as a check, you are said to pay them "in kind." Payments in kind may be in the form of goods, lodging, food, clothing, or services. Generally, the fair market value of such payments at the time that they are provided is subject to federal income tax withholding and social security, Medicare, and FUTA taxes.

However, noncash payments for household work, agricultural labor, and service not in the employer's trade or business are exempt from social security, Medicare, and FUTA taxes. Withhold income tax on these payments only if you and the employee agree to do so. Nonetheless, noncash payments for agricultural labor, such as commodity wages, are treated as cash payments subject to employment taxes if the substance of the transaction is a cash payment.

Moving expenses. Reimbursed and employer-paid qualified moving expenses (those that would otherwise be deductible by the employee) are not includible in an employee's income unless you have knowledge that the employee deducted the expenses in a prior year. Reimbursed and employer-paid nonqualified moving expenses are includible in income and are subject to employment taxes and income tax withholding. For more information on moving expenses, see Publication 521, Moving Expenses.

Meals and lodging. The value of meals is not taxable income and is not subject to income tax withholding and social security, Medicare, and FUTA taxes if the meals are furnished for the employer's convenience and on the employer's premises. The value of lodging is not subject to income tax withholding and social security, Medicare, and FUTA taxes if the lodging is furnished for the employer's

IRS Publication 15, Circular E (continued)

convenience, on the employer's premises, and as a condition of employment.

"For the convenience of the employer" means that you have a substantial business reason for providing the meals and lodging other than to provide additional compensation to the employee. For example, meals that you provide at the place of work so that an employee is available for emergencies during his or her lunch period are generally considered to be for your convenience.

However, whether meals or lodging are provided for the convenience of the employer depends on all of the facts and circumstances. A written statement that the meals or lodging are for your convenience is not sufficient.

50% test. If over 50% of the employees who are provided meals on an employer's business premises receive these meals for the convenience of the employer, all meals provided on the premises are treated as furnished for the convenience of the employer. If this 50% test is met, the value of the meals is excludable from income for all employees and is not subject to federal income tax withholding or employment taxes.

For more information, see Publication 15-B, Employer's Tax Guide to Fringe Benefits.

Health insurance plans. If you pay the cost of an accident or health insurance plan for your employees, that may include an employee's spouse and dependents, your payments are not wages and are not subject to social security, Medicare, and FUTA taxes, or federal income tax withholding. Generally, this exclusion also applies to qualified long-term care insurance contracts. However, the cost of health insurance benefits must be included in the wages of S corporation employees who own more than 2% of the S corporation (2% shareholders).

Health Savings Accounts and medical savings accounts. Your contributions to an employee's Health Savings Account (HSA) or medical savings account (Archer MSA) are not subject to social security, Medicare, or FUTA taxes, or federal income tax withholding if it is reasonable to believe at the time of payment of the contributions that they will be excludable from the income of the employee. To the extent that it is not reasonable to believe that they will be excludable, your contributions are subject to these taxes. Employee contributions to their HSAs or MSAs through a payroll deduction plan must be included in wages and are subject to social security, Medicare, and FUTA taxes, and income tax withholding. For more information, see the Instructions for Form 8889.

Medical care reimbursements. Generally, medical care reimbursements paid for an employee under an employer's self-insured medical reimbursement plan are not wages and are not subject to social security, Medicare, and FUTA taxes, or income tax withholding. See Publication 15-B for an exception for highly compensated employees.

Fringe benefits. You generally must include fringe benefits in an employee's gross income (but see *Nontaxable fringe benefits* next). The benefits are subject to income tax withholding and employment taxes. Fringe benefits include cars that you provide, flights on aircraft that you provide, free or discounted commercial flights, vacations, discounts on property or services, memberships in country clubs or other social clubs, and tickets to entertainment or sporting events. In general, the amount that you must include is the amount by which the fair market value of the benefits is more than the sum of what the employee paid for it plus any amount that the law excludes. There are other special rules that you and your employees may use to value certain fringe benefits. See Publication 15-B for more information.

Nontaxable fringe benefits. Some fringe benefits are not taxable (or are minimally taxable) if certain conditions are met. See Publication 15-B for details. Examples include:

1. Services provided to your employees at no additional cost to you,

2. Qualified employee discounts,

3. Working condition fringes that are property or services that the employee could deduct as a business expense if he or she had paid for it. Examples include a company car for business use and subscriptions to business magazines.

4. Minimal value fringes (including an occasional cab ride when an employee must work overtime, local transportation benefits provided because of unsafe conditions and unusual circumstances, and meals that you provide at eating places that you run for your employees if the meals are not furnished at below cost),

5. Qualified transportation fringes subject to specified conditions and dollar limitations (including transportation in a commuter highway vehicle, any transit pass, and qualified parking),

6. Qualified moving expense reimbursement. See *Moving expenses,* above for details,

7. The use of on-premises athletic facilities, if substantially all of the use is by employees, their spouses, and their dependent children, and

8. Qualified tuition reduction that an educational organization provides to its employees for education. For more information, see Publication 970, Tax Benefits for Education.

However, do not exclude the following fringe benefits from the income of highly compensated employees unless the benefit is available to other employees on a nondiscriminatory basis.

- No-additional-cost services (item 1 above).

- Qualified employee discounts (item 2 above).

- Meals provided at an employer operated eating facility (included in item 4 above).

- Reduced tuition for education (item 8 above).

For more information, including the definition of a highly compensated employee, see Publication 15-B.

When fringe benefits are treated as paid. You may choose to treat certain noncash fringe benefits as paid by the pay period, by the quarter, or on any other basis that you choose as long as you treat the benefits as paid at least once a year. You do not have to make a formal choice

IRS Publication 15, Circular E (continued)

of payment dates or notify the IRS of the dates that you choose. You do not have to make this choice for all employees. You may change methods as often as you like, as long as you treat all benefits provided in a calendar year as paid by December 31 of the calendar year. See Publication 15-B for more information, including a discussion of the special accounting rule for fringe benefits provided during November and December.

Valuation of fringe benefits. Generally, you must determine the value of fringe benefits no later than January 31 of the next year. Prior to January 31, you may reasonably estimate the value of the fringe benefits for purposes of withholding and depositing on time.

Withholding on fringe benefits. You may add the value of fringe benefits to regular wages for a payroll period and figure withholding taxes on the total, or you may withhold federal income tax on the value of the fringe benefits at the flat 25% supplemental wage rate. However, see *Supplemental wage payments exceeding $1,000,000* in section 7.

You may choose not to withhold income tax on the value of an employee's personal use of a vehicle that you provide. You must, however, withhold social security and Medicare taxes on the use of the vehicle. See Publication 15-B for more information on this election.

Depositing taxes on fringe benefits. Once you choose payment dates for fringe benefits (discussed above), you must deposit taxes in the same deposit period that you treat the fringe benefits as paid. To avoid a penalty, deposit the taxes following the general deposit rules for that deposit period.

If you determine by January 31 that you overestimated the value of a fringe benefit at the time you withheld and deposited for it, you may claim a refund for the overpayment or have it applied to your next employment tax return. See *Valuation of fringe benefits* above. If you underestimated the value and deposited too little, you may be subject to a failure to deposit penalty. See section 11 for information on deposit penalties.

If you deposited the required amount of taxes but withheld a lesser amount from the employee, you can recover from the employee the social security, Medicare, or income taxes that you deposited on his or her behalf, and included in the employee's Form W-2. However, you must recover the income taxes before April 1 of the following year.

Sick pay. In general, sick pay is any amount that you pay under a plan to an employee who is unable to work because of sickness or injury. These amounts are sometimes paid by a third party, such as an insurance company or an employees' trust. In either case, these payments are subject to social security, Medicare, and FUTA taxes. Sick pay becomes exempt from these taxes after the end of six calendar months after the calendar month that the employee last worked for the employer. The payments are also subject to federal income tax. See Publication 15-A for more information.

6. Tips

Tips that your employee receives from customers are generally subject to withholding. Your employee must re-

port cash tips to you by the 10th of the month after the month that the tips are received. The report should include tips that you paid over to the employee for charge customers and tips that the employee received directly from customers. No report is required for months when tips are less than $20. Your employee reports the tips on Form 4070, Employee's Report of Tips to Employer, or on a similar statement. The statement must be signed by the employee and must show the following:

- The employee's name, address, and SSN.
- Your name and address.
- The month or period that the report covers.
- The total of tips received during the month or period.

Both Forms 4070 and 4070-A, Employee's Daily Record of Tips, are included in Publication 1244, Employee's Daily Record of Tips and Report to Employer.

You must collect income tax, employee social security tax, and employee Medicare tax on the employee's tips. You can collect these taxes from the employee's wages or from other funds that he or she makes available. See *Tips treated as supplemental wages* in section 7 for further information. Stop collecting the employee social security tax when his or her wages and tips for tax year 2005 reach $90,000; collect the income and employee Medicare taxes for the whole year on all wages and tips. You are responsible for the employer social security tax on wages and tips until the wages (including tips) reach the limit. You are responsible for the employer Medicare tax for the whole year on all wages and tips. File Form 941 to report withholding and employment taxes on tips.

If, by the 10th of the month after the month for which you received an employee's report on tips, you do not have enough employee funds available to deduct the employee tax, you no longer have to collect it. If there are not enough funds available, withhold taxes in the following order.

1. Withhold on regular wages and other compensation.
2. Withhold social security and Medicare taxes on tips.
3. Withhold income tax on tips.

Show these tips and any uncollected social security and Medicare taxes on Form W-2 and on lines 5b and 5c of Form 941. Report an adjustment on line 7c of Form 941 for the uncollected social security and Medicare taxes. Enter the amount of uncollected social security and Medicare taxes in box 12 of Form W-2 with codes A and B. See section 13 and the Instructions for Forms W-2 and W-3.

If an employee reports to you in writing $20 or more of tips in a month, the tips are also subject to FUTA tax.

Note. You are permitted to establish a system for electronic tip reporting by employees. See Regulations section 31.6053-1(d).

Allocated tips. If you operate a large food or beverage establishment, you must report allocated tips under certain circumstances. However, do not withhold income, social security, or Medicare taxes on allocated tips.

A large food or beverage establishment is one that provides food or beverages for consumption on the premises, where tipping is customary, and where there were

IRS Publication 15, Circular E (continued)

normally more than 10 employees on a typical business day during the preceding year.

The tips may be allocated by one of three methods—hours worked, gross receipts, or good faith agreement. For information about these allocation methods, including the requirement to file Forms 8027 on magnetic media or electronically if 250 or more forms are filed, see the separate Instructions for Form 8027.

Tip Rate Determination and Education Program. Employers may participate in the Tip Rate Determination and Education Program. The program consists of two voluntary agreements developed to improve tip income reporting by helping taxpayers to understand and meet their tip reporting responsibilities. The two agreements are the Tip Rate Determination Agreement (TRDA) and the Tip Reporting Alternative Commitment (TRAC). To find out more about this program, or to identify the IRS Tip Coordinator for your state, call the IRS at 1-800-829-4933. To get more information about TRDA or TRAC agreements, access the IRS website at *www.irs.gov* and search for Market Segment Understanding (MSU) agreements.

7. Supplemental Wages

Supplemental wages are compensation paid in addition to an employee's regular wages. They include, but are not limited to, bonuses, commissions, overtime pay, payments for accumulated sick leave, severance pay, awards, prizes, back pay and retroactive pay increases for current employees, and payments for nondeductible moving expenses. Other payments subject to the supplemental wage rules include taxable fringe benefits and expense allowances paid under a nonaccountable plan. How you withhold on supplemental payments depends on whether the supplemental payment is identified as a separate payment from regular wages.

Supplemental wages combined with regular wages. If you pay supplemental wages with regular wages but do not specify the amount of each, withhold federal income tax as if the total were a single payment for a regular payroll period.

Supplemental wages identified separately from regular wages. If you pay supplemental wages separately (or combine them in a single payment and specify the amount of each), the federal income tax withholding method depends partly on whether you withhold income tax from your employee's regular wages. However, separate rules apply to the extent the supplemental wages paid to any one employee during the year exceed $1,000,000. The American Jobs Creation Act of 2004 provides that if a supplemental wage payment, together with other supplemental wage payments made to the employee during the calendar year exceeds $1,000,000, the excess will be subject to withholding at 35 percent (or the highest rate of income tax for the year). This provision is effective with respect to payments made after December 31, 2004. The Internal Revenue Service will be providing guidance about this provision in the near future.

1. If you withheld income tax from an employee's regular wages, you can use one of the following methods for the supplemental wages.

   a. Withhold a flat 25% (no other percentage allowed).

   b. Add the supplemental and regular wages for the most recent payroll period this year. Then figure the income tax withholding as if the total was a single payment. Subtract the tax already withheld from the regular wages. Withhold the remaining tax from the supplemental wages.

2. If you did not withhold income tax from the employee's regular wages, use method 1-b above. This would occur, for example, when the value of the employee's withholding allowances claimed on Form W-4 is more than the wages.

Regardless of the method that you use to withhold income tax on supplemental wages, they are subject to social security, Medicare, and FUTA taxes.

Example 1. You pay John Peters a base salary on the 1st of each month. He is single and claims one withholding allowance. In January of 2005, he is paid $1,000. Using the wage bracket tables, you withhold $53 from this amount. In February 2005, he receives salary of $1,000 plus a commission of $2,000, which you include in regular wages. You figure the withholding based on the total of $3,000. The correct withholding from the tables is $363.

Example 2. You pay Sharon Warren a base salary on the 1st of each month. She is single and claims one allowance. Her May 1, 2005, pay is $2,000. Using the wage bracket tables, you withhold $200. On May 14, 2005, she receives a bonus of $2,000. Electing to use supplemental payment method 1-b, you:

1. Add the bonus amount to the amount of wages from the most recent pay date ($2,000 + $2,000 = $4,000),

2. Determine the amount of withholding on the combined $4,000 amount to be $613 using the wage bracket tables,

3. Subtract the amount withheld from wages on the most recent pay date from the combined withholding amount ($613 − $200 = $413), and

4. Withhold $413 from the bonus payment.

Example 3. The facts are the same as in Example 2, except that you elect to use the flat rate method of withholding on the bonus. You withhold 25% of $2,000, or $500, from Sharon's bonus payment.

Supplemental wage payments exceeding $1,000,000. You must withhold federal income tax of 35% on any supplemental wages exceeding $1,000,000 that you pay to an individual during the year. Withhold using the 35% rate without regard to the employee's Form W-4. In determining supplemental wages paid to the employee during the year, include payments from all businesses under common control.

Page 13

IRS Publication 15, Circular E (continued)

Tips treated as supplemental wages. Withhold income tax on tips from wages or from other funds that the employee makes available. If an employee receives regular wages and reports tips, figure income tax as if the tips were supplemental wages. If you have not withheld income tax from the regular wages, add the tips to the regular wages. Then withhold income tax on the total. If you withheld income tax from the regular wages, you can withhold on the tips by method 1-a or 1-b above.

Vacation pay. Vacation pay is subject to withholding as if it were a regular wage payment. When vacation pay is in addition to regular wages for the vacation period, treat it as a supplemental wage payment. If the vacation pay is for a time longer than your usual payroll period, spread it over the pay periods for which you pay it.

8. Payroll Period

Your payroll period is a period of service for which you usually pay wages. When you have a regular payroll period, withhold income tax for that time period even if your employee does not work the full period.

When you do not have a regular payroll period, withhold the tax as if you paid wages for a daily or miscellaneous payroll period. Figure the number of days (including Sundays and holidays) in the period covered by the wage payment. If the wages are unrelated to a specific length of time (for example, commissions paid on completion of a sale), count back the number of days from the payment period to the latest of:

- The last wage payment made during the same calendar year,

- The date employment began, if during the same calendar year, or

- January 1 of the same year.

When you pay an employee for a period of less than one week, and the employee signs a statement under penalties of perjury indicating that he or she is not working for any other employer during the same week for wages subject to withholding, figure withholding based on a weekly payroll period. If the employee later begins to work for another employer for wages subject to withholding, the employee must notify you within 10 days. You then figure withholding based on the daily or miscellaneous period.

9. Withholding From Employees' Wages

Income Tax Withholding

To know how much federal income tax to withhold from employees' wages, you should have a Form W-4, Employee's Withholding Allowance Certificate, on file for each employee. Encourage your employees to file an updated Form W-4 for 2005, especially if they owed taxes or received a large refund when filing their 2004 tax return. Advise your employees to use the Withholding Calculator on the IRS website at *www.irs.gov/individuals* for help in determining how many withholding allowances to claim on their Form W-4.

Ask all new employees to give you a signed Form W-4 when they start work. Make the form effective with the first wage payment. If a new employee does not give you a completed Form W-4, withhold income tax as if he or she is single, with no withholding allowances.

You may establish a system to electronically receive Forms W-4 from your employees. See Regulations section 31.3402(f)(5)-1(c) for more information.

A Form W-4 remains in effect until the employee gives you a new one. If an employee gives you a Form W-4 that replaces an existing Form W-4, begin withholding no later than the start of the first payroll period ending on or after the 30th day from the date when you received the replacement Form W-4. For exceptions, see *Exemption from federal income tax withholding, Sending certain Forms W-4 to the IRS,* and *Invalid Forms W-4* later.

The amount of any federal income tax withholding must be based on marital status and withholding allowances. Your employees may not base their withholding amounts on a fixed dollar amount or percentage. However, an employee may specify a dollar amount to be withheld in addition to the amount of withholding based on filing status and withholding allowances claimed on Form W-4.

Employees may claim fewer withholding allowances than they are entitled to claim. They may wish to claim fewer allowances to ensure that they have enough withholding or to offset the tax on other sources of taxable income that are not subject to adequate withholding.

Note. A Form W-4 that makes a change for the next calendar year will not take effect in the current calendar year.

See Publication 505, Tax Withholding and Estimated Tax, for detailed instructions for completing Form W-4. Along with Form W-4, you may wish to order Publication 505 and Publication 919, How Do I Adjust My Tax Withholding, for use by your employees.

When you receive a new Form W-4 from an employee, do not adjust withholding for pay periods before the effective date of the new form. Also, do not accept any withholding or estimated tax payments from your employees in addition to withholding based on their Form W-4. If they require additional withholding, they should submit a new Form W-4 and, if necessary, pay estimated tax by filing Form 1040-ES, Estimated Tax for Individuals.

Exemption from federal income tax withholding. Generally, an employee may claim exemption from federal income tax withholding because he or she had no income tax liability last year and expects none this year. See the Form W-4 instructions for more information. However, the wages are still subject to social security and Medicare taxes.

A Form W-4 claiming exemption from withholding is valid for only one calendar year. To continue to be exempt from withholding in the next year, an employee must give you a new Form W-4 by February 15 of that year. If the employee does not give you a new Form W-4, withhold tax as if the employee is single with zero withholding allowances or withhold based on the last valid Form W-4 you have for the employee.

IRS Publication 15, Circular E (continued)

Withholding on nonresident aliens. In general, if you pay wages to nonresident aliens, you must withhold federal income tax, social security, and Medicare taxes as you would for a U.S. citizen. However, see Publication 515, Withholding of Tax on Nonresident Aliens and Foreign Entities, for exceptions to these general rules.

Form W-4. When completing Form W-4, nonresident aliens are required to:

- Not claim exemption from income tax withholding,

- Request withholding as if they are single, regardless of their actual marital status,

- Claim only one allowance (if the nonresident alien is a resident of Canada, Mexico, Japan, or South Korea, he or she may claim more than one allowance), and

- Request an additional income tax withholding amount, depending on the payroll period, as follows:

Payroll Period	Additional Withholding
Weekly	7.60
Biweekly	15.30
Semimonthly	16.60
Monthly	33.10
Quarterly	99.40
Semiannually	198.80
Annually	397.50
Daily or Miscellaneous (each day of the payroll period)	1.50

Note. Nonresident alien students from India are not subject to the additional income tax withholding requirement.

Form 8233. If a nonresident alien employee claims a tax treaty exemption from withholding, the employee must submit Form 8233, Exemption from Withholding or Compensation for Independent (and Certain Dependent) Personal Services of a Nonresident Alien Individual, with respect to the income exempt under the treaty, instead of Form W-4. See Publication 515 for details.

Sending certain Forms W-4 to the IRS. Generally, you must send to the IRS copies of certain Forms W-4 that you received during the quarter from employees still employed by you at the end of the quarter. Send copies of Form W-4 when the employee claims (a) more than 10 withholding allowances or (b) exemption from withholding and his or her wages would normally be more than $200 per week. Send the copies to the IRS office where you file your Form 941. You are not required to send any other Forms W-4 unless the IRS notifies you in writing to do so.

Send in Forms W-4 that meet either of the above conditions each quarter with Form 941. Complete boxes 8 and 10 on any Forms W-4 that you send in. You may use box 9 to identify the office responsible for processing the employee's payroll information. Also send copies of any written statements from employees in support of the claims made on their Forms W-4. Send these statements even if the Forms W-4 are not in effect at the end of the quarter. You can send them to the IRS more often if you like. If you do so, include a cover letter giving your name, address, EIN, and the number of forms included. In certain cases, the IRS may notify you in writing that you must submit specified Forms W-4 more frequently, separate from your Form 941.

Note. Please make sure that the copies of Form W-4 that you send to the IRS are clear and legible.

If your Forms 941 are filed electronically, this Form W-4 information also should be filed with the IRS on magnetic media or electronically. See *Filing Form W-4 on magnetic media or electronically* below. Electronic filers of Form 941 may send paper Forms W-4 to the IRS with a cover letter if they are unable to file them electronically. If you file Form 941 by 941TeleFile, send your paper Forms W-4 to the IRS with a cover letter.

Note. Any Form W-4 that you send to the IRS without a Form 941 should be mailed to the "Return Without A Payment" address in the instructions for Form 941.

Base any employee federal income tax withholding on the Forms W-4 that you send in unless the IRS notifies you in writing to do otherwise. If the IRS notifies you about a particular employee, base his or her income tax withholding on the number of withholding allowances shown in the IRS notice. The employee will get a similar notice directly from the IRS. If the employee later gives you a new Form W-4, follow it only if: (a) exempt status is not claimed and (b) the number of withholding allowances is equal to or lower than the number in the IRS notice. Otherwise, disregard it and do not submit it to the IRS. Continue to follow the IRS notice.

If the employee prepares a new Form W-4 explaining any difference with the IRS notice, he or she may either submit it to the IRS or to you. If submitted to you, send the Form W-4 and an explanation to the IRS office shown in the notice. Continue to withhold based on the notice until the IRS tells you to follow the new Form W-4.

Filing Form W-4 on magnetic media or electronically. Form W-4 information may be filed with the IRS electronically. If you wish to file electronically, you must submit Form 4419, Application for Filing Information Returns Electronically/Magnetically, to request authorization. See Publication 1245, Specification for Filing Form W-4, Employee's Withholding Allowance Certificate, Magnetically or Electronically. To get more information about electronic filing, call the IRS Martinsburg Computing Center at 1-866-455-7438 (toll free) or 304-263-8700 (not toll free).

Note. Any Forms W-4 with employee supporting statements that you are required to submit to the IRS must be submitted on paper. They cannot be submitted on magnetic media or electronically.

Invalid Forms W-4. Any unauthorized change or addition to Form W-4 makes it invalid. This includes taking out any language by which the employee certifies that the form is correct. A Form W-4 is also invalid if, by the date an employee gives it to you, he or she indicates in any way that it is false. An employee who files a false Form W-4 may be subject to a $500 penalty.

When you get an invalid Form W-4, do not use it to figure federal income tax withholding. Tell the employee

IRS Publication 15, Circular E (continued)

that it is invalid and ask for another one. If the employee does not give you a valid one, withhold taxes as if the employee was single and claiming no withholding allowances. However, if you have an earlier Form W-4 for this worker that is valid, withhold as you did before.

Amounts exempt from levy on wages, salary, and other income. If you receive a Notice of Levy on Wages, Salary, and Other Income (Forms 668-W(c), or 668-W(c)(DO)), you must withhold amounts as described in the instructions for these forms. Publication 1494, Table for Figuring Amount Exempt From Levy on Wages, Salary, and Other Income (Forms 668-W(c), 668-W(c)(DO) and 668-W(ICS)) 2005, shows the exempt amount. If a levy issued in a prior year is still in effect and the taxpayer submits a new Statement of Exemptions and Filing Status, use the current year Publication 1494 to compute the exempt amount.

Social Security and Medicare Taxes

The Federal Insurance Contributions Act (FICA) provides for a federal system of old-age, survivors, disability, and hospital insurance. The old-age, survivors, and disability insurance part is financed by the social security tax. The hospital insurance part is financed by the Medicare tax. Each of these taxes is reported separately.

Generally, you are required to withhold social security and Medicare taxes from your employees' wages and you must also pay a matching amount of these taxes. Certain types of wages and compensation are not subject to social security taxes. See sections 5 and 15 for details. Generally, employee wages are subject to social security and Medicare taxes regardless of the employee's age or whether he or she is receiving social security benefits. If the employee reported tips, see section 6.

Tax rates and the social security wage base limit. Social security and Medicare taxes have different rates and only the social security tax has a wage base limit. The wage base limit is the maximum wage that is subject to the tax for the year. Determine the amount of withholding for social security and Medicare taxes by multiplying each payment by the employee tax rate. There are no withholding allowances for social security and Medicare taxes.

The employee tax rate for social security is 6.2% (amount withheld). The employer tax rate for social security is also 6.2% (12.4% total). The 2004 wage base limit was $87,900. For 2005, the wage base limit is $90,000.

The employee tax rate for Medicare is 1.45% (amount withheld). The employer tax rate for Medicare is also 1.45% (2.9% total). There is no wage base limit for Medicare tax; all covered wages are subject to Medicare tax.

Successor employer. If you received all or most of the property used in the trade or business of another employer, or a unit of that employer's trade or business, you may include the wages that the other employer paid to your acquired employees before the transfer of property when you figure the annual wage base limit for social security. You should determine whether or not you should file Schedule D (Form 941), Report of Discrepancies Caused by Acquisitions, Statutory Mergers, or Consolidations, by reviewing the Instructions for Schedule D (Form 941). See Regulations section 31.3121(a)(1)-1(b) for more information. Also see Rev. Proc. 2004-53 for more information.

You can find Rev. Proc. 2004-53 on page 320 of Internal Revenue Bulletin 2004-34 at *www.irs.gov/pub/irs-irbs/ irb04-34.pdf.*

Example. Early in 2005, you bought all of the assets of a plumbing business from Mr. Martin. Mr. Brown, who had been employed by Mr. Martin and received $2,000 in wages before the date of purchase, continued to work for you. The wages that you paid to Mr. Brown are subject to social security taxes on the first $88,000 ($90,000 minus $2,000). Medicare tax is due on all of the wages that you pay him during the calendar year.

International social security agreements. The United States has social security agreements with many countries that eliminate dual taxation and dual coverage. Compensation subject to social security and Medicare taxes may be exempt under one of these agreements. You can get more information and a list of agreement countries from SSA at *www.socialsecurity.gov/international* or see section 7 of Publication 15-A, Employer's Supplemental Tax Guide.

Part-Time Workers

For federal income tax withholding and social security, Medicare, and federal unemployment (FUTA) tax purposes, there are no differences among full-time employees, part-time employees, and employees hired for short periods. It does not matter whether the worker has another job or has the maximum amount of social security tax withheld by another employer. Income tax withholding may be figured the same way as for full-time workers. Or it may be figured by the part-year employment method explained in section 9 of Publication 15-A.

---

10. Advance Earned Income Credit (EIC) Payment

An employee who expects to be eligible for the earned income credit (EIC) and expects to have a qualifying child is entitled to receive EIC payments with his or her pay during the year. To get these payments, the employee must provide to you a properly completed Form W-5, Earned Income Credit Advance Payment Certificate, using either the paper form or an approved electronic format. You are required to make advance EIC payments to employees who give you a completed and signed Form W-5. You may establish a system to electronically receive Forms W-5 from your employees. See Announcement 99-3 for information on electronic requirements for Form W-5. You can find Announcement 99-3 on page 15 of Internal Revenue Bulletin 1999-3 at *www.irs.gov/pub/ irs-irbs/irb99-03.pdf.*

Certain employees who do not have a qualifying child may be able to claim the EIC on their tax return. However, they cannot get advance EIC payments.

For 2005, the advance payment can be as much as $1,597. The tables that begin on page 58 reflect that limit.

Form W-5. Form W-5 states the eligibility requirements for receiving advance EIC payments. On Form W-5, an employee states that he or she expects to be eligible to

IRS Publication 15, Circular E (continued)

claim the EIC and shows whether he or she has another Form W-5 in effect with any other current employer. The employee also shows the following:

- Whether he or she expects to have a qualifying child.
- Whether he or she will file a joint return.
- If the employee is married, whether his or her spouse has a Form W-5 in effect with any employer.

An employee may have only one certificate in effect with a current employer at one time. If an employee is married and his or her spouse also works, each spouse should file a separate Form W-5.

Length of effective period. Form W-5 is effective for the first payroll period ending on or after the date the employee gives you the form (or the first wage payment made without regard to a payroll period). It remains in effect until the end of the calendar year unless the employee revokes it or files another one. Eligible employees must file a new Form W-5 each year.

Change of status. If an employee gives you a signed Form W-5 and later becomes ineligible for advance EIC payments, he or she must revoke Form W-5 within 10 days after learning about the change of circumstances. The employee must give you a new Form W-5 stating that he or she is no longer eligible for or no longer wants advance EIC payments.

If an employee's situation changes because his or her spouse files a Form W-5, the employee must file a new Form W-5 showing that his or her spouse has a Form W-5 in effect with an employer. This will reduce the maximum amount of advance payments that you can make to that employee.

If an employee's spouse has filed a Form W-5 that is no longer in effect, the employee may file a new Form W-5 with you, but is not required to do so. A new form will certify that the spouse does not have a Form W-5 in effect and will increase the maximum amount of advance payments you can make to that employee.

Invalid Form W-5. The Form W-5 is invalid if it is incomplete, unsigned, or has an alteration or unauthorized addition. The form has been altered if any of the language has been deleted. Any writing added to the form other than the requested entries is an unauthorized addition.

You should consider a Form W-5 invalid if an employee has made an oral or written statement that clearly shows the Form W-5 to be false. If you receive an invalid form, tell the employee that it is invalid as of the date that he or she made the oral or written statement. For advance EIC payment purposes, the invalid Form W-5 is considered void.

You are not required to determine if a completed and signed Form W-5 is correct. However, you should contact the IRS if you have reason to believe that it contains an incorrect statement.

How to figure the advance EIC payment. To figure the amount of the advance EIC payment to include with the employee's pay, you must consider:

- Wages, including reported tips, for the same period. Generally, figure advance EIC payments using the amount of wages subject to income tax withholding. If an employee's wages are not subject to income

tax withholding, use the amount of wages subject to withholding for social security and Medicare taxes.

- Whether the employee is married or single.
- Whether a married employee's spouse has a Form W-5 in effect with an employer.

Do not consider combat zone pay received by the employee and excluded from income as earned income when figuring the advance EIC payment.

Note. If during the year you have paid an employee total wages of at least $31,030 ($33,030 if married filing jointly), you must stop making advance EIC payments to that employee for the rest of the year.

Figure the amount of advance EIC to include in the employee's pay by using the tables that begin on page 58. There are separate tables for employees whose spouses have a Form W-5 in effect. See page 35 for instructions on using the advance EIC payment tables. The amount of advance EIC paid to an employee during 2005 cannot exceed $1,597.

Paying the advance EIC to employees. An advance EIC payment is not wages and is not subject to withholding of income, social security, or Medicare taxes. An advance EIC payment does not change the amount of income, social security, or Medicare taxes that you withheld from the employee's wages. You add the EIC payment to the employee's **net** pay for the pay period. At the end of the year, you show the total advance EIC payments in box 9 on Form W-2. Do not include this amount as wages in box 1.

Employer's returns. Show the total payments that you made to employees on the advance EIC payments line (line 9) of your Form 941. Subtract this amount from your total taxes on line 8. See the separate Instructions for Form 941. Reduce the amounts reported on line 15 of Form 941 or on appropriate lines of Schedule B (Form 941), Report of Tax Liability for Semiweekly Schedule Depositors, by any advance EIC paid to your employees.

Generally, employers will make the advance EIC payment from withheld income tax and employee and employer social security and Medicare taxes. These taxes are normally required to be paid over to the IRS either through federal tax deposits or with employment tax returns. For purposes of deposit due dates, advance EIC payments are treated as deposits of these taxes on the day that you pay wages (including the advance EIC payment) to your employees. The payments are treated as deposits of these taxes in the following order: (1) income tax withholding, (2) withheld employee social security and Medicare taxes, and (3) the employer's share of social security and Medicare taxes.

Example. You have 10 employees, each entitled to an advance EIC payment of $10. The total amount of advance EIC payments that you make for the payroll period is $100. The total amount of income tax withholding for the payroll period is $90. The total employee and employer social security and Medicare taxes for the payroll period is $122.60 ($61.30 each).

You are considered to have made a deposit of $100 advance EIC payment on the day that you paid wages. The $100 is treated as if you deposited the $90 total income tax withholding and $10 of the employee social security and

IRS Publication 15, Circular E (continued)

Medicare taxes. You remain liable for depositing the remaining $112.60 of the social security and Medicare taxes ($51.30 + $61.30 = $112.60).

Advance EIC payments more than taxes due. For any payroll period, if the total advance EIC payments are more than the total payroll taxes (withheld income tax and both employee and employer shares of social security and Medicare taxes), you may choose either to:

1. Reduce each employee's advance payment proportionally so that the total advance EIC payments equal the amount of taxes due or

2. Elect to make full payment of the advance EIC and treat the excess as an advance payment of employment taxes.

Example. You have 10 employees who are each entitled to an advance EIC payment of $10. The total amount of advance EIC payable for the payroll period is $100. The total employment tax for the payroll period is $90 (including income tax withholding and social security and Medicare taxes). The advance EIC payable is $10 more than the total employment tax. The $10 excess is 10% of the advance EIC payable ($100). You may—

- Reduce each employee's payment by 10% (to $9 each) so that the advance EIC payments equal your total employment tax ($90) or

- Pay each employee $10, and treat the excess $10 as an advance payment of employment taxes. Attach a statement to Form 941 showing the excess advance EIC payments and the pay period(s) to which the excess applies.

U.S. territories. If you are in American Samoa, the Commonwealth of the Northern Mariana Islands, Guam, or the U.S. Virgin Islands, consult your local tax office for information on the EIC. You cannot take advance EIC payments into account on Form 941-SS.

Required Notice to Employees

You must notify employees who have no federal income tax withheld that they may be able to claim a tax refund because of the EIC. Although you do not have to notify employees who claim exemption from withholding on Form W-4, Employee's Withholding Allowance Certificate, about the EIC, you are encouraged to notify any employees whose wages for 2004 were less than $34,458 ($35,458 if married filing jointly) that they may be eligible to claim the credit for 2004. This is because eligible employees may get a refund of the amount of EIC that is more than the tax that they owe.

You will meet this notification requirement if you issue to the employee IRS Form W-2 with the EIC notice on the back of Copy B, or a substitute Form W-2 with the same statement. You will also meet the requirement by providing Notice 797, Possible Federal Tax Refund Due to the Earned Income Credit (EIC), or your own statement that contains the same wording.

If a substitute Form W-2 is given to the employee on time but does not have the required statement, you must

notify the employee within one week of the date that the substitute Form W-2 is given. If Form W-2 is required but is not given on time, you must give the employee Notice 797 or your written statement by the date that Form W-2 is required to be given. If Form W-2 is not required, you must notify the employee by February 7, 2005.

11. Depositing Taxes

In general, you must deposit federal income tax withheld and both the employer and employee social security and Medicare taxes plus or minus any prior period adjustments to your tax liability (minus any advance EIC payments) by mailing or delivering a check, money order, or cash to a financial institution that is an authorized depositary for federal taxes. However, some taxpayers are required to deposit using the Electronic Federal Tax Payment System (EFTPS). See *How To Deposit* on page 21 for information on electronic deposit requirements for 2005.

Payment with return. You may make a payment with Form 941 instead of depositing if one of the following applies.

- You report less than a $2,500 tax liability for the quarter on line 10 of Form 941, and you pay in full with a timely filed return. (However, if you are unsure that you will report less than $2,500, deposit under the appropriate rules so that you will not be subject to failure to deposit penalties.)

- You are a monthly schedule depositor (defined below) and make a payment in accordance with the *Accuracy of Deposits Rule* discussed on page 21. This payment may be $2,500 or more.

Separate deposit requirements for nonpayroll (Form 945) tax liabilities. Separate deposits are required for nonpayroll and payroll income tax withholding. Do not combine deposits for Forms 941 and 945 tax liabilities. Generally, the deposit rules for nonpayroll liabilities are the same as discussed below, except that the rules apply to an annual rather than a quarterly return period. Thus, the $2,500 threshold for the deposit requirement discussed above applies to Form 945 on an annual basis. See the separate Instructions for Form 945 for more information.

When To Deposit

There are two deposit schedules—monthly or semiweekly—for determining when you deposit social security, Medicare, and withheld income taxes. These schedules tell you when a deposit is due after a tax liability arises (for example, when you have a payday). Prior to the beginning of each calendar year, you must determine which of the two deposit schedules that you are required to use. The deposit schedule that you must use is based on the total tax liability that you reported on Form 941 during a four-quarter lookback period discussed below. Your deposit schedule is not determined by how often you pay your employees or make deposits. See *Application of Monthly and Semiweekly Schedules* on page 20.

IRS Publication 15, Circular E (continued)

 These rules do not apply to federal unemployment (FUTA) tax. See section 14 for information on depositing FUTA tax.

Lookback period. Your deposit schedule for a calendar year is determined from the total taxes (that is, not reduced by any advance EIC payments) reported on line 8 of your Forms 941 in a four-quarter lookback period. (Refer to line 11 on pre-2005 versions of Form 941.) The lookback period begins July 1 and ends June 30 as shown in Table 1 below. If you reported $50,000 or less of taxes for the lookback period, you are a monthly schedule depositor; if you reported more than $50,000, you are a semiweekly schedule depositor.

Table 1. **Lookback Period for Calendar Year 2005**

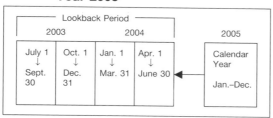

Adjustments and the lookback rule. Determine your tax liability for the four quarters in the lookback period based on the tax liability as reported on your Form 941. If you made adjustments to correct errors on previously filed Forms 941, these adjustments do not affect the amount of tax liability for purposes of the lookback rule.

If you report adjustments on your current Form 941 to correct errors on prior Forms 941, include these adjustments as part of your tax liability for the current quarter and adjust your deposits accordingly. If you filed Form 843 to claim a refund for a prior period overpayment, your tax liability does not change for either the prior period or the current period for purposes of the lookback rule.

Example. An employer originally reported a tax liability of $45,000 for the four quarters in the lookback period ending June 30, 2004. The employer discovered during January 2005 that the tax during one of the lookback period quarters was understated by $10,000 and corrected this error with an adjustment on the 2005 first quarter return. This employer is a monthly schedule depositor for 2005 because the lookback period tax liabilities are based on the amounts originally reported, and they were $50,000 or less. The $10,000 adjustment is part of the 2005 first quarter tax liability.

Deposit period. The term deposit period refers to the period during which tax liabilities are accumulated for each required deposit due date. For monthly schedule depositors, the deposit period is a calendar month. The deposit periods for semiweekly schedule depositors are Wednesday through Friday and Saturday through Tuesday.

Monthly Deposit Schedule

You are a monthly schedule depositor for a calendar year if the total taxes on line 8 of Form 941 for the four quarters in your lookback period were $50,000 or less. (Refer to line 11 on pre-2005 versions of Form 941.) Under the monthly deposit schedule, deposit Form 941 taxes on payments made during a month by the 15th day of the following month. See also *Deposits on Banking Days Only* later.

Monthly schedule depositors should not file Form 941 on a monthly basis. Also, do not file Form 941-M, Employer's Monthly Federal Tax Return, unless you are instructed to do so by an IRS representative.

New employers. During the first calendar year of your business, your tax liability for each quarter in the lookback period is considered to be zero. Therefore, you are a monthly schedule depositor for the first calendar year of your business. But see the *$100,000 Next-Day Deposit Rule* on page 20.

Semiweekly Deposit Schedule

You are a semiweekly schedule depositor for a calendar year if the total taxes on line 8 of Form 941 during your lookback period were more than $50,000. (Refer to line 11 on pre-2005 versions of Form 941.) Under the semiweekly deposit schedule, deposit Form 941 taxes for payments made on Wednesday, Thursday, and/or Friday by the following Wednesday. Deposit amounts accumulated for payments made on Saturday, Sunday, Monday, and/or Tuesday by the following Friday. See also *Deposits on Banking Days Only* later.

Note. Semiweekly schedule depositors must complete Schedule B (Form 941), Report of Tax Liability for Semiweekly Schedule Depositors, and submit it with Form 941.

Table 2. **Semiweekly Deposit Schedule**

IF the payday falls on a . . .	THEN deposit taxes by the following . . .
Wednesday, Thursday, and/or Friday	Wednesday
Saturday, Sunday, Monday, and/or Tuesday	Friday

Semiweekly deposit period spanning two quarters. If you have more than one pay date during a semiweekly period and the pay dates fall in different calendar quarters, you will need to make **separate deposits** for the separate liabilities. For example, if you have a pay date on Wednesday, March 30, 2005 (first quarter), and another pay date on Friday, April 1, 2005 (second quarter), two separate deposits would be required even though the pay dates fall within the same semiweekly period. Both deposits would be due Wednesday, April 6, 2005 (three banking days from the end of the semiweekly deposit period).

Page 19

IRS Publication 15, Circular E (continued)

Summary of Steps To Determine Your Deposit Schedule

1. Identify your lookback period (see Table 1).
2. Add the total taxes (line 11 of Form 941) you reported during the lookback period.
3. Determine if you are a monthly or semiweekly schedule depositor:

If the total taxes you reported in the lookback period were . . .	Then you are a . . .
$50,000 or less	Monthly Schedule Depositor
More than $50,000	Semiweekly Schedule Depositor

Example of Monthly and Semiweekly Schedules

Rose Co. reported Form 941 taxes as follows:

2004 Lookback Period		2005 Lookback Period	
3rd Quarter 2002	$12,000	3rd Quarter 2003	$12,000
4th Quarter 2002	$12,000	4th Quarter 2003	$12,000
1st Quarter 2003	$12,000	1st Quarter 2004	$12,000
2nd Quarter 2003	$12,000	2nd Quarter 2004	$15,000
	$48,000		$51,000

Rose Co. is a monthly schedule depositor for 2004 because its tax liability for the four quarters in its lookback period (third quarter 2002 through second quarter 2003) was not more than $50,000. However, for 2005, Rose Co. is a semiweekly schedule depositor because the total taxes exceeded $50,000 for the four quarters in its lookback period (third quarter 2003 through second quarter 2004).

Deposits on Banking Days Only

If a deposit is required to be made on a day that is not a banking day, the deposit is considered timely if it is made by the close of the next banking day. In addition to federal and state bank holidays, Saturdays and Sundays are treated as nonbanking days. For example, if a deposit is required to be made on a Friday and Friday is not a banking day, the deposit will be considered timely if it is made by the following Monday (if that Monday is a banking day).

Semiweekly schedule depositors have at least three banking days to make a deposit. That is, if any of the three weekdays after the end of a semiweekly period is a banking holiday, you will have one additional banking day to deposit. For example, if a semiweekly schedule depositor accumulated taxes for payments made on Friday and the following Monday is not a banking day, the deposit normally due on Wednesday may be made on Thursday (allowing three banking days to make the deposit).

Application of Monthly and Semiweekly Schedules

The terms "monthly schedule depositor" and "semiweekly schedule depositor" do not refer to how often your business pays its employees or even how often you are required to make deposits. The terms identify which set of deposit rules that you must follow when an employment tax liability arises. The deposit rules are based on the dates when wages are paid (for example, cash basis); not on when tax liabilities are accrued for accounting purposes.

Monthly schedule example. Spruce Co. is a monthly schedule depositor with seasonal employees. It paid wages each Friday. During March it paid wages but did not pay any wages during April. Under the monthly deposit schedule, Spruce Co. must deposit the combined tax liabilities for the four March paydays by April 15. Spruce Co. does not have a deposit requirement for April (due by May 15) because no wages were paid and, therefore, it did not have a tax liability for April.

Semiweekly schedule example. Green, Inc., which has a semiweekly deposit schedule, pays wages once each month on the last day of the month. Although Green, Inc. has a semiweekly deposit schedule, it will deposit just once a month because it pays wages only once a month. The deposit, however, will be made under the semiweekly deposit schedule as follows: Green, Inc.'s tax liability for the April 29, 2005 (Friday) payday must be deposited by May 4, 2005 (Wednesday). Under the semiweekly deposit schedule, liabilities for wages paid on Wednesday through Friday must be deposited by the following Wednesday.

$100,000 Next-Day Deposit Rule

If you accumulate a tax liability (reduced by any advance EIC payments) of $100,000 or more on any day during a deposit period, you must deposit the tax by the next banking day, whether you are a monthly or semiweekly schedule depositor.

For purposes of the $100,000 rule, do not continue accumulating a tax liability after the end of a deposit period. For example, if a semiweekly schedule depositor has accumulated a liability of $95,000 on a Tuesday (of a Saturday-through-Tuesday deposit period) and accumulated a $10,000 liability on Wednesday, the $100,000 next-day deposit rule does not apply. Thus, $95,000 must be deposited by Friday and $10,000 must be deposited by the following Wednesday.

However, once you accumulate at least $100,000 in a deposit period, stop accumulating at the end of that day and begin to accumulate anew on the next day. For example, Fir Co. is a semiweekly schedule depositor. On Monday, Fir Co. accumulates taxes of $110,000 and must deposit this amount on Tuesday, the next banking day. On Tuesday, Fir Co. accumulates additional taxes of $30,000. Because the $30,000 is not added to the previous $110,000 and is less than $100,000, Fir Co. must deposit the $30,000 by Friday (following the semiweekly deposit schedule).

IRS Publication 15, Circular E (continued)

 If you are a monthly schedule depositor and accumulate a $100,000 tax liability on any day, you become a semiweekly schedule depositor on the next day and remain so for at least the rest of the calendar year and for the following calendar year.

Example. Elm, Inc. started its business on April 1, 2005. On April 15, it paid wages for the first time and accumulated a tax liability of $40,000. On April 22, 2005, Elm, Inc. paid wages and accumulated a liability of $60,000, bringing its accumulated tax liability to $100,000. Because this was the first year of its business, the tax liability for its lookback period is considered to be zero, and it would be a monthly schedule depositor based on the lookback rules. However, since Elm, Inc. accumulated a $100,000 liability on April 22, it became a semiweekly schedule depositor on April 23. It will be a semiweekly schedule depositor for the remainder of 2005 and for 2006. Elm, Inc. is required to deposit the $100,000 by April 23, the next banking day.

Accuracy of Deposits Rule

You are required to deposit 100% of your tax liability on or before the deposit due date. However, penalties will not be applied for depositing less than 100% if both of the following conditions are met.

- Any deposit shortfall does not exceed the greater of $100 or 2% of the amount of taxes otherwise required to be deposited and

- The deposit shortfall is paid or deposited by the shortfall makeup date as described below.

Makeup Date for Deposit Shortfall:

1. **Monthly schedule depositor.** Deposit the shortfall or pay it with your return by the due date of your Form 941 for the quarter in which the shortfall occurred. You may pay the shortfall with Form 941 even if the amount is $2,500 or more.

2. **Semiweekly schedule depositor.** Deposit by the earlier of:

   a. The first Wednesday or Friday (whichever comes first) that falls on or after the 15th of the month following the month in which the shortfall occurred or

   b. The due date of Form 941 (for the quarter of the tax liability).

For example, if a semiweekly schedule depositor has a deposit shortfall during July 2005, the shortfall makeup date is August 17, 2005 (Wednesday). However, if the shortfall occurred on the required October 5 (Wednesday) deposit due date for a September 30 (Friday) pay date, the return due date for the September 30 pay date (October 31) would come before the November 16 (Wednesday) shortfall makeup date. In this case, the shortfall must be deposited by October 31.

How To Deposit

The two methods of depositing employment taxes, including Form 945 taxes, are discussed below. See *Payment with return* on page 18 for exceptions explaining when taxes may be paid with the tax return instead of being deposited.

Electronic deposit requirement. You must make electronic deposits of all depository taxes (such as employment tax, excise tax, and corporate income tax) using the Electronic Federal Tax Payment System (EFTPS) in 2005 if:

- Your total deposits of such taxes in 2003 were more than $200,000 or

- You were required to use EFTPS in 2004.

If you are required to use EFTPS and fail to do so, you may be subject to a 10% penalty. EFTPS is a free service provided by the Department of Treasury. If you are not required to use EFTPS, you may participate voluntarily. To get more information or to enroll in EFTPS, call 1-800-555-4477 or 1-800-945-8400. You can also visit the EFTPS website at *www.eftps.gov.*

Depositing on time. For deposits made by EFTPS to be on time, you must initiate the transaction at least one business day before the date that the deposit is due.

Deposit record. For your records an Electronic Funds Transfer (EFT) Trace Number will be provided with each successful payment that can be used as a receipt or to trace the payment.

Making deposits with FTD coupons. If you are not making deposits by EFTPS, use Form 8109, Federal Tax Deposit Coupon, to make the deposits at an authorized financial institution.

For new employers, if you would like to receive a Federal Tax Deposit (FTD) coupon booklet, call 1-800-829-4933. Allow 5 to 6 weeks for delivery. The IRS will keep track of the number of FTD coupons that you use and automatically will send you additional coupons when you need them. If you do not receive your resupply of FTD coupons, call 1-800-829-4933. You can have the FTD coupon books sent to a branch office, tax preparer, or service bureau that is making your deposits by showing that address on Form 8109-C, FTD Address Change, which is in the FTD coupon book. (Filing Form 8109-C will not change your address of record; it will change only the address where the FTD coupons are mailed.) The FTD coupons will be preprinted with your name, address, and EIN. They have entry boxes for indicating the type of tax and the tax period for which the deposit is made.

It is very important to clearly mark the correct type of tax and tax period on each FTD coupon. This information is used by the IRS to credit your account.

If you have branch offices depositing taxes, give them FTD coupons and complete instructions so that they can deposit the taxes when due.

Please use only your FTD coupons. If you use anyone else's FTD coupon, you may be subject to a failure to deposit penalty. This is because your account will be underpaid by the amount of the deposit credited to the other person's account. See *Deposit Penalties* below for penalty amounts.

IRS Publication 15, Circular E (continued)

How to deposit with an FTD coupon. Mail or deliver each FTD coupon and a single payment covering the taxes to be deposited to an authorized depositary. An authorized depositary is a financial institution (for example, a commercial bank) that is authorized to accept federal tax deposits. Follow the instructions in the FTD coupon book. Make your check or money order payable to the depositary. To help ensure proper crediting of your account, include your EIN, the type of tax (for example, Form 941), and the tax period to which the payment applies on your check or money order.

Authorized depositaries must accept cash, a postal money order drawn to the order of the depositary, or a check or draft drawn on and to the order of the depositary. You may deposit taxes with a check drawn on another financial institution only if the depositary is willing to accept that form of payment. Be sure that the financial institution where you make deposits is an authorized depositary. Deposits made at an unauthorized institution may be subject to the failure to deposit penalty.

If you prefer, you may mail your coupon and payment to: Financial Agent, Federal Tax Deposit Processing, P.O. Box 970030, St. Louis, MO 63197. Make your check or money order payable to "Financial Agent."

Depositing on time. The IRS determines whether deposits are on time by the date that they are received by an authorized depositary. To be considered timely, the funds must be available to the depositary on the deposit due date before the institution's daily cutoff deadline. Contact your local depositary for information concerning check clearance and cutoff schedules. However, a deposit received by the authorized depositary after the due date will be considered timely if the taxpayer establishes that it was mailed in the United States at least two days before the due date.

Note. If you are required to deposit any taxes more than once a month, any deposit of $20,000 or more must be received by the authorized depositary by its due date to be timely. See section 7502(e)(3).

Depositing without an EIN. If you have applied for an EIN but have not received it and you must make a deposit, make the deposit with the IRS. Do not make the deposit at an authorized depositary. Make it payable to the "United States Treasury" and show on it your name (as shown on Form SS-4), address, kind of tax, period covered, and date you applied for an EIN. Send your deposit with an explanation to your local IRS office or the service center where you will file Form 941. The service center addresses are in the Instructions for Form 941 and are also available on the IRS website at *www.irs.gov*. Do not use Form 8109-B, Federal Tax Deposit Coupon, in this situation.

Depositing without Form 8109. If you have an EIN but do not have a preprinted Form 8109, you may use Form 8109-B to make deposits. Form 8109-B is an over-the-counter FTD coupon that is not preprinted with your identifying information. You may get this form by calling 1-800-829-4933. Be sure to have your EIN ready when you call. You will not be able to obtain Form 8109-B by calling 1-800-TAX-FORM.

Use Form 8109-B to make deposits only if:

- You are a new employer and you have been assigned an EIN, but you have not received your initial supply of Forms 8109 or

- You have not received your resupply of preprinted Forms 8109.

Deposit record. For your records, a stub is provided with each FTD coupon in the coupon book. The FTD coupon itself will not be returned. It is used to credit your account. Your check, bank receipt, or money order is your receipt.

How to claim credit for overpayments. If you deposited more than the right amount of taxes for a quarter, you can choose on Form 941 for that quarter to have the overpayment refunded or applied as a credit to your next return. Do not ask the depositary or EFTPS to request a refund from the IRS for you.

Deposit Penalties

Penalties may apply if you do not make required deposits on time, if you make deposits for less than the required amount, or if you do not use EFTPS when required. The penalties do not apply if any failure to make a proper and timely deposit was due to reasonable cause and not to willful neglect. For amounts not properly or timely deposited, the penalty rates are as follows.

2% - Deposits made 1 to 5 days late.

5% - Deposits made 6 to 15 days late.

10% - Deposits made 16 or more days late. Also applies to amounts paid within 10 days of the date of the first notice the IRS sent asking for the tax due.

10% - Deposits made at an unauthorized financial institution, paid directly to the IRS, or paid with your tax return. But see *Depositing without an EIN* on page 22 and *Payment with return* on page 18 for exceptions.

10% - Amounts subject to electronic deposit requirements but not deposited using EFTPS.

15% - Amounts still unpaid more than 10 days after the date of the first notice that the IRS sent asking for the tax due or the day on which you received notice and demand for immediate payment, whichever is earlier.

Note. Late deposit penalty amounts are determined using calendar days, starting from the due date of the liability.

Order in which deposits are applied. Deposits generally are applied to the most recent tax liability within the quarter. If you receive a failure-to-deposit penalty notice, you may designate how your payment is to be applied in order to minimize the amount of the penalty. Follow the instructions on the penalty notice that you received. For more information on designating deposits, see Rev. Proc. 2001-58. You can find Rev. Proc. 2001-58 on page 579 of Internal Revenue Bulletin 2001-50 at *www.irs.gov/pub/ irs-irbs/irb01-50.pdf*.

Example. Cedar, Inc. is required to make a deposit of $1,000 on June 15 and $1,500 on July 15. It does not make the deposit on June 15. On July 15, Cedar, Inc. deposits $2,000. Under the deposits rule, which applies deposits to the most recent tax liability, $1,500 of the deposit is applied to the July 15 deposit and the remaining $500 is applied to the June deposit. Accordingly, $500 of the June 15 liability

IRS Publication 15, Circular E (continued)

remains undeposited. The penalty on this underdeposit will apply as explained above.

Trust fund recovery penalty. If income, social security, and Medicare taxes that must be withheld are not withheld or are not deposited or paid to the United States Treasury, the trust fund recovery penalty may apply. The penalty is the full amount of the unpaid trust fund tax. This penalty may apply to you if these unpaid taxes cannot be immediately collected from the employer or business.

The trust fund recovery penalty may be imposed on all persons who are determined by the IRS to be responsible for collecting, accounting for, and paying over these taxes, and who acted willfully in not doing so.

A **responsible person** can be an officer or employee of a corporation, a partner or employee of a partnership, an accountant a volunteer director/trustee, or an employee of a sole proprietorship. A responsible person also may include one who signs checks for the business or otherwise has authority to cause the spending of business funds.

Willfully means voluntarily, consciously, and intentionally. A responsible person acts willfully if the person knows that the required actions are not taking place.

Separate accounting when deposits are not made or withheld taxes are not paid. Separate accounting may be required if you do not pay over withheld employee social security, Medicare, or income taxes; deposit required taxes; make required payments; or file tax returns. In this case, you would receive written notice from the IRS requiring you to deposit taxes into a special trust account for the U.S. Government. You would also have to file monthly tax returns on Form 941-M, Employer's Monthly Federal Tax Return.

"Averaged" failure to deposit penalty. IRS may assess an "averaged" failure to deposit (FTD) penalty of 2% to 10% if you are a monthly schedule depositor and did not properly complete line 15 of Form 941 when your tax liability (line 10) shown on Form 941 was $2,500 or more. IRS may also assess this penalty of 2% to 10% if you are a semiweekly schedule depositor and your tax liability (line 10) shown on Form 941 was $2,500 or more and you did any of the following.

- Completed line 15 of Form 941 instead of Schedule B (Form 941).

- Failed to attach a properly completed Schedule B (Form 941).

- Completed Schedule B (Form 941) incorrectly, for example, by entering tax deposits instead of tax liabilities in the numbered spaces.

IRS figures the penalty by allocating your total tax liability on line 10, Form 941 equally throughout the tax period. Your deposits and payments may not be counted as timely because IRS does not know the actual dates of your tax liabilities.

You can avoid the penalty by reviewing your return before filing it. Follow these steps before filing your Form 941.

- If you are a monthly schedule depositor, report your tax liabilities (not your deposits) in the monthly entry spaces on line 15.

- If you are a semiweekly schedule depositor, report your tax liabilities (not your deposits) on Schedule B (Form 941) in the lines that represent the dates you paid your employees.

- Verify that your total liability shown on line 15 of Form 941 or the bottom of Schedule B (Form 941) equals your tax liability shown on line 10 of Form 941.

- Do not show negative amounts on line 15 or Schedule B (Form 941). If a prior period adjustment results in a decrease in your tax liability, reduce your liability for the day you discovered the error by the tax decrease resulting from the error, but not below zero. Apply any remaining decrease to subsequent liabilities.

12. Filing Form 941

Each quarter, all employers who pay wages subject to income tax withholding (including withholding on sick pay and supplemental unemployment benefits) or social security and Medicare taxes must file Form 941, Employer's Quarterly Federal Tax Return, by the last day of the month that follows the end of the quarter. See the *Calendar* on page 2. However, the following exceptions apply:

- **Seasonal employers who no longer file for quarters when they regularly have no tax liability because they have paid no wages.** To alert the IRS that you will not have to file a return for one or more quarters during the year, check the "Seasonal employer" box on line 17 of Form 941. The IRS will mail two Forms 941 to the seasonal filer once a year after March 1. The preprinted forms will not include the date that the quarter ended. You must enter the date that the quarter ended when you file the return. Generally, the IRS will not inquire about unfiled returns if at least one taxable return is filed each year. However, you must check the "Seasonal employer" box on every Form 941 you file. Otherwise, the IRS will expect a return to be filed for each quarter.

- **Household employers reporting social security and Medicare taxes and/or withheld income tax.** If you are a sole proprietor and file Form 941 for business employees, you may include taxes for household employees on your Form 941. Otherwise, report social security and Medicare taxes and income tax withholding for household employees on Schedule H (Form 1040), Household Employment Taxes. See Publication 926, Household Employer's Tax Guide, for more information.

- **Employers reporting wages for employees in American Samoa, Guam, the Commonwealth of the Northern Mariana Islands, the U.S. Virgin Islands, or Puerto Rico.** If your employees are not subject to U.S. income tax withholding, use Form 941-SS. Employers in Puerto Rico use Form 941-PR.

- **Agricultural employers reporting social security, Medicare, and withheld income taxes.** Report

IRS Publication 15, Circular E (continued)

these taxes on Form 943, Employer's Annual Federal Tax Return for Agricultural Employees.

Form 941 e-file. The Form 941 e-file program allows a taxpayer to electronically file Form 941 using a personal computer, modem, and commercial tax preparation software. Contact the IRS at 1-866-255-0654 or visit the IRS website at *www.irs.gov/efile* for more information. See Publication 1855, Technical Specifications Guide for the Electronic Filing of Form 941, Employee's Quarterly Federal Tax Return, for technical specifications.

941TeleFile. You may be able to file Form 941 and pay any balance due by phone. If you received 941TeleFile materials with your Form 941 Package, check page TEL-1 of the 941TeleFile Instructions to see if you qualify for this method of filing. If you have questions related to filing Form 941 using 941TeleFile, call 1-866-255-0654. This phone number is for 941TeleFile information only and is not the number used to file the return.

Electronic filing by reporting agents. Reporting agents filing Forms 941 for groups of taxpayers can file them electronically. See *Reporting Agents* in section 7 of Publication 15-A, Employer's Supplemental Tax Guide, for more information.

Penalties. For each whole or part month that a return is not filed when required (disregarding any extensions of the filing deadline), there is a penalty of 5% of the unpaid tax due with that return. The maximum penalty is generally 25% of the tax due. Also, for each whole or part month that the tax is paid late (disregarding any extensions of the payment deadline), a penalty of 0.5% per month of the amount of tax generally applies. This penalty is 0.25% per month, and applies to individual filers only, if an installment agreement is in effect. You must have filed your return on or before the due date of the return to qualify for the reduced penalty. The maximum amount of this penalty is also 25% of the tax due. If both penalties apply in any month, the failure-to-file penalty is reduced by the amount of the failure-to-pay penalty. The penalties will not be charged if you have a reasonable cause for failing to file or pay. If you file or pay late, attach an explanation to your Form 941.

Note. In addition to any penalties, interest accrues from the due date of the tax on any unpaid balance.

If income, social security, or Medicare taxes that must be withheld are not withheld or are not paid, you may be personally liable for the trust fund recovery penalty. See *Trust fund recovery penalty* in section 11.

Use of a reporting agent or other third-party payroll service provider does not relieve an employer of the responsibility to ensure that tax returns are filed and all taxes are paid or deposited correctly and on time.

Do not file more than one Form 941 per quarter. Employers with multiple locations or divisions must file only one Form 941 per quarter. Filing more than one return may result in processing delays and may require correspondence between you and the IRS. For information on making adjustments to previously filed returns, see section 13.

Hints on filing.

- Do not report more than one calendar quarter on a return.
- Use the preaddressed form mailed to you. If you do not have the form, get one from the IRS in time to file the return when due.
- If you use a form that is not preaddressed, show your name and EIN on it. Be sure that they are exactly as they appeared on earlier returns.
- See the Instructions for Form 941 for information on preparing the form.

Final return. If you go out of business, you must file a final return for the last quarter in which wages are paid. If you continue to pay wages or other compensation for quarters following termination of your business, you must file returns for those quarters. See the Instructions for Form 941 for details on how to file a final return.

Note. If you are required to file a final Form 941, you are also required to furnish Forms W-2 to your employees by the due date of your final Form 941. File Forms W-2 and W-3 with the SSA by the last day of the month that follows the due date of your final Form 941. Do not send an original or copy of Form 941 to the SSA. See the Instructions for Forms W-2 and W-3 for more information.

Filing late Forms 941 for prior years. If possible, get a copy of Form 941 (and separate instructions) with a revision date showing the year for which your delinquent return is being filed. See *Quick and Easy Access to Tax Help and Forms* on page 68 for various ways to secure any necessary forms and instructions.

However, if you are filing an original return for a quarter in a prior year and you are using the current year form, you will have to modify Form 941. (Do not modify post-2004 versions of Form 941 for pre-2005 quarters.) A form for a particular year generally can be used without modification for any quarter within that year. For example, a form with any 2005 revision date (for example, January or October 2005) generally can be used without modification for any quarter of 2005.

In all cases, be sure to correctly fill out the "Date quarter ended" section at the top of the form. If you are modifying a form with preprinted information, change the date. The date is shown with the month and year the quarter ends; for example, JUN05 would be for the quarter ending June 30, 2005. Cross out any inapplicable tax rate(s) shown on the form and write in the rate from Table 3 below. You can get tax rates and wage base limits for years not shown in the table from the IRS.

 The instructions on the form may be inappropriate for the year that you are reporting taxes because of changes in the law, regulations, or procedures. The revision date (found under the form number at the top of the form) will tell you the year for which the form was developed. Contact the IRS at 1-800-829-4933 if you have any questions.

IRS Publication 15, Circular E (continued)

Table 3. **Social Security and Medicare Tax Rates** *(For 3 prior years)*

Calendar Year	Wage Base Limit (each employee)	Tax Rate on Taxable Wages and Tips
2004 – Social Security	$87,900	12.4%
2004 – Medicare	All Wages	2.9%
2003 – Social Security	$87,000	12.4%
2003 – Medicare	All Wages	2.9%
2002 – Social Security	$84,900	12.4%
2002 – Medicare	All Wages	2.9%

Reconciling Forms W-2, W-3, and 941. When there are discrepancies between Forms 941 filed with the IRS and Forms W-2 and W-3 filed with the SSA, the IRS must contact you to resolve the discrepancies. This costs time and money for the Government and for you.

To help reduce discrepancies:

1. Report bonuses as wages and as social security and Medicare wages on Forms W-2 and 941,

2. Report both social security and Medicare wages and taxes separately on Forms W-2, W-3, and 941,

3. Report employee share of social security taxes on Form W-2 in the box for social security tax withheld (box 4), not as social security wages,

4. Report employee share of Medicare taxes on Form W-2 in the box for Medicare tax withheld (box 6), not as Medicare wages,

5. Make sure the social security wage amount for each employee does not exceed the annual social security wage base limit (for example, $87,900 for 2004),

6. Do not report noncash wages that are not subject to social security or Medicare taxes as social security or Medicare wages,

7. If you used an EIN on any Form 941 for the year that is different from the EIN reported on Form W-3, enter the other EIN on Form W-3 in the box for "Other EIN used this year,"

8. Be sure that the amounts on Form W-3 are the total of amounts from Forms W-2, and

9. Reconcile Form W-3 with your four quarterly Forms 941 by comparing amounts reported for:

    a. Income tax withholding;

    b. Social security wages, social security tips, and Medicare wages and tips. Form W-3 should include Form 941 adjustments only for the current year (that is, if the Form 941 adjustments include amounts for a prior year, do not report those prior year adjustments on the current-year Forms W-2 and W-3);

    c. Social security and Medicare taxes. The amounts shown on the four quarterly Forms 941, including current-year adjustments, should be approximately twice the amounts shown on Form W-3. This is because Form 941 includes both the employer and employee shares of social security and Medicare taxes; and

    d. Advance earned income credit (EIC).

Do not report on Form 941 backup withholding or income tax withholding on nonpayroll payments such as pensions, annuities, and gambling winnings. Nonpayroll withholding must be reported on Form 945, Annual Return of Withheld Federal Income Tax. See the separate Instructions for Form 945 for details. Income tax withholding required to be reported on Forms 1099 or W-2G must be reported on Form 945. Only taxes and withholding properly reported on Form W-2 should be reported on Form 941.

Amounts reported on Forms W-2, W-3, and 941 may not match for valid reasons. If they do not match, you should determine that the reasons are valid. Keep your reconciliation so that you will have a record of why amounts did not match in case there are inquiries from the IRS or the SSA. See the Instructions for Schedule D (Form 941) if you need to explain any discrepancies that were caused by an acquisition, statutory merger, or consolidation.

13. Reporting Adjustments on Form 941

There are two types of adjustments reported on Form 941: current period adjustments and prior period adjustments to correct errors. See the Instructions for Form 941 and the Instructions for Form 941c, Supporting Statement to Correct Information, for more information on how to report these adjustments.

Current Period Adjustments

In certain cases, amounts reported as social security and Medicare taxes in column 2 of lines 5a, 5b, and 5c of Form 941 must be adjusted to arrive at your correct tax liability (for example, excluding amounts withheld by a third-party payer or amounts you were not required to withhold). Current period adjustments are reported on lines 7a, 7b, and 7c of Form 941 and include the following:

Adjustment of tax on tips. If, by the 10th of the month after the month you received an employee's report on tips, you do not have enough employee funds available to withhold the employee's share of social security and Medicare taxes, you no longer have to collect it. However, report the entire amount of these tips on lines 5b (social security tips) and 5c (Medicare wages and tips). Include as a negative adjustment on line 7c the total uncollected employee share of the social security and Medicare taxes.

Adjustment of tax on group-term life insurance premiums paid for former employees. The employee share of social security and Medicare taxes on group-term life insurance over $50,000 for a former employee is paid by the former employee with his or her tax return and is not collected by the employer. However, include all social

IRS Publication 15, Circular E (continued)

security and Medicare taxes for such coverage on lines 5a and 5c (social security and Medicare taxes), and back out the amount of the employee share of these taxes as a negative adjustment on line 7c. See Publication 15-B for more information on group-term life insurance.

Adjustment of tax on third-party sick pay. Report both the employer and employee shares of social security and Medicare taxes for sick pay on lines 5a and 5c of Form 941. Show as a negative adjustment on line 7b the social security and Medicare taxes withheld on sick pay by a third-party payer. See section 6 of Publication 15-A for more information.

Fractions of cents adjustment. If there is a small difference between total taxes after adjustment for advance EIC (line 10) and total deposits (line 11), it may have been caused, all or in part, by rounding to the nearest cent each time you computed payroll. This rounding occurs when you figure the amount of social security and Medicare tax to be withheld and deposited from each employee's wages. IRS refers to rounding differences relating to employee withholding of social security and Medicare taxes as "fractions-of-cents" adjustments. (If you pay your taxes with Form 941 instead of making deposits because your total taxes for the quarter are less than $2,500, you also may report a fractions-of-cents adjustment.)

To determine if you have a fractions-of-cents adjustment, multiply the total wages and tips for the quarter subject to:

- Social security tax (reported on lines 5a, column 1 and 5b, column 1) by 6.2% (.062) and
- Medicare tax (reported on line 5c column 1) by 1.45% (.0145).

Compare these amounts (the employee share of social security and Medicare taxes) with the total social security and Medicare taxes actually withheld from employees for the quarter (from your payroll records). The difference, positive or negative, is your fractions-of-cents adjustment to be reported on line 7a. If the actual amount withheld is less, report a negative adjustment in parentheses (if possible) in the entry space. If the actual amount is more, report a positive adjustment.

Note. For the above adjustments, prepare and retain a brief supporting statement explaining the nature and amount of each. Do not attach the statement to Form 941.

Example of reporting current period adjustments. Cedar, Inc. was entitled to the following current period adjustments.

- **Third-party sick pay.** Cedar, Inc. included taxes of $2,000 for sick pay on lines 5a, column 2 and 5c, column 2 for social security and Medicare taxes. However, the third-party payer of the sick pay withheld and paid the employee share ($1,000) of these taxes. Cedar, Inc. is entitled to a $1,000 sick pay adjustment (negative) on line 7b.

- **Fractions of cents.** Cedar, Inc. determined that the amounts withheld and deposited for social security and Medicare taxes during the quarter were a net $1.44 more than the employee share of the amount figured on lines 5a, column 2, 5b, column 2, and 5c, column 2 (social security and Medicare taxes). This difference was caused by adding or dropping fractions of cents when figuring social security and Medicare taxes for each wage payment. Cedar, Inc. must report a positive $1.44 fractions-of-cents adjustment on line 7a.

- **Life insurance premiums.** Cedar, Inc. paid group-term life insurance premiums for policies in excess of $50,000 for former employees. The former employees must pay the employee share of the social security and Medicare taxes ($200) on the policies. However, Cedar, Inc. must include the employee share of these taxes with the social security and Medicare taxes reported on lines 5a, column 2 and 5c, column 2 of Form 941. Therefore, Cedar, Inc. is entitled to a negative $200 adjustment on line 7c.

Cedar, Inc. reported these adjustments on line 7 of Form 941 as shown in the *Current Period Adjustment Example* below.

Note. Do not make any changes to your record of federal tax liability reported on line 15 or Schedule B (Form 941) for current period adjustments. The amounts reported on the record reflect the actual amounts you withheld from employees' wages for social security and Medicare taxes. Because the current period adjustments make the amounts reported on lines 5a, column 2, 5b, column 2, and 5c, column 2 of Form 941 equal the actual amounts you withheld (the amounts reported on the record), no additional changes to the record of federal tax liability are necessary for these adjustments.

Current Period Adjustment Example

7 Tax adjustments (If your answer is a negative number, write it in brackets.):

7a Current quarter's fractions of cents	1.44
7b Current quarter's sick pay	(1000.00)
7c Current quarter's adjustments for tips and group-term life insurance	(200.00)
7d Current year's income tax withholding (Attach Form 941c) . . .	.
7e Prior quarter's social security and Medicare taxes (Attach Form 941c)	.
7f Special additions to federal income tax (reserved use)	.
7g Special additions to social security and Medicare (reserved use) .	.
7h Total adjustments (Combine all amounts: lines 7a through 7g.) 7h	(1198.56)

IRS Publication 15, Circular E (continued)

Prior Period Adjustments

Generally, you can correct errors on prior period Forms 941 by making an adjustment on your Form 941 for the quarter during which the error was discovered. For example, if you made an error in reporting social security tax on your second quarter 2004 Form 941 and discovered the error during January 2005, correct the error by making an adjustment on your first quarter 2005 Form 941.

The adjustment increases or decreases your tax liability for the quarter in which it is reported (that is, the quarter the error is discovered) and is interest free. The net adjustments reported on Form 941 may include any number of corrections for one or more previous quarters, including both overpayments and underpayments.

You are required to provide background information and certifications supporting prior quarter adjustments. File with Form 941 a Form 941c, Supporting Statement To Correct Information, or attach a statement that shows:

- What the error was,

- Quarter in which the error was made,

- The amount of the error for each quarter,

- Date on which you found the error,

- That you repaid the employee tax or received from each affected employee a written consent to this refund or credit, if the entry corrects an overcollection, and

- If the entry corrects social security and Medicare taxes overcollected in an earlier year, that you received from the employee a written statement that he or she will not claim a refund or credit for the amount.

Do not file Form 941c separately. The IRS will not be able to process your adjustments on Form 941 without this supporting information. See the instructions for Form 941c for more information.

Income tax withholding adjustments. Correct prior quarter income tax withholding errors by making an adjustment on line 7d of Form 941 for the quarter during which you discovered the error.

Note. You may make an adjustment to correct income tax withholding errors only for quarters during the same calendar year. This is because the employee uses the amount shown on Form W-2 as a credit when filing his or her income tax return (Form 1040, etc.).

You cannot adjust amounts reported as income tax withheld in a prior calendar year unless it is to correct an administrative error. An administrative error occurs if the amount you entered on Form 941 is not the amount you actually withheld. For example, if the total income tax actually withheld was incorrectly reported on Form 941 due to a mathematical or transposition error, this would be an administrative error. The administrative error adjustment corrects the amount reported on Form 941 to agree with the amount actually withheld from employees.

Social security and Medicare tax adjustments. Correct prior quarter social security and Medicare tax errors by making an adjustment on line 7e of Form 941 for the quarter during which you discovered the error. You may report adjustments on the current quarter Form 941 for previous quarters in the current and prior years.

Reporting prior quarter adjustments on the record of federal tax liability. Adjustments to correct errors in prior quarters must be taken into account on either Form 941, line 15, or on Schedule B (Form 941), Report of Tax Liability for Semiweekly Schedule Depositors.

If the adjustment corrects an underreported liability in a prior quarter, report the adjustment on the entry space corresponding to the date the error was discovered. If the adjustment corrects an overreported liability, use the adjustment amount as a credit to offset subsequent liabilities until it is used up.

Example of reporting prior period adjustments. Elm Co., a monthly schedule depositor, discovered on January 7, 2005, that it overreported social security tax on a prior quarter return by $5,000. Its total tax liabilities for the first quarter of 2005 were: January—$4,500, February—$4,500, and March—$4,500. Elm Co. completed line 15 of Form 941 as shown in the *Prior Period Adjustment Example* below.

The adjustment for the $5,000 overreported liability offset the January liability, so the $4,500 liability was not deposited and a "-0-" liability was reported on line 15, Month 1. The remaining $500 of the $5,000 adjustment

Prior Period Adjustment Example

15   Check one: ☐   Line 10 is less than $2,500, go to Part 3.

☑   **You were a monthly schedule depositor for the entire quarter and line 10 is $2,500 or more, fill out the tax liability for each month.** Then go to Part 3.

Tax liability:	Month 1	-0- .
	Month 2	4000.00
	Month 3	4500.00
	Total	8500.00

Total must equal line 10.

☐   **You were a semiweekly schedule depositor for any part of this quarter.** Fill out *Schedule B (Form 941): Report of Tax Liability for Semiweekly Schedule Depositors* and attach it to this form.

IRS Publication 15, Circular E (continued)

credit was used to partially offset the liability for February, so only $4,000 of the $4,500 liability was deposited and reported on line 15, Month 2.

Filing a claim for overreported prior period liabilities. If you discover an error on a prior quarter return resulting in a tax overpayment, you may file Form 843, Claim for Refund and Request for Abatement, for a refund. This form also can be used to request an abatement of an overassessment of employment taxes, interest, and/or penalties. You must file Form 941c, or an equivalent statement, with Form 843. See the separate Instructions for Form 843.

Collecting underwithheld taxes from employees. If you withheld no income, social security, or Medicare taxes or less than the right amount from an employee's wages, you can make it up from later pay to that employee. But you are the one who owes the underpayment. Reimbursement is a matter for settlement between you and the employee. Underwithheld income tax must be recovered from the employee on or before the last day of the calendar year. There are special rules for tax on tips (see section 6) and fringe benefits (see section 5).

Refunding amounts incorrectly withheld from employees. If you withheld more than the right amount of income, social security, or Medicare taxes from wages paid, give the employee the excess. Any excess income tax withholding must be reimbursed to the employee before the end of the calendar year in which it was withheld. Keep in your records the employee's written receipt showing the date and amount of the repayment. If you do not have a receipt, you must report and pay each excess amount when you file Form 941 for the quarter in which you withheld too much tax.

Correcting filed Forms W-2 and W-3. When adjustments are made to correct social security and Medicare taxes because of a change in the wage totals reported for a previous year, you also may need to file Form W-2c, Corrected Wage and Tax Statement, and Form W-3c, Transmittal of Corrected Wage and Tax Statements, with the SSA. Up to five Forms W-2c per Form W-3c may be filed over the Internet. For more information, visit the Social Security Administration's Employer Reporting Instructions and Information page at *www.socialsecurity.gov/employer*.

Special additions to tax liability. The revised Form 941 includes new lines to report special additions to federal income tax and social security and Medicare tax. However, these lines are specifically reserved for special circumstances and are to be used only if the IRS sends the employer a notice instructing the employer to use them.

Wage Repayments

If an employee repays you for wages received in error, do not offset the repayments against current-year wages unless the repayments are for amounts received in error in the current year.

Repayment of current year wages. If you receive repayments for wages paid during a prior quarter in the current year, report adjustments on Form 941 to recover income tax withholding and social security and Medicare taxes for the repaid wages (as discussed earlier). Report the adjust-ments on Form 941 for the quarter during which the repayment occurred.

Repayment of prior year wages. If you receive repayments for wages paid during a prior year, report an adjustment on the Form 941 for the quarter during which the repayment was made to recover the social security and Medicare taxes. Instead of making an adjustment on Form 941, you may file a claim for these taxes using Form 843. You may not make an adjustment for income tax withholding because the wages were paid during a prior year.

You also must file Forms W-2c and W-3c with the SSA to correct social security and Medicare wages and taxes. Do not correct wages(box 1) on Form W-2c for the amount paid in error. Give a copy of Form W-2c to the employee.

Note. The wages paid in error in the prior year remain taxable to the employee for that year. This is because the employee received and had use of those funds during that year. The employee is not entitled to file an amended return (Form 1040X) to recover the income tax on these wages. Instead, the employee is entitled to a deduction (or credit in some cases) for the repaid wages on his or her income tax return for the year of repayment.

14. Federal Unemployment (FUTA) Tax

The Federal Unemployment Tax Act (FUTA), with state unemployment systems, provides for payments of unemployment compensation to workers who have lost their jobs. Most employers pay both a federal and a state unemployment tax. A list of state unemployment tax agencies, including addresses and phone numbers, is available in Publication 926, Household Employer's Tax Guide. Only the employer pays FUTA tax; it is not withheld from the employee's wages. For more information, see the Instructions for Form 940.

Note. Services rendered after December 20, 2000, to a federally recognized Indian tribal government (or any subdivision, subsidiary, or business wholly owned by such an Indian tribe) are exempt from FUTA tax, subject to the tribe's compliance with state law. For more information, see Code section 3309(d).

Use the following three tests to determine whether you must pay FUTA tax. Each test applies to a different category of employee, and each is independent of the others. If a test describes your situation, you are subject to FUTA tax on the wages that you pay to employees in that category during the current calendar year.

1. General test.

   You are subject to FUTA tax in 2005 on the wages that you pay employees who are not farmworkers or household workers if in the current or preceding calendar year:

   a. You paid wages of $1,500 or more in any calendar quarter in 2004 or 2005 or

IRS Publication 15, Circular E (continued)

b. You had one or more employees for at least some part of a day in any 20 or more different weeks in 2004 or 20 or more different weeks in 2005.

2. Household employees test.

You are subject to FUTA tax only if you paid total cash wages of $1,000 or more (for all household employees) in any calendar quarter in 2004 or 2005. A household worker is an employee who performs household work in a private home, local college club, or local fraternity or sorority chapter.

3. Farmworkers test.

You are subject to FUTA tax on the wages that you pay to farmworkers if:

a. You paid cash wages of $20,000 or more to farmworkers during any calendar quarter in 2004 or 2005 or

b. You employed 10 or more farmworkers during at least some part of a day (whether or not at the same time) during any 20 or more different weeks in 2004 or 20 or more different weeks in 2005.

Computing FUTA tax. For 2004 and 2005, the FUTA tax rate is 6.2%. The tax applies to the first $7,000 that you pay to each employee as wages during the year. The $7,000 is the federal wage base. Your state wage base may be different. Generally, you can take a credit against your FUTA tax for amounts that you paid into state unemployment funds. This credit cannot be more than 5.4% of taxable wages. If you are entitled to the maximum 5.4% credit, the FUTA tax rate after the credit is 0.8%.

Successor employer. If you acquired a business from an employer who was liable for FUTA tax, you may be able to count the wages that employer paid to the employees who continue to work for you when you figure the $7,000 FUTA wage base. See the Instructions for Form 940.

Depositing FUTA tax. For deposit purposes, figure FUTA tax quarterly. Determine your FUTA tax liability by multiplying the amount of wages paid during the quarter by .008 (0.8%). Stop depositing FUTA tax on an employee's wages when he or she reaches $7,000 in wages for the calendar year. If any part of the wages subject to FUTA is exempt from state unemployment tax, you may have to deposit more than the tax using the 0.8% rate. For example, in certain states, wages paid to corporate officers, certain payments of sick pay by unions, and certain fringe benefits, are exempt from state unemployment tax.

If your FUTA tax liability for a quarter after 2004 is $500 or less, you do not have to deposit the tax. Instead, you may carry it forward and add it to the liability figured in the next quarter to see if you must make a deposit. If your FUTA tax liability for any calendar quarter in 2005 is over $500 (including any FUTA tax carried forward from an earlier quarter), you must deposit the tax by electronic funds transfer (EFTPS) or in an authorized financial institution using Form 8109, Federal Tax Deposit Coupon. See section 11 for information on these two deposit methods.

Note. You are not required to deposit FUTA taxes for household employees unless you report their wages on Form 941 or Form 943. See Publication 926, Household Employer's Tax Guide, for more information.

When to deposit. Deposit the FUTA tax by the last day of the first month that follows the end of the quarter. If the due date (below) for making your deposit falls on a Saturday, Sunday, or legal holiday, you may make your deposit on the next business day.

If your liability for the fourth quarter (plus any undeposited amount from any earlier quarter) is over $500, deposit the entire amount by the due date of Form 940 or Form 940-EZ (January 31). If it is $500 or less, you can either make a deposit or pay the tax with your Form 940 or Form 940-EZ by January 31.

Table 4. **When To Deposit FUTA Taxes**

Quarter	Ending	Due Date
Jan.–Feb.–Mar.	Mar. 31	Apr. 30
Apr.–May–June	June 30	July 31
July–Aug.–Sept.	Sept. 30	Oct. 31
Oct.–Nov.–Dec.	Dec. 31	Jan. 31

Reporting FUTA tax. Use Form 940 or Form 940-EZ, Employer's Annual Federal Unemployment (FUTA) Tax Return, to report FUTA tax. File Form 940 or Form 940-EZ by January 31. However, if you deposited all FUTA tax when due, you may file on or before February 10. The IRS will mail a preaddressed Form 940 or Form 940-EZ to you if you filed a return for the year before. If you do not receive Form 940 or Form 940-EZ, you can get a form by calling 1-800-TAX-FORM (1-800-829-3676).

Form 940-EZ requirements. You may be able to use Form 940-EZ instead of Form 940 if (a) you paid unemployment taxes ("contributions") to only one state, (b) you paid state unemployment taxes by the due date of Form 940 or Form 940-EZ, (c) all wages that were taxable for FUTA tax purposes were also taxable for your state's unemployment tax, and (d) you did not make contributions to a credit reduction state. For example, if you paid wages to corporate officers (these wages are subject to FUTA tax) in a state that exempts these wages from its unemployment taxes, you cannot use Form 940-EZ.

Household employees. If you did not report employment taxes for household employees on Form 941 or Form 943, report FUTA tax for these employees on Schedule H (Form 1040), Household Employment Taxes. See Publication 926 for more information.

Electronic filing by Reporting Agents. Reporting agents filing Forms 940 for groups of taxpayers can file them electronically. See the *Reporting Agent* discussion in section 7 of Publication 15-A, Employer's Supplemental Tax Guide, for more information.

IRS Publication 15, Circular E (continued)

15. Special Rules for Various Types of Services and Payments

(Section references are to the Internal Revenue Code unless otherwise noted.)

Special Classes of Employment and Special Types of Payments	Treatment Under Employment Taxes		
	Income Tax Withholding	Social Security and Medicare	Federal Unemployment
Aliens, nonresident.	See page 14 and Publication 515, Withholding of Tax on Nonresident Aliens and Foreign Entities, and Publication 519, U.S. Tax Guide for Aliens.		
Aliens, resident: 1. Service performed in the U.S.	Same as U.S. citizen.	Same as U.S. citizen. (Exempt if any part of service as crew member of foreign vessel or aircraft is performed outside U.S.)	Same as U.S. citizen.
2. Service performed outside U.S.	Withhold	Taxable if (1) working for an American employer or (2) an American employer by agreement covers U.S. citizens and residents employed by its foreign affiliates.	Exempt unless on or in connection with an American vessel or aircraft and either performed under contract made in U.S., or alien is employed on such vessel or aircraft when it touches U.S. port.
Cafeteria plan benefits under section 125.	If employee chooses cash, subject to all employment taxes. If employee chooses another benefit, the treatment is the same as if the benefit was provided outside the plan. See Publication 15-B for more information.		
Deceased worker: 1. Wages paid to beneficiary or estate in same calendar year as worker's death. See Instructions for Forms W-2 and W-3 for details.	Exempt	Taxable	Taxable
2. Wages paid to beneficiary or estate after calendar year of worker's death.	Exempt	Exempt	Exempt
Dependent care assistance programs (limited to $5,000; $2,500 if married filing separately).	Exempt to the extent that it is reasonable to believe that amounts are excludable from gross income under section 129.		
Disabled worker's wages paid after year in which worker became entitled to disability insurance benefits under the Social Security Act.	Withhold	Exempt, if worker did not perform any service for employer during period for which payment is made.	Taxable
Employee business expense reimbursement: 1. Accountable plan. a. Amounts not exceeding specified government rate for per diem or standard mileage.	Exempt	Exempt	Exempt
b. Amounts in excess of specified government rate for per diem or standard mileage.	Withhold	Taxable	Taxable
2. Nonaccountable plan. See page 10 for details.	Withhold	Taxable	Taxable
Family employees: 1. Child employed by parent (or partnership in which each partner is a parent of the child).	Withhold	Exempt until age 18; age 21 for domestic service.	Exempt until age 21
2. Parent employed by child.	Withhold	Taxable if in course of the son's or daughter's business. For domestic services, see section 3.	Exempt
3. Spouse employed by spouse. See section 3 for more information.	Withhold	Taxable if in course of spouse's business.	Exempt
Fishing and related activities.	See Publication 595, Tax Highlights for Commercial Fishermen.		
Foreign governments and international organizations.	Exempt	Exempt	Exempt

IRS Publication 15, Circular E (continued)

Special Classes of Employment and Special Types of Payments	Treatment Under Employment Taxes		
	Income Tax Withholding	**Social Security and Medicare**	**Federal Unemployment**
Foreign service by U.S. citizens: 1. As U.S. government employee.	Withhold	Same as within U.S.	Exempt
2. For foreign affiliates of American employers and other private employers.	Exempt if at time of payment (1) it is reasonable to believe employee is entitled to exclusion from income under section 911 or (2) the employer is required by law of the foreign country to withhold income tax on such payment.	Exempt unless (1) an American employer by agreement covers U.S. citizens employed by its foreign affiliates or (2) U.S. citizen works for American employer.	Exempt unless (1) on American vessel or aircraft and work is performed under contract made in U.S. or worker is employed on vessel when it touches U.S. port or (2) U.S. citizen works for American employer (except in a contiguous country with which the U.S. has an agreement for unemployment compensation) or in the U.S. Virgin Islands.
Homeworkers (industrial, cottage industry): 1. Common law employees.	Withhold	Taxable	Taxable
2. Statutory employees. See page 7 for details.	Exempt	Taxable if paid $100 or more in cash in a year.	Exempt
Hospital employees: 1. Interns	Withhold	Taxable	Exempt
2. Patients	Withhold	Taxable (Exempt for state or local government hospitals.)	Exempt
Household employees: 1. Domestic service in private homes. Farmers, see Publication 51 (Circular A).	Exempt (withhold if both employer and employee agree).	Taxable if paid $1,400 or more in cash in 2005. Exempt if performed by an individual under age 18 during any portion of the calendar year and is not the principal occupation of the employee.	Taxable if employer paid total cash wages of $1,000 or more (for all household employees) in any quarter in the current or preceding calendar year.
2. Domestic service in college clubs, fraternities, and sororities.	Exempt (withhold if both employer and employee agree).	Exempt if paid to regular student; also exempt if employee is paid less than $100 in a year by an income-tax-exempt employer.	Taxable if employer paid total cash wages of $1,000 or more (for all household employees) in any quarter in the current or preceding calendar year.
Insurance for employees: 1. Accident and health insurance premiums under a plan or system for employees and their dependents generally or for a class or classes of employees and their dependents.	Exempt (except 2% shareholder-employees of S corporations).	Exempt	Exempt
2. Group-term life insurance costs. See Publication 15-B for details.	Exempt	Exempt, except for the cost of group-term life insurance that is includible in the employee's gross income. (Special rules apply for former employees.)	Exempt
Insurance agents or solicitors: 1. Full-time life insurance salesperson.	Withhold only if employee under common law. See page 7.	Taxable	Taxable if (1) employee under common law and (2) not paid solely by commissions.
2. Other salesperson of life, casualty, etc., insurance.	Withhold only if employee under common law.	Taxable only if employee under common law.	Taxable if (1) employee under common law and (2) not paid solely by commissions.

IRS Publication 15, Circular E (continued)

Special Classes of Employment and Special Types of Payments	Treatment Under Employment Taxes		
	Income Tax Withholding	Social Security and Medicare	Federal Unemployment
Interest on loans with below-market interest rates (foregone interest and deemed original issue discount).	See Publication 15-A.		
Leave-sharing plans: Amounts paid to an employee under a leave-sharing plan.	Withhold	Taxable	Taxable
Newspaper carriers and vendors: Newspaper carriers under age 18; newspaper and magazine vendors buying at fixed prices and retaining receipts from sales to customers. See Publication 15-A for information on statutory nonemployee status.	Exempt (withhold if both employer and employee voluntarily agree).	Exempt	Exempt
Noncash payments: 1. For household work, agricultural labor, and service not in the course of the employer's trade or business.	Exempt (withhold if both employer and employee voluntarily agree).	Exempt	Exempt
2. To certain retail commission salespersons ordinarily paid solely on a cash commission basis.	Optional with employer.	Taxable	Taxable
Nonprofit organizations.	See Publication 15-A.		
Officers or shareholders of an S Corporation. Distributions and other payments by an S corporation to a corporate officer or shareholder must be treated as wages to the extent the amounts are reasonable compensation for services to the corporation by an employee. (See the Instructions for Form 1120S.)	Withhold	Taxable	Taxable
Partners: Payments to general or limited partners of a partnership. (See Publication 541, Partnerships, and Publication 533, Self-Employment Tax, for partner reporting rules.)	Exempt	Exempt	Exempt
Railroads: Payments subject to the Railroad Retirement Act.	Withhold	Exempt	Exempt
Religious exemptions.	See Publication 15-A.		
Retirement and pension plans: 1. Employer contributions to a qualified plan.	Exempt	Exempt	Exempt
2. Elective employee contributions and deferrals to a plan containing a qualified cash or deferred compensation arrangement (for example, 401(k)).	Generally exempt, but see section 402(g) for limitation.	Taxable	Taxable
3. Employer contributions to individual retirement accounts under simplified employee pension plan (SEP).	Generally exempt, but see section 402(g) for salary reduction SEP limitation.	Exempt, except for amounts contributed under a salary reduction SEP agreement.	
4. Employer contributions to section 403(b) annuities.	Generally exempt, but see section 402(g) for limitation.	Taxable if paid through a salary reduction agreement (written or otherwise).	
5. Employee salary reduction contributions to a SIMPLE retirement account.	Exempt	Taxable	Taxable
6. Distributions from qualified retirement and pension plans and section 403(b) annuities. See Publication 15-A for information on pensions, annuities, and employer contributions to nonqualified deferred compensation arrangements.	Withhold, but recipient may elect exemption on Form W-4P in certain cases; mandatory 20% withholding applies to an eligible rollover distribution that is not a direct rollover; exempt for direct rollover. See Publication 15-A.	Exempt	Exempt
Salespersons: 1. Common law employees.	Withhold	Taxable	Taxable
2. Statutory employees.	Exempt	Taxable	Taxable, except for full-time life insurance sales agents.
3. Statutory nonemployees (qualified real estate agents and direct sellers). See page 8 for details.	Exempt	Exempt	Exempt
Scholarships and fellowship grants: (includible in income under section 117(c)).	Withhold	Taxability depends on the nature of the employment and the status of the organization. See Students on next page.	

IRS Publication 15, Circular E (continued)

Special Classes of Employment and Special Types of Payments	Treatment Under Employment Taxes		
	Income Tax Withholding	Social Security and Medicare	Federal Unemployment
Severance or dismissal pay.	Withhold	Taxable	Taxable
Service not in the course of the employer's trade or business, other than on a farm operated for profit or for household employment in private homes.	Withhold only if employee earns $50 or more in cash in a quarter and works on 24 or more different days in that quarter or in the preceding quarter.	Taxable if employee receives $100 or more in cash in a calendar year.	Taxable only if employee earns $50 or more in cash in a quarter and works on 24 or more different days in that quarter or in the preceding quarter.
Sick pay. (See Publication 15-A for more information.)	Withhold	Exempt after end of 6 calendar months after the calendar month employee last worked for employer.	
State governments and political subdivisions, employees of: 1. Salaries and wages. (Includes payments to most elected and appointed officials. See chapter 3 of Publication 963, Federal-State Reference Guide.)	Withhold	Taxable (1) for services performed by employees who are either (a) covered under a section 218 agreement or (b) not a member of a public retirement system, and (2) (for Medicare tax only) for employees hired after 3/31/86 who are members of a public retirement system not covered by a section 218 social security agreement.	Exempt
2. Election workers. Election workers are individuals who are employed to perform services for state or local governments at election booths in connection with national, state or local elections. **Note.** File Form W-2 for payments of $600 or more even if no social security or Medicare taxes were withheld.	Exempt	Taxable if paid $1,200 or more in 2005 (lesser amount if specified by a section 218 social security agreement).	Exempt
Students, scholars, trainees, teachers, etc.: 1. Student enrolled and regularly attending classes, performing services for: a. Private school, college, or university.	Withhold	Exempt	Exempt
b. Auxiliary nonprofit organization operated for and controlled by school, college, or university.	Withhold	Exempt unless services are covered by a section 218 (Social Security Act) agreement	Exempt
c. Public school, college, or university.	Withhold	Exempt unless services are covered by a section 218 (Social Security Act) agreement	Exempt
2. Full-time student performing service for academic credit, combining instruction with work experience as an integral part of the program.	Withhold	Taxable	Exempt unless program was established for or on behalf of an employer or group of employers.
3. Student nurse performing part-time services for nominal earnings at hospital as incidental part of training.	Withhold	Exempt	Exempt
4. Student employed by organized camps.	Withhold	Taxable	Exempt
5. Student, scholar, trainee, teacher, etc., as nonimmigrant alien under section 101(a)(15)(F), (J), (M), or (Q) of Immigration and Nationality Act (that is, aliens holding F-1, J-1, M-1, or Q-1 visas).	Withhold unless excepted by regulations.	Exempt if service is performed for purpose specified in section 101(a)(15)(F), (J), (M), or (Q) of Immigration and Nationality Act. However, these taxes may apply if the employee becomes a resident alien. See the special residency tests for exempt individuals in chapter 1 of Publication 519.	
Supplemental unemployment compensation plan benefits.	Withhold	Exempt under certain conditions. See Publication 15-A.	
Tips: 1. If $20 or more in a month.	Withhold	Taxable	Taxable for all tips reported in writing to employer.
2. If less than $20 in a month. See section 6 for more information.	Exempt	Exempt	Exempt
Worker's compensation.	Exempt	Exempt	Exempt

IRS Publication 15, Circular E (continued)

16. How To Use the Income Tax Withholding and Advance Earned Income Credit (EIC) Payment Tables

Income Tax Withholding

There are several ways to figure income tax withholding. The following methods of withholding are based on the information that you get from your employees on Form W-4, Employee's Withholding Allowance Certificate. See section 9 for more information on Form W-4.

Wage Bracket Method

Under the wage bracket method, find the proper table (on pages 38-57) for your payroll period and the employee's marital status as shown on his or her Form W-4. Then, based on the number of withholding allowances claimed on the Form W-4 and the amount of wages, find the amount of federal tax to withhold. If your employee is claiming more than 10 withholding allowances, see below.

Note. If you cannot use the wage bracket tables because wages exceed the amount shown in the last bracket of the table, use the percentage method of withholding described below. Be sure to reduce wages by the amount of total withholding allowances in Table 5 on this page before using the percentage method tables (pages 36-37).

Adjusting wage bracket withholding for employees claiming more than 10 withholding allowances. The wage bracket tables can be used if an employee claims up to 10 allowances. More than 10 allowances may be claimed because of the special withholding allowance, additional allowances for deductions and credits, and the system itself.

Adapt the tables to more than 10 allowances as follows:

1. Multiply the number of withholding allowances over 10 by the allowance value for the payroll period. (The allowance values are in *Table 5, Percentage Method—2005 Amount for One Withholding Allowance* later.)

2. Subtract the result from the employee's wages.

3. On this amount, find and withhold the tax in the column for 10 allowances.

This is a voluntary method. If you use the wage bracket tables, you may continue to withhold the amount in the "10" column when your employee has more than 10 allowances, using the method above. You can also use any other method described below.

Percentage Method

If you do not want to use the wage bracket tables on pages 38 through 57 to figure how much income tax to withhold, you can use a percentage computation based on Table 5 below and the appropriate rate table. This method works for any number of withholding allowances the employee claims and any amount of wages.

Use these steps to figure the income tax to withhold under the percentage method.

1. Multiply one withholding allowance for your payroll period (see Table 5 below) by the number of allowances that the employee claims.

2. Subtract that amount from the employee's wages.

3. Determine the amount to withhold from the appropriate table on page 36 or 37.

Table 5. Percentage Method—2005 Amount for One Withholding Allowance

Payroll Period	One Withholding Allowance
Weekly	$61.54
Biweekly	123.08
Semimonthly	133.33
Monthly	266.67
Quarterly	800.00
Semiannually	1,600.00
Annually	3,200.00
Daily or miscellaneous (each day of the payroll period)	12.31

Example: An unmarried employee is paid $600 weekly. This employee has in effect a Form W-4 claiming two withholding allowances. Using the percentage method, figure the income tax to withhold as follows:

1. Total wage payment $600.00
2. One allowance $61.54
3. Allowances claimed on Form W-4 __2__
4. Multiply line 2 by line 3 . . . . . . $123.08
5. Amount subject to withholding (subtract line 4 from line 1) $476.92
6. Tax to be withheld on $476.92 from Table 1—single person, page 36 . . . . . . $ 57.04

To figure the income tax to withhold, you may reduce the last digit of the wages to zero, or figure the wages to the nearest dollar.

Annual income tax withholding. Figure the income tax to withhold on annual wages under the *Percentage Method* for an annual payroll period. Then prorate the tax back to the payroll period.

Example. A married person claims four withholding allowances. She is paid $1,000 a week. Multiply the weekly wages by 52 weeks to figure the annual wage of $52,000. Subtract $12,800 (the value of four withholding allowances for 2005) for a balance of $39,200. Using the table for the annual payroll period on page 37, $3,950 is withheld. Divide the annual tax by 52. The weekly income tax to withhold is $75.96.

Alternative Methods of Income Tax Withholding

Rather than the *Wage Bracket Method* or *Percentage Method* described above, you can use an alternative method to withhold income tax. Publication 15-A,

IRS Publication 15, Circular E (continued)

Employer's Supplemental Tax Guide, describes these alternative methods and contains:

- Formula tables for percentage method withholding (for automated payroll systems),
- Wage bracket percentage method tables (for automated payroll systems), and
- Combined income, social security, and Medicare tax withholding tables.

Some of the alternative methods explained in Publication 15-A are annualized wages, average estimated wages, cumulative wages, and part-year employment.

Advance Payment Methods for the Earned Income Credit (EIC)

To figure the advance EIC payment, you may use either the *Wage Bracket Method* or the *Percentage Method* as explained below. You may use other methods for figuring advance EIC payments if the amount of the payment is about the same as it would be using tables in this booklet. See the tolerances allowed in the chart in section 9 of Publication 15-A. See also section 10 in this booklet for an explanation of the advance payment of the EIC.

The number of withholding allowances that an employee claims on Form W-4 is not used in figuring the advance EIC payment. Nor does it matter that the employee has claimed exemption from income tax withholding on Form W-4.

Wage Bracket Method

If you use the wage bracket tables on pages 60 through 65, figure the advance EIC payment as follows.

Find the employee's gross wages before any deductions using the appropriate table. There are different tables for (a) single or head of household, (b) married without spouse filing certificate, and (c) married with both spouses filing certificates. Determine the amount of the advance EIC payment shown in the appropriate table for the amount of wages paid.

Percentage Method

If you do not want to use the wage bracket tables to figure how much to include in an employee's wages for the advance EIC payment, you can use the percentage method based on the appropriate rate table on pages 58 and 59.

Find the employee's gross wages before any deductions in the appropriate table on pages 58 and 59. There are different tables for (a) single or head of household, (b) married without spouse filing certificate, and (c) married with both spouses filing certificates. Find the advance EIC payment shown in the appropriate table for the amount of wages paid.

Whole-Dollar Withholding and Paying Advance EIC (Rounding)

The income tax withholding amounts in the Wage Bracket Tables (pages 38-57) have been rounded to whole-dollar amounts.

When employers use the Percentage Method (pages 36-37) or an alternative method of income tax withholding, the tax for the pay period may be rounded to the nearest dollar.

The Wage Bracket Tables for advance EIC payments (pages 60-65) have also been rounded to whole-dollar amounts. If you use the Tables for Percentage Method of Advance EIC Payments (pages 58-59), the payments may be rounded to the nearest dollar.

IRS Publication 15, Circular E (continued)

Tables for Percentage Method of Withholding
(For Wages Paid in 2005)

TABLE 1—WEEKLY Payroll Period

(a) SINGLE person (including head of household)—

If the amount of wages (after subtracting withholding allowances) is:
The amount of income tax to withhold is:

Not over $51 . . . . . $0

Over—	But not over—		of excess over—
$51	—$188 . .	10%	—$51
$188	—$606 . .	$13.70 plus 15%	—$188
$606	—$1,341 . .	$76.40 plus 25%	—$606
$1,341	—$2,922 . .	$260.15 plus 28%	—$1,341
$2,922	—$6,313 . .	$702.83 plus 33%	—$2,922
$6,313	. . . . . .	$1,821.86 plus 35%	—$6,313

(b) MARRIED person—

If the amount of wages (after subtracting withholding allowances) is:
The amount of income tax to withhold is:

Not over $154 . . . . $0

Over—	But not over—		of excess over—
$154	—$435 . .	10%	—$154
$435	—$1,273 . .	$28.10 plus 15%	—$435
$1,273	—$2,322 . .	$153.80 plus 25%	—$1,273
$2,322	—$3,646 . .	$416.05 plus 28%	—$2,322
$3,646	—$6,409 . .	$786.77 plus 33%	—$3,646
$6,409	. . .	$1,698.56 plus 35%	—$6,409

TABLE 2—BIWEEKLY Payroll Period

(a) SINGLE person (including head of household)—

If the amount of wages (after subtracting withholding allowances) is:
The amount of income tax to withhold is:

Not over $102 . . . . $0

Over—	But not over—		of excess over—
$102	—$377 . .	10%	—$102
$377	—$1,212 . .	$27.50 plus 15%	—$377
$1,212	—$2,683 . .	$152.75 plus 25%	—$1,212
$2,683	—$5,844 . .	$520.50 plus 28%	—$2,683
$5,844	—$12,625 . .	$1,405.58 plus 33%	—$5,844
$12,625	. . . . .	$3,643.31 plus 35%	—$12,625

(b) MARRIED person—

If the amount of wages (after subtracting withholding allowances) is:
The amount of income tax to withhold is:

Not over $308 . . . . $0

Over—	But not over—		of excess over—
$308	—$869 . .	10%	—$308
$869	—$2,546 . .	$56.10 plus 15%	—$869
$2,546	—$4,644 . .	$307.65 plus 25%	—$2,546
$4,644	—$7,292 . .	$832.15 plus 28%	—$4,644
$7,292	—$12,817 . .	$1,573.59 plus 33%	—$7,292
$12,817	. . .	$3,396.84 plus 35%	—$12,817

TABLE 3—SEMIMONTHLY Payroll Period

(a) SINGLE person (including head of household)—

If the amount of wages (after subtracting withholding allowances) is:
The amount of income tax to withhold is:

Not over $110 . . . . $0

Over—	But not over—		of excess over—
$110	—$408 . .	10%	—$110
$408	—$1,313 . .	$29.80 plus 15%	—$408
$1,313	—$2,906 . .	$165.55 plus 25%	—$1,313
$2,906	—$6,331 . .	$563.80 plus 28%	—$2,906
$6,331	—$13,677 . .	$1,522.80 plus 33%	—$6,331
$13,677	. . . . .	$3,946.98 plus 35%	—$13,677

(b) MARRIED person—

If the amount of wages (after subtracting withholding allowances) is:
The amount of income tax to withhold is:

Not over $333 . . . . $0

Over—	But not over—		of excess over—
$333	—$942 . .	10%	—$333
$942	—$2,758 . .	$60.90 plus 15%	—$942
$2,758	—$5,031 . .	$333.30 plus 25%	—$2,758
$5,031	—$7,900 . .	$901.55 plus 28%	—$5,031
$7,900	—$13,885 . .	$1,704.87 plus 33%	—$7,900
$13,885	. . . . .	$3,679.92 plus 35%	—$13,885

TABLE 4—MONTHLY Payroll Period

(a) SINGLE person (including head of household)—

If the amount of wages (after subtracting withholding allowances) is:
The amount of income tax to withhold is:

Not over $221 . . . . $0

Over—	But not over—		of excess over—
$221	—$817 . .	10%	—$221
$817	—$2,625 . .	$59.60 plus 15%	—$817
$2,625	—$5,813 . .	$330.80 plus 25%	—$2,625
$5,813	—$12,663 . .	$1,127.80 plus 28%	—$5,813
$12,663	—$27,354 . .	$3,045.80 plus 33%	—$12,663
$27,354	. . . . . .	$7,893.83 plus 35%	—$27,354

(b) MARRIED person—

If the amount of wages (after subtracting withholding allowances) is:
The amount of income tax to withhold is:

Not over $667 . . . . $0

Over—	But not over—		of excess over—
$667	—$1,883 . .	10%	—$667
$1,883	—$5,517 . .	$121.60 plus 15%	—$1,883
$5,517	—$10,063 . .	$666.70 plus 25%	—$5,517
$10,063	—$15,800 . .	$1,803.20 plus 28%	—$10,063
$15,800	—$27,771 . .	$3,409.56 plus 33%	—$15,800
$27,771	. . . . .	$7,359.99 plus 35%	—$27,771

IRS Publication 15, Circular E (continued)

Tables for Percentage Method of Withholding (Continued)
(For Wages Paid in 2005)

TABLE 5—QUARTERLY Payroll Period

(a) SINGLE person (including head of household)—

If the amount of wages (after subtracting withholding allowances) is: The amount of income tax to withhold is:

Not over $663 . . . . $0

Over—	But not over—		of excess over—
$663	—$2,450	. 10%	—$663
$2,450	—$7,875	. $178.70 plus 15%	—$2,450
$7,875	—$17,438	. $992.45 plus 25%	—$7,875
$17,438	—$37,988	. $3,383.20 plus 28%	—$17,438
$37,988	—$82,063	. $9,137.20 plus 33%	—$37,988
$82,063	. . . . .	. $23,681.95 plus 35%	—$82,063

(b) MARRIED person—

If the amount of wages (after subtracting withholding allowances) is: The amount of income tax to withhold is:

Not over $2,000 . . . . $0

Over—	But not over—		of excess over—
$2,000	—$5,650	. 10%	—$2,000
$5,650	—$16,550	. $365.00 plus 15%	—$5,650
$16,550	—$30,188	. $2,000.00 plus 25%	—$16,550
$30,188	—$47,400	. $5,409.50 plus 28%	—$30,188
$47,400	—$83,313	. $10,228.86 plus 33%	—$47,400
$83,313	. . . . .	. $22,080.15 plus 35%	—$83,313

TABLE 6—SEMIANNUAL Payroll Period

(a) SINGLE person (including head of household)—

If the amount of wages (after subtracting withholding allowances) is: The amount of income tax to withhold is:

Not over $1,325 . . . . $0

Over—	But not over—		of excess over—
$1,325	—$4,900	. 10%	—$1,325
$4,900	—$15,750	. $357.50 plus 15%	—$4,900
$15,750	—$34,875	. $1,985.00 plus 25%	—$15,750
$34,875	—$75,975	. $6,766.25 plus 28%	—$34,875
$75,975	—$164,125	. $18,274.25 plus 33%	—$75,975
$164,125	. . . . .	. $47,363.75 plus 35%	—$164,125

(b) MARRIED person—

If the amount of wages (after subtracting withholding allowances) is: The amount of income tax to withhold is:

Not over $4,000 . . . . $0

Over—	But not over—		of excess over—
$4,000	—$11,300	. 10%	—$4,000
$11,300	—$33,100	. $730.00 plus 15%	—$11,300
$33,100	—$60,375	. $4,000.00 plus 25%	—$33,100
$60,375	—$94,800	. $10,818.75 plus 28%	—$60,375
$94,800	—$166,625	. $20,457.75 plus 33%	—$94,800
$166,625	. . . . .	. $44,160.00 plus 35%	—$166,625

TABLE 7—ANNUAL Payroll Period

(a) SINGLE person (including head of household)—

If the amount of wages (after subtracting withholding allowances) is: The amount of income tax to withhold is:

Not over $2,650 . . . . $0

Over—	But not over—		of excess over—
$2,650	—$9,800	. 10%	—$2,650
$9,800	—$31,500	. $715.00 plus 15%	—$9,800
$31,500	—$69,750	. $3,970.00 plus 25%	—$31,500
$69,750	—$151,950	. $13,532.50 plus 28%	—$69,750
$151,950	—$328,250	. $36,548.50 plus 33%	—$151,950
$328,250	. . . . .	. $94,727.50 plus 35%	—$328,250

(b) MARRIED person—

If the amount of wages (after subtracting withholding allowances) is: The amount of income tax to withhold is:

Not over $8,000 . . . . $0

Over—	But not over—		of excess over—
$8,000	—$22,600	. 10%	—$8,000
$22,600	—$66,200	. $1,460.00 plus 15%	—$22,600
$66,200	—$120,750	. $8,000.00 plus 25%	—$66,200
$120,750	—$189,600	. $21,637.50 plus 28%	—$120,750
$189,600	—$333,250	. $40,915.50 plus 33%	—$189,600
$333,250	. . . . .	. $88,320.00 plus 35%	—$333,250

TABLE 8—DAILY or MISCELLANEOUS Payroll Period

(a) SINGLE person (including head of household)—

If the amount of wages (after subtracting withholding allowances) divided by the number of days in the payroll period is: The amount of income tax to withhold per day is:

Not over $10.20 . . . . $0

Over—	But not over—		of excess over—
$10.20	—$37.70	. 10%	—$10.20
$37.70	—$121.20	. $2.75 plus 15%	—$37.70
$121.20	—$268.30	. $15.28 plus 25%	—$121.20
$268.30	—$584.40	. $52.06 plus 28%	—$268.30
$584.40	—$1,262.50	. $140.57 plus 33%	—$584.40
$1,262.50	. . . . .	. $364.34 plus 35%	—$1,262.50

(b) MARRIED person—

If the amount of wages (after subtracting withholding allowances) divided by the number of days in the payroll period is: The amount of income tax to withhold per day is:

Not over $30.80 . . . . $0

Over—	But not over—		of excess over—
$30.80	—$86.90	. 10%	—$30.80
$86.90	—$254.60	. $5.61 plus 15%	—$86.90
$254.60	—$464.40	. $30.77 plus 25%	—$254.60
$464.40	—$729.20	. $83.22 plus 28%	—$464.40
$729.20	—$1,281.70	. $157.36 plus 33%	—$729.20
$1,281.70	. . . . .	. $339.69 plus 35%	—$1,281.70

IRS Publication 15, Circular E (continued)

SINGLE Persons—WEEKLY Payroll Period

(For Wages Paid in 2005)

If the wages are—		And the number of withholding allowances claimed is—										
At least	But less than	0	1	2	3	4	5	6	7	8	9	10
		The amount of income tax to be withheld is—										
$0	$55	$0	$0	$0	$0	$0	$0	$0	$0	$0	$0	$0
55	60	1	0	0	0	0	0	0	0	0	0	0
60	65	1	0	0	0	0	0	0	0	0	0	0
65	70	2	0	0	0	0	0	0	0	0	0	0
70	75	2	0	0	0	0	0	0	0	0	0	0
75	80	3	0	0	0	0	0	0	0	0	0	0
80	85	3	0	0	0	0	0	0	0	0	0	0
85	90	4	0	0	0	0	0	0	0	0	0	0
90	95	4	0	0	0	0	0	0	0	0	0	0
95	100	5	0	0	0	0	0	0	0	0	0	0
100	105	5	0	0	0	0	0	0	0	0	0	0
105	110	6	0	0	0	0	0	0	0	0	0	0
110	115	6	0	0	0	0	0	0	0	0	0	0
115	120	7	1	0	0	0	0	0	0	0	0	0
120	125	7	1	0	0	0	0	0	0	0	0	0
125	130	8	2	0	0	0	0	0	0	0	0	0
130	135	8	2	0	0	0	0	0	0	0	0	0
135	140	9	3	0	0	0	0	0	0	0	0	0
140	145	9	3	0	0	0	0	0	0	0	0	0
145	150	10	4	0	0	0	0	0	0	0	0	0
150	155	10	4	0	0	0	0	0	0	0	0	0
155	160	11	5	0	0	0	0	0	0	0	0	0
160	165	11	5	0	0	0	0	0	0	0	0	0
165	170	12	6	0	0	0	0	0	0	0	0	0
170	175	12	6	0	0	0	0	0	0	0	0	0
175	180	13	7	0	0	0	0	0	0	0	0	0
180	185	13	7	1	0	0	0	0	0	0	0	0
185	190	14	8	1	0	0	0	0	0	0	0	0
190	195	14	8	2	0	0	0	0	0	0	0	0
195	200	15	9	2	0	0	0	0	0	0	0	0
200	210	16	9	3	0	0	0	0	0	0	0	0
210	220	18	10	4	0	0	0	0	0	0	0	0
220	230	19	11	5	0	0	0	0	0	0	0	0
230	240	21	12	6	0	0	0	0	0	0	0	0
240	250	22	13	7	1	0	0	0	0	0	0	0
250	260	24	15	8	2	0	0	0	0	0	0	0
260	270	25	16	9	3	0	0	0	0	0	0	0
270	280	27	18	10	4	0	0	0	0	0	0	0
280	290	28	19	11	5	0	0	0	0	0	0	0
290	300	30	21	12	6	0	0	0	0	0	0	0
300	310	31	22	13	7	1	0	0	0	0	0	0
310	320	33	24	14	8	2	0	0	0	0	0	0
320	330	34	25	16	9	3	0	0	0	0	0	0
330	340	36	27	17	10	4	0	0	0	0	0	0
340	350	37	28	19	11	5	0	0	0	0	0	0
350	360	39	30	20	12	6	0	0	0	0	0	0
360	370	40	31	22	13	7	1	0	0	0	0	0
370	380	42	33	23	14	8	2	0	0	0	0	0
380	390	43	34	25	16	9	3	0	0	0	0	0
390	400	45	36	26	17	10	4	0	0	0	0	0
400	410	46	37	28	19	11	5	0	0	0	0	0
410	420	48	39	29	20	12	6	0	0	0	0	0
420	430	49	40	31	22	13	7	0	0	0	0	0
430	440	51	42	32	23	14	8	1	0	0	0	0
440	450	52	43	34	25	15	9	2	0	0	0	0
450	460	54	45	35	26	17	10	3	0	0	0	0
460	470	55	46	37	28	18	11	4	0	0	0	0
470	480	57	48	38	29	20	12	5	0	0	0	0
480	490	58	49	40	31	21	13	6	0	0	0	0
490	500	60	51	41	32	23	14	7	1	0	0	0
500	510	61	52	43	34	24	15	8	2	0	0	0
510	520	63	54	44	35	26	17	9	3	0	0	0
520	530	64	55	46	37	27	18	10	4	0	0	0
530	540	66	57	47	38	29	20	11	5	0	0	0
540	550	67	58	49	40	30	21	12	6	0	0	0
550	560	69	60	50	41	32	23	13	7	1	0	0
560	570	70	61	52	43	33	24	15	8	2	0	0
570	580	72	63	53	44	35	26	16	9	3	0	0
580	590	73	64	55	46	36	27	18	10	4	0	0
590	600	75	66	56	47	38	29	19	11	5	0	0

IRS Publication 15, Circular E (continued)

SINGLE Persons—WEEKLY Payroll Period

(For Wages Paid in 2005)

If the wages are–		And the number of withholding allowances claimed is—										
At least	But less than	0	1	2	3	4	5	6	7	8	9	10
		The amount of income tax to be withheld is—										
$600	$610	$76	$67	$58	$49	$39	$30	$21	$12	$6	$0	$0
610	620	79	69	59	50	41	32	22	13	7	1	0
620	630	81	70	61	52	42	33	24	15	8	2	0
630	640	84	72	62	53	44	35	25	16	9	3	0
640	650	86	73	64	55	45	36	27	18	10	4	0
650	660	89	75	65	56	47	38	28	19	11	5	0
660	670	91	76	67	58	48	39	30	21	12	6	0
670	680	94	78	68	59	50	41	31	22	13	7	1
680	690	96	81	70	61	51	42	33	24	14	8	2
690	700	99	83	71	62	53	44	34	25	16	9	3
700	710	101	86	73	64	54	45	36	27	17	10	4
710	720	104	88	74	65	56	47	37	28	19	11	5
720	730	106	91	76	67	57	48	39	30	20	12	6
730	740	109	93	78	68	59	50	40	31	22	13	7
740	750	111	96	80	70	60	51	42	33	23	14	8
750	760	114	98	83	71	62	53	43	34	25	16	9
760	770	116	101	85	73	63	54	45	36	26	17	10
770	780	119	103	88	74	65	56	46	37	28	19	11
780	790	121	106	90	76	66	57	48	39	29	20	12
790	800	124	108	93	78	68	59	49	40	31	22	13
800	810	126	111	95	80	69	60	51	42	32	23	14
810	820	129	113	98	83	71	62	52	43	34	25	15
820	830	131	116	100	85	72	63	54	45	35	26	17
830	840	134	118	103	88	74	65	55	46	37	28	18
840	850	136	121	105	90	75	66	57	48	38	29	20
850	860	139	123	108	93	77	68	58	49	40	31	21
860	870	141	126	110	95	80	69	60	51	41	32	23
870	880	144	128	113	98	82	71	61	52	43	34	24
880	890	146	131	115	100	85	72	63	54	44	35	26
890	900	149	133	118	103	87	74	64	55	46	37	27
900	910	151	136	120	105	90	75	66	57	47	38	29
910	920	154	138	123	108	92	77	67	58	49	40	30
920	930	156	141	125	110	95	79	69	60	50	41	32
930	940	159	143	128	113	97	82	70	61	52	43	33
940	950	161	146	130	115	100	84	72	63	53	44	35
950	960	164	148	133	118	102	87	73	64	55	46	36
960	970	166	151	135	120	105	89	75	66	56	47	38
970	980	169	153	138	123	107	92	76	67	58	49	39
980	990	171	156	140	125	110	94	79	69	59	50	41
990	1,000	174	158	143	128	112	97	81	70	61	52	42
1,000	1,010	176	161	145	130	115	99	84	72	62	53	44
1,010	1,020	179	163	148	133	117	102	86	73	64	55	45
1,020	1,030	181	166	150	135	120	104	89	75	65	56	47
1,030	1,040	184	168	153	138	122	107	91	76	67	58	48
1,040	1,050	186	171	155	140	125	109	94	78	68	59	50
1,050	1,060	189	173	158	143	127	112	96	81	70	61	51
1,060	1,070	191	176	160	145	130	114	99	83	71	62	53
1,070	1,080	194	178	163	148	132	117	101	86	73	64	54
1,080	1,090	196	181	165	150	135	119	104	88	74	65	56
1,090	1,100	199	183	168	153	137	122	106	91	76	67	57
1,100	1,110	201	186	170	155	140	124	109	93	78	68	59
1,110	1,120	204	188	173	158	142	127	111	96	81	70	60
1,120	1,130	206	191	175	160	145	129	114	98	83	71	62
1,130	1,140	209	193	178	163	147	132	116	101	86	73	63
1,140	1,150	211	196	180	165	150	134	119	103	88	74	65
1,150	1,160	214	198	183	168	152	137	121	106	91	76	66
1,160	1,170	216	201	185	170	155	139	124	108	93	78	68
1,170	1,180	219	203	188	173	157	142	126	111	96	80	69
1,180	1,190	221	206	190	175	160	144	129	113	98	83	71
1,190	1,200	224	208	193	178	162	147	131	116	101	85	72
1,200	1,210	226	211	195	180	165	149	134	118	103	88	74
1,210	1,220	229	213	198	183	167	152	136	121	106	90	75
1,220	1,230	231	216	200	185	170	154	139	123	108	93	77
1,230	1,240	234	218	203	188	172	157	141	126	111	95	80
1,240	1,250	236	221	205	190	175	159	144	128	113	98	82

$1,250 and over Use Table 1(a) for a **SINGLE person** on page 36. Also see the instructions on page 34.

IRS Publication 15, Circular E (continued)

MARRIED Persons—WEEKLY Payroll Period
(For Wages Paid in 2005)

If the wages are—		And the number of withholding allowances claimed is—										
At least	But less than	0	1	2	3	4	5	6	7	8	9	10
		The amount of income tax to be withheld is—										
$0	$125	$0	$0	$0	$0	$0	$0	$0	$0	$0	$0	$0
125	130	0	0	0	0	0	0	0	0	0	0	0
130	135	0	0	0	0	0	0	0	0	0	0	0
135	140	0	0	0	0	0	0	0	0	0	0	0
140	145	0	0	0	0	0	0	0	0	0	0	0
145	150	0	0	0	0	0	0	0	0	0	0	0
150	155	0	0	0	0	0	0	0	0	0	0	0
155	160	0	0	0	0	0	0	0	0	0	0	0
160	165	1	0	0	0	0	0	0	0	0	0	0
165	170	1	0	0	0	0	0	0	0	0	0	0
170	175	2	0	0	0	0	0	0	0	0	0	0
175	180	2	0	0	0	0	0	0	0	0	0	0
180	185	3	0	0	0	0	0	0	0	0	0	0
185	190	3	0	0	0	0	0	0	0	0	0	0
190	195	4	0	0	0	0	0	0	0	0	0	0
195	200	4	0	0	0	0	0	0	0	0	0	0
200	210	5	0	0	0	0	0	0	0	0	0	0
210	220	6	0	0	0	0	0	0	0	0	0	0
220	230	7	1	0	0	0	0	0	0	0	0	0
230	240	8	2	0	0	0	0	0	0	0	0	0
240	250	9	3	0	0	0	0	0	0	0	0	0
250	260	10	4	0	0	0	0	0	0	0	0	0
260	270	11	5	0	0	0	0	0	0	0	0	0
270	280	12	6	0	0	0	0	0	0	0	0	0
280	290	13	7	1	0	0	0	0	0	0	0	0
290	300	14	8	2	0	0	0	0	0	0	0	0
300	310	15	9	3	0	0	0	0	0	0	0	0
310	320	16	10	4	0	0	0	0	0	0	0	0
320	330	17	11	5	0	0	0	0	0	0	0	0
330	340	18	12	6	0	0	0	0	0	0	0	0
340	350	19	13	7	1	0	0	0	0	0	0	0
350	360	20	14	8	2	0	0	0	0	0	0	0
360	370	21	15	9	3	0	0	0	0	0	0	0
370	380	22	16	10	4	0	0	0	0	0	0	0
380	390	23	17	11	5	0	0	0	0	0	0	0
390	400	24	18	12	6	0	0	0	0	0	0	0
400	410	25	19	13	7	1	0	0	0	0	0	0
410	420	26	20	14	8	2	0	0	0	0	0	0
420	430	27	21	15	9	3	0	0	0	0	0	0
430	440	28	22	16	10	4	0	0	0	0	0	0
440	450	30	23	17	11	5	0	0	0	0	0	0
450	460	31	24	18	12	6	0	0	0	0	0	0
460	470	33	25	19	13	7	0	0	0	0	0	0
470	480	34	26	20	14	8	1	0	0	0	0	0
480	490	36	27	21	15	9	2	0	0	0	0	0
490	500	37	28	22	16	10	3	0	0	0	0	0
500	510	39	29	23	17	11	4	0	0	0	0	0
510	520	40	31	24	18	12	5	0	0	0	0	0
520	530	42	32	25	19	13	6	0	0	0	0	0
530	540	43	34	26	20	14	7	1	0	0	0	0
540	550	45	35	27	21	15	8	2	0	0	0	0
550	560	46	37	28	22	16	9	3	0	0	0	0
560	570	48	38	29	23	17	10	4	0	0	0	0
570	580	49	40	31	24	18	11	5	0	0	0	0
580	590	51	41	32	25	19	12	6	0	0	0	0
590	600	52	43	34	26	20	13	7	1	0	0	0
600	610	54	44	35	27	21	14	8	2	0	0	0
610	620	55	46	37	28	22	15	9	3	0	0	0
620	630	57	47	38	29	23	16	10	4	0	0	0
630	640	58	49	40	30	24	17	11	5	0	0	0
640	650	60	50	41	32	25	18	12	6	0	0	0
650	660	61	52	43	33	26	19	13	7	1	0	0
660	670	63	53	44	35	27	20	14	8	2	0	0
670	680	64	55	46	36	28	21	15	9	3	0	0
680	690	66	56	47	38	29	22	16	10	4	0	0
690	700	67	58	49	39	30	23	17	11	5	0	0
700	710	69	59	50	41	32	24	18	12	6	0	0
710	720	70	61	52	42	33	25	19	13	7	1	0
720	730	72	62	53	44	35	26	20	14	8	2	0
730	740	73	64	55	45	36	27	21	15	9	3	0

IRS Publication 15, Circular E (continued)

MARRIED Persons—WEEKLY Payroll Period

(For Wages Paid in 2005)

If the wages are—		And the number of withholding allowances claimed is—										
At least	But less than	0	1	2	3	4	5	6	7	8	9	10
		The amount of income tax to be withheld is—										
$740	$750	$75	$65	$56	$47	$38	$28	$22	$16	$10	$4	$0
750	760	76	67	58	48	39	30	23	17	11	5	0
760	770	78	68	59	50	41	31	24	18	12	6	0
770	780	79	70	61	51	42	33	25	19	13	7	1
780	790	81	71	62	53	44	34	26	20	14	8	2
790	800	82	73	64	54	45	36	27	21	15	9	3
800	810	84	74	65	56	47	37	28	22	16	10	4
810	820	85	76	67	57	48	39	30	23	17	11	5
820	830	87	77	68	59	50	40	31	24	18	12	6
830	840	88	79	70	60	51	42	33	25	19	13	7
840	850	90	80	71	62	53	43	34	26	20	14	8
850	860	91	82	73	63	54	45	36	27	21	15	9
860	870	93	83	74	65	56	46	37	28	22	16	10
870	880	94	85	76	66	57	48	39	30	23	17	11
880	890	96	86	77	68	59	49	40	31	24	18	12
890	900	97	88	79	69	60	51	42	33	25	19	13
900	910	99	89	80	71	62	52	43	34	26	20	14
910	920	100	91	82	72	63	54	45	36	27	21	15
920	930	102	92	83	74	65	55	46	37	28	22	16
930	940	103	94	85	75	66	57	48	39	29	23	17
940	950	105	95	86	77	68	58	49	40	31	24	18
950	960	106	97	88	78	69	60	51	42	32	25	19
960	970	108	98	89	80	71	61	52	43	34	26	20
970	980	109	100	91	81	72	63	54	45	35	27	21
980	990	111	101	92	83	74	64	55	46	37	28	22
990	1,000	112	103	94	84	75	66	57	48	38	29	23
1,000	1,010	114	104	95	86	77	67	58	49	40	31	24
1,010	1,020	115	106	97	87	78	69	60	51	41	32	25
1,020	1,030	117	107	98	89	80	70	61	52	43	34	26
1,030	1,040	118	109	100	90	81	72	63	54	44	35	27
1,040	1,050	120	110	101	92	83	73	64	55	46	37	28
1,050	1,060	121	112	103	93	84	75	66	57	47	38	29
1,060	1,070	123	113	104	95	86	76	67	58	49	40	30
1,070	1,080	124	115	106	96	87	78	69	60	50	41	32
1,080	1,090	126	116	107	98	89	79	70	61	52	43	33
1,090	1,100	127	118	109	99	90	81	72	63	53	44	35
1,100	1,110	129	119	110	101	92	82	73	64	55	46	36
1,110	1,120	130	121	112	102	93	84	75	66	56	47	38
1,120	1,130	132	122	113	104	95	85	76	67	58	49	39
1,130	1,140	133	124	115	105	96	87	78	69	59	50	41
1,140	1,150	135	125	116	107	98	88	79	70	61	52	42
1,150	1,160	136	127	118	108	99	90	81	72	62	53	44
1,160	1,170	138	128	119	110	101	91	82	73	64	55	45
1,170	1,180	139	130	121	111	102	93	84	75	65	56	47
1,180	1,190	141	131	122	113	104	94	85	76	67	58	48
1,190	1,200	142	133	124	114	105	96	87	78	68	59	50
1,200	1,210	144	134	125	116	107	97	88	79	70	61	51
1,210	1,220	145	136	127	117	108	99	90	81	71	62	53
1,220	1,230	147	137	128	119	110	100	91	82	73	64	54
1,230	1,240	148	139	130	120	111	102	93	84	74	65	56
1,240	1,250	150	140	131	122	113	103	94	85	76	67	57
1,250	1,260	151	142	133	123	114	105	96	87	77	68	59
1,260	1,270	153	143	134	125	116	106	97	88	79	70	60
1,270	1,280	154	145	136	126	117	108	99	90	80	71	62
1,280	1,290	157	146	137	128	119	109	100	91	82	73	63
1,290	1,300	159	148	139	129	120	111	102	93	83	74	65
1,300	1,310	162	149	140	131	122	112	103	94	85	76	66
1,310	1,320	164	151	142	132	123	114	105	96	86	77	68
1,320	1,330	167	152	143	134	125	115	106	97	88	79	69
1,330	1,340	169	154	145	135	126	117	108	99	89	80	71
1,340	1,350	172	156	146	137	128	118	109	100	91	82	72
1,350	1,360	174	159	148	138	129	120	111	102	92	83	74
1,360	1,370	177	161	149	140	131	121	112	103	94	85	75
1,370	1,380	179	164	151	141	132	123	114	105	95	86	77
1,380	1,390	182	166	152	143	134	124	115	106	97	88	78
1,390	1,400	184	169	154	144	135	126	117	108	98	89	80

$1,400 and over   Use Table 1(b) for a **MARRIED person** on page 36. Also see the instructions on page 34.

IRS Publication 15, Circular E (continued)

SINGLE Persons—BIWEEKLY Payroll Period

(For Wages Paid in 2005)

If the wages are–		And the number of withholding allowances claimed is—										
At least	But less than	0	1	2	3	4	5	6	7	8	9	10
		The amount of income tax to be withheld is—										
$0	$105	$0	$0	$0	$0	$0	$0	$0	$0	$0	$0	$0
105	110	1	0	0	0	0	0	0	0	0	0	0
110	115	1	0	0	0	0	0	0	0	0	0	0
115	120	2	0	0	0	0	0	0	0	0	0	0
120	125	2	0	0	0	0	0	0	0	0	0	0
125	130	3	0	0	0	0	0	0	0	0	0	0
130	135	3	0	0	0	0	0	0	0	0	0	0
135	140	4	0	0	0	0	0	0	0	0	0	0
140	145	4	0	0	0	0	0	0	0	0	0	0
145	150	5	0	0	0	0	0	0	0	0	0	0
150	155	5	0	0	0	0	0	0	0	0	0	0
155	160	6	0	0	0	0	0	0	0	0	0	0
160	165	6	0	0	0	0	0	0	0	0	0	0
165	170	7	0	0	0	0	0	0	0	0	0	0
170	175	7	0	0	0	0	0	0	0	0	0	0
175	180	8	0	0	0	0	0	0	0	0	0	0
180	185	8	0	0	0	0	0	0	0	0	0	0
185	190	9	0	0	0	0	0	0	0	0	0	0
190	195	9	0	0	0	0	0	0	0	0	0	0
195	200	10	0	0	0	0	0	0	0	0	0	0
200	205	10	0	0	0	0	0	0	0	0	0	0
205	210	11	0	0	0	0	0	0	0	0	0	0
210	215	11	0	0	0	0	0	0	0	0	0	0
215	220	12	0	0	0	0	0	0	0	0	0	0
220	225	12	0	0	0	0	0	0	0	0	0	0
225	230	13	0	0	0	0	0	0	0	0	0	0
230	235	13	1	0	0	0	0	0	0	0	0	0
235	240	14	1	0	0	0	0	0	0	0	0	0
240	245	14	2	0	0	0	0	0	0	0	0	0
245	250	15	2	0	0	0	0	0	0	0	0	0
250	260	15	3	0	0	0	0	0	0	0	0	0
260	270	16	4	0	0	0	0	0	0	0	0	0
270	280	17	5	0	0	0	0	0	0	0	0	0
280	290	18	6	0	0	0	0	0	0	0	0	0
290	300	19	7	0	0	0	0	0	0	0	0	0
300	310	20	8	0	0	0	0	0	0	0	0	0
310	320	21	9	0	0	0	0	0	0	0	0	0
320	330	22	10	0	0	0	0	0	0	0	0	0
330	340	23	11	0	0	0	0	0	0	0	0	0
340	350	24	12	0	0	0	0	0	0	0	0	0
350	360	25	13	1	0	0	0	0	0	0	0	0
360	370	26	14	2	0	0	0	0	0	0	0	0
370	380	27	15	3	0	0	0	0	0	0	0	0
380	390	29	16	4	0	0	0	0	0	0	0	0
390	400	30	17	5	0	0	0	0	0	0	0	0
400	410	32	18	6	0	0	0	0	0	0	0	0
410	420	33	19	7	0	0	0	0	0	0	0	0
420	430	35	20	8	0	0	0	0	0	0	0	0
430	440	36	21	9	0	0	0	0	0	0	0	0
440	450	38	22	10	0	0	0	0	0	0	0	0
450	460	39	23	11	0	0	0	0	0	0	0	0
460	470	41	24	12	0	0	0	0	0	0	0	0
470	480	42	25	13	0	0	0	0	0	0	0	0
480	490	44	26	14	1	0	0	0	0	0	0	0
490	500	45	27	15	2	0	0	0	0	0	0	0
500	520	47	29	16	4	0	0	0	0	0	0	0
520	540	50	32	18	6	0	0	0	0	0	0	0
540	560	53	35	20	8	0	0	0	0	0	0	0
560	580	56	38	22	10	0	0	0	0	0	0	0
580	600	59	41	24	12	0	0	0	0	0	0	0
600	620	62	44	26	14	2	0	0	0	0	0	0
620	640	65	47	29	16	4	0	0	0	0	0	0
640	660	68	50	32	18	6	0	0	0	0	0	0
660	680	71	53	35	20	8	0	0	0	0	0	0
680	700	74	56	38	22	10	0	0	0	0	0	0
700	720	77	59	41	24	12	0	0	0	0	0	0
720	740	80	62	44	26	14	1	0	0	0	0	0
740	760	83	65	47	28	16	3	0	0	0	0	0
760	780	86	68	50	31	18	5	0	0	0	0	0
780	800	89	71	53	34	20	7	0	0	0	0	0

IRS Publication 15, Circular E (continued)

SINGLE Persons—BIWEEKLY Payroll Period

(For Wages Paid in 2005)

If the wages are—		And the number of withholding allowances claimed is—										
At least	But less than	0	1	2	3	4	5	6	7	8	9	10
		The amount of income tax to be withheld is—										
$800	$820	$92	$74	$56	$37	$22	$9	$0	$0	$0	$0	$0
820	840	95	77	59	40	24	11	0	0	0	0	0
840	860	98	80	62	43	26	13	1	0	0	0	0
860	880	101	83	65	46	28	15	3	0	0	0	0
880	900	104	86	68	49	31	17	5	0	0	0	0
900	920	107	89	71	52	34	19	7	0	0	0	0
920	940	110	92	74	55	37	21	9	0	0	0	0
940	960	113	95	77	58	40	23	11	0	0	0	0
960	980	116	98	80	61	43	25	13	1	0	0	0
980	1,000	119	101	83	64	46	27	15	3	0	0	0
1,000	1,020	122	104	86	67	49	30	17	5	0	0	0
1,020	1,040	125	107	89	70	52	33	19	7	0	0	0
1,040	1,060	128	110	92	73	55	36	21	9	0	0	0
1,060	1,080	131	113	95	76	58	39	23	11	0	0	0
1,080	1,100	134	116	98	79	61	42	25	13	0	0	0
1,100	1,120	137	119	101	82	64	45	27	15	2	0	0
1,120	1,140	140	122	104	85	67	48	30	17	4	0	0
1,140	1,160	143	125	107	88	70	51	33	19	6	0	0
1,160	1,180	146	128	110	91	73	54	36	21	8	0	0
1,180	1,200	149	131	113	94	76	57	39	23	10	0	0
1,200	1,220	152	134	116	97	79	60	42	25	12	0	0
1,220	1,240	157	137	119	100	82	63	45	27	14	2	0
1,240	1,260	162	140	122	103	85	66	48	29	16	4	0
1,260	1,280	167	143	125	106	88	69	51	32	18	6	0
1,280	1,300	172	146	128	109	91	72	54	35	20	8	0
1,300	1,320	177	149	131	112	94	75	57	38	22	10	0
1,320	1,340	182	152	134	115	97	78	60	41	24	12	0
1,340	1,360	187	157	137	118	100	81	63	44	26	14	2
1,360	1,380	192	162	140	121	103	84	66	47	29	16	4
1,380	1,400	197	167	143	124	106	87	69	50	32	18	6
1,400	1,420	202	172	146	127	109	90	72	53	35	20	8
1,420	1,440	207	177	149	130	112	93	75	56	38	22	10
1,440	1,460	212	182	152	133	115	96	78	59	41	24	12
1,460	1,480	217	187	156	136	118	99	81	62	44	26	14
1,480	1,500	222	192	161	139	121	102	84	65	47	28	16
1,500	1,520	227	197	166	142	124	105	87	68	50	31	18
1,520	1,540	232	202	171	145	127	108	90	71	53	34	20
1,540	1,560	237	207	176	148	130	111	93	74	56	37	22
1,560	1,580	242	212	181	151	133	114	96	77	59	40	24
1,580	1,600	247	217	186	155	136	117	99	80	62	43	26
1,600	1,620	252	222	191	160	139	120	102	83	65	46	28
1,620	1,640	257	227	196	165	142	123	105	86	68	49	31
1,640	1,660	262	232	201	170	145	126	108	89	71	52	34
1,660	1,680	267	237	206	175	148	129	111	92	74	55	37
1,680	1,700	272	242	211	180	151	132	114	95	77	58	40
1,700	1,720	277	247	216	185	154	135	117	98	80	61	43
1,720	1,740	282	252	221	190	159	138	120	101	83	64	46
1,740	1,760	287	257	226	195	164	141	123	104	86	67	49
1,760	1,780	292	262	231	200	169	144	126	107	89	70	52
1,780	1,800	297	267	236	205	174	147	129	110	92	73	55
1,800	1,820	302	272	241	210	179	150	132	113	95	76	58
1,820	1,840	307	277	246	215	184	153	135	116	98	79	61
1,840	1,860	312	282	251	220	189	158	138	119	101	82	64
1,860	1,880	317	287	256	225	194	163	141	122	104	85	67
1,880	1,900	322	292	261	230	199	168	144	125	107	88	70
1,900	1,920	327	297	266	235	204	173	147	128	110	91	73
1,920	1,940	332	302	271	240	209	178	150	131	113	94	76
1,940	1,960	337	307	276	245	214	183	153	134	116	97	79
1,960	1,980	342	312	281	250	219	188	158	137	119	100	82
1,980	2,000	347	317	286	255	224	193	163	140	122	103	85
2,000	2,020	352	322	291	260	229	198	168	143	125	106	88
2,020	2,040	357	327	296	265	234	203	173	146	128	109	91
2,040	2,060	362	332	301	270	239	208	178	149	131	112	94
2,060	2,080	367	337	306	275	244	213	183	152	134	115	97
2,080	2,100	372	342	311	280	249	218	188	157	137	118	100

$2,100 and over   Use Table 2(a) for a **SINGLE person** on page 36. Also see the instructions on page 34.

IRS Publication 15, Circular E (continued)

MARRIED Persons—BIWEEKLY Payroll Period

(For Wages Paid in 2005)

If the wages are—		And the number of withholding allowances claimed is—										
At least	But less than	0	1	2	3	4	5	6	7	8	9	10
		The amount of income tax to be withheld is—										
$0	$250	$0	$0	$0	$0	$0	$0	$0	$0	$0	$0	$0
250	260	0	0	0	0	0	0	0	0	0	0	0
260	270	0	0	0	0	0	0	0	0	0	0	0
270	280	0	0	0	0	0	0	0	0	0	0	0
280	290	0	0	0	0	0	0	0	0	0	0	0
290	300	0	0	0	0	0	0	0	0	0	0	0
300	310	0	0	0	0	0	0	0	0	0	0	0
310	320	1	0	0	0	0	0	0	0	0	0	0
320	330	2	0	0	0	0	0	0	0	0	0	0
330	340	3	0	0	0	0	0	0	0	0	0	0
340	350	4	0	0	0	0	0	0	0	0	0	0
350	360	5	0	0	0	0	0	0	0	0	0	0
360	370	6	0	0	0	0	0	0	0	0	0	0
370	380	7	0	0	0	0	0	0	0	0	0	0
380	390	8	0	0	0	0	0	0	0	0	0	0
390	400	9	0	0	0	0	0	0	0	0	0	0
400	410	10	0	0	0	0	0	0	0	0	0	0
410	420	11	0	0	0	0	0	0	0	0	0	0
420	430	12	0	0	0	0	0	0	0	0	0	0
430	440	13	0	0	0	0	0	0	0	0	0	0
440	450	14	1	0	0	0	0	0	0	0	0	0
450	460	15	2	0	0	0	0	0	0	0	0	0
460	470	16	3	0	0	0	0	0	0	0	0	0
470	480	17	4	0	0	0	0	0	0	0	0	0
480	490	18	5	0	0	0	0	0	0	0	0	0
490	500	19	6	0	0	0	0	0	0	0	0	0
500	520	20	8	0	0	0	0	0	0	0	0	0
520	540	22	10	0	0	0	0	0	0	0	0	0
540	560	24	12	0	0	0	0	0	0	0	0	0
560	580	26	14	2	0	0	0	0	0	0	0	0
580	600	28	16	4	0	0	0	0	0	0	0	0
600	620	30	18	6	0	0	0	0	0	0	0	0
620	640	32	20	8	0	0	0	0	0	0	0	0
640	660	34	22	10	0	0	0	0	0	0	0	0
660	680	36	24	12	0	0	0	0	0	0	0	0
680	700	38	26	14	1	0	0	0	0	0	0	0
700	720	40	28	16	3	0	0	0	0	0	0	0
720	740	42	30	18	5	0	0	0	0	0	0	0
740	760	44	32	20	7	0	0	0	0	0	0	0
760	780	46	34	22	9	0	0	0	0	0	0	0
780	800	48	36	24	11	0	0	0	0	0	0	0
800	820	50	38	26	13	1	0	0	0	0	0	0
820	840	52	40	28	15	3	0	0	0	0	0	0
840	860	54	42	30	17	5	0	0	0	0	0	0
860	880	56	44	32	19	7	0	0	0	0	0	0
880	900	59	46	34	21	9	0	0	0	0	0	0
900	920	62	48	36	23	11	0	0	0	0	0	0
920	940	65	50	38	25	13	1	0	0	0	0	0
940	960	68	52	40	27	15	3	0	0	0	0	0
960	980	71	54	42	29	17	5	0	0	0	0	0
980	1,000	74	56	44	31	19	7	0	0	0	0	0
1,000	1,020	77	59	46	33	21	9	0	0	0	0	0
1,020	1,040	80	62	48	35	23	11	0	0	0	0	0
1,040	1,060	83	65	50	37	25	13	0	0	0	0	0
1,060	1,080	86	68	52	39	27	15	2	0	0	0	0
1,080	1,100	89	71	54	41	29	17	4	0	0	0	0
1,100	1,120	92	74	56	43	31	19	6	0	0	0	0
1,120	1,140	95	77	58	45	33	21	8	0	0	0	0
1,140	1,160	98	80	61	47	35	23	10	0	0	0	0
1,160	1,180	101	83	64	49	37	25	12	0	0	0	0
1,180	1,200	104	86	67	51	39	27	14	2	0	0	0
1,200	1,220	107	89	70	53	41	29	16	4	0	0	0
1,220	1,240	110	92	73	55	43	31	18	6	0	0	0
1,240	1,260	113	95	76	58	45	33	20	8	0	0	0
1,260	1,280	116	98	79	61	47	35	22	10	0	0	0
1,280	1,300	119	101	82	64	49	37	24	12	0	0	0
1,300	1,320	122	104	85	67	51	39	26	14	2	0	0
1,320	1,340	125	107	88	70	53	41	28	16	4	0	0
1,340	1,360	128	110	91	73	55	43	30	18	6	0	0
1,360	1,380	131	113	94	76	57	45	32	20	8	0	0

IRS Publication 15, Circular E (continued)

MARRIED Persons—BIWEEKLY Payroll Period
(For Wages Paid in 2005)

If the wages are—		And the number of withholding allowances claimed is—										
At least	But less than	0	1	2	3	4	5	6	7	8	9	10
		The amount of income tax to be withheld is—										
$1,380	$1,400	$134	$116	$97	$79	$60	$47	$34	$22	$10	$0	$0
1,400	1,420	137	119	100	82	63	49	36	24	12	0	0
1,420	1,440	140	122	103	85	66	51	38	26	14	1	0
1,440	1,460	143	125	106	88	69	53	40	28	16	3	0
1,460	1,480	146	128	109	91	72	55	42	30	18	5	0
1,480	1,500	149	131	112	94	75	57	44	32	20	7	0
1,500	1,520	152	134	115	97	78	60	46	34	22	9	0
1,520	1,540	155	137	118	100	81	63	48	36	24	11	0
1,540	1,560	158	140	121	103	84	66	50	38	26	13	1
1,560	1,580	161	143	124	106	87	69	52	40	28	15	3
1,580	1,600	164	146	127	109	90	72	54	42	30	17	5
1,600	1,620	167	149	130	112	93	75	57	44	32	19	7
1,620	1,640	170	152	133	115	96	78	60	46	34	21	9
1,640	1,660	173	155	136	118	99	81	63	48	36	23	11
1,660	1,680	176	158	139	121	102	84	66	50	38	25	13
1,680	1,700	179	161	142	124	105	87	69	52	40	27	15
1,700	1,720	182	164	145	127	108	90	72	54	42	29	17
1,720	1,740	185	167	148	130	111	93	75	56	44	31	19
1,740	1,760	188	170	151	133	114	96	78	59	46	33	21
1,760	1,780	191	173	154	136	117	99	81	62	48	35	23
1,780	1,800	194	176	157	139	120	102	84	65	50	37	25
1,800	1,820	197	179	160	142	123	105	87	68	52	39	27
1,820	1,840	200	182	163	145	126	108	90	71	54	41	29
1,840	1,860	203	185	166	148	129	111	93	74	56	43	31
1,860	1,880	206	188	169	151	132	114	96	77	59	45	33
1,880	1,900	209	191	172	154	135	117	99	80	62	47	35
1,900	1,920	212	194	175	157	138	120	102	83	65	49	37
1,920	1,940	215	197	178	160	141	123	105	86	68	51	39
1,940	1,960	218	200	181	163	144	126	108	89	71	53	41
1,960	1,980	221	203	184	166	147	129	111	92	74	55	43
1,980	2,000	224	206	187	169	150	132	114	95	77	58	45
2,000	2,020	227	209	190	172	153	135	117	98	80	61	47
2,020	2,040	230	212	193	175	156	138	120	101	83	64	49
2,040	2,060	233	215	196	178	159	141	123	104	86	67	51
2,060	2,080	236	218	199	181	162	144	126	107	89	70	53
2,080	2,100	239	221	202	184	165	147	129	110	92	73	55
2,100	2,120	242	224	205	187	168	150	132	113	95	76	58
2,120	2,140	245	227	208	190	171	153	135	116	98	79	61
2,140	2,160	248	230	211	193	174	156	138	119	101	82	64
2,160	2,180	251	233	214	196	177	159	141	122	104	85	67
2,180	2,200	254	236	217	199	180	162	144	125	107	88	70
2,200	2,220	257	239	220	202	183	165	147	128	110	91	73
2,220	2,240	260	242	223	205	186	168	150	131	113	94	76
2,240	2,260	263	245	226	208	189	171	153	134	116	97	79
2,260	2,280	266	248	229	211	192	174	156	137	119	100	82
2,280	2,300	269	251	232	214	195	177	159	140	122	103	85
2,300	2,320	272	254	235	217	198	180	162	143	125	106	88
2,320	2,340	275	257	238	220	201	183	165	146	128	109	91
2,340	2,360	278	260	241	223	204	186	168	149	131	112	94
2,360	2,380	281	263	244	226	207	189	171	152	134	115	97
2,380	2,400	284	266	247	229	210	192	174	155	137	118	100
2,400	2,420	287	269	250	232	213	195	177	158	140	121	103
2,420	2,440	290	272	253	235	216	198	180	161	143	124	106
2,440	2,460	293	275	256	238	219	201	183	164	146	127	109
2,460	2,480	296	278	259	241	222	204	186	167	149	130	112
2,480	2,500	299	281	262	244	225	207	189	170	152	133	115
2,500	2,520	302	284	265	247	228	210	192	173	155	136	118
2,520	2,540	305	287	268	250	231	213	195	176	158	139	121
2,540	2,560	309	290	271	253	234	216	198	179	161	142	124
2,560	2,580	314	293	274	256	237	219	201	182	164	145	127
2,580	2,600	319	296	277	259	240	222	204	185	167	148	130
2,600	2,620	324	299	280	262	243	225	207	188	170	151	133
2,620	2,640	329	302	283	265	246	228	210	191	173	154	136
2,640	2,660	334	305	286	268	249	231	213	194	176	157	139
2,660	2,680	339	308	289	271	252	234	216	197	179	160	142
2,680	2,700	344	313	292	274	255	237	219	200	182	163	145

$2,700 and over   Use Table 2(b) for a **MARRIED person** on page 36. Also see the instructions on page 34.

IRS Publication 15, Circular E (continued)

SINGLE Persons—SEMIMONTHLY Payroll Period

(For Wages Paid in 2005)

If the wages are—		And the number of withholding allowances claimed is—										
At least	But less than	0	1	2	3	4	5	6	7	8	9	10
		The amount of income tax to be withheld is—										
$0	$115	$0	$0	$0	$0	$0	$0	$0	$0	$0	$0	$0
115	120	1	0	0	0	0	0	0	0	0	0	0
120	125	1	0	0	0	0	0	0	0	0	0	0
125	130	2	0	0	0	0	0	0	0	0	0	0
130	135	2	0	0	0	0	0	0	0	0	0	0
135	140	3	0	0	0	0	0	0	0	0	0	0
140	145	3	0	0	0	0	0	0	0	0	0	0
145	150	4	0	0	0	0	0	0	0	0	0	0
150	155	4	0	0	0	0	0	0	0	0	0	0
155	160	5	0	0	0	0	0	0	0	0	0	0
160	165	5	0	0	0	0	0	0	0	0	0	0
165	170	6	0	0	0	0	0	0	0	0	0	0
170	175	6	0	0	0	0	0	0	0	0	0	0
175	180	7	0	0	0	0	0	0	0	0	0	0
180	185	7	0	0	0	0	0	0	0	0	0	0
185	190	8	0	0	0	0	0	0	0	0	0	0
190	195	8	0	0	0	0	0	0	0	0	0	0
195	200	9	0	0	0	0	0	0	0	0	0	0
200	205	9	0	0	0	0	0	0	0	0	0	0
205	210	10	0	0	0	0	0	0	0	0	0	0
210	215	10	0	0	0	0	0	0	0	0	0	0
215	220	11	0	0	0	0	0	0	0	0	0	0
220	225	11	0	0	0	0	0	0	0	0	0	0
225	230	12	0	0	0	0	0	0	0	0	0	0
230	235	12	0	0	0	0	0	0	0	0	0	0
235	240	13	0	0	0	0	0	0	0	0	0	0
240	245	13	0	0	0	0	0	0	0	0	0	0
245	250	14	0	0	0	0	0	0	0	0	0	0
250	260	14	1	0	0	0	0	0	0	0	0	0
260	270	15	2	0	0	0	0	0	0	0	0	0
270	280	16	3	0	0	0	0	0	0	0	0	0
280	290	17	4	0	0	0	0	0	0	0	0	0
290	300	18	5	0	0	0	0	0	0	0	0	0
300	310	19	6	0	0	0	0	0	0	0	0	0
310	320	20	7	0	0	0	0	0	0	0	0	0
320	330	21	8	0	0	0	0	0	0	0	0	0
330	340	22	9	0	0	0	0	0	0	0	0	0
340	350	23	10	0	0	0	0	0	0	0	0	0
350	360	24	11	0	0	0	0	0	0	0	0	0
360	370	25	12	0	0	0	0	0	0	0	0	0
370	380	26	13	0	0	0	0	0	0	0	0	0
380	390	27	14	1	0	0	0	0	0	0	0	0
390	400	28	15	2	0	0	0	0	0	0	0	0
400	410	29	16	3	0	0	0	0	0	0	0	0
410	420	31	17	4	0	0	0	0	0	0	0	0
420	430	32	18	5	0	0	0	0	0	0	0	0
430	440	34	19	6	0	0	0	0	0	0	0	0
440	450	35	20	7	0	0	0	0	0	0	0	0
450	460	37	21	8	0	0	0	0	0	0	0	0
460	470	38	22	9	0	0	0	0	0	0	0	0
470	480	40	23	10	0	0	0	0	0	0	0	0
480	490	41	24	11	0	0	0	0	0	0	0	0
490	500	43	25	12	0	0	0	0	0	0	0	0
500	520	45	27	13	0	0	0	0	0	0	0	0
520	540	48	29	15	2	0	0	0	0	0	0	0
540	560	51	31	17	4	0	0	0	0	0	0	0
560	580	54	34	19	6	0	0	0	0	0	0	0
580	600	57	37	21	8	0	0	0	0	0	0	0
600	620	60	40	23	10	0	0	0	0	0	0	0
620	640	63	43	25	12	0	0	0	0	0	0	0
640	660	66	46	27	14	1	0	0	0	0	0	0
660	680	69	49	29	16	3	0	0	0	0	0	0
680	700	72	52	32	18	5	0	0	0	0	0	0
700	720	75	55	35	20	7	0	0	0	0	0	0
720	740	78	58	38	22	9	0	0	0	0	0	0
740	760	81	61	41	24	11	0	0	0	0	0	0
760	780	84	64	44	26	13	0	0	0	0	0	0
780	800	87	67	47	28	15	1	0	0	0	0	0
800	820	90	70	50	30	17	3	0	0	0	0	0
820	840	93	73	53	33	19	5	0	0	0	0	0

IRS Publication 15, Circular E (continued)

SINGLE Persons—SEMIMONTHLY Payroll Period
(For Wages Paid in 2005)

If the wages are–		And the number of withholding allowances claimed is—										
At least	But less than	0	1	2	3	4	5	6	7	8	9	10
		The amount of income tax to be withheld is—										
$840	$860	$96	$76	$56	$36	$21	$7	$0	$0	$0	$0	$0
860	880	99	79	59	39	23	9	0	0	0	0	0
880	900	102	82	62	42	25	11	0	0	0	0	0
900	920	105	85	65	45	27	13	0	0	0	0	0
920	940	108	88	68	48	29	15	2	0	0	0	0
940	960	111	91	71	51	31	17	4	0	0	0	0
960	980	114	94	74	54	34	19	6	0	0	0	0
980	1,000	117	97	77	57	37	21	8	0	0	0	0
1,000	1,020	120	100	80	60	40	23	10	0	0	0	0
1,020	1,040	123	103	83	63	43	25	12	0	0	0	0
1,040	1,060	126	106	86	66	46	27	14	1	0	0	0
1,060	1,080	129	109	89	69	49	29	16	3	0	0	0
1,080	1,100	132	112	92	72	52	32	18	5	0	0	0
1,100	1,120	135	115	95	75	55	35	20	7	0	0	0
1,120	1,140	138	118	98	78	58	38	22	9	0	0	0
1,140	1,160	141	121	101	81	61	41	24	11	0	0	0
1,160	1,180	144	124	104	84	64	44	26	13	0	0	0
1,180	1,200	147	127	107	87	67	47	28	15	1	0	0
1,200	1,220	150	130	110	90	70	50	30	17	3	0	0
1,220	1,240	153	133	113	93	73	53	33	19	5	0	0
1,240	1,260	156	136	116	96	76	56	36	21	7	0	0
1,260	1,280	159	139	119	99	79	59	39	23	9	0	0
1,280	1,300	162	142	122	102	82	62	42	25	11	0	0
1,300	1,320	165	145	125	105	85	65	45	27	13	0	0
1,320	1,340	170	148	128	108	88	68	48	29	15	2	0
1,340	1,360	175	151	131	111	91	71	51	31	17	4	0
1,360	1,380	180	154	134	114	94	74	54	34	19	6	0
1,380	1,400	185	157	137	117	97	77	57	37	21	8	0
1,400	1,420	190	160	140	120	100	80	60	40	23	10	0
1,420	1,440	195	163	143	123	103	83	63	43	25	12	0
1,440	1,460	200	166	146	126	106	86	66	46	27	14	1
1,460	1,480	205	171	149	129	109	89	69	49	29	16	3
1,480	1,500	210	176	152	132	112	92	72	52	32	18	5
1,500	1,520	215	181	155	135	115	95	75	55	35	20	7
1,520	1,540	220	186	158	138	118	98	78	58	38	22	9
1,540	1,560	225	191	161	141	121	101	81	61	41	24	11
1,560	1,580	230	196	164	144	124	104	84	64	44	26	13
1,580	1,600	235	201	168	147	127	107	87	67	47	28	15
1,600	1,620	240	206	173	150	130	110	90	70	50	30	17
1,620	1,640	245	211	178	153	133	113	93	73	53	33	19
1,640	1,660	250	216	183	156	136	116	96	76	56	36	21
1,660	1,680	255	221	188	159	139	119	99	79	59	39	23
1,680	1,700	260	226	193	162	142	122	102	82	62	42	25
1,700	1,720	265	231	198	165	145	125	105	85	65	45	27
1,720	1,740	270	236	203	170	148	128	108	88	68	48	29
1,740	1,760	275	241	208	175	151	131	111	91	71	51	31
1,760	1,780	280	246	213	180	154	134	114	94	74	54	34
1,780	1,800	285	251	218	185	157	137	117	97	77	57	37
1,800	1,820	290	256	223	190	160	140	120	100	80	60	40
1,820	1,840	295	261	228	195	163	143	123	103	83	63	43
1,840	1,860	300	266	233	200	166	146	126	106	86	66	46
1,860	1,880	305	271	238	205	171	149	129	109	89	69	49
1,880	1,900	310	276	243	210	176	152	132	112	92	72	52
1,900	1,920	315	281	248	215	181	155	135	115	95	75	55
1,920	1,940	320	286	253	220	186	158	138	118	98	78	58
1,940	1,960	325	291	258	225	191	161	141	121	101	81	61
1,960	1,980	330	296	263	230	196	164	144	124	104	84	64
1,980	2,000	335	301	268	235	201	168	147	127	107	87	67
2,000	2,020	340	306	273	240	206	173	150	130	110	90	70
2,020	2,040	345	311	278	245	211	178	153	133	113	93	73
2,040	2,060	350	316	283	250	216	183	156	136	116	96	76
2,060	2,080	355	321	288	255	221	188	159	139	119	99	79
2,080	2,100	360	326	293	260	226	193	162	142	122	102	82
2,100	2,120	365	331	298	265	231	198	165	145	125	105	85
2,120	2,140	370	336	303	270	236	203	170	148	128	108	88

$2,140 and over   Use Table 3(a) for a **SINGLE person** on page 36. Also see the instructions on page 34.

IRS Publication 15, Circular E (continued)

MARRIED Persons—SEMIMONTHLY Payroll Period

(For Wages Paid in 2005)

If the wages are—		And the number of withholding allowances claimed is—										
At least	But less than	0	1	2	3	4	5	6	7	8	9	10
		The amount of income tax to be withheld is—										
$0	$270	$0	$0	$0	$0	$0	$0	$0	$0	$0	$0	$0
270	280	0	0	0	0	0	0	0	0	0	0	0
280	290	0	0	0	0	0	0	0	0	0	0	0
290	300	0	0	0	0	0	0	0	0	0	0	0
300	310	0	0	0	0	0	0	0	0	0	0	0
310	320	0	0	0	0	0	0	0	0	0	0	0
320	330	0	0	0	0	0	0	0	0	0	0	0
330	340	0	0	0	0	0	0	0	0	0	0	0
340	350	1	0	0	0	0	0	0	0	0	0	0
350	360	2	0	0	0	0	0	0	0	0	0	0
360	370	3	0	0	0	0	0	0	0	0	0	0
370	380	4	0	0	0	0	0	0	0	0	0	0
380	390	5	0	0	0	0	0	0	0	0	0	0
390	400	6	0	0	0	0	0	0	0	0	0	0
400	410	7	0	0	0	0	0	0	0	0	0	0
410	420	8	0	0	0	0	0	0	0	0	0	0
420	430	9	0	0	0	0	0	0	0	0	0	0
430	440	10	0	0	0	0	0	0	0	0	0	0
440	450	11	0	0	0	0	0	0	0	0	0	0
450	460	12	0	0	0	0	0	0	0	0	0	0
460	470	13	0	0	0	0	0	0	0	0	0	0
470	480	14	1	0	0	0	0	0	0	0	0	0
480	490	15	2	0	0	0	0	0	0	0	0	0
490	500	16	3	0	0	0	0	0	0	0	0	0
500	520	18	4	0	0	0	0	0	0	0	0	0
520	540	20	6	0	0	0	0	0	0	0	0	0
540	560	22	8	0	0	0	0	0	0	0	0	0
560	580	24	10	0	0	0	0	0	0	0	0	0
580	600	26	12	0	0	0	0	0	0	0	0	0
600	620	28	14	1	0	0	0	0	0	0	0	0
620	640	30	16	3	0	0	0	0	0	0	0	0
640	660	32	18	5	0	0	0	0	0	0	0	0
660	680	34	20	7	0	0	0	0	0	0	0	0
680	700	36	22	9	0	0	0	0	0	0	0	0
700	720	38	24	11	0	0	0	0	0	0	0	0
720	740	40	26	13	0	0	0	0	0	0	0	0
740	760	42	28	15	2	0	0	0	0	0	0	0
760	780	44	30	17	4	0	0	0	0	0	0	0
780	800	46	32	19	6	0	0	0	0	0	0	0
800	820	48	34	21	8	0	0	0	0	0	0	0
820	840	50	36	23	10	0	0	0	0	0	0	0
840	860	52	38	25	12	0	0	0	0	0	0	0
860	880	54	40	27	14	0	0	0	0	0	0	0
880	900	56	42	29	16	2	0	0	0	0	0	0
900	920	58	44	31	18	4	0	0	0	0	0	0
920	940	60	46	33	20	6	0	0	0	0	0	0
940	960	62	48	35	22	8	0	0	0	0	0	0
960	980	65	50	37	24	10	0	0	0	0	0	0
980	1,000	68	52	39	26	12	0	0	0	0	0	0
1,000	1,020	71	54	41	28	14	1	0	0	0	0	0
1,020	1,040	74	56	43	30	16	3	0	0	0	0	0
1,040	1,060	77	58	45	32	18	5	0	0	0	0	0
1,060	1,080	80	60	47	34	20	7	0	0	0	0	0
1,080	1,100	83	63	49	36	22	9	0	0	0	0	0
1,100	1,120	86	66	51	38	24	11	0	0	0	0	0
1,120	1,140	89	69	53	40	26	13	0	0	0	0	0
1,140	1,160	92	72	55	42	28	15	2	0	0	0	0
1,160	1,180	95	75	57	44	30	17	4	0	0	0	0
1,180	1,200	98	78	59	46	32	19	6	0	0	0	0
1,200	1,220	101	81	61	48	34	21	8	0	0	0	0
1,220	1,240	104	84	64	50	36	23	10	0	0	0	0
1,240	1,260	107	87	67	52	38	25	12	0	0	0	0
1,260	1,280	110	90	70	54	40	27	14	0	0	0	0
1,280	1,300	113	93	73	56	42	29	16	2	0	0	0
1,300	1,320	116	96	76	58	44	31	18	4	0	0	0
1,320	1,340	119	99	79	60	46	33	20	6	0	0	0
1,340	1,360	122	102	82	62	48	35	22	8	0	0	0
1,360	1,380	125	105	85	65	50	37	24	10	0	0	0
1,380	1,400	128	108	88	68	52	39	26	12	0	0	0
1,400	1,420	131	111	91	71	54	41	28	14	1	0	0

IRS Publication 15, Circular E (continued)

MARRIED Persons—SEMIMONTHLY Payroll Period
(For Wages Paid in 2005)

If the wages are—		And the number of withholding allowances claimed is—										
At least	But less than	0	1	2	3	4	5	6	7	8	9	10
		The amount of income tax to be withheld is—										
$1,420	$1,440	$134	$114	$94	$74	$56	$43	$30	$16	$3	$0	$0
1,440	1,460	137	117	97	77	58	45	32	18	5	0	0
1,460	1,480	140	120	100	80	60	47	34	20	7	0	0
1,480	1,500	143	123	103	83	63	49	36	22	9	0	0
1,500	1,520	146	126	106	86	66	51	38	24	11	0	0
1,520	1,540	149	129	109	89	69	53	40	26	13	0	0
1,540	1,560	152	132	112	92	72	55	42	28	15	2	0
1,560	1,580	155	135	115	95	75	57	44	30	17	4	0
1,580	1,600	158	138	118	98	78	59	46	32	19	6	0
1,600	1,620	161	141	121	101	81	61	48	34	21	8	0
1,620	1,640	164	144	124	104	84	64	50	36	23	10	0
1,640	1,660	167	147	127	107	87	67	52	38	25	12	0
1,660	1,680	170	150	130	110	90	70	54	40	27	14	0
1,680	1,700	173	153	133	113	93	73	56	42	29	16	2
1,700	1,720	176	156	136	116	96	76	58	44	31	18	4
1,720	1,740	179	159	139	119	99	79	60	46	33	20	6
1,740	1,760	182	162	142	122	102	82	62	48	35	22	8
1,760	1,780	185	165	145	125	105	85	65	50	37	24	10
1,780	1,800	188	168	148	128	108	88	68	52	39	26	12
1,800	1,820	191	171	151	131	111	91	71	54	41	28	14
1,820	1,840	194	174	154	134	114	94	74	56	43	30	16
1,840	1,860	197	177	157	137	117	97	77	58	45	32	18
1,860	1,880	200	180	160	140	120	100	80	60	47	34	20
1,880	1,900	203	183	163	143	123	103	83	63	49	36	22
1,900	1,920	206	186	166	146	126	106	86	66	51	38	24
1,920	1,940	209	189	169	149	129	109	89	69	53	40	26
1,940	1,960	212	192	172	152	132	112	92	72	55	42	28
1,960	1,980	215	195	175	155	135	115	95	75	57	44	30
1,980	2,000	218	198	178	158	138	118	98	78	59	46	32
2,000	2,020	221	201	181	161	141	121	101	81	61	48	34
2,020	2,040	224	204	184	164	144	124	104	84	64	50	36
2,040	2,060	227	207	187	167	147	127	107	87	67	52	38
2,060	2,080	230	210	190	170	150	130	110	90	70	54	40
2,080	2,100	233	213	193	173	153	133	113	93	73	56	42
2,100	2,120	236	216	196	176	156	136	116	96	76	58	44
2,120	2,140	239	219	199	179	159	139	119	99	79	60	46
2,140	2,160	242	222	202	182	162	142	122	102	82	62	48
2,160	2,180	245	225	205	185	165	145	125	105	85	65	50
2,180	2,200	248	228	208	188	168	148	128	108	88	68	52
2,200	2,220	251	231	211	191	171	151	131	111	91	71	54
2,220	2,240	254	234	214	194	174	154	134	114	94	74	56
2,240	2,260	257	237	217	197	177	157	137	117	97	77	58
2,260	2,280	260	240	220	200	180	160	140	120	100	80	60
2,280	2,300	263	243	223	203	183	163	143	123	103	83	63
2,300	2,320	266	246	226	206	186	166	146	126	106	86	66
2,320	2,340	269	249	229	209	189	169	149	129	109	89	69
2,340	2,360	272	252	232	212	192	172	152	132	112	92	72
2,360	2,380	275	255	235	215	195	175	155	135	115	95	75
2,380	2,400	278	258	238	218	198	178	158	138	118	98	78
2,400	2,420	281	261	241	221	201	181	161	141	121	101	81
2,420	2,440	284	264	244	224	204	184	164	144	124	104	84
2,440	2,460	287	267	247	227	207	187	167	147	127	107	87
2,460	2,480	290	270	250	230	210	190	170	150	130	110	90
2,480	2,500	293	273	253	233	213	193	173	153	133	113	93
2,500	2,520	296	276	256	236	216	196	176	156	136	116	96
2,520	2,540	299	279	259	239	219	199	179	159	139	119	99
2,540	2,560	302	282	262	242	222	202	182	162	142	122	102
2,560	2,580	305	285	265	245	225	205	185	165	145	125	105
2,580	2,600	308	288	268	248	228	208	188	168	148	128	108
2,600	2,620	311	291	271	251	231	211	191	171	151	131	111
2,620	2,640	314	294	274	254	234	214	194	174	154	134	114
2,640	2,660	317	297	277	257	237	217	197	177	157	137	117
2,660	2,680	320	300	280	260	240	220	200	180	160	140	120
2,680	2,700	323	303	283	263	243	223	203	183	163	143	123
2,700	2,720	326	306	286	266	246	226	206	186	166	146	126
2,720	2,740	329	309	289	269	249	229	209	189	169	149	129

$2,740 and over   Use Table 3(b) for a **MARRIED person** on page 36. Also see the instructions on page 34.

IRS Publication 15, Circular E (continued)

SINGLE Persons—MONTHLY Payroll Period
(For Wages Paid in 2005)

If the wages are–		And the number of withholding allowances claimed is—										
At least	But less than	0	1	2	3	4	5	6	7	8	9	10
		The amount of income tax to be withheld is—										
$0	$230	$0	$0	$0	$0	$0	$0	$0	$0	$0	$0	$0
230	240	1	0	0	0	0	0	0	0	0	0	0
240	250	2	0	0	0	0	0	0	0	0	0	0
250	260	3	0	0	0	0	0	0	0	0	0	0
260	270	4	0	0	0	0	0	0	0	0	0	0
270	280	5	0	0	0	0	0	0	0	0	0	0
280	290	6	0	0	0	0	0	0	0	0	0	0
290	300	7	0	0	0	0	0	0	0	0	0	0
300	320	9	0	0	0	0	0	0	0	0	0	0
320	340	11	0	0	0	0	0	0	0	0	0	0
340	360	13	0	0	0	0	0	0	0	0	0	0
360	380	15	0	0	0	0	0	0	0	0	0	0
380	400	17	0	0	0	0	0	0	0	0	0	0
400	420	19	0	0	0	0	0	0	0	0	0	0
420	440	21	0	0	0	0	0	0	0	0	0	0
440	460	23	0	0	0	0	0	0	0	0	0	0
460	480	25	0	0	0	0	0	0	0	0	0	0
480	500	27	0	0	0	0	0	0	0	0	0	0
500	520	29	2	0	0	0	0	0	0	0	0	0
520	540	31	4	0	0	0	0	0	0	0	0	0
540	560	33	6	0	0	0	0	0	0	0	0	0
560	580	35	8	0	0	0	0	0	0	0	0	0
580	600	37	10	0	0	0	0	0	0	0	0	0
600	640	40	13	0	0	0	0	0	0	0	0	0
640	680	44	17	0	0	0	0	0	0	0	0	0
680	720	48	21	0	0	0	0	0	0	0	0	0
720	760	52	25	0	0	0	0	0	0	0	0	0
760	800	56	29	3	0	0	0	0	0	0	0	0
800	840	60	33	7	0	0	0	0	0	0	0	0
840	880	66	37	11	0	0	0	0	0	0	0	0
880	920	72	41	15	0	0	0	0	0	0	0	0
920	960	78	45	19	0	0	0	0	0	0	0	0
960	1,000	84	49	23	0	0	0	0	0	0	0	0
1,000	1,040	90	53	27	0	0	0	0	0	0	0	0
1,040	1,080	96	57	31	4	0	0	0	0	0	0	0
1,080	1,120	102	62	35	8	0	0	0	0	0	0	0
1,120	1,160	108	68	39	12	0	0	0	0	0	0	0
1,160	1,200	114	74	43	16	0	0	0	0	0	0	0
1,200	1,240	120	80	47	20	0	0	0	0	0	0	0
1,240	1,280	126	86	51	24	0	0	0	0	0	0	0
1,280	1,320	132	92	55	28	1	0	0	0	0	0	0
1,320	1,360	138	98	59	32	5	0	0	0	0	0	0
1,360	1,400	144	104	64	36	9	0	0	0	0	0	0
1,400	1,440	150	110	70	40	13	0	0	0	0	0	0
1,440	1,480	156	116	76	44	17	0	0	0	0	0	0
1,480	1,520	162	122	82	48	21	0	0	0	0	0	0
1,520	1,560	168	128	88	52	25	0	0	0	0	0	0
1,560	1,600	174	134	94	56	29	3	0	0	0	0	0
1,600	1,640	180	140	100	60	33	7	0	0	0	0	0
1,640	1,680	186	146	106	66	37	11	0	0	0	0	0
1,680	1,720	192	152	112	72	41	15	0	0	0	0	0
1,720	1,760	198	158	118	78	45	19	0	0	0	0	0
1,760	1,800	204	164	124	84	49	23	0	0	0	0	0
1,800	1,840	210	170	130	90	53	27	0	0	0	0	0
1,840	1,880	216	176	136	96	57	31	4	0	0	0	0
1,880	1,920	222	182	142	102	62	35	8	0	0	0	0
1,920	1,960	228	188	148	108	68	39	12	0	0	0	0
1,960	2,000	234	194	154	114	74	43	16	0	0	0	0
2,000	2,040	240	200	160	120	80	47	20	0	0	0	0
2,040	2,080	246	206	166	126	86	51	24	0	0	0	0
2,080	2,120	252	212	172	132	92	55	28	1	0	0	0
2,120	2,160	258	218	178	138	98	59	32	5	0	0	0
2,160	2,200	264	224	184	144	104	64	36	9	0	0	0
2,200	2,240	270	230	190	150	110	70	40	13	0	0	0
2,240	2,280	276	236	196	156	116	76	44	17	0	0	0
2,280	2,320	282	242	202	162	122	82	48	21	0	0	0
2,320	2,360	288	248	208	168	128	88	52	25	0	0	0
2,360	2,400	294	254	214	174	134	94	56	29	3	0	0
2,400	2,440	300	260	220	180	140	100	60	33	7	0	0
2,440	2,480	306	266	226	186	146	106	66	37	11	0	0

IRS Publication 15, Circular E (continued)

SINGLE Persons—MONTHLY Payroll Period
(For Wages Paid in 2005)

If the wages are—		And the number of withholding allowances claimed is—										
At least	But less than	0	1	2	3	4	5	6	7	8	9	10
		The amount of income tax to be withheld is—										
$2,480	$2,520	$312	$272	$232	$192	$152	$112	$72	$41	$15	$0	$0
2,520	2,560	318	278	238	198	158	118	78	45	19	0	0
2,560	2,600	324	284	244	204	164	124	84	49	23	0	0
2,600	2,640	330	290	250	210	170	130	90	53	27	0	0
2,640	2,680	340	296	256	216	176	136	96	57	31	4	0
2,680	2,720	350	302	262	222	182	142	102	62	35	8	0
2,720	2,760	360	308	268	228	188	148	108	68	39	12	0
2,760	2,800	370	314	274	234	194	154	114	74	43	16	0
2,800	2,840	380	320	280	240	200	160	120	80	47	20	0
2,840	2,880	390	326	286	246	206	166	126	86	51	24	0
2,880	2,920	400	333	292	252	212	172	132	92	55	28	1
2,920	2,960	410	343	298	258	218	178	138	98	59	32	5
2,960	3,000	420	353	304	264	224	184	144	104	64	36	9
3,000	3,040	430	363	310	270	230	190	150	110	70	40	13
3,040	3,080	440	373	316	276	236	196	156	116	76	44	17
3,080	3,120	450	383	322	282	242	202	162	122	82	48	21
3,120	3,160	460	393	328	288	248	208	168	128	88	52	25
3,160	3,200	470	403	336	294	254	214	174	134	94	56	29
3,200	3,240	480	413	346	300	260	220	180	140	100	60	33
3,240	3,280	490	423	356	306	266	226	186	146	106	66	37
3,280	3,320	500	433	366	312	272	232	192	152	112	72	41
3,320	3,360	510	443	376	318	278	238	198	158	118	78	45
3,360	3,400	520	453	386	324	284	244	204	164	124	84	49
3,400	3,440	530	463	396	330	290	250	210	170	130	90	53
3,440	3,480	540	473	406	340	296	256	216	176	136	96	57
3,480	3,520	550	483	416	350	302	262	222	182	142	102	62
3,520	3,560	560	493	426	360	308	268	228	188	148	108	68
3,560	3,600	570	503	436	370	314	274	234	194	154	114	74
3,600	3,640	580	513	446	380	320	280	240	200	160	120	80
3,640	3,680	590	523	456	390	326	286	246	206	166	126	86
3,680	3,720	600	533	466	400	333	292	252	212	172	132	92
3,720	3,760	610	543	476	410	343	298	258	218	178	138	98
3,760	3,800	620	553	486	420	353	304	264	224	184	144	104
3,800	3,840	630	563	496	430	363	310	270	230	190	150	110
3,840	3,880	640	573	506	440	373	316	276	236	196	156	116
3,880	3,920	650	583	516	450	383	322	282	242	202	162	122
3,920	3,960	660	593	526	460	393	328	288	248	208	168	128
3,960	4,000	670	603	536	470	403	336	294	254	214	174	134
4,000	4,040	680	613	546	480	413	346	300	260	220	180	140
4,040	4,080	690	623	556	490	423	356	306	266	226	186	146
4,080	4,120	700	633	566	500	433	366	312	272	232	192	152
4,120	4,160	710	643	576	510	443	376	318	278	238	198	158
4,160	4,200	720	653	586	520	453	386	324	284	244	204	164
4,200	4,240	730	663	596	530	463	396	330	290	250	210	170
4,240	4,280	740	673	606	540	473	406	340	296	256	216	176
4,280	4,320	750	683	616	550	483	416	350	302	262	222	182
4,320	4,360	760	693	626	560	493	426	360	308	268	228	188
4,360	4,400	770	703	636	570	503	436	370	314	274	234	194
4,400	4,440	780	713	646	580	513	446	380	320	280	240	200
4,440	4,480	790	723	656	590	523	456	390	326	286	246	206
4,480	4,520	800	733	666	600	533	466	400	333	292	252	212
4,520	4,560	810	743	676	610	543	476	410	343	298	258	218
4,560	4,600	820	753	686	620	553	486	420	353	304	264	224
4,600	4,640	830	763	696	630	563	496	430	363	310	270	230
4,640	4,680	840	773	706	640	573	506	440	373	316	276	236
4,680	4,720	850	783	716	650	583	516	450	383	322	282	242
4,720	4,760	860	793	726	660	593	526	460	393	328	288	248
4,760	4,800	870	803	736	670	603	536	470	403	336	294	254
4,800	4,840	880	813	746	680	613	546	480	413	346	300	260
4,840	4,880	890	823	756	690	623	556	490	423	356	306	266
4,880	4,920	900	833	766	700	633	566	500	433	366	312	272
4,920	4,960	910	843	776	710	643	576	510	443	376	318	278
4,960	5,000	920	853	786	720	653	586	520	453	386	324	284
5,000	5,040	930	863	796	730	663	596	530	463	396	330	290
5,040	5,080	940	873	806	740	673	606	540	473	406	340	296

$5,080 and over   Use Table 4(a) for a **SINGLE person** on page 36. Also see the instructions on page 34.

IRS Publication 15, Circular E (continued)

MARRIED Persons—MONTHLY Payroll Period

(For Wages Paid in 2005)

If the wages are—		And the number of withholding allowances claimed is—										
At least	But less than	0	1	2	3	4	5	6	7	8	9	10
		The amount of income tax to be withheld is—										
$0	$540	$0	$0	$0	$0	$0	$0	$0	$0	$0	$0	$0
540	560	0	0	0	0	0	0	0	0	0	0	0
560	580	0	0	0	0	0	0	0	0	0	0	0
580	600	0	0	0	0	0	0	0	0	0	0	0
600	640	0	0	0	0	0	0	0	0	0	0	0
640	680	0	0	0	0	0	0	0	0	0	0	0
680	720	3	0	0	0	0	0	0	0	0	0	0
720	760	7	0	0	0	0	0	0	0	0	0	0
760	800	11	0	0	0	0	0	0	0	0	0	0
800	840	15	0	0	0	0	0	0	0	0	0	0
840	880	19	0	0	0	0	0	0	0	0	0	0
880	920	23	0	0	0	0	0	0	0	0	0	0
920	960	27	1	0	0	0	0	0	0	0	0	0
960	1,000	31	5	0	0	0	0	0	0	0	0	0
1,000	1,040	35	9	0	0	0	0	0	0	0	0	0
1,040	1,080	39	13	0	0	0	0	0	0	0	0	0
1,080	1,120	43	17	0	0	0	0	0	0	0	0	0
1,120	1,160	47	21	0	0	0	0	0	0	0	0	0
1,160	1,200	51	25	0	0	0	0	0	0	0	0	0
1,200	1,240	55	29	2	0	0	0	0	0	0	0	0
1,240	1,280	59	33	6	0	0	0	0	0	0	0	0
1,280	1,320	63	37	10	0	0	0	0	0	0	0	0
1,320	1,360	67	41	14	0	0	0	0	0	0	0	0
1,360	1,400	71	45	18	0	0	0	0	0	0	0	0
1,400	1,440	75	49	22	0	0	0	0	0	0	0	0
1,440	1,480	79	53	26	0	0	0	0	0	0	0	0
1,480	1,520	83	57	30	3	0	0	0	0	0	0	0
1,520	1,560	87	61	34	7	0	0	0	0	0	0	0
1,560	1,600	91	65	38	11	0	0	0	0	0	0	0
1,600	1,640	95	69	42	15	0	0	0	0	0	0	0
1,640	1,680	99	73	46	19	0	0	0	0	0	0	0
1,680	1,720	103	77	50	23	0	0	0	0	0	0	0
1,720	1,760	107	81	54	27	1	0	0	0	0	0	0
1,760	1,800	111	85	58	31	5	0	0	0	0	0	0
1,800	1,840	115	89	62	35	9	0	0	0	0	0	0
1,840	1,880	119	93	66	39	13	0	0	0	0	0	0
1,880	1,920	124	97	70	43	17	0	0	0	0	0	0
1,920	1,960	130	101	74	47	21	0	0	0	0	0	0
1,960	2,000	136	105	78	51	25	0	0	0	0	0	0
2,000	2,040	142	109	82	55	29	2	0	0	0	0	0
2,040	2,080	148	113	86	59	33	6	0	0	0	0	0
2,080	2,120	154	117	90	63	37	10	0	0	0	0	0
2,120	2,160	160	121	94	67	41	14	0	0	0	0	0
2,160	2,200	166	126	98	71	45	18	0	0	0	0	0
2,200	2,240	172	132	102	75	49	22	0	0	0	0	0
2,240	2,280	178	138	106	79	53	26	0	0	0	0	0
2,280	2,320	184	144	110	83	57	30	3	0	0	0	0
2,320	2,360	190	150	114	87	61	34	7	0	0	0	0
2,360	2,400	196	156	118	91	65	38	11	0	0	0	0
2,400	2,440	202	162	122	95	69	42	15	0	0	0	0
2,440	2,480	208	168	128	99	73	46	19	0	0	0	0
2,480	2,520	214	174	134	103	77	50	23	0	0	0	0
2,520	2,560	220	180	140	107	81	54	27	1	0	0	0
2,560	2,600	226	186	146	111	85	58	31	5	0	0	0
2,600	2,640	232	192	152	115	89	62	35	9	0	0	0
2,640	2,680	238	198	158	119	93	66	39	13	0	0	0
2,680	2,720	244	204	164	124	97	70	43	17	0	0	0
2,720	2,760	250	210	170	130	101	74	47	21	0	0	0
2,760	2,800	256	216	176	136	105	78	51	25	0	0	0
2,800	2,840	262	222	182	142	109	82	55	29	2	0	0
2,840	2,880	268	228	188	148	113	86	59	33	6	0	0
2,880	2,920	274	234	194	154	117	90	63	37	10	0	0
2,920	2,960	280	240	200	160	121	94	67	41	14	0	0
2,960	3,000	286	246	206	166	126	98	71	45	18	0	0
3,000	3,040	292	252	212	172	132	102	75	49	22	0	0
3,040	3,080	298	258	218	178	138	106	79	53	26	0	0
3,080	3,120	304	264	224	184	144	110	83	57	30	3	0
3,120	3,160	310	270	230	190	150	114	87	61	34	7	0
3,160	3,200	316	276	236	196	156	118	91	65	38	11	0
3,200	3,240	322	282	242	202	162	122	95	69	42	15	0

IRS Publication 15, Circular E (continued)

MARRIED Persons—MONTHLY Payroll Period
(For Wages Paid in 2005)

At least	But less than	0	1	2	3	4	5	6	7	8	9	10
\$3,240	\$3,280	\$328	\$288	\$248	\$208	\$168	\$128	\$99	\$73	\$46	\$19	\$0
3,280	3,320	334	294	254	214	174	134	103	77	50	23	0
3,320	3,360	340	300	260	220	180	140	107	81	54	27	1
3,360	3,400	346	306	266	226	186	146	111	85	58	31	5
3,400	3,440	352	312	272	232	192	152	115	89	62	35	9
3,440	3,480	358	318	278	238	198	158	119	93	66	39	13
3,480	3,520	364	324	284	244	204	164	124	97	70	43	17
3,520	3,560	370	330	290	250	210	170	130	101	74	47	21
3,560	3,600	376	336	296	256	216	176	136	105	78	51	25
3,600	3,640	382	342	302	262	222	182	142	109	82	55	29
3,640	3,680	388	348	308	268	228	188	148	113	86	59	33
3,680	3,720	394	354	314	274	234	194	154	117	90	63	37
3,720	3,760	400	360	320	280	240	200	160	121	94	67	41
3,760	3,800	406	366	326	286	246	206	166	126	98	71	45
3,800	3,840	412	372	332	292	252	212	172	132	102	75	49
3,840	3,880	418	378	338	298	258	218	178	138	106	79	53
3,880	3,920	424	384	344	304	264	224	184	144	110	83	57
3,920	3,960	430	390	350	310	270	230	190	150	114	87	61
3,960	4,000	436	396	356	316	276	236	196	156	118	91	65
4,000	4,040	442	402	362	322	282	242	202	162	122	95	69
4,040	4,080	448	408	368	328	288	248	208	168	128	99	73
4,080	4,120	454	414	374	334	294	254	214	174	134	103	77
4,120	4,160	460	420	380	340	300	260	220	180	140	107	81
4,160	4,200	466	426	386	346	306	266	226	186	146	111	85
4,200	4,240	472	432	392	352	312	272	232	192	152	115	89
4,240	4,280	478	438	398	358	318	278	238	198	158	119	93
4,280	4,320	484	444	404	364	324	284	244	204	164	124	97
4,320	4,360	490	450	410	370	330	290	250	210	170	130	101
4,360	4,400	496	456	416	376	336	296	256	216	176	136	105
4,400	4,440	502	462	422	382	342	302	262	222	182	142	109
4,440	4,480	508	468	428	388	348	308	268	228	188	148	113
4,480	4,520	514	474	434	394	354	314	274	234	194	154	117
4,520	4,560	520	480	440	400	360	320	280	240	200	160	121
4,560	4,600	526	486	446	406	366	326	286	246	206	166	126
4,600	4,640	532	492	452	412	372	332	292	252	212	172	132
4,640	4,680	538	498	458	418	378	338	298	258	218	178	138
4,680	4,720	544	504	464	424	384	344	304	264	224	184	144
4,720	4,760	550	510	470	430	390	350	310	270	230	190	150
4,760	4,800	556	516	476	436	396	356	316	276	236	196	156
4,800	4,840	562	522	482	442	402	362	322	282	242	202	162
4,840	4,880	568	528	488	448	408	368	328	288	248	208	168
4,880	4,920	574	534	494	454	414	374	334	294	254	214	174
4,920	4,960	580	540	500	460	420	380	340	300	260	220	180
4,960	5,000	586	546	506	466	426	386	346	306	266	226	186
5,000	5,040	592	552	512	472	432	392	352	312	272	232	192
5,040	5,080	598	558	518	478	438	398	358	318	278	238	198
5,080	5,120	604	564	524	484	444	404	364	324	284	244	204
5,120	5,160	610	570	530	490	450	410	370	330	290	250	210
5,160	5,200	616	576	536	496	456	416	376	336	296	256	216
5,200	5,240	622	582	542	502	462	422	382	342	302	262	222
5,240	5,280	628	588	548	508	468	428	388	348	308	268	228
5,280	5,320	634	594	554	514	474	434	394	354	314	274	234
5,320	5,360	640	600	560	520	480	440	400	360	320	280	240
5,360	5,400	646	606	566	526	486	446	406	366	326	286	246
5,400	5,440	652	612	572	532	492	452	412	372	332	292	252
5,440	5,480	658	618	578	538	498	458	418	378	338	298	258
5,480	5,520	664	624	584	544	504	464	424	384	344	304	264
5,520	5,560	673	630	590	550	510	470	430	390	350	310	270
5,560	5,600	683	636	596	556	516	476	436	396	356	316	276
5,600	5,640	693	642	602	562	522	482	442	402	362	322	282
5,640	5,680	703	648	608	568	528	488	448	408	368	328	288
5,680	5,720	713	654	614	574	534	494	454	414	374	334	294
5,720	5,760	723	660	620	580	540	500	460	420	380	340	300
5,760	5,800	733	666	626	586	546	506	466	426	386	346	306
5,800	5,840	743	676	632	592	552	512	472	432	392	352	312
5,840	5,880	753	686	638	598	558	518	478	438	398	358	318

\$5,880 and over   Use Table 4(b) for a **MARRIED person** on page 36. Also see the instructions on page 34.

IRS Publication 15, Circular E (continued)

SINGLE Persons—DAILY OR MISCELLANEOUS Payroll Period
(For Wages Paid in 2005)

If the wages are—		And the number of withholding allowances claimed is—										
At least	But less than	0	1	2	3	4	5	6	7	8	9	10
		The amount of income tax to be withheld is—										
$0	$15	$0	$0	$0	$0	$0	$0	$0	$0	$0	$0	$0
15	18	1	0	0	0	0	0	0	0	0	0	0
18	21	1	0	0	0	0	0	0	0	0	0	0
21	24	1	0	0	0	0	0	0	0	0	0	0
24	27	2	0	0	0	0	0	0	0	0	0	0
27	30	2	1	0	0	0	0	0	0	0	0	0
30	33	2	1	0	0	0	0	0	0	0	0	0
33	36	2	1	0	0	0	0	0	0	0	0	0
36	39	3	2	0	0	0	0	0	0	0	0	0
39	42	3	2	1	0	0	0	0	0	0	0	0
42	45	4	2	1	0	0	0	0	0	0	0	0
45	48	4	2	1	0	0	0	0	0	0	0	0
48	51	5	3	1	0	0	0	0	0	0	0	0
51	54	5	3	2	1	0	0	0	0	0	0	0
54	57	5	4	2	1	0	0	0	0	0	0	0
57	60	6	4	2	1	0	0	0	0	0	0	0
60	63	6	4	3	1	0	0	0	0	0	0	0
63	66	7	5	3	2	1	0	0	0	0	0	0
66	69	7	5	4	2	1	0	0	0	0	0	0
69	72	8	6	4	2	1	0	0	0	0	0	0
72	75	8	6	4	3	1	0	0	0	0	0	0
75	78	9	7	5	3	2	0	0	0	0	0	0
78	81	9	7	5	3	2	1	0	0	0	0	0
81	84	9	8	6	4	2	1	0	0	0	0	0
84	87	10	8	6	4	3	1	0	0	0	0	0
87	90	10	9	7	5	3	2	0	0	0	0	0
90	93	11	9	7	5	3	2	1	0	0	0	0
93	96	11	9	8	6	4	2	1	0	0	0	0
96	99	12	10	8	6	4	3	1	0	0	0	0
99	102	12	10	8	7	5	3	2	0	0	0	0
102	105	13	11	9	7	5	3	2	1	0	0	0
105	108	13	11	9	8	6	4	2	1	0	0	0
108	111	14	12	10	8	6	4	3	1	0	0	0
111	114	14	12	10	8	7	5	3	2	0	0	0
114	117	14	13	11	9	7	5	3	2	1	0	0
117	120	15	13	11	9	7	6	4	2	1	0	0
120	123	15	13	12	10	8	6	4	3	1	0	0
123	126	16	14	12	10	8	7	5	3	2	0	0
126	129	17	14	13	11	9	7	5	3	2	1	0
129	132	18	15	13	11	9	7	6	4	2	1	0
132	135	18	15	13	12	10	8	6	4	2	1	0
135	138	19	16	14	12	10	8	6	5	3	2	0
138	141	20	17	14	12	11	9	7	5	3	2	1
141	144	21	18	15	13	11	9	7	6	4	2	1
144	147	21	18	15	13	12	10	8	6	4	2	1
147	150	22	19	16	14	12	10	8	6	5	3	2
150	153	23	20	17	14	12	11	9	7	5	3	2
153	156	24	21	17	15	13	11	9	7	6	4	2
156	159	24	21	18	15	13	11	10	8	6	4	2
159	162	25	22	19	16	14	12	10	8	6	5	3
162	165	26	23	20	17	14	12	11	9	7	5	3
165	168	27	24	20	17	15	13	11	9	7	5	4
168	171	27	24	21	18	15	13	11	10	8	6	4
171	174	28	25	22	19	16	14	12	10	8	6	5
174	177	29	26	23	20	17	14	12	10	9	7	5
177	180	30	27	23	20	17	15	13	11	9	7	5
180	183	30	27	24	21	18	15	13	11	10	8	6
183	186	31	28	25	22	19	16	14	12	10	8	6
186	189	32	29	26	23	20	16	14	12	10	9	7
189	192	33	30	26	23	20	17	15	13	11	9	7
192	195	33	30	27	24	21	18	15	13	11	10	8
195	198	34	31	28	25	22	19	16	14	12	10	8
198	201	35	32	29	26	23	19	16	14	12	10	9
201	204	36	33	29	26	23	20	17	15	13	11	9
204	207	36	33	30	27	24	21	18	15	13	11	9
207	210	37	34	31	28	25	22	19	16	14	12	10
210	213	38	35	32	29	26	22	19	16	14	12	10
213	216	39	36	32	29	26	23	20	17	15	13	11
216	219	39	36	33	30	27	24	21	18	15	13	11
219	222	40	37	34	31	28	25	22	19	15	14	12

IRS Publication 15, Circular E (continued)

SINGLE Persons—DAILY OR MISCELLANEOUS Payroll Period

(For Wages Paid in 2005)

If the wages are—		And the number of withholding allowances claimed is—										
At least	But less than	0	1	2	3	4	5	6	7	8	9	10
		The amount of income tax to be withheld is—										
$222	$225	$41	$38	$35	$32	$29	$25	$22	$19	$16	$14	$12
225	228	42	39	35	32	29	26	23	20	17	14	13
228	231	42	39	36	33	30	27	24	21	18	15	13
231	234	43	40	37	34	31	28	25	22	18	15	14
234	237	44	41	38	35	32	28	25	22	19	16	14
237	240	45	42	38	35	32	29	26	23	20	17	14
240	243	45	42	39	36	33	30	27	24	21	18	15
243	246	46	43	40	37	34	31	28	25	21	18	15
246	249	47	44	41	38	35	31	28	25	22	19	16
249	252	48	45	41	38	35	32	29	26	23	20	17
252	255	48	45	42	39	36	33	30	27	24	21	18
255	258	49	46	43	40	37	34	31	28	24	21	18
258	261	50	47	44	41	38	34	31	28	25	22	19
261	264	51	48	44	41	38	35	32	29	26	23	20
264	267	51	48	45	42	39	36	33	30	27	24	21
267	270	52	49	46	43	40	37	34	31	27	24	21
270	273	53	50	47	44	41	37	34	31	28	25	22
273	276	54	51	47	44	41	38	35	32	29	26	23
276	279	55	51	48	45	42	39	36	33	30	27	24
279	282	55	52	49	46	43	40	37	34	30	27	24
282	285	56	53	50	47	44	40	37	34	31	28	25
285	288	57	54	50	47	44	41	38	35	32	29	26
288	291	58	55	51	48	45	42	39	36	33	30	27
291	294	59	55	52	49	46	43	40	37	33	30	27
294	297	60	56	53	50	47	43	40	37	34	31	28
297	300	61	57	54	50	47	44	41	38	35	32	29
300	303	61	58	54	51	48	45	42	39	36	33	30
303	306	62	59	55	52	49	46	43	40	36	33	30
306	309	63	60	56	53	50	46	43	40	37	34	31
309	312	64	60	57	54	50	47	44	41	38	35	32
312	315	65	61	58	54	51	48	45	42	39	36	33
315	318	66	62	59	55	52	49	46	43	39	36	33
318	321	66	63	60	56	53	49	46	43	40	37	34
321	324	67	64	60	57	53	50	47	44	41	38	35
324	327	68	65	61	58	54	51	48	45	42	39	36
327	330	69	65	62	59	55	52	49	46	42	39	36
330	333	70	66	63	59	56	53	49	46	43	40	37
333	336	71	67	64	60	57	53	50	47	44	41	38
336	339	71	68	65	61	58	54	51	48	45	42	39
339	341	72	69	65	62	58	55	52	48	45	42	39
341	343	73	69	66	62	59	55	52	49	46	43	40
343	345	73	70	66	63	59	56	53	49	46	43	40
345	347	74	70	67	63	60	57	53	50	47	44	41
347	349	74	71	67	64	61	57	54	50	47	44	41
349	351	75	71	68	65	61	58	54	51	48	45	42
351	353	75	72	69	65	62	58	55	51	48	45	42
353	355	76	73	69	66	62	59	55	52	49	46	43
355	357	77	73	70	66	63	59	56	52	49	46	43
357	359	77	74	70	67	63	60	56	53	50	47	44
359	361	78	74	71	67	64	61	57	54	50	47	44
361	363	78	75	71	68	65	61	58	54	51	48	45
363	365	79	75	72	69	65	62	58	55	51	48	45
365	367	79	76	73	69	66	62	59	55	52	49	46
367	369	80	77	73	70	66	63	59	56	52	49	46
369	371	81	77	74	70	67	63	60	56	53	50	47
371	373	81	78	74	71	67	64	60	57	54	50	47
373	375	82	78	75	71	68	64	61	58	54	51	48
375	377	82	79	75	72	68	65	62	58	55	51	48
377	379	83	79	76	72	69	66	62	59	55	52	49
379	381	83	80	76	73	70	66	63	59	56	52	49
381	383	84	80	77	74	70	67	63	60	56	53	50
383	385	84	81	78	74	71	67	64	60	57	53	50
385	387	85	82	78	75	71	68	64	61	57	54	51
387	389	86	82	79	75	72	68	65	61	58	55	51
389	391	86	83	79	76	72	69	65	62	59	55	52

$391 and over   Use Table 8(a) for a **SINGLE person** on page 37. Also see the instructions on page 34.

IRS Publication 15, Circular E (continued)

MARRIED Persons—DAILY OR MISCELLANEOUS Payroll Period

(For Wages Paid in 2005)

If the wages are—		And the number of withholding allowances claimed is—										
At least	But less than	0	1	2	3	4	5	6	7	8	9	10
		The amount of income tax to be withheld is—										
$0	$27	$0	$0	$0	$0	$0	$0	$0	$0	$0	$0	$0
27	30	0	0	0	0	0	0	0	0	0	0	0
30	33	0	0	0	0	0	0	0	0	0	0	0
33	36	0	0	0	0	0	0	0	0	0	0	0
36	39	1	0	0	0	0	0	0	0	0	0	0
39	42	1	0	0	0	0	0	0	0	0	0	0
42	45	1	0	0	0	0	0	0	0	0	0	0
45	48	2	0	0	0	0	0	0	0	0	0	0
48	51	2	1	0	0	0	0	0	0	0	0	0
51	54	2	1	0	0	0	0	0	0	0	0	0
54	57	2	1	0	0	0	0	0	0	0	0	0
57	60	3	2	0	0	0	0	0	0	0	0	0
60	63	3	2	1	0	0	0	0	0	0	0	0
63	66	3	2	1	0	0	0	0	0	0	0	0
66	69	4	2	1	0	0	0	0	0	0	0	0
69	72	4	3	2	0	0	0	0	0	0	0	0
72	75	4	3	2	1	0	0	0	0	0	0	0
75	78	5	3	2	1	0	0	0	0	0	0	0
78	81	5	4	2	1	0	0	0	0	0	0	0
81	84	5	4	3	1	0	0	0	0	0	0	0
84	87	5	4	3	2	1	0	0	0	0	0	0
87	90	6	5	3	2	1	0	0	0	0	0	0
90	93	6	5	4	2	1	0	0	0	0	0	0
93	96	7	5	4	3	1	0	0	0	0	0	0
96	99	7	5	4	3	2	1	0	0	0	0	0
99	102	8	6	5	3	2	1	0	0	0	0	0
102	105	8	6	5	4	2	1	0	0	0	0	0
105	108	9	7	5	4	3	1	0	0	0	0	0
108	111	9	7	5	4	3	2	0	0	0	0	0
111	114	9	8	6	4	3	2	1	0	0	0	0
114	117	10	8	6	5	4	2	1	0	0	0	0
117	120	10	9	7	5	4	3	1	0	0	0	0
120	123	11	9	7	5	4	3	2	0	0	0	0
123	126	11	9	8	6	4	3	2	1	0	0	0
126	129	12	10	8	6	5	4	2	1	0	0	0
129	132	12	10	8	7	5	4	3	1	0	0	0
132	135	13	11	9	7	5	4	3	2	0	0	0
135	138	13	11	9	8	6	4	3	2	1	0	0
138	141	14	12	10	8	6	5	3	2	1	0	0
141	144	14	12	10	8	7	5	4	3	1	0	0
144	147	14	13	11	9	7	5	4	3	2	0	0
147	150	15	13	11	9	7	6	4	3	2	1	0
150	153	15	13	12	10	8	6	5	3	2	1	0
153	156	16	14	12	10	8	7	5	4	3	1	0
156	159	16	14	13	11	9	7	5	4	3	2	0
159	162	17	15	13	11	9	7	6	4	3	2	1
162	165	17	15	13	12	10	8	6	5	3	2	1
165	168	18	16	14	12	10	8	6	5	4	2	1
168	171	18	16	14	12	11	9	7	5	4	3	2
171	174	18	17	15	13	11	9	7	6	4	3	2
174	177	19	17	15	13	12	10	8	6	5	3	2
177	180	19	18	16	14	12	10	8	6	5	4	2
180	183	20	18	16	14	12	11	9	7	5	4	3
183	186	20	18	17	15	13	11	9	7	6	4	3
186	189	21	19	17	15	13	11	10	8	6	5	3
189	192	21	19	17	16	14	12	10	8	6	5	4
192	195	22	20	18	16	14	12	11	9	7	5	4
195	198	22	20	18	17	15	13	11	9	7	5	4
198	201	23	21	19	17	15	13	11	10	8	6	5
201	204	23	21	19	17	16	14	12	10	8	6	5
204	207	23	22	20	18	16	14	12	10	9	7	5
207	210	24	22	20	18	16	15	13	11	9	7	5
210	213	24	22	21	19	17	15	13	11	10	8	6
213	216	25	23	21	19	17	16	14	12	10	8	6
216	219	25	23	22	20	18	16	14	12	10	9	7
219	222	26	24	22	20	18	16	15	13	11	9	7
222	225	26	24	22	21	19	17	15	13	11	9	8
225	228	27	25	23	21	19	17	15	14	12	10	8
228	231	27	25	23	21	20	18	16	14	12	10	9
231	234	27	26	24	22	20	18	16	15	13	11	9

IRS Publication 15, Circular E (continued)

MARRIED Persons—DAILY OR MISCELLANEOUS Payroll Period
(For Wages Paid in 2005)

If the wages are—		And the number of withholding allowances claimed is—										
At least	But less than	0	1	2	3	4	5	6	7	8	9	10
		The amount of income tax to be withheld is—										
$234	$237	$28	$26	$24	$22	$21	$19	$17	$15	$13	$11	$9
237	240	28	27	25	23	21	19	17	15	14	12	10
240	243	29	27	25	23	21	20	18	16	14	12	10
243	246	29	27	26	24	22	20	18	16	14	13	11
246	249	30	28	26	24	22	20	19	17	15	13	11
249	252	30	28	26	25	23	21	19	17	15	14	12
252	255	31	29	27	25	23	21	20	18	16	14	12
255	258	31	29	27	26	24	22	20	18	16	14	13
258	261	32	30	28	26	24	22	20	19	17	15	13
261	264	33	30	28	26	25	23	21	19	17	15	13
264	267	33	31	29	27	25	23	21	19	18	16	14
267	270	34	31	29	27	25	24	22	20	18	16	14
270	273	35	32	30	28	26	24	22	20	19	17	15
273	276	36	33	30	28	26	25	23	21	19	17	15
276	279	36	33	31	29	27	25	23	21	19	18	16
279	282	37	34	31	29	27	25	24	22	20	18	16
282	285	38	35	32	30	28	26	24	22	20	18	17
285	288	39	36	33	30	28	26	26	24	23	21	17
288	291	39	36	33	30	29	27	25	23	21	19	18
291	294	40	37	34	31	29	27	25	24	22	20	18
294	297	41	38	35	32	30	28	26	24	22	20	18
297	300	42	39	36	33	30	28	26	24	23	21	19
300	303	42	39	36	33	30	29	27	25	23	21	19
303	306	43	40	37	34	31	29	27	25	23	22	20
306	309	44	41	38	35	32	29	28	26	24	22	20
309	312	45	42	39	36	32	30	28	26	24	23	21
312	315	45	42	39	36	33	30	29	27	25	23	21
315	318	46	43	40	37	34	31	29	27	25	23	22
318	321	47	44	41	38	35	32	29	28	26	24	22
321	324	48	45	42	39	35	32	30	28	26	24	22
324	327	48	45	42	39	36	33	30	28	27	25	23
327	330	49	46	43	40	37	34	31	29	27	25	23
330	333	50	47	44	41	38	35	32	29	28	26	24
333	336	51	48	45	42	38	35	32	30	28	26	24
336	339	51	48	45	42	39	36	33	30	28	27	25
339	341	52	49	46	43	40	37	34	31	29	27	25
341	343	53	50	46	43	40	37	34	31	29	27	25
343	345	53	50	47	44	41	38	35	32	29	28	26
345	347	54	51	47	44	41	38	35	32	30	28	26
347	349	54	51	48	45	42	39	36	33	30	28	26
349	351	55	52	48	45	42	39	36	33	30	28	27
351	353	55	52	49	46	43	40	37	34	31	29	27
353	355	56	53	49	46	43	40	37	34	31	29	27
355	357	56	53	50	47	44	41	38	35	32	29	28
357	359	57	54	50	47	44	41	38	35	32	30	28
359	361	57	54	51	48	45	42	39	36	33	30	28
361	363	58	55	51	48	45	42	39	36	33	30	28
363	365	58	55	52	49	46	43	40	37	34	31	29
365	367	59	56	52	49	46	43	40	37	34	31	29
367	369	59	56	53	50	47	44	41	38	35	31	29
369	371	60	57	53	50	47	44	41	38	35	32	30
371	373	60	57	54	51	48	45	42	39	36	32	30
373	375	61	58	54	51	48	45	42	39	36	33	30
375	377	61	58	55	52	49	46	43	40	37	33	31
377	379	62	59	55	52	49	46	43	40	37	34	31
379	381	62	59	56	53	50	47	44	41	38	34	31
381	383	63	60	56	53	50	47	44	41	38	35	32
383	385	63	60	57	54	51	48	45	42	39	35	32
385	387	64	61	57	54	51	48	45	42	39	36	33
387	389	64	61	58	55	52	49	46	43	40	36	33
389	391	65	62	58	55	52	49	46	43	40	37	34
391	393	65	62	59	56	53	50	47	44	41	37	34
393	395	66	63	59	56	53	50	47	44	41	38	35
395	397	66	63	60	57	54	51	48	45	42	38	35
397	399	67	64	60	57	54	51	48	45	42	39	36
399	401	67	64	61	58	55	52	49	46	43	39	36

$401 and over — Use Table 8(b) for a **MARRIED person** on page 37. Also see the instructions on page 34.

IRS Publication 15, Circular E (continued)

Tables for Percentage Method of Advance EIC Payments
(For Wages Paid in 2005)

Table 1. WEEKLY Payroll Period

(a) SINGLE or HEAD OF HOUSEHOLD		(b) MARRIED Without Spouse Filing Certificate		(c) MARRIED With Both Spouses Filing Certificate	
If the amount of wages (before deducting withholding allowances) is:	The amount of payment to be made is:	If the amount of wages (before deducting withholding allowances) is:	The amount of payment to be made is:	If the amount of wages (before deducting withholding allowances) is:	The amount of payment to be made is:
Over— But not over—		Over— But not over—		Over— But not over—	
$0 $150	20.40% of wages	$0 $150	20.40% of wages	$0 $75	20.40% of wages
$150 $276	$31	$150 $314	$31	$75 $157	$15
$276	$31 less 9.588% of wages in excess of $276	$314	$31 less 9.588% of wages in excess of $314	$157	$15 less 9.588% of wages in excess of $157

Table 2. BIWEEKLY Payroll Period

(a) SINGLE or HEAD OF HOUSEHOLD		(b) MARRIED Without Spouse Filing Certificate		(c) MARRIED With Both Spouses Filing Certificate	
If the amount of wages (before deducting withholding allowances) is:	The amount of payment to be made is:	If the amount of wages (before deducting withholding allowances) is:	The amount of payment to be made is:	If the amount of wages (before deducting withholding allowances) is:	The amount of payment to be made is:
Over— But not over—		Over— But not over—		Over— But not over—	
$0 $301	20.40% of wages	$0 $301	20.40% of wages	$0 $150	20.40% of wages
$301 $552	$61	$301 $629	$61	$150 $314	$31
$552	$61 less 9.588% of wages in excess of $552	$629	$61 less 9.588% of wages in excess of $629	$314	$31 less 9.588% of wages in excess of $314

Table 3. SEMIMONTHLY Payroll Period

(a) SINGLE or HEAD OF HOUSEHOLD		(b) MARRIED Without Spouse Filing Certificate		(c) MARRIED With Both Spouses Filing Certificate	
If the amount of wages (before deducting withholding allowances) is:	The amount of payment to be made is:	If the amount of wages (before deducting withholding allowances) is:	The amount of payment to be made is:	If the amount of wages (before deducting withholding allowances) is:	The amount of payment to be made is:
Over— But not over—		Over— But not over—		Over— But not over—	
$0 $326	20.40% of wages	$0 $326	20.40% of wages	$0 $163	20.40% of wages
$326 $598	$67	$326 $682	$67	$163 $341	$33
$598	$67 less 9.588% of wages in excess of $598	$682	$67 less 9.588% of wages in excess of $682	$341	$33 less 9.588% of wages in excess of $341

Table 4. MONTHLY Payroll Period

(a) SINGLE or HEAD OF HOUSEHOLD		(b) MARRIED Without Spouse Filing Certificate		(c) MARRIED With Both Spouses Filing Certificate	
If the amount of wages (before deducting withholding allowances) is:	The amount of payment to be made is:	If the amount of wages (before deducting withholding allowances) is:	The amount of payment to be made is:	If the amount of wages (before deducting withholding allowances) is:	The amount of payment to be made is:
Over— But not over—		Over— But not over—		Over— But not over—	
$0 $652	20.40% of wages	$0 $652	20.40% of wages	$0 $326	20.40% of wages
$652 $1,197	$133	$652 $1,364	$133	$326 $682	$67
$1,197	$133 less 9.588% of wages in excess of $1,197	$1,364	$133 less 9.588% of wages in excess of $1,364	$682	$67 less 9.588% of wages in excess of $682

IRS Publication 15, Circular E (continued)

Tables for Percentage Method of Advance EIC Payments (Continued)
(For Wages Paid in 2005)

Table 5. QUARTERLY Payroll Period

(a) SINGLE or HEAD OF HOUSEHOLD		(b) MARRIED Without Spouse Filing Certificate		(c) MARRIED With Both Spouses Filing Certificate	
If the amount of wages (before deducting withholding allowances) is:	The amount of payment to be made is:	If the amount of wages (before deducting withholding allowances) is:	The amount of payment to be made is:	If the amount of wages (before deducting withholding allowances) is:	The amount of payment to be made is:
Over— But not over—		Over— But not over—		Over— But not over—	
$0 $1,957	20.40% of wages	$0 $1,957	20.40% of wages	$0 $978	20.40% of wages
$1,957 $3,592	$399	$1,957 $4,092	$399	$978 $2,046	$200
$3,592	$399 less 9.588% of wages in excess of $3,592	$4,092	$399 less 9.588% of wages in excess of $4,092	$2,046	$200 less 9.588% of wages in excess of $2,046

Table 6. SEMIANNUAL Payroll Period

(a) SINGLE or HEAD OF HOUSEHOLD		(b) MARRIED Without Spouse Filing Certificate		(c) MARRIED With Both Spouses Filing Certificate	
If the amount of wages (before deducting withholding allowances) is:	The amount of payment to be made is:	If the amount of wages (before deducting withholding allowances) is:	The amount of payment to be made is:	If the amount of wages (before deducting withholding allowances) is:	The amount of payment to be made is:
Over— But not over—		Over— But not over—		Over— But not over—	
$0 $3,915	20.40% of wages	$0 $3,915	20.40% of wages	$0 $1,957	20.40% of wages
$3,915 $7,185	$799	$3,915 $8,185	$799	$1,957 $4,092	$399
$7,185	$799 less 9.588% of wages in excess of $7,185	$8,185	$799 less 9.588% of wages in excess of $8,185	$4,092	$399 less 9.588% of wages in excess of $4,092

Table 7. ANNUAL Payroll Period

(a) SINGLE or HEAD OF HOUSEHOLD		(b) MARRIED Without Spouse Filing Certificate		(c) MARRIED With Both Spouses Filing Certificate	
If the amount of wages (before deducting withholding allowances) is:	The amount of payment to be made is:	If the amount of wages (before deducting withholding allowances) is:	The amount of payment to be made is:	If the amount of wages (before deducting withholding allowances) is:	The amount of payment to be made is:
Over— But not over—		Over— But not over—		Over— But not over—	
$0 $7,830	20.40% of wages	$0 $7,830	20.40% of wages	$0 $3,915	20.40% of wages
$7,830 $14,370	$1,597	$7,830 $16,370	$1,597	$3,915 $8,185	$799
$14,370	$1,597 less 9.588% of wages in excess of $14,370	$16,370	$1,597 less 9.588% of wages in excess of $16,370	$8,185	$799 less 9.588% of wages in excess of $8,185

Table 8. DAILY or MISCELLANEOUS Payroll Period

(a) SINGLE or HEAD OF HOUSEHOLD		(b) MARRIED Without Spouse Filing Certificate		(c) MARRIED With Both Spouses Filing Certificate	
If the wages divided by the number of days in such period (before deducting withholding allowances) are:	The amount of payment to be made is the following amount multiplied by the number of days in such period:	If the wages divided by the number of days in such period (before deducting withholding allowances) are:	The amount of payment to be made is the following amount multiplied by the number of days in such period:	If the wages divided by the number of days in such period (before deducting withholding allowances) are:	The amount of payment to be made is the following amount multiplied by the number of days in such period:
Over— But not over—		Over— But not over—		Over— But not over—	
$0 $30	20.40% of wages	$0 $30	20.40% of wages	$0 $15	20.40% of wages
$30 $55	$6	$30 $62	$6	$15 $31	$3
$55	$6 less 9.588% of wages in excess of $55	$62	$6 less 9.588% of wages in excess of $62	$31	$3 less 9.588% of wages in excess of $31

IRS Publication 15, Circular E (continued)

Tables for Wage Bracket Method of Advance EIC Payments (For Wages Paid in 2005)

WEEKLY Payroll Period

SINGLE or HEAD OF HOUSEHOLD

Wages— At least	But less than	Payment to be made	Wages— At least	But less than	Payment to be made	Wages— At least	But less than	Payment to be made	Wages— At least	But less than	Payment to be made	Wages— At least	But less than	Payment to be made
$0	$5	$0	$65	$70	$13	$130	$135	$27	$355	$365	$22	$485	$495	$10
5	10	1	70	75	14	135	140	28	365	375	21	495	505	9
10	15	2	75	80	15	140	145	29	375	385	20	505	515	8
15	20	3	80	85	16	145	150	30	385	395	19	515	525	7
20	25	4	85	90	17	150	275	31	395	405	18	525	535	6
25	30	5	90	95	18	275	285	30	405	415	17	535	545	5
30	35	6	95	100	19	285	295	29	415	425	16	545	555	4
35	40	7	100	105	20	295	305	28	425	435	15	555	565	3
40	45	8	105	110	21	305	315	27	435	445	15	565	575	2
45	50	9	110	115	22	315	325	26	445	455	14	575	585	1
50	55	10	115	120	23	325	335	25	455	465	13	585	- - -	0
55	60	11	120	125	24	335	345	24	465	475	12			
60	65	12	125	130	26	345	355	23	475	485	11			

MARRIED Without Spouse Filing Certificate

Wages— At least	But less than	Payment to be made	Wages— At least	But less than	Payment to be made	Wages— At least	But less than	Payment to be made	Wages— At least	But less than	Payment to be made	Wages— At least	But less than	Payment to be made
$0	$5	$0	$65	$70	$13	$130	$135	$27	$390	$400	$23	$520	$530	$10
5	10	1	70	75	14	135	140	28	400	410	22	530	540	9
10	15	2	75	80	15	140	145	29	410	420	21	540	550	8
15	20	3	80	85	16	145	150	30	420	430	20	550	560	7
20	25	4	85	90	17	150	310	31	430	440	19	560	570	6
25	30	5	90	95	18	310	320	30	440	450	18	570	580	5
30	35	6	95	100	19	320	330	29	450	460	17	580	590	4
35	40	7	100	105	20	330	340	28	460	470	16	590	600	3
40	45	8	105	110	21	340	350	27	470	480	15	600	610	2
45	50	9	110	115	22	350	360	26	480	490	14	610	620	1
50	55	10	115	120	23	360	370	25	490	500	13	620	- - -	0
55	60	11	120	125	24	370	380	24	500	510	12			
60	65	12	125	130	26	380	390	24	510	520	11			

MARRIED With Both Spouses Filing Certificate

Wages— At least	But less than	Payment to be made	Wages— At least	But less than	Payment to be made	Wages— At least	But less than	Payment to be made	Wages— At least	But less than	Payment to be made	Wages— At least	But less than	Payment to be made
$0	$5	$0	$35	$40	$7	$70	$75	$14	$205	$215	$10	$275	$285	$3
5	10	1	40	45	8	75	155	15	215	225	9	285	295	2
10	15	2	45	50	9	155	165	15	225	235	8	295	305	1
15	20	3	50	55	10	165	175	14	235	245	7	305	- - -	0
20	25	4	55	60	11	175	185	13	245	255	6			
25	30	5	60	65	12	185	195	12	255	265	5			
30	35	6	65	70	13	195	205	11	265	275	4			

BIWEEKLY Payroll Period

SINGLE or HEAD OF HOUSEHOLD

Wages— At least	But less than	Payment to be made	Wages— At least	But less than	Payment to be made	Wages— At least	But less than	Payment to be made	Wages— At least	But less than	Payment to be made	Wages— At least	But less than	Payment to be made
$0	$5	$0	$50	$55	$10	$100	$105	$20	$150	$155	$31	$200	$205	$41
5	10	1	55	60	11	105	110	21	155	160	32	205	210	42
10	15	2	60	65	12	110	115	22	160	165	33	210	215	43
15	20	3	65	70	13	115	120	23	165	170	34	215	220	44
20	25	4	70	75	14	120	125	24	170	175	35	220	225	45
25	30	5	75	80	15	125	130	26	175	180	36	225	230	46
30	35	6	80	85	16	130	135	27	180	185	37	230	235	47
35	40	7	85	90	17	135	140	28	185	190	38	235	240	48
40	45	8	90	95	18	140	145	29	190	195	39	240	245	49
45	50	9	95	100	19	145	150	30	195	200	40	245	250	50

(continued on next page)

IRS Publication 15, Circular E (continued)

BIWEEKLY Payroll Period

SINGLE or HEAD OF HOUSEHOLD

At least	But less than	Payment to be made	At least	But less than	Payment to be made	At least	But less than	Payment to be made	At least	But less than	Payment to be made	At least	But less than	Payment to be made
$250	$255	$51	$590	$600	$57	$740	$750	$43	$890	$900	$28	$1,040	$1,050	$14
255	260	52	600	610	56	750	760	42	900	910	27	1,050	1,060	13
260	265	53	610	620	55	760	770	41	910	920	26	1,060	1,070	12
265	270	54	620	630	54	770	780	40	920	930	25	1,070	1,080	11
270	275	55	630	640	53	780	790	39	930	940	24	1,080	1,090	10
275	280	56	640	650	52	790	800	38	940	950	23	1,090	1,100	9
280	285	57	650	660	51	800	810	37	950	960	22	1,100	1,110	8
285	290	58	660	670	50	810	820	36	960	970	21	1,110	1,120	7
290	295	59	670	680	49	820	830	35	970	980	20	1,120	1,130	6
295	300	60	680	690	48	830	840	34	980	990	19	1,130	1,140	5
300	550	61	690	700	47	840	850	33	990	1,000	19	1,140	1,150	4
550	560	61	700	710	46	850	860	32	1,000	1,010	18	1,150	1,160	3
560	570	60	710	720	45	860	870	31	1,010	1,020	17	1,160	1,170	2
570	580	59	720	730	44	870	880	30	1,020	1,030	16	1,170	1,180	1
580	590	58	730	740	43	880	890	29	1,030	1,040	15	1,180	- - -	0

MARRIED Without Spouse Filing Certificate

At least	But less than	Payment to be made	At least	But less than	Payment to be made	At least	But less than	Payment to be made	At least	But less than	Payment to be made	At least	But less than	Payment to be made
$0	$5	$0	$130	$135	$27	$260	$265	$53	$795	$805	$45	$1,055	$1,065	$20
5	10	1	135	140	28	265	270	54	805	815	44	1,065	1,075	19
10	15	2	140	145	29	270	275	55	815	825	43	1,075	1,085	18
15	20	3	145	150	30	275	280	56	825	835	42	1,085	1,095	17
20	25	4	150	155	31	280	285	57	835	845	41	1,095	1,105	16
25	30	5	155	160	32	285	290	58	845	855	40	1,105	1,115	15
30	35	6	160	165	33	290	295	59	855	865	39	1,115	1,125	14
35	40	7	165	170	34	295	300	60	865	875	38	1,125	1,135	13
40	45	8	170	175	35	300	625	61	875	885	37	1,135	1,145	12
45	50	9	175	180	36	625	635	61	885	895	36	1,145	1,155	11
50	55	10	180	185	37	635	645	60	895	905	35	1,155	1,165	10
55	60	11	185	190	38	645	655	59	905	915	34	1,165	1,175	9
60	65	12	190	195	39	655	665	58	915	925	33	1,175	1,185	8
65	70	13	195	200	40	665	675	57	925	935	32	1,185	1,195	7
70	75	14	200	205	41	675	685	56	935	945	31	1,195	1,205	6
75	80	15	205	210	42	685	695	55	945	955	30	1,205	1,215	5
80	85	16	210	215	43	695	705	54	955	965	29	1,215	1,225	4
85	90	17	215	220	44	705	715	53	965	975	28	1,225	1,235	3
90	95	18	220	225	45	715	725	52	975	985	27	1,235	1,245	2
95	100	19	225	230	46	725	735	51	985	995	26	1,245	1,255	1
100	105	20	230	235	47	735	745	50	995	1,005	25	1,255	1,265	1
105	110	21	235	240	48	745	755	49	1,005	1,015	24	1,265	- - -	0
110	115	22	240	245	49	755	765	48	1,015	1,025	24			
115	120	23	245	250	50	765	775	47	1,025	1,035	23			
120	125	24	250	255	51	775	785	47	1,035	1,045	22			
125	130	26	255	260	52	785	795	46	1,045	1,055	21			

MARRIED With Both Spouses Filing Certificate

At least	But less than	Payment to be made	At least	But less than	Payment to be made	At least	But less than	Payment to be made	At least	But less than	Payment to be made	At least	But less than	Payment to be made
$0	$5	$0	$65	$70	$13	$130	$135	$27	$390	$400	$23	$520	$530	$10
5	10	1	70	75	14	135	140	28	400	410	22	530	540	9
10	15	2	75	80	15	140	145	29	410	420	21	540	550	8
15	20	3	80	85	16	145	150	30	420	430	20	550	560	7
20	25	4	85	90	17	150	310	31	430	440	19	560	570	6
25	30	5	90	95	18	310	320	30	440	450	18	570	580	5
30	35	6	95	100	19	320	330	29	450	460	17	580	590	4
35	40	7	100	105	20	330	340	28	460	470	16	590	600	3
40	45	8	105	110	21	340	350	27	470	480	15	600	610	2
45	50	9	110	115	22	350	360	26	480	490	14	610	620	1
50	55	10	115	120	23	360	370	25	490	500	13	620	630	1
55	60	11	120	125	24	370	380	24	500	510	12	630	- - -	0
60	65	12	125	130	26	380	390	23	510	520	11			

IRS Publication 15, Circular E (continued)

SEMIMONTHLY Payroll Period

SINGLE or HEAD OF HOUSEHOLD

At least	But less than	Payment to be made	At least	But less than	Payment to be made	At least	But less than	Payment to be made	At least	But less than	Payment to be made	At least	But less than	Payment to be made
$0	$5	$0	$140	$145	$29	$280	$285	$57	$775	$785	$49	$1,055	$1,065	$22
5	10	1	145	150	30	285	290	58	785	795	48	1,065	1,075	21
10	15	2	150	155	31	290	295	59	795	805	47	1,075	1,085	20
15	20	3	155	160	32	295	300	60	805	815	46	1,085	1,095	19
20	25	4	160	165	33	300	305	61	815	825	45	1,095	1,105	18
25	30	5	165	170	34	305	310	62	825	835	44	1,105	1,115	17
30	35	6	170	175	35	310	315	63	835	845	43	1,115	1,125	16
35	40	7	175	180	36	315	320	64	845	855	42	1,125	1,135	15
40	45	8	180	185	37	320	325	65	855	865	41	1,135	1,145	14
45	50	9	185	190	38	325	595	66	865	875	40	1,145	1,155	13
50	55	10	190	195	39	595	605	66	875	885	39	1,155	1,165	12
55	60	11	195	200	40	605	615	65	885	895	38	1,165	1,175	11
60	65	12	200	205	41	615	625	64	895	905	37	1,175	1,185	10
65	70	13	205	210	42	625	635	63	905	915	36	1,185	1,195	9
70	75	14	210	215	43	635	645	62	915	925	35	1,195	1,205	8
75	80	15	215	220	44	645	655	61	925	935	34	1,205	1,215	7
80	85	16	220	225	45	655	665	60	935	945	33	1,215	1,225	6
85	90	17	225	230	46	665	675	59	945	955	32	1,225	1,235	6
90	95	18	230	235	47	675	685	58	955	965	31	1,235	1,245	5
95	100	19	235	240	48	685	695	57	965	975	30	1,245	1,255	4
100	105	20	240	245	49	695	705	56	975	985	30	1,255	1,265	3
105	110	21	245	250	50	705	715	55	985	995	29	1,265	1,275	2
110	115	22	250	255	51	715	725	54	995	1,005	28	1,275	1,285	1
115	120	23	255	260	52	725	735	53	1,005	1,015	27	1,285	- - -	0
120	125	24	260	265	53	735	745	53	1,015	1,025	26			
125	130	26	265	270	54	745	755	52	1,025	1,035	25			
130	135	27	270	275	55	755	765	51	1,035	1,045	24			
135	140	28	275	280	56	765	775	50	1,045	1,055	23			

MARRIED Without Spouse Filing Certificate

At least	But less than	Payment to be made	At least	But less than	Payment to be made	At least	But less than	Payment to be made	At least	But less than	Payment to be made	At least	But less than	Payment to be made
$0	$5	$0	$140	$145	$29	$280	$285	$57	$860	$870	$49	$1,140	$1,150	$22
5	10	1	145	150	30	285	290	58	870	880	48	1,150	1,160	21
10	15	2	150	155	31	290	295	59	880	890	47	1,160	1,170	20
15	20	3	155	160	32	295	300	60	890	900	46	1,170	1,180	19
20	25	4	160	165	33	300	305	61	900	910	45	1,180	1,190	18
25	30	5	165	170	34	305	310	62	910	920	44	1,190	1,200	17
30	35	6	170	175	35	310	315	63	920	930	43	1,200	1,210	16
35	40	7	175	180	36	315	320	64	930	940	42	1,210	1,220	15
40	45	8	180	185	37	320	325	65	940	950	41	1,220	1,230	14
45	50	9	185	190	38	325	680	66	950	960	40	1,230	1,240	13
50	55	10	190	195	39	680	690	66	960	970	39	1,240	1,250	12
55	60	11	195	200	40	690	700	65	970	980	38	1,250	1,260	11
60	65	12	200	205	41	700	710	64	980	990	37	1,260	1,270	10
65	70	13	205	210	42	710	720	63	990	1,000	36	1,270	1,280	9
70	75	14	210	215	43	720	730	62	1,000	1,010	35	1,280	1,290	8
75	80	15	215	220	44	730	740	61	1,010	1,020	34	1,290	1,300	7
80	85	16	220	225	45	740	750	60	1,020	1,030	33	1,300	1,310	6
85	90	17	225	230	46	750	760	59	1,030	1,040	32	1,310	1,320	5
90	95	18	230	235	47	760	770	58	1,040	1,050	31	1,320	1,330	4
95	100	19	235	240	48	770	780	57	1,050	1,060	30	1,330	1,340	3
100	105	20	240	245	49	780	790	56	1,060	1,070	29	1,340	1,350	3
105	110	21	245	250	50	790	800	55	1,070	1,080	28	1,350	1,360	2
110	115	22	250	255	51	800	810	54	1,080	1,090	27	1,360	1,370	1
115	120	23	255	260	52	810	820	53	1,090	1,100	26	1,370	- - -	0
120	125	24	260	265	53	820	830	52	1,100	1,110	26			
125	130	26	265	270	54	830	840	51	1,110	1,120	25			
130	135	27	270	275	55	840	850	50	1,120	1,130	24			
135	140	28	275	280	56	850	860	49	1,130	1,140	23			

IRS Publication 15, Circular E (continued)

SEMIMONTHLY Payroll Period

MARRIED With Both Spouses Filing Certificate

Wages— At least	But less than	Payment to be made	Wages— At least	But less than	Payment to be made	Wages— At least	But less than	Payment to be made	Wages— At least	But less than	Payment to be made	Wages— At least	But less than	Payment to be made
$0	$5	$0	$70	$75	$14	$140	$145	$29	$430	$440	$24	$570	$580	$10
5	10	1	75	80	15	145	150	30	440	450	23	580	590	9
10	15	2	80	85	16	150	155	31	450	460	22	590	600	8
15	20	3	85	90	17	155	160	32	460	470	21	600	610	8
20	25	4	90	95	18	160	340	33	470	480	20	610	620	7
25	30	5	95	100	19	340	350	32	480	490	19	620	630	6
30	35	6	100	105	20	350	360	31	490	500	18	630	640	5
35	40	7	105	110	21	360	370	31	500	510	17	640	650	4
40	45	8	110	115	22	370	380	30	510	520	16	650	660	3
45	50	9	115	120	23	380	390	29	520	530	15	660	670	2
50	55	10	120	125	24	390	400	28	530	540	14	670	680	1
55	60	11	125	130	26	400	410	27	540	550	13	680	- - -	0
60	65	12	130	135	27	410	420	26	550	560	12			
65	70	13	135	140	28	420	430	25	560	570	11			

MONTHLY Payroll Period

SINGLE or HEAD OF HOUSEHOLD

Wages— At least	But less than	Payment to be made	Wages— At least	But less than	Payment to be made	Wages— At least	But less than	Payment to be made	Wages— At least	But less than	Payment to be made	Wages— At least	But less than	Payment to be made
$0	$5	$0	$215	$220	$44	$430	$435	$88	$645	$650	$132	$1,605	$1,615	$93
5	10	1	220	225	45	435	440	89	650	1,195	133	1,615	1,625	92
10	15	2	225	230	46	440	445	90	1,195	1,205	132	1,625	1,635	91
15	20	3	230	235	47	445	450	91	1,205	1,215	131	1,635	1,645	90
20	25	4	235	240	48	450	455	92	1,215	1,225	130	1,645	1,655	89
25	30	5	240	245	49	455	460	93	1,225	1,235	129	1,655	1,665	88
30	35	6	245	250	50	460	465	94	1,235	1,245	129	1,665	1,675	87
35	40	7	250	255	51	465	470	95	1,245	1,255	128	1,675	1,685	86
40	45	8	255	260	52	470	475	96	1,255	1,265	127	1,685	1,695	85
45	50	9	260	265	53	475	480	97	1,265	1,275	126	1,695	1,705	84
50	55	10	265	270	54	480	485	98	1,275	1,285	125	1,705	1,715	83
55	60	11	270	275	55	485	490	99	1,285	1,295	124	1,715	1,725	83
60	65	12	275	280	56	490	495	100	1,295	1,305	123	1,725	1,735	82
65	70	13	280	285	57	495	500	101	1,305	1,315	122	1,735	1,745	81
70	75	14	285	290	58	500	505	102	1,315	1,325	121	1,745	1,755	80
75	80	15	290	295	59	505	510	103	1,325	1,335	120	1,755	1,765	79
80	85	16	295	300	60	510	515	104	1,335	1,345	119	1,765	1,775	78
85	90	17	300	305	61	515	520	105	1,345	1,355	118	1,775	1,785	77
90	95	18	305	310	62	520	525	106	1,355	1,365	117	1,785	1,795	76
95	100	19	310	315	63	525	530	107	1,365	1,375	116	1,795	1,805	75
100	105	20	315	320	64	530	535	108	1,375	1,385	115	1,805	1,815	74
105	110	21	320	325	65	535	540	109	1,385	1,395	114	1,815	1,825	73
110	115	22	325	330	66	540	545	110	1,395	1,405	113	1,825	1,835	72
115	120	23	330	335	67	545	550	111	1,405	1,415	112	1,835	1,845	71
120	125	24	335	340	68	550	555	112	1,415	1,425	111	1,845	1,855	70
125	130	26	340	345	69	555	560	113	1,425	1,435	110	1,855	1,865	69
130	135	27	345	350	70	560	565	114	1,435	1,445	109	1,865	1,875	68
135	140	28	350	355	71	565	570	115	1,445	1,455	108	1,875	1,885	67
140	145	29	355	360	72	570	575	116	1,455	1,465	107	1,885	1,895	66
145	150	30	360	365	73	575	580	117	1,465	1,475	106	1,895	1,905	65
150	155	31	365	370	74	580	585	118	1,475	1,485	106	1,905	1,915	64
155	160	32	370	375	75	585	590	119	1,485	1,495	105	1,915	1,925	63
160	165	33	375	380	77	590	595	120	1,495	1,505	104	1,925	1,935	62
165	170	34	380	385	78	595	600	121	1,505	1,515	103	1,935	1,945	61
170	175	35	385	390	79	600	605	122	1,515	1,525	102	1,945	1,955	60
175	180	36	390	395	80	605	610	123	1,525	1,535	101	1,955	1,965	59
180	185	37	395	400	81	610	615	124	1,535	1,545	100	1,965	1,975	59
185	190	38	400	405	82	615	620	125	1,545	1,555	99	1,975	1,985	58
190	195	39	405	410	83	620	625	126	1,555	1,565	98	1,985	1,995	57
195	200	40	410	415	84	625	630	128	1,565	1,575	97	1,995	2,005	56
200	205	41	415	420	85	630	635	129	1,575	1,585	96	2,005	2,015	55
205	210	42	420	425	86	635	640	130	1,585	1,595	95	2,015	2,025	54
210	215	43	425	430	87	640	645	131	1,595	1,605	94	(Continued on next page)		

IRS Publication 15, Circular E (continued)

MONTHLY Payroll Period

SINGLE or HEAD OF HOUSEHOLD

At least	But less than	Payment to be made	At least	But less than	Payment to be made	At least	But less than	Payment to be made	At least	But less than	Payment to be made	At least	But less than	Payment to be made
$2,025	$2,035	$53	$2,145	$2,155	$41	$2,265	$2,275	$30	$2,385	$2,395	$18	$2,505	$2,515	$7
2,035	2,045	52	2,155	2,165	40	2,275	2,285	29	2,395	2,405	17	2,515	2,525	6
2,045	2,055	51	2,165	2,175	39	2,285	2,295	28	2,405	2,415	16	2,525	2,535	5
2,055	2,065	50	2,175	2,185	38	2,295	2,305	27	2,415	2,425	15	2,535	2,545	4
2,065	2,075	49	2,185	2,195	37	2,305	2,315	26	2,425	2,435	14	2,545	2,555	3
2,075	2,085	48	2,195	2,205	36	2,315	2,325	25	2,435	2,445	13	2,555	2,565	2
2,085	2,095	47	2,205	2,215	36	2,325	2,335	24	2,445	2,455	13	2,565	2,575	1
2,095	2,105	46	2,215	2,225	35	2,335	2,345	23	2,455	2,465	12	2,575	- - -	0
2,105	2,115	45	2,225	2,235	34	2,345	2,355	22	2,465	2,475	11			
2,115	2,125	44	2,235	2,245	33	2,355	2,365	21	2,475	2,485	10			
2,125	2,135	43	2,245	2,255	32	2,365	2,375	20	2,485	2,495	9			
2,135	2,145	42	2,255	2,265	31	2,375	2,385	19	2,495	2,505	8			

MARRIED Without Spouse Filing Certificate

At least	But less than	Payment to be made	At least	But less than	Payment to be made	At least	But less than	Payment to be made	At least	But less than	Payment to be made	At least	But less than	Payment to be made
$0	$5	$0	$225	$230	$46	$450	$455	$92	$1,400	$1,410	$129	$1,850	$1,860	$86
5	10	1	230	235	47	455	460	93	1,410	1,420	128	1,860	1,870	85
10	15	2	235	240	48	460	465	94	1,420	1,430	127	1,870	1,880	84
15	20	3	240	245	49	465	470	95	1,430	1,440	126	1,880	1,890	83
20	25	4	245	250	50	470	475	96	1,440	1,450	125	1,890	1,900	82
25	30	5	250	255	51	475	480	97	1,450	1,460	124	1,900	1,910	81
30	35	6	255	260	52	480	485	98	1,460	1,470	123	1,910	1,920	80
35	40	7	260	265	53	485	490	99	1,470	1,480	122	1,920	1,930	79
40	45	8	265	270	54	490	495	100	1,480	1,490	121	1,930	1,940	78
45	50	9	270	275	55	495	500	101	1,490	1,500	120	1,940	1,950	77
50	55	10	275	280	56	500	505	102	1,500	1,510	119	1,950	1,960	76
55	60	11	280	285	57	505	510	103	1,510	1,520	118	1,960	1,970	75
60	65	12	285	290	58	510	515	104	1,520	1,530	117	1,970	1,980	74
65	70	13	290	295	59	515	520	105	1,530	1,540	116	1,980	1,990	73
70	75	14	295	300	60	520	525	106	1,540	1,550	115	1,990	2,000	72
75	80	15	300	305	61	525	530	107	1,550	1,560	114	2,000	2,010	71
80	85	16	305	310	62	530	535	108	1,560	1,570	113	2,010	2,020	70
85	90	17	310	315	63	535	540	109	1,570	1,580	112	2,020	2,030	69
90	95	18	315	320	64	540	545	110	1,580	1,590	111	2,030	2,040	68
95	100	19	320	325	65	545	550	111	1,590	1,600	110	2,040	2,050	67
100	105	20	325	330	66	550	555	112	1,600	1,610	110	2,050	2,060	66
105	110	21	330	335	67	555	560	113	1,610	1,620	109	2,060	2,070	65
110	115	22	335	340	68	560	565	114	1,620	1,630	108	2,070	2,080	64
115	120	23	340	345	69	565	570	115	1,630	1,640	107	2,080	2,090	63
120	125	24	345	350	70	570	575	116	1,640	1,650	106	2,090	2,100	63
125	130	26	350	355	71	575	580	117	1,650	1,660	105	2,100	2,110	62
130	135	27	355	360	72	580	585	118	1,660	1,670	104	2,110	2,120	61
135	140	28	360	365	73	585	590	119	1,670	1,680	103	2,120	2,130	60
140	145	29	365	370	74	590	595	120	1,680	1,690	102	2,130	2,140	59
145	150	30	370	375	75	595	600	121	1,690	1,700	101	2,140	2,150	58
150	155	31	375	380	77	600	605	122	1,700	1,710	100	2,150	2,160	57
155	160	32	380	385	78	605	610	123	1,710	1,720	99	2,160	2,170	56
160	165	33	385	390	79	610	615	124	1,720	1,730	98	2,170	2,180	55
165	170	34	390	395	80	615	620	125	1,730	1,740	97	2,180	2,190	54
170	175	35	395	400	81	620	625	126	1,740	1,750	96	2,190	2,200	53
175	180	36	400	405	82	625	630	128	1,750	1,760	95	2,200	2,210	52
180	185	37	405	410	83	630	635	129	1,760	1,770	94	2,210	2,220	51
185	190	38	410	415	84	635	640	130	1,770	1,780	93	2,220	2,230	50
190	195	39	415	420	85	640	645	131	1,780	1,790	92	2,230	2,240	49
195	200	40	420	425	86	645	650	132	1,790	1,800	91	2,240	2,250	48
200	205	41	425	430	87	650	1,360	133	1,800	1,810	90	2,250	2,260	47
205	210	42	430	435	88	1,360	1,370	133	1,810	1,820	89	2,260	2,270	46
210	215	43	435	440	89	1,370	1,380	132	1,820	1,830	88	2,270	2,280	45
215	220	44	440	445	90	1,380	1,390	131	1,830	1,840	87	2,280	2,290	44
220	225	45	445	450	91	1,390	1,400	130	1,840	1,850	87	2,290	2,300	43

(Continued on next page)

IRS Publication 15, Circular E (continued)

MONTHLY Payroll Period

MARRIED Without Spouse Filing Certificate

Wages— At least	But less than	Payment to be made	Wages— At least	But less than	Payment to be made	Wages— At least	But less than	Payment to be made	Wages— At least	But less than	Payment to be made	Wages— At least	But less than	Payment to be made
$2,300	$2,310	$42	$2,390	$2,400	$34	$2,480	$2,490	$25	$2,570	$2,580	$17	$2,660	$2,670	$8
2,310	2,320	41	2,400	2,410	33	2,490	2,500	24	2,580	2,590	16	2,670	2,680	7
2,320	2,330	40	2,410	2,420	32	2,500	2,510	23	2,590	2,600	15	2,680	2,690	6
2,330	2,340	40	2,420	2,430	31	2,510	2,520	22	2,600	2,610	14	2,690	2,700	5
2,340	2,350	39	2,430	2,440	30	2,520	2,530	21	2,610	2,620	13	2,700	2,710	4
2,350	2,360	38	2,440	2,450	29	2,530	2,540	20	2,620	2,630	12	2,710	2,720	3
2,360	2,370	37	2,450	2,460	28	2,540	2,550	19	2,630	2,640	11	2,720	2,730	2
2,370	2,380	36	2,460	2,470	27	2,550	2,560	18	2,640	2,650	10	2,730	2,740	1
2,380	2,390	35	2,470	2,480	26	2,560	2,570	17	2,650	2,660	9	2,740	- - -	0

MARRIED With Both Spouses Filing Certificate

Wages— At least	But less than	Payment to be made	Wages— At least	But less than	Payment to be made	Wages— At least	But less than	Payment to be made	Wages— At least	But less than	Payment to be made	Wages— At least	But less than	Payment to be made
$0	$5	$0	$140	$145	$29	$280	$285	$57	$860	$870	$49	$1,140	$1,150	$22
5	10	1	145	150	30	285	290	58	870	880	48	1,150	1,160	21
10	15	2	150	155	31	290	295	59	880	890	47	1,160	1,170	20
15	20	3	155	160	32	295	300	60	890	900	46	1,170	1,180	19
20	25	4	160	165	33	300	305	61	900	910	45	1,180	1,190	18
25	30	5	165	170	34	305	310	62	910	920	44	1,190	1,200	17
30	35	6	170	175	35	310	315	63	920	930	43	1,200	1,210	16
35	40	7	175	180	36	315	320	64	930	940	42	1,210	1,220	15
40	45	8	180	185	37	320	325	65	940	950	41	1,220	1,230	14
45	50	9	185	190	38	325	680	66	950	960	40	1,230	1,240	13
50	55	10	190	195	39	680	690	66	960	970	39	1,240	1,250	12
55	60	11	195	200	40	690	700	65	970	980	38	1,250	1,260	11
60	65	12	200	205	41	700	710	64	980	990	37	1,260	1,270	10
65	70	13	205	210	42	710	720	63	990	1,000	36	1,270	1,280	9
70	75	14	210	215	43	720	730	62	1,000	1,010	35	1,280	1,290	8
75	80	15	215	220	44	730	740	61	1,010	1,020	34	1,290	1,300	7
80	85	16	220	225	45	740	750	60	1,020	1,030	33	1,300	1,310	6
85	90	17	225	230	46	750	760	59	1,030	1,040	32	1,310	1,320	5
90	95	18	230	235	47	760	770	58	1,040	1,050	31	1,320	1,330	4
95	100	19	235	240	48	770	780	57	1,050	1,060	30	1,330	1,340	4
100	105	20	240	245	49	780	790	56	1,060	1,070	29	1,340	1,350	3
105	110	21	245	250	50	790	800	55	1,070	1,080	28	1,350	1,360	2
110	115	22	250	255	51	800	810	54	1,080	1,090	27	1,360	1,370	1
115	120	23	255	260	52	810	820	53	1,090	1,100	27	1,370	- - -	0
120	125	24	260	265	53	820	830	52	1,100	1,110	26			
125	130	26	265	270	54	830	840	51	1,110	1,120	25			
130	135	27	270	275	55	840	850	50	1,120	1,130	24			
135	140	28	275	280	56	850	860	50	1,130	1,140	23			

DAILY Payroll Period

SINGLE or HEAD OF HOUSEHOLD

Wages— At least	But less than	Payment to be made	Wages— At least	But less than	Payment to be made
$0	$5	$0	$65	$75	$4
5	10	1	75	85	3
10	15	2	85	95	2
15	20	3	95	105	1
20	25	4	105	- - -	0
25	30	5			
30	55	6			
55	65	5			

MARRIED Without Spouse Filing Certificate

Wages— At least	But less than	Payment to be made	Wages— At least	But less than	Payment to be made
$0	$5	$0	$70	$80	$5
5	10	1	80	90	4
10	15	2	90	100	3
15	20	3	100	110	2
20	25	4	110	120	1
25	30	5	120	- - -	0
30	60	6			
60	70	5			

MARRIED With Both Spouses Filing Certificate

Wages— At least	But less than	Payment to be made	Wages— At least	But less than	Payment to be made
$0	$5	$0	$30	$40	$2
5	10	1	40	50	1
10	15	2	50	- - -	0
15	30	3			

Page 65

IRS Publication 15, Circular E (continued)

Index To help us develop a more useful index, please let us know if you have ideas for index entries. See "Comments and Suggestions" in the "Introduction" for the ways you can reach us.

A
Accuracy of deposits rule 21
Adjustments, Form 941 25
Advance earned income credit 16
Advance EIC tables, instructions 35
Aliens, nonresident................. 15
Allocated tips....................... 12
Archer MSAs 11

B
Backup withholding 5
Business expenses, employee 10

C
Calendar 2
Change of address 5
Claim for refund 28
Correcting errors, (prior period adjustments) Form 941 27

D
Delivery services, private 5
Depositing taxes:
  Coupons 21
  Penalties 22
  Rules 18

E
Electronic........................... 21
Electronic deposit requirement 21
Electronic Federal Tax Payment System (EFTPS) 21
Electronic filing.................. 4, 24
Electronic filing of Form W-4 15
Eligibility for employment 4
Employees defined 7
Employer identification number (EIN) 7
Employer responsibilities 4

F
Family employees 8
Final return, Form 941 24
Form 941 e-file 24
Form 941TeleFile 4, 24
Fringe benefits 11
FTD coupons 21
FUTA tax........................... 28

G
Government employers 7

H
Health insurance plans 11
Health Savings Accounts (HSAs)............................ 11
Hiring new employees 4
Household employees 23

I
Income tax withholding 14, 34
Information returns 4
International social security agreements....................... 16

L
Long-term care insurance 11
Lookback period, Form 941 19

M
Magnetic media filing, Form W-4 15
Meals and lodging 10
Medical care 11
Medical savings accounts 11
Medicare tax 16
Mileage 10
Monthly deposit schedule 19
Moving expenses 10

N
New employees 4
Noncash wages 10
Nonemployee compensation 5
Nonpayroll withholding 4

P
Part-time workers 16
Payroll period 14
Penalties........................ 22, 24
Private delivery services 5

R
Reconciling Forms W-2 and 941 25
Recordkeeping 5
Reimbursements 10
Repayments, wages 28

S
Seasonal employers 23
Semiweekly deposit schedule 19
Sick pay 12
Social security and Medicare taxes 16

Social security number, employee 8
Standard mileage rate 10
Statutory employees 7
Statutory nonemployees 8
Successor employer 16, 29
Supplemental wages 2, 13

T
Telephone help 5
Tip Rate Determination Agreement 13
Tip Rate Determination and Education Program 13
Tip Reporting Alternative Commitment 13
Tips............................. 12, 14
Trust fund recovery penalty 23

U
Unemployment tax, federal 2, 28
Unresolved tax issues 6

V
Vacation pay....................... 14

W
Wage repayments 28
Wages defined..................... 9
Wages not paid in money 10
Withholding:
  Backup........................... 5
  Certificate 14
  Exemption........................ 14
  Fringe benefits 12
  Income tax 14
  Levies........................... 16
  Nonpayroll payments 4
  Nonresident aliens................ 15
  Pensions and annuities 4
  Percentage method 34
  Social security and Medicare taxes........................... 16
  Table instructions................. 34
  Tips 14
  Wage bracket method 34

Z
Zero wage return 4

IRS Publication 15, Circular E (continued)

Form **7018-A**
(Rev. November 2004)

Department of the Treasury
Internal Revenue Service

Employer's Order Blank for 2004 Forms
Visit the IRS website at www.irs.gov.

OMB No. 1545–1059

Instructions. Enter the quantity next to the form you are ordering. **Please order the number of forms needed, not the number of sheets. Note:** None of the items on the order blank are available from the IRS in a continuous-feed version. All forms on this order blank that require multiple copies are carbonized so that you will not have to insert carbons. You will automatically receive one instruction with any form on this order blank. **Type or print** your name and complete mail delivery address in the space provided below. An accurate mail delivery address is necessary to ensure delivery of your order.

USE THIS PORTION FOR 2004 FORMS ONLY

Item	Quantity	Title	Item	Quantity	Title
W-2		Wage and Tax Statement	1099 H		Health Insurance Advance Payments
W-2 C		Corrected Wage and Tax Statement	1099 INT		Interest Income
W-3		Transmittal of Wage and Tax Statements	1099 LTC		Long-Term Care and Accelerated Death Benefits
W-3 C		Transmittal of Corrected Wage and Tax Statements	1099 MISC		Miscellaneous Income
W-4		Employee's Withholding Allowance Certificate	1099 MSA		Distributions From an Archer MSA or Medicare+Choice MSA
W-4 P		Withholding Certificate for Pension or Annuity Payments	1099 OID		Original Issue Discount
W-4 S		Request for Federal Income Tax Withholding From Sick Pay	1099 PATR		Taxable Distributions Received From Cooperatives
W-5		Earned Income Credit Advance Payment Certificate	1099 Q		Payments From Qualified Education Programs (Under Sections 529 and 530)
1096		Annual Summary and Transmittal of U.S. Information Returns	1099 R		Distributions From Pensions, Annuities, Retirement or Profit-Sharing Plans, IRAs, Insurance Contracts, etc.
1098		Mortgage Interest Statement	1099 S		Proceeds From Real Estate Transactions
1098 E		Student Loan Interest Statement	5498		IRA Contribution Information
1098 T		Tuition Statement	5498 ESA		Coverdell ESA Contribution Information
1099 A		Acquisition or Abandonment of Secured Property	5498 MSA		Archer MSA or Medicare+Choice MSA Information
1099 B		Proceeds From Broker and Barter Exchange Transactions	Pub 15 A		Employer's Supplemental Tax Guide
1099 C		Cancellation of Debt	Pub 15 B		Employer's Tax Guide to Fringe Benefits
1099 DIV		Dividends and Distributions	Pub 1494		Table for Figuring Amount Exempt From Levy On Wages, Salary, and Other Income (Forms 668-W(c) and 668-W(c)(DO))
1099 G		Certain Government Payments			

Print or Type Only

Attention: _____

Daytime Telephone Number: ( )

Company Name: _____

Postal Mailing Address: _____   Ste/Room _____

City: _____   State: _____   Zip Code: _____

Foreign Country: _____   International Postal Code: _____

Where To Send Your Order

Send your order to the Internal Revenue Service address for the Area Distribution Center closest to your state.

Central Area Distribution Center
P.O. Box 8908
Bloomington, IL 61702-8908

Eastern Area Distribution Center
P.O. Box 85075
Richmond, VA 23261-5075

Western Area Distribution Center
Rancho Cordova, CA 95743-0001

Paperwork Reduction Act Notice. We ask for the information on this form to carry out the Internal Revenue laws of the United States. Your response is voluntary.

You are not required to provide the information requested on a form that is subject to the Paperwork Reduction Act unless the form displays a valid OMB control number. Books or records relating to a form or its instructions must be retained as long as their contents may become material in the administration of any Internal Revenue law. Generally, tax returns and return information are confidential, as required by Code section 6103.

The time needed to complete this form will vary depending on the individual circumstances. The estimated average time is 3 minutes. If you have comments concerning the accuracy of this time estimate or suggestions for making this form simpler, we would be happy to hear from you. You can write to the Internal Revenue Service, Tax Products Coordinating Committee, SE:W:CAR:MP:T:T:SP 1111 Constitution Ave. NW Washington, DC 20224

Do not send your order Form 7018-A to the Tax Products Coordinating Committee. Instead, send your forms order to the IRS Area Distribution Center closest to your state.

Cat. No. 43709Q

IRS Publication 15, Circular E (continued)

Quick and Easy Access to Tax Help and Forms

Personal Computer

You can access the IRS website 24 hours a day, 7 days a week, at **www.irs.gov** to:

- Download forms, instructions, and publications
- Order IRS products on-line.
- See answers to frequently asked tax questions
- Search publications on-line by topic or keyword
- Figure your withholding allowances using our W-4 calculator
- Send us comments or request help by e-mail
- Sign up to receive local and national tax news by e-mail

Fax

You can get over 100 of the most requested forms and instructions 24 hours a day, 7 days a week, by fax. Just call **703-368-9694** from the telephone connected to the fax machine.

For help with transmission problems, call **703-487-4608.**

Long-distance charges may apply.

Mail

You can order forms, instructions, and publications by completing the order blank inside the back cover. You should receive your order within 10 days after we receive your request.

Phone

You can order forms and publications and receive automated information 24 hours a day, 7 days a week, by phone.

Forms and Publications

Call **1-800-829-4933** to order current year forms, instructions, and publications, and prior year forms and instructions. You should receive your order within 10 days.

TeleTax Topics

Call **1-800-829-4477** to listen to pre-recorded messages covering about 150 tax topics. See page 6 for a list of the topics.

Walk-In

You can pick up some of the most requested forms, instructions, and publications at many IRS offices, post offices, and libraries. Some city and county government offices, credit unions, grocery stores, office supply stores, and copy centers have an extensive collection of products available to photocopy or print from a CD-ROM.

CD-ROM

Order **Pub. 1796,** Federal Tax Products on CD-ROM, and get:

- Current year forms, instructions, and publications
- Prior year forms, instructions, and publications
- Frequently requested tax forms that may be filled in electronically, printed out for submission, and saved for recordkeeping
- The Internal Revenue Bulletin

Buy the CD-ROM on the Internet at **www.irs.gov/cdorders** from the National Technical Information Service (NTIS) for $22 (no handling fee) or call **1-877-CDFORMS** (1-877-233-6767) toll free to buy the CD-ROM for $22 (plus a $5 handling fee).

Internal Revenue Service
NDC–8903
Bloomington, IL 61702-8903

Official Business
Penalty for Private Use $300

Deliver to Payroll Department

| **PRSRT STD** |
| Postage and Fees Paid |
| Internal Revenue Service |
| **Permit No. G-48** |

Form W-4

Form W-4 (2005)

Purpose. Complete Form W-4 so that your employer can withhold the correct federal income tax from your pay. Because your tax situation may change, you may want to refigure your withholding each year.

Exemption from withholding. If you are exempt, complete only lines 1, 2, 3, 4, and 7 and sign the form to validate it. Your exemption for 2005 expires February 16, 2006. See Pub. 505, Tax Withholding and Estimated Tax.

Note. You cannot claim exemption from withholding if (a) your income exceeds $800 and includes more than $250 of unearned income (for example, interest and dividends) and (b) another person can claim you as a dependent on their tax return.

Basic instructions. If you are not exempt, complete the **Personal Allowances Worksheet** below. The worksheets on page 2 adjust your withholding allowances based on itemized deductions, certain credits, adjustments to income, or two-

earner/two-job situations. Complete all worksheets that apply. However, you may claim fewer (or zero) allowances.

Head of household. Generally, you may claim head of household filing status on your tax return only if you are unmarried and pay more than 50% of the costs of keeping up a home for yourself and your dependent(s) or other qualifying individuals. See line **E** below.

Tax credits. You can take projected tax credits into account in figuring your allowable number of withholding allowances. Credits for child or dependent care expenses and the child tax credit may be claimed using the **Personal Allowances Worksheet** below. See Pub. 919, How Do I Adjust My Tax Withholding? for information on converting your other credits into withholding allowances.

Nonwage income. If you have a large amount of nonwage income, such as interest or dividends, consider making estimated tax payments using Form 1040-ES, Estimated Tax for Individuals. Otherwise, you may owe additional tax.

Two earners/two jobs. If you have a working spouse or more than one job, figure the total number of allowances you are entitled to claim on all jobs using worksheets from only one Form W-4. Your withholding usually will be most accurate when all allowances are claimed on the Form W-4 for the highest paying job and zero allowances are claimed on the others.

Nonresident alien. If you are a nonresident alien, see the Instructions for Form 8233 before completing this Form W-4.

Check your withholding. After your Form W-4 takes effect, use Pub. 919 to see how the dollar amount you are having withheld compares to your projected total tax for 2005. See Pub. 919, especially if your earnings exceed $125,000 (Single) or $175,000 (Married).

Recent name change? If your name on line 1 differs from that shown on your social security card, call 1-800-772-1213 to initiate a name change and obtain a social security card showing your correct name.

Personal Allowances Worksheet (Keep for your records.)

A Enter "1" for **yourself** if no one else can claim you as a dependent . . . . **A** _____

B Enter "1" if:
- You are single and have only one job; or
- You are married, have only one job, and your spouse does not work; or
- Your wages from a second job or your spouse's wages (or the total of both) are $1,000 or less.
    . . **B** _____

C Enter "1" for your **spouse.** But, you may choose to enter "-0-" if you are married and have either a working spouse or more than one job. (Entering "-0-" may help you avoid having too little tax withheld.) . . . . **C** _____

D Enter number of **dependents** (other than your spouse or yourself) you will claim on your tax return . . . . . . **D** _____

E Enter "1" if you will file as **head of household** on your tax return (see conditions under **Head of household** above) . **E** _____

F Enter "1" if you have at least $1,500 of **child or dependent care expenses** for which you plan to claim a credit . . **F** _____
(**Note.** Do **not** include child support payments. See **Pub. 503,** Child and Dependent Care Expenses, for details.)

G **Child Tax Credit** (including additional child tax credit):
- If your total income will be less than $54,000 ($79,000 if married), enter "2" for each eligible child.
- If your total income will be between $54,000 and $84,000 ($79,000 and $119,000 if married), enter "1" for each eligible child plus "1" **additional** if you have four or more eligible children. **G** _____

H Add lines A through G and enter total here. (**Note.** This may be different from the number of exemptions you claim on your tax return.) ▶ **H** _____

For accuracy, complete all worksheets that apply.
- If you plan to **itemize or claim adjustments to income** and want to reduce your withholding, see the **Deductions and Adjustments Worksheet** on page 2.
- If you have **more than one job** or are **married and you and your spouse both work** and the combined earnings from all jobs exceed $35,000 ($25,000 if married) see the **Two-Earner/Two-Job Worksheet** on page 2 to avoid having too little tax withheld.
- If **neither** of the above situations applies, **stop here** and enter the number from line H on line 5 of Form W-4 below.

- - - - - - - - - - - - - - - - - **Cut here and give Form W-4 to your employer. Keep the top part for your records.** - - - - - - - - - - - - - - -

Form **W-4**

Department of the Treasury
Internal Revenue Service

Employee's Withholding Allowance Certificate

▶ Whether you are entitled to claim a certain number of allowances or exemption from withholding is subject to review by the IRS. Your employer may be required to send a copy of this form to the IRS.

OMB No. 1545-0010

2005

1 Type or print your first name and middle initial	Last name	2 Your social security number

Home address (number and street or rural route)	3 ☐ Single ☐ Married ☐ Married, but withhold at higher Single rate.
	Note. If married, but legally separated, or spouse is a nonresident alien, check the "Single" box.
City or town, state, and ZIP code	4 If your last name differs from that shown on your social security card, check here. You must call 1-800-772-1213 for a new card. ▶ ☐

5	Total number of allowances you are claiming (from line **H** above **or** from the applicable worksheet on page 2)	**5**	
6	Additional amount, if any, you want withheld from each paycheck	**6**	$

7 I claim exemption from withholding for 2005, and I certify that I meet **both** of the following conditions for exemption.
- Last year I had a right to a refund of **all** federal income tax withheld because I had **no** tax liability **and**
- This year I expect a refund of **all** federal income tax withheld because I expect to have **no** tax liability.

If you meet both conditions, write "Exempt" here . . . . ▶ **7**

Under penalties of perjury, I declare that I have examined this certificate and to the best of my knowledge and belief, it is true, correct, and complete.

Employee's signature
(Form is not valid
unless you sign it.) ▶ _____   Date ▶ _____

8 Employer's name and address (Employer: Complete lines 8 and 10 only if sending to the IRS.)	9 Office code (optional)	10 Employer identification number (EIN)

For Privacy Act and Paperwork Reduction Act Notice, see page 2.   Cat. No. 10220Q   Form **W-4** (2005)

Form W-4 (continued)

Deductions and Adjustments Worksheet

Note. Use this worksheet *only* if you plan to itemize deductions, claim certain credits, or claim adjustments to income on your 2005 tax return.

1	Enter an estimate of your 2005 itemized deductions. These include qualifying home mortgage interest, charitable contributions, state and local taxes, medical expenses in excess of 7.5% of your income, and miscellaneous deductions. (For 2005, you may have to reduce your itemized deductions if your income is over $145,950 ($72,975 if married filing separately). See *Worksheet 3* in Pub. 919 for details.) . . .	**1**	$ _____
2	Enter: { $10,000 if married filing jointly or qualifying widow(er) / $ 7,300 if head of household / $ 5,000 if single or married filing separately }	**2**	$ _____
3	**Subtract** line 2 from line 1. If line 2 is greater than line 1, enter "-0-"	**3**	$ _____
4	Enter an estimate of your 2005 adjustments to income, including alimony, deductible IRA contributions, and student loan interest	**4**	$ _____
5	**Add** lines 3 and 4 and enter the total. (Include any amount for credits from *Worksheet 7* in Pub. 919) .	**5**	$ _____
6	Enter an estimate of your 2005 nonwage income (such as dividends or interest)	**6**	$ _____
7	**Subtract** line 6 from line 5. Enter the result, but not less than "-0-"	**7**	$ _____
8	**Divide** the amount on line 7 by $3,200 and enter the result here. Drop any fraction	**8**	_____
9	Enter the number from the **Personal Allowances Worksheet,** line H, page 1	**9**	_____
10	**Add** lines 8 and 9 and enter the total here. If you plan to use the **Two-Earner/Two-Job Worksheet,** also enter this total on line 1 below. Otherwise, **stop here** and enter this total on Form W-4, line 5, page 1 .	**10**	_____

Two-Earner/Two-Job Worksheet (See *Two earners/two jobs* on page 1.)

Note. Use this worksheet *only* if the instructions under line H on page 1 direct you here.

1	Enter the number from line H, page 1 (or from line 10 above if you used the **Deductions and Adjustments Worksheet**)	**1**	_____
2	Find the number in **Table 1** below that applies to the **LOWEST** paying job and enter it here	**2**	_____
3	If line 1 is **more than or equal to** line 2, subtract line 2 from line 1. Enter the result here (if zero, enter "-0-") and on Form W-4, line 5, page 1. **Do not** use the rest of this worksheet	**3**	_____

Note. If line 1 is *less than* line 2, enter "-0-" on Form W-4, line 5, page 1. Complete lines 4–9 below to calculate the additional withholding amount necessary to avoid a year-end tax bill.

4	Enter the number from line 2 of this worksheet	**4**	_____
5	Enter the number from line 1 of this worksheet	**5**	_____
6	**Subtract** line 5 from line 4	**6**	_____
7	Find the amount in **Table 2** below that applies to the **HIGHEST** paying job and enter it here	**7**	$ _____
8	**Multiply** line 7 by line 6 and enter the result here. This is the additional annual withholding needed . .	**8**	$ _____
9	Divide line 8 by the number of pay periods remaining in 2005. For example, divide by 26 if you are paid every two weeks and you complete this form in December 2004. Enter the result here and on Form W-4, line 6, page 1. This is the additional amount to be withheld from each paycheck	**9**	$ _____

Table 1: Two-Earner/Two-Job Worksheet

Married Filing Jointly						All Others	
If wages from **HIGHEST** paying job are—	AND, wages from **LOWEST** paying job are—	Enter on line 2 above	If wages from **HIGHEST** paying job are—	AND, wages from **LOWEST** paying job are—	Enter on line 2 above	If wages from **LOWEST** paying job are—	Enter on line 2 above
$0 - $40,000	$0 - $4,000	0	$40,001 and over	30,001 - 36,000	6	$0 - $6,000	0
	4,001 - 8,000	1		36,001 - 45,000	7	6,001 - 12,000	1
	8,001 - 18,000	2		45,001 - 50,000	8	12,001 - 18,000	2
	18,001 and over	3		50,001 - 60,000	9	18,001 - 24,000	3
				60,001 - 65,000	10	24,001 - 31,000	4
$40,001 and over	$0 - $4,000	0		65,001 - 75,000	11	31,001 - 45,000	5
	4,001 - 8,000	1		75,001 - 90,000	12	45,001 - 60,000	6
	8,001 - 18,000	2		90,001 - 100,000	13	60,001 - 75,000	7
	18,001 - 22,000	3		100,001 - 115,000	14	75,001 - 80,000	8
	22,001 - 25,000	4		115,001 and over	15	80,001 - 100,000	9
	25,001 - 30,000	5				100,001 and over	10

Table 2: Two-Earner/Two-Job Worksheet

Married Filing Jointly		All Others	
If wages from **HIGHEST** paying job are—	Enter on line 7 above	If wages from **HIGHEST** paying job are—	Enter on line 7 above
$0 - $60,000	$480	$0 - $30,000	$480
60,001 - 110,000	800	30,001 - 70,000	800
110,001 - 160,000	900	70,001 - 140,000	900
160,001 - 280,000	1,060	140,001 - 320,000	1,060
280,001 and over	1,120	320,001 and over	1,120

Privacy Act and Paperwork Reduction Act Notice. We ask for the information on this form to carry out the Internal Revenue laws of the United States. The Internal Revenue Code requires this information under sections 3402(f)(2)(A) and 6109 and their regulations. Failure to provide a properly completed form will result in your being treated as a single person who claims no withholding allowances; providing fraudulent information may also subject you to penalties. Routine uses of this information include giving it to the Department of Justice for civil and criminal litigation, to cities, states, and the District of Columbia for use in administering their tax laws, and using it in the National Directory of New Hires. We may also disclose this information to other countries under a tax treaty, to federal and state agencies to enforce federal nontax criminal laws, or to federal law enforcement and intelligence agencies to combat terrorism.

You are not required to provide the information requested on a form that is subject to the Paperwork Reduction Act unless the form displays a valid OMB control number. Books or records relating to a form or its instructions must be retained as long as their contents may become material in the administration of any Internal Revenue law. Generally, tax returns and return information are confidential, as required by Code section 6103.

The time needed to complete this form will vary depending on individual circumstances. The estimated average time is: Recordkeeping, 45 min.; Learning about the law or the form, 12 min.; Preparing the form, 58 min. If you have comments concerning the accuracy of these time estimates or suggestions for making this form simpler, we would be happy to hear from you. You can write to: Internal Revenue Service, Tax Products Coordinating Committee, SE:W:CAR:MP:T:T:SP, 1111 Constitution Ave. NW, IR-6406, Washington, DC 20224. **Do not** send Form W-4 to this address. Instead, give it to your employer.

 Printed on recycled paper

APPENDIX D

EMPLOYMENT LAW

Handy Reference Guide to the Fair Labor Standards Act

The Fair Labor Standards Act (FLSA) establishes minimum wage, overtime pay, recordkeeping, and child labor standards affecting full-time and part-time workers in the private sector and in Federal, State, and local governments.

The Wage and Hour Division (Wage-Hour) administers and enforces FLSA with respect to private employment, State and local government employment, and Federal employees of the Library of Congress, U.S. Postal Service, Postal Rate Commission, and the Tennessee Valley Authority. The FLSA is enforced by the U.S. Office of Personnel Management for employees of other Executive Branch agencies, and by the U.S. Congress for covered employees of the Legislative Branch.

Special rules apply to State and local government employment involving fire protection and law enforcement activities, volunteer services, and compensatory time off instead of cash overtime pay.

Basic Wage Standards

Covered nonexempt workers are entitled to a minimum wage of not less than $4.75 an hour, effective October 1, 1996, and not less than $5.15 an hour, effective September 1, 1997. Overtime pay at a rate of not less than one and one-half times their regular rates of pay is required after 40 hours of work in a workweek.

Wages required by FLSA are due on the regular payday for the pay period covered. Deductions made from wages for such items as cash or merchandise shortages, employer-required uniforms, and tools of the trade, are not legal to the extent that they reduce the wages of employees below the minimum rate required by FLSA or reduce the amount of overtime pay due under FLSA.

The FLSA contains some exemptions from these basic standards. Some apply to specific types of businesses; others apply to specific kinds of work.

While FLSA does set basic minimum wage and overtime pay standards and regulates the employment of minors, there are a number of employment practices which FLSA does not regulate. For example, FLSA does *not* require:
- vacation, holiday, severance, or sick pay;
- meal or rest periods, holidays off, or vacations;
- premium pay for weekend or holiday work;
- pay raises or fringe benefits; and
- a discharge notice, reason for discharge, or immediate payment of final wages to terminated employees.

The FLSA does not provide wage payment or collection procedures for an employee's usual or promised wages or commissions in excess of those required by the FLSA. However, some States do have laws under which such claims (sometimes including fringe benefits) may be filed.

Also, FLSA does not limit the number of hours in a day or days in a week an employee may be required or scheduled to work, including overtime hours, if the employee is at least 16 years old.

The above matters are for agreement between the employer and the employees or their authorized representatives.

Handy Reference Guide to the
Fair Labor Standards Act (continued)

Who is Covered?

All employees of certain enterprises having workers engaged in interstate commerce, producing goods for interstate commerce, or handling, selling, or otherwise working on goods or materials that have been moved in or produced for such commerce by any person are covered by FLSA.

A covered enterprise is the related activities performed through unified operation or common control by any person or persons for a common business purpose and --
- whose annual gross volume of sales made or business done is not less than $500,000 (exclusive of excise taxes at the retail level that are separately stated); or
- is engaged in the operation of a hospital, an institution primarily engaged in the care of the sick, the aged, or the mentally ill who reside on the premises; a school for mentally or physically disabled or gifted children; a preschool, an elementary or secondary school, or an institution of higher education (whether operated for profit or not for profit); or
- is an activity of a public agency.

Construction and laundry/dry cleaning enterprises, which had been previously covered regardless of their annual dollar volume of business, became subject to the $500,000 test on April 1, 1990.

Any enterprise that was covered by FLSA on March 31, 1990, and that ceased to be covered because of the $500,000 test, continues to be subject to the overtime pay, child labor and recordkeeping provisions of FLSA.

Employees of firms which are not covered enterprises under FLSA still may be subject to its minimum wage, overtime pay, and child labor provisions if they are individually engaged in interstate commerce or in the production of goods for interstate commerce, or in any closely-related process or occupation directly essential to such production. Such employees include those who: work in communications or transportation; regularly use the mails, telephones, or telegraph for interstate communication, or keep records of interstate transactions; handle, ship, or receive goods moving in interstate commerce; regularly cross State lines in the course of employment; or work for independent employers who contract to do clerical, custodial, maintenance, or other work for firms engaged in interstate commerce or in the production of goods for interstate commerce.

Domestic service workers such as day workers, housekeepers, chauffeurs, cooks, or full-time babysitters are covered if
- their cash wages from one employer are at least $1,000 in a calendar year (or the amount designated pursuant to an adjustment provision in the Internal Revenue Code), or
- they work a total of more than 8 hours a week for one or more employers.

Tipped Employees

Tipped employees are those who customarily and regularly receive more than $30 a month in tips. The employer may consider tips as part of wages, but the employer must pay at least $2.13 an hour in direct wages.

Handy Reference Guide to the
Fair Labor Standards Act (continued)

The employer who elects to use the tip credit provision, must inform the employee in advance and must be able to show that the employee receives at least the minimum wage when direct wages and the tip credit allowance are combined. If an employee's tips combined with the employer's direct wages of at least $2.13 an hour do not equal the minimum hourly wage, the employer must make up the difference. Also, employees must retain all of their tips, except to the extent that they participate in a valid tip pooling or sharing arrangement.

Employer-Furnished Facilities

The reasonable cost or fair value of board, lodging, or other facilities customarily furnished by the employer for the employee's benefit may be considered part of wages.

Industrial Homework

The performance of certain types of work in an employee's home is prohibited under the law unless the employer has obtained prior certification from the Department of Labor. Restrictions apply in the manufacture of knitted outerwear, gloves and mittens, buttons and buckles, handkerchiefs, embroideries, and jewelry (where safety and health hazards are not involved). The manufacture of women's apparel (and jewelry under hazardous conditions) is generally prohibited. If you have questions on whether a certain type of work is restricted, or who is eligible for a homework certificate, or how to obtain a certificate, you may contact the local Wage-Hour office.

Subminimum Wage Provisions

The FLSA provides for the employment of certain individuals at wage rates below the statutory minimum. Such individuals include student-learners (vocational education students), as well as full-time students in retail or service establishments, agriculture, or institutions of higher education. Also included are individuals whose earning or productive capacity is impaired by a physical or mental disability, including those related to age or injury, for the work to be performed. Employment at less than the minimum wage is authorized to prevent curtailment of opportunities for employment. Such employment is permitted only under certificates issued by Wage-Hour.

Youth Minimum Wage

A minimum wage of not less than $4.25 an hour is permitted for employees under 20 years of age during their first 90 consecutive calendar days of employment with an employer. Employers are prohibited from taking any action to displace employees in order to hire employees at the youth minimum wage. Also prohibited are partial displacements such as reducing employees' hours, wages, or employment benefits.

Exemptions

Some employees are exempt from the overtime pay provisions or both the minimum wage and overtime pay provisions.

Handy Reference Guide to the
Fair Labor Standards Act (continued)

Because exemptions are generally narrowly defined under FLSA, an employer should carefully check the exact terms and conditions for each. Detailed information is available from local Wage-Hour offices.

Following are examples of exemptions which are illustrative, but not all-inclusive. These examples do *not* define the conditions for each exemption.

Exemptions from Both Minimum Wage and Overtime Pay

- Executive, administrative, and professional employees (including teachers and academic administrative personnel in elementary and secondary schools), outside sales employees, and employees in certain computer-related occupations (as defined in Department of Labor regulations);
- Employees of certain seasonal amusement or recreational establishments, employees of certain small newspapers, seamen employed on foreign vessels, employees engaged in fishing operations, and employees engaged in newspaper delivery;
- Farm workers employed by anyone who used no more than 500 "man-days" of farm labor in any calendar quarter of the preceding calendar year;
- Casual babysitters and persons employed as companions to the elderly or infirm.

Exemptions from Overtime Pay Only

- Certain commissioned employees of retail or service establishments; auto, truck, trailer, farm implement, boat, or aircraft salesworkers, or parts-clerks and mechanics servicing autos, trucks, or farm implements, who are employed by nonmanufacturing establishments primarily engaged in selling these items to ultimate purchasers;
- Employees of railroads and air carriers, taxi drivers, certain employees of motor carriers, seamen on American vessels, and local delivery employees paid on approved trip rate plans;
- Announcers, news editors, and chief engineers of certain nonmetropolitan broadcasting stations;
- Domestic service workers living in the employer's residence;
- Employees of motion picture theaters; and
- Farmworkers.

Partial Exemptions from Overtime Pay

Partial overtime pay exemptions apply to employees engaged in certain operations on agricultural commodities and to employees of certain bulk petroleum distributors.

Hospitals and residential care establishments may adopt, by agreement with their employees, a 14-day work period instead of the usual 7-day workweek, if the employees are paid at least time and one-half their regular rates for hours worked over 8 in a day or 80 in a 14-day work period, whichever is the greater number of overtime hours.

Employees who lack a high school diploma, or who have not attained the educational level of the 8th grade, can be required to spend up to 10 hours in a workweek engaged in remedial reading or training in other basic skills without receiving time and one-half overtime pay for these hours. However, the employees must receive their normal wages for hours spent in such training and the training must not be job specific.

Handy Reference Guide to the
Fair Labor Standards Act (continued)

Child Labor Provisions

The FLSA child labor provisions are designed to protect the educational opportunities of minors and prohibit their employment in jobs and under conditions detrimental to their health or well-being. The provisions include restrictions on hours of work for minors under 16 and lists of hazardous occupations orders for both farm and nonfarm jobs declared by the Secretary of Labor to be too dangerous for minors to perform. Further information on prohibited occupations is available from local Wage-Hour offices.

Nonagricultural Jobs (Child Labor)

Regulations governing youth employment in nonfarm jobs differ somewhat from those pertaining to agricultural employment. In nonfarm work, the permissible jobs and hours of work, by age, are as follows:
- Youths 18 years or older may perform any job, whether hazardous or not, for unlimited hours;
- Youths 16 and 17 years old may perform any nonhazardous job, for unlimited hours; and
- Youths 14 and 15 years old may work outside school hours in various nonmanufacturing, nonmining, nonhazardous jobs under the following conditions: no more than 3 hours on a school day, 18 hours in a school week, 8 hours on a nonschool day, or 40 hours in a nonschool week. Also, work may not begin before 7 a.m., nor end after 7 p.m., except from June 1 through Labor Day, when evening hours are extended to 9 p.m. Under a special provision, youths 14 and 15 years old enrolled in an approved Work Experience and Career Exploration Program (WECEP) may be employed for up to 23 hours in school weeks and 3 hours on school days (including during school hours).

Fourteen is the minimum age for most nonfarm work. However, at any age, youths may deliver newspapers; perform in radio, television, movie, or theatrical productions; work for parents in their solely-owned nonfarm business (except in manufacturing or on hazardous jobs); or, gather evergreens and make evergreen wreaths.

Farm Jobs (Child Labor)

In farm work, permissible jobs and hours of work, by age, are as follows:
- Youths 16 years and older may perform any job, whether hazardous or not, for unlimited hours;
- Youths 14 and 15 years old may perform any nonhazardous farm job outside of school hours;
- Youths 12 and 13 years old may work outside of school hours in nonhazardous jobs, either with a parent's written consent or on the same farm as the parent(s);
- Youths under 12 years old may perform jobs on farms owned or operated by parent(s), or with a parent's written consent, outside of school hours in nonhazardous jobs on farms not covered by minimum wage requirements.

Minors of any age may be employed by their parents at any time in any occupation on a farm owned or operated by their parents.

Handy Reference Guide to the
Fair Labor Standards Act (continued)

Recordkeeping

The FLSA requires employers to keep records on wages, hours, and other items, as specified in Department of Labor recordkeeping regulations. Most of the information is of the kind generally maintained by employers in ordinary business practice and in compliance with other laws and regulations. The records do not have to be kept in any particular form and time clocks need not be used. With respect to an employee subject to the minimum wage provisions or both the minimum wage and overtime pay provisions, the following records must be kept:

- personal information, including employee's name, home address, occupation, sex, and birth date if under 19 years of age;
- hour and day when workweek begins;
- total hours worked each workday and each workweek;
- total daily or weekly straight-time earnings;
- regular hourly pay rate for any week when overtime is worked;
- total overtime pay for the workweek;
- deductions from or additions to wages;
- total wages paid each pay period; and
- date of payment and pay period covered.

Records required for exempt employees differ from those for nonexempt workers. Special information is required for homeworkers, for employees working under uncommon pay arrangements, for employees to whom lodging or other facilities are furnished, and for employees receiving remedial education.

Terms Used in FLSA

Workweek -- A workweek is a period of 168 hours during 7 consecutive 24-hour periods. It may begin on any day of the week and at any hour of the day established by the employer. Generally, for purposes of minimum wage and overtime payment each workweek stands alone; there can be no averaging of 2 or more workweeks. Employee coverage, compliance with wage payment requirements, and the application of most exemptions are determined on a workweek basis.

Hours Worked -- Covered employees must be paid for all hours worked in a workweek. In general, "hours worked" includes all time an employee must be on duty, or on the employer's premises or at any other prescribed place of work. Also included is any additional time the employee is allowed (i.e., suffered or permitted) to work.

Computing Overtime Pay

Overtime must be paid at a rate of at least one and one-half times the employee's regular rate of pay for each hour worked in a workweek in excess of the maximum allowable in a given type of employment. Generally, the regular rate includes all payments made by the employer to or on behalf of the employee (except for certain statutory exclusions). The following examples are based on a maximum 40-hour workweek.

Hourly rate -- (regular pay rate for an employee paid by the hour). If more than 40 hours are worked, at least one and one-half times the regular rate for each hour over 40 is due.

Handy Reference Guide to the
Fair Labor Standards Act (continued)

Example: An employee paid $8.00 an hour works 44 hours in a workweek. The employee is entitled to at least one and one-half times $8.00, or $12.00, for each hour over 40. Pay for the week would be $320 for the first 40 hours, plus $48.00 for the four hours of overtime--a total of $368.00.

Piece rate -- The regular rate of pay for an employee paid on a piecework basis is obtained by dividing the total weekly earnings by the total number of hours worked in that week. The employee is entitled to an additional one-half times this regular rate for each hour over 40, plus the full piecework earnings.

Example: An employee paid on a piecework basis works 45 hours in a week and earns $315. The regular rate of pay for that week is $315 divided by 45, or $7.00 an hour. In addition to the straight-time pay, the employee is also entitled to $3.50 (half the regular rate) for each hour over 40 -- an additional $17.50 for the 5 overtime hours -- for a total of $332.50.

Another way to compensate pieceworkers for overtime, if agreed to before the work is performed, is to pay one and one-half times the piece rate for each piece produced during the overtime hours. The piece rate must be the one actually paid during nonovertime hours and must be enough to yield at least the minimum wage per hour.

Salary -- the regular rate for an employee paid a salary for a regular or specified number of hours a week is obtained by dividing the salary by the number of hours for which the salary is intended to compensate.

If, under the employment agreement, a salary sufficient to meet the minimum wage requirement in every workweek is paid as straight time for whatever number of hours are worked in a workweek, the regular rate is obtained by dividing the salary by the number of hours worked each week. To illustrate, suppose an employee's hours of work vary each week and the agreement with the employer is that the employee will be paid $420 a week for whatever number of hours of work are required. Under this agreement, the regular rate will vary in overtime weeks. If the employee works 50 hours, the regular rate is $8.40 ($420 divided by 50 hours). In addition to the salary, half the regular rate, or $4.20 is due for each of the 10 overtime hours, for a total of $462 for the week. If the employee works 60 hours, the regular rate is $7.00 ($420 divided by 60 hours). In that case, an additional $3.50 is due for each of the 20 overtime hours, for a total of $490 for the week.

In no case may the regular rate be less than the minimum wage required by FLSA.

If a salary is paid on other than a weekly basis, the weekly pay must be determined in order to compute the regular rate and overtime pay. If the salary is for a half month, it must be multiplied by 24 and the product divided by 52 weeks to get the weekly equivalent. A monthly salary should be multiplied by 12 and the product divided by 52.

Enforcement

Wage-Hour's enforcement of FLSA is carried out by investigators stationed across the U.S. As Wage-Hour's authorized representatives, they conduct investigations and gather data on

Handy Reference Guide to the
Fair Labor Standards Act (continued)

wages, hours, and other employment conditions or practices, in order to determine compliance with the law. Where violations are found, they also may recommend changes in employment practices to bring an employer into compliance.

It is a violation to fire or in any other manner discriminate against an employee for filing a complaint or for participating in a legal proceeding under FLSA.

Willful violations may be prosecuted criminally and the violator fined up to $10,000. A second conviction may result in imprisonment.

Violators of the child labor provisions are subject to a civil money penalty of up to $10,000 for each employee who was the subject of a violation.

Employers who willfully or repeatedly violate the minimum wage or overtime pay requirements are subject to a civil money penalty of up to $1,000 for each such violation.

The FLSA prohibits the shipment of goods in interstate commerce which were produced in violation of the minimum wage, overtime pay, child labor, or special minimum wage provisions.

Recovery of Back Wages

Listed below are methods which FLSA provides for recovering unpaid minimum and/or overtime wages.

- Wage-Hour may supervise payment of back wages.
- The Secretary of Labor may bring suit for back wages and an equal amount as liquidated damages.
- An employee may file a private suit for back pay and an equal amount as liquidated damages, plus attorney's fees and court costs.
- The Secretary of Labor may obtain an injunction to restrain any person from violating FLSA, including the unlawful withholding of proper minimum wage and overtime pay.

An employee may not bring suit if he or she has been paid back wages under the supervision of Wage-Hour or if the Secretary of Labor has already filed suit to recover the wages.

A 2-year statute of limitations applies to the recovery of back pay, except in the case of willful violation, in which case a 3-year statute applies.

Other Labor Laws

In addition to FLSA, Wage-Hour enforces and administers a number of other labor laws. Among these are:

- the **Davis-Bacon and Related Acts**, which require payment of prevailing wage rates and fringe benefits on federally-financed or assisted construction;
- the **Walsh-Healey Public Contracts Act**, which requires payment of minimum wage rates and overtime pay on contracts to provide goods to the Federal Government;
- the **Service Contract Act**, which requires payment of prevailing wage rates and fringe benefits on contracts to provide services to the Federal Government;
- the **Contract Work Hours and Safety Standards Act**, which sets overtime standards for service and construction contracts;

Handy Reference Guide to the
Fair Labor Standards Act (continued)

- the **Migrant and Seasonal Agricultural Worker Protection Act**, which protects farm workers by imposing certain requirements on agricultural employers and associations and requires the registration of crewleaders who must also provide the same worker protections;

- the **Wage Garnishment Law**, which limits the amount of an individual's income that may be legally garnished and prohibits firing an employee whose pay is garnished for payment of a single debt;

- the **Employee Polygraph Protection Act**, which prohibits most private employers from using any type of lie detector test either for pre-employment screening of job applicants or for testing current employees during the course of employment;

- the **Family and Medical Leave Act**, which entitles eligible employees of covered employers to take up to 12 weeks of unpaid job-protected leave each year, with maintenance of group health insurance, for the birth and care of a child, for the placement of a child for adoption or foster care, for the care of a child, spouse, or parent with a serious health condition, or for the employee's serious health condition; and

- the **Immigration and Nationality Act**, as amended, which: *under the employment eligibility provisions*, requires employers to verify the employment eligibility of all individuals hired and keep Immigration and Naturalization Service forms (I-9) on file for at least 3 years and for one year after an employee is terminated;

under the H-2A provisions, provides for the enforcement of contractual obligations of job offers which have been certified to by employers of temporary alien nonimmigrant agricultural workers;

under the H-1C provisions, provides for the enforcement of employment conditions attested to by employers in disadvantages areas employing H-1C temporary alien nonimmigrant registered nurses;

under the D-1 provisions, provides for the enforcement of employment conditions attested to by employers seeking to employ alien crewmembers to perform specified longshore activity at U.S. ports; and

under the H-1B provisions, provides for the enforcement of labor condition applications filed by employers wishing to employ aliens in specialty occupations and as fashion models of distinguished merit and ability.

More detailed information on FLSA and other laws administered by Wage-Hour is available from local Wage-Hour offices, which are listed in most telephone directories under U.S. Government, Department of Labor, Wage and Hour Division. For those who have access to the Internet, further information may also be obtained on the Wage and Hour Division Internet Home Page which can be located at the following address: www.wagehour.dol.gov.

Handy Reference Guide to the
Fair Labor Standards Act (continued)

Small Business Regulatory Enforcement Fairness Act of 1996 (SBREFA)

In accordance with the provisions of the SBREFA, the Small Business Administration has established a National Small Business and Agriculture Regulatory Ombudsman and 10 Regional Fairness Boards to receive comments from small businesses about federal agency enforcement actions. The Ombudsman annually evaluates enforcement activities and rates each agency's responsiveness to small business. Small businesses wishing to comment on the enforcement activities of the Wage and Hour Division may call 1-888-REG-FAIR (1-888-734-3247), or write to the Ombudsman at 500 W. Madison Street, Suite 1240, Chicago, Illinois 60661.

The right to file a comment with the Ombudsman is in addition to any other rights a small business may have, including the right to contest the assessment of a civil money penalty. Filing a comment with the Ombudsman neither extends the maximum time period for contesting the assessment of a penalty, nor takes the place of filing the response required to secure an administrative hearing on a penalty.

Equal Pay Provisions

The equal pay provisions of FLSA prohibit sex-based wage differentials between men and women employed in the same establishment who perform jobs that require equal skill, effort, and responsibility and which are performed under similar working conditions. These provisions, as well as other statutes prohibiting discrimination in employment, are enforced by the Equal Employment Opportunity Commission. More detailed information is available from its offices which are listed in most telephone directories under U.S. Government.

General Information about Form I-9

U.S. Citizenship and Immigration Services

OFFICE OF BUSINESS LIAISON

Employer Information Bulletin 101 **Basic Information about the Form I-9** **December 8, 2004**	**EBISS: (800) 357-2099** **NCSC: (800) 375-5283** **TDD: (800) 767-1833** **Fax: (202) 272-1864** **Order Forms: (800) 870-3676** **Website: www.uscis.gov**

> **The following is not intended to be legal advice pertaining to your situation and should not be construed as such. The information provided is intended merely as a general overview with regard to the subject matter covered.**

GENERAL INFORMATION ABOUT THE FORM I-9

What is Form I-9?
Form I-9 is the Employment Eligibility Verification Form issued by the Department of Homeland Security, U.S. Citizenship and Immigration Services. By law all US employers are responsible for completion and retention of Forms I-9 for **all** US citizen as well as non-citizen employees it has hired for employment in the US after November 6, 1986. This process, which includes an employee's attestation of work authorization and an employer's review of documents presented by that employee to demonstrate identity and work authorization, is the means by which US employers document that they have verified whether a newly hired employee is eligible to work in the US. The employee and employer both must provide information and signatures as indicated on the form.

How do I obtain the Form I-9?
Copies of the Form I-9 can be ordered at **(800) 870-3676**. They may also be downloaded from the U.S. Citizenship and Immigration Services Internet website at http://www.uscis.gov.

How do I administer the Form I-9 process?
Instructions accompany the Form I-9. Additionally, the "Handbook for Employers", Form M-274, is another available resource. Detailed information about the employment eligibility verification process also appears in the Employer Information Bulletins (EIB 101-112).

Can I verify an employee's work authorization?
ONLY officially registered participants in the Department of Homeland Security's automated verification system pilot projects are permitted to verify the work authorization of a newly hired employee. Questions about participation in the Department of Homeland Security verification pilot programs may be directed to the Department of Homeland Security, SAVE Program at (202) 514-2317 or (888) 464-4218. For more information see Employer Information Bulletin 103.

Where do I send the Form I-9?
The employer must retain the Form I-9 for each employee either for three years after the date of hire or for one year after employment is terminated, whichever is later. (See Employer Information Bulletin 102).

Can I reproduce Form I-9?
Employers are permitted to electronically generate the Form I-9, provided that the resulting form is legible, the content and sequence of the data elements and instructions match those on the official Department of Homeland Security document (Form I-9, revised 11/21/91, OMB No. 1111-0136) and the paper is of retention quality. Copies of the Form I-9 may be reproduced in either double-sided or single-sided format.

Can I store Forms I-9 electronically?
Currently, the only storage options are hard copy or microfiche or microfilm.

Are changes anticipated in the Form I-9?
Changes in the Form I-9 are expected in late 2005 or early 2006, including a reduction in the number of documents that can be submitted by new employees to demonstrate their employment eligibility. (The interim rule of September 30, 1997, reduced the number of documents that are acceptable for the I-9; however these changes are not reflected on the Form I-9. See 8 C.F.R. 274a.2(b)(1)(v) for the most up to date list of acceptable documents.)

The I-9 Process in a Nutshell

 ## U.S. Citizenship and Immigration Services

OFFICE OF BUSINESS LIAISON

U.S. DEPARTMENT OF HOMELAND SECURITY
U.S. CITIZENSHIP AND IMMIGRATION SERVICES

Employer Information Bulletin 102 **The I-9 Process In A Nutshell** **December 2, 2003**	**EBISS: (800) 357-2099** **NCSC: (800) 375-5283** **TDD: (800) 767-1833** **Fax: (202) 272-1864** **Order Forms: (800) 870-3676** **Website: www.uscis.gov**

> **The following is not intended to be legal advice pertaining to your situation and should not be construed as such. The information provided is intended merely as a general overview with regard to the subject matter covered.**

THE I-9 PROCESS IN A NUTSHELL

Purpose

- This bulletin supplements the 1991 version of the "Handbook for Employers" (Form M-274) and the 1991 version of the I-9 instructions and form, which may both be downloaded from the U.S. Citizenship and Immigration Services web site.
- This bulletin provides employers with basic guidance for compliance with requirements to complete, update, and retain I-9 forms for all employees, whether US citizens or non-citizens.
- **NOTE:** The "receipt rule" described in this bulletin is the most up-to-date receipt rule. The receipt rule stated in the Form I-9 instructions and the "Handbook for Employers" (Form M-274) is **NOT** the current rule. See Receipt Rule below.

Introduction to Worksite Enforcement and Employment Eligibility Verification

The 1986 Immigration Reform and Control Act ("IRCA") sought to control illegal migration by eliminating employment opportunity as a key incentive for unauthorized persons to come to the US. IRCA's core prohibition is against the hire or continued employment in the US of an alien whom the employer knows is unauthorized for the employment. IRCA makes all US employers responsible for verifying through a specific process the identity and work authorization or eligibility of all individuals, whether U.S. citizens or not, hired after November 6, 1986. To implement this, employers are required to complete Employment Eligibility Verification Forms I-9 for all employees. An employer's obligation to review documents is not triggered until a person has been **hired**, whereupon the new employee is entitled to submit a document or combination of documents of his choice **(from List A or a combination of a List B and List C document on the reverse side of the I-9 form)** to verify his identity and work eligibility.

Hired = Actual commencement of employment of an employee for wages or other remuneration. The employee must complete Section 1 of the I-9 Form by the date of hire (i.e. no later than the date on which employment services start). (See Completing the I-9 Form below.)

Protection from Discrimination[1]

IRCA also prohibits employers with 4 or more employees from discriminating against any person (other than an unauthorized alien) in hiring, discharging, or recruiting or referring for a fee because of a person's national origin or, in the case of a citizen or protected individual, citizenship status. Employers with 15 or more employees may not discriminate against any person on the basis of national origin in hiring, discharge, recruitment, assignment, compensation, or other terms and conditions of employment. The I-9 process may not be used to **pre-screen** employees for hiring. Furthermore, an employer may not demand more or different documents than an employee chooses to present, provided that the documents presented are acceptable under the I-9 requirements. An employer may not demand documents issued by the Department of Homeland Security **(formerly the Immigration and Naturalization Service)** in lieu of other acceptable document(s) from List(s) A or B and C and may not consider the fact that work authorization documents have future expiration dates as cause not to hire or to terminate.

---

[1] The Office of Special Counsel for Immigration Related Unfair Employment Practices ("OSC") investigates charges of job discrimination related to an individual's immigration status or national origin. It also investigates charges of document abuse discrimination--when employers request more or different documents than are required to verify employment eligibility and identity, reject reasonably genuine-looking documents or specify certain documents over others. All work-authorized individuals are protected from document abuse. OSC can be accessed via the Internet at http://www.usdoj.gov/crt/osc/htm/aboutosc.htm.

The I-9 Process in a Nutshell (continued)

Changes effective after 11/91 Publication of Form I-9 and "Handbook for Employers"[2]

FORM I-151: Form I-151 has been withdrawn from circulation and is no longer a valid List A document.[3]

FORM I-766: Form I-766 was introduced in January 1997 as an Employment Authorization Document (EAD). It should be recorded on the I-9 Form under List A. A previous version of the EAD is the Form I-688B, which continues to be an acceptable List A document. (See Employer Information Bulletin 104.)

FORM I-551: The **Permanent Resident Card** (new version of Form I-551) was introduced in 1990 as documentation issued to lawful permanent residents of the US. Older versions of Form I-551 remain valid until expiration, if any. The Form I-551 should be recorded on the I-9 Form under List A. On the back of the Form I-9, it is listed under List A #5 as an Alien Registration Receipt Card. (See Employer Information Bulletin 104.)

REMOVED DOCUMENTS FROM I-9 LIST: *Effective September 30, 1997* via interim rule published at 62 Fed. Reg. 51001-51006, the following documents were removed from the list of acceptable identity and work authorization documents (listed on the 11/91 version of the Form I-9) to comply with the *Illegal Immigration Reform and Alien Responsibility Act of 1996 (IIRIRA)*: Certificate of US Citizenship (**List A #2**), Certificate of Naturalization (**List A #3**), Unexpired Reentry Permit (**List A #8**), and Unexpired Refugee Travel Document (**List A #9**). In addition, the acceptability of an unexpired foreign passport with Form I-94 indicating unexpired work authorization (List A #4) was made more limiting. Such combination of documents is only acceptable where the individual is employment authorized incident to status for a specific employer.

RECEIPT RULE: Originally effective September 30, 1997, amended by interim rule of *February 9, 1999*; the rule explaining **when receipts may be used** in lieu of original documents in the I-9 process (*receipt rule[4]*) now provides that:

- If an individual's document has been **lost**, **stolen**, or **damaged**, then he/she can present a receipt for the application for a replacement document. The replacement document needs to be presented to the employer within 90 days of hire or, in the case of reverification, the date employment authorization expires.
- If the individual presents as a receipt, the arrival portion of the Form I-94 containing an unexpired temporary I-551 stamp (indicating temporary evidence of permanent resident status) and photograph of the individual, such document satisfies the I-9 documentation presentation requirement until the expiration date on the Form I-94. If no expiration date is indicated, an employer may accept the receipt for one year from the issue date of the I-94 Form.
- Form I-94 with a refugee admission stamp is acceptable as a receipt for 90 days, within which time the employee must present an unrestricted Social Security card together with a List B identity document, or an Employment Authorization Document (Form I-688B or I-766). To indicate refugee status, the stamp may include a reference to Section 207 of the Immigration and Nationality Act (INA) rather than use the words "refugee."

THE I-9 PROCESS

General

Employers are responsible for the completion and retention of Forms I-9 for all employees, regardless of citizenship or national origin, hired for employment in the United States. An employee is any individual compensated for services or labor by an employer, whether by payment in the form of wages or other remuneration (such as goods or services such as food and lodging).

For whom is a Form I-9 unnecessary?

- Employees hired before November 6, 1986, and continuously employed by the same employer;
- Individuals performing casual employment who provide domestic service in a private home that is sporadic, irregular or intermittent;
- Independent contractors (see Employer Information Bulletin 110);
- Workers provided to employers by individuals or entities providing contract services, such as temporary agencies (in such cases, the contracting party is the employer for I-9 purposes)

Note:

- An employer is not permitted under the law to contract for the labor of an individual whom he knows is not authorized for employment. Employers who violate this prohibition may be subject to civil and criminal penalties.
- Employers are not permitted to request more or different documents than are required or to refuse to honor documents tendered that on their face reasonably appear to be genuine and to relate to the individual presenting the document.

---

[2] These changes are not reflected on the current 1991 version of the I-9 Form, its instructions or the "Handbook for Employers" since the changes occurred after 1991.
[3] To replace their "green cards", holders of Form I-151 Alien Registration Receipt Card must submit a completed Form I-90 along with the current filing fee to their local District Office. (To download I-90 go to www.uscis.gov.)
[4] For more information on the receipt rule request Employer Information Bulletin 107; see more on Receipt Rule below.

The I-9 Process in a Nutshell (continued)

Retention of I-9 Records

An employer must retain the I-9 form of each employee **either** for three (3) years after the date of hire **or** for one (1) year after employment is terminated, <u>whichever is later.</u>   All current employees, therefore, must have I-9's on file with the employer. Upon request, all Forms I-9 subject to the retention requirement must be made available to an authorized official of the Department of Homeland Security, Department of Labor, and/or the Office of Special Counsel for Unfair Immigration-Related Employment Practices of the Department of Justice.

Examples for terminated employees:
     Step one: Identify hire date and add 3-years = [date A]
       1.   11/01/93 + 3 years = 11/01/96   or   03/27/99 + 3 years = 03/27/02

     Step two: Identify termination date and add 1 year = [date B]
       1. 07/05/94 + 1 year = 07/05/95   or   05/19/03 + 1 year = 05/19/04

     Step three: Compare date [A] and [B]
       1. Compare 11/01/96 and 07/05/95
       2. Compare 03/27/02 and 05/19/04

     Step four: Determine the later date [A] or [B] in each case. The later of the two becomes the retention
         date for the corresponding Form I-9.

     Example results:
       1. 11/01/96 is later than 07/05/95, so 11/01/96 is the retention date for this terminated employee's I-9.
       2. 05/19/04 is later than 03/27/02, so 05/19/04 is the retention date for this terminated employee's I-9.

Missing I-9 Forms

An employer who discovers that an I-9 form is not on file for a given employee should request the employee to complete section 1 of an I-9 form immediately and submit documentation as required in Section 2. The new form should be dated when completed--**never** post-dated[5]. When an employee does not provide acceptable documentation, the employer must terminate employment of risk being subject to penalties for "knowingly" continuing to employ an unauthorized worker if the individual is not in fact authorized to work.

Discovering an Unauthorized Employee

An employer who discovers that an employee has been working without authorization should reverify work authorization by allowing such an employee another opportunity to present acceptable documentation and complete a new I-9. However, employers should be aware that if it knows or should have known that an employee is unauthorized to work in the United, they may be subject to serious penalties for "knowingly continuing to employ" an unauthorized worker.

Successive Employers and Reorganizations

Employers that acquire a business as a result of a corporate reorganization, merger, or sale of stock or assets, and retain the predecessor's employees are not required to complete new I-9's for those employees and may rely on the I-9s completed by the predecessor employer if the employees are continuing in employment, and they have a reasonable expectation of employment at all times. However, the successor employer will be held responsible if the predecessor's I-9s are deficient or defective.

---

[5] Employers may provide an explanatory annotation to an untimely-completed Form I-9.

The I-9 Process in a Nutshell (continued)

COMPLETING THE I-9 FORM

There are three sections of the Form I-9. The employee must complete Section 1. The employer must complete sections 2 and 3. The employer is required to ensure that **all** sections of the Form I-9 are timely and properly completed. **The Form I-9 is available in ENGLISH ONLY.**

SECTION 1: EMPLOYEE INFORMATION AND VERIFICATION
Responsibility of the Employer

Employers must ensure that Section 1 is completed by the employee upon **date of hire** (i.e. 1st day of paid work). The signature and attestation under penalty of perjury portions of Section 1 are very important, and employers should take special care to ensure that employees complete these in full. Although employers are held responsible for deficiencies of information in Section 1 (i.e. where required information is not provided by the employee), they may not require employees to produce documents to verify Section 1 information.

NOTE: An employee's signature and attestation of status under penalty of perjury are particularly important. If a given employee refuses to provide his/her signature or attestation, there is no reason for the employer to proceed to complete Section 2, and the employer should not continue to employ the individual.

NOTE: An employee may not be able to provide a social security number if the Social Security administration has not yet issued the individual a social security card.[6] This information block is optional. Therefore, an employer cannot require an employee to complete it.

Responsibility of the Employee

Employees need to provide the information requested in Section 1. In particular, they must attest to their status by checking the applicable box indicating that they are:
- Citizen/national of the United States (**top box**),
- Lawful permanent resident with a "green card" (**middle box**), or
- Alien authorized to work in the United States until a specified date (**bottom box**).

Employees **must sign and date** this Section of the Form I-9 when completed.

Note: Employers should remind employees of format conventions such as providing dates in the format of month/day/year, since date formats in their countries of origin may have a different order.

Note: Certain aliens, such as asylees and refugees, are work authorized incident to their status and may not have an expiration date to fill-in for the bottom box of the attestation block in Section 1.

Responsibility of Translator or Preparer

If used by the employee to fill out Section 1, translators or prepares must also sign, date, and provide requested information in the Preparer/Translator Certification Block at the bottom of Section 1. Employers themselves must fill in and sign this block if they have assisted employees with Section 1.

---

[6] Some local Social Security Administration offices will give the individual their social security number upon request before the actual social security card is issued.

The I-9 Process in a Nutshell (continued)

SECTION 2: EMPLOYER REVIEW AND VERIFICATION

- The second part of the form requires the employer to list the documents that were produced by the worker to verify his or her identity and employment eligibility. There are three groups of documents that a worker may use for this purpose. The documents that can be presented by employees are listed on the reverse side of the Form I-9.[7] A worker may choose to provide a List A document (which establishes both identity and work authorization), or he/she may choose to provide one List B document (which establishes identity) and one List C document (which establishes work eligibility). Documentation must be rejected if it is expired, with two exceptions: the U.S. passport (a List A document) and all List B documents. Employers who fail to complete the Form I-9 or who hire or continue to employ workers they know are unauthorized to work in the United States may be subject to civil and, in certain cases, criminal penalties. See Employer Information Bulletin 111.

- Employers cannot refuse to hire an individual because the individual's document has an expiration date.

Original Documents Only - The employer or employer's representative/agent[8] must ***personally***[9] review *original* document(s) that demonstrate an employee's identity and eligibility to work in the US.[10] Photocopies, or numbers representing original documents, are not acceptable. Exception: List C, #3, a certified copy of a birth certificate issued by a state, county, municipal authority or outlying possession of the US bearing an official seal is acceptable. All identifying information, including the document title, the issuing authority, the document number, and/or the expiration date (if applicable) must be provided in full.

RECEIPT RULE: Employees who do not possess the required documentation when employment begins **may not submit receipts showing that they have applied for initial applications for documents or for applications for extension of documents**. An employer may only accept receipts for:

- A **replacement document** in lieu of the required document if a document was ***lost, stolen, or damaged***. The replacement document must be presented within 90 days of the hire or, in the case or reverification; the date employment authorization expires.

- The individual presents as a receipt, the arrival portion of the Form I-94 containing an unexpired temporary I-551 ADIT stamp (indicating temporary evidence of permanent resident status) and photograph of the individual, until the expiration date. If no expiration date is indicated, an employer may accept the receipt for one year from the issue date of the I-94 form. The "green card" itself should be presented at the expiration date on the Form I-94.

- Someone granted refugee status will be issued a Form I-94 containing a refugee admission stamp. The employer can accept this as a receipt as long as the employee presents: 1) the departure portion of Form I-94 containing an unexpired refugee admission stamp, which is designated for purposes of this section as a receipt for the Form I-766, Form I-688B, or a social security card that contains no employment restrictions; and 2) within 90-days of the hire, or in the case of reverification, the date employment authorization expires, presents an unexpired Form I-766 or From I-688B, or a social security card that contains no employment restrictions together with a document described under List B. This type of receipt is sufficient to evidence both identity and employment authorization for the 90-day receipt validity period.

Common example: An EAD (Form I-688B or I-766) is generally valid as evidence of work authorization for one year. The EAD may be renewed by the submission of a new application to the U.S. Citizenship and Immigration Services. Accordingly, a receipt acknowledging such an application is unacceptable.

Note: A receipt is never acceptable for employment lasting less than 3 working days.

Source of Confusion:
(1) Social Security Cards. Please request Employer Information Bulletin 112.
(2) Multiple entries for document #'s and expiration dates must be filled out only where an employee has presented more than one document under one List (e.g., an unexpired passport with an unexpired I-94; unexpired passport with an unexpired I-94 and Form I-20 endorsed by the Designated School Official). All document numbers and expiration dates must be recorded.
(3) List A or B documents from which the bearer cannot be identified are never acceptable even if unexpired.
(4) Unexpired foreign passport containing an unexpired I-551 stamp. This constitutes temporary evidence of permanent resident status and must be reverified at the time the stamp expires; it does not constitute a receipt. The actual Form I-551, or "green card," should not be reverified even if it contains an expiration date.

---

[7] See "Changes effective after 11/91 Publication of Form I-9 and *Handbook for Employers*" on page two for changes.

[8] Employers may not use agents to shield themselves from responsibility.

[9] Employers with remote hires may designate agents such as notaries public, attorneys, or other trusted individuals to exercise the Section 2 review of documents on their behalf. An employer is bound by the actions of such agent. What is key is that whoever fills out section 2 of the I-9 must personally review the employee's document(s).

[10] **Anti-Discrimination Warning:** Employers are not permitted to require a particular document(s) or combination of documents. The employer must accept any document from List A or combination of documents from Lists B and C, at the employee's discretion. Likewise, employers may neither require nor accept any more documentation than the minimum necessary to substantiate identity and work eligibility.

5

The I-9 Process in a Nutshell (continued)

Standards of Review[11]

The employer must review and accept documents that reasonably appear to be genuine and to relate to the person presenting them (e.g., the name on the Social Security card should be compared to the name on the state driver's permit and the photo on the driver's permit compared to the appearance of the person who presented the documents). Employers may reject documents it they do not reasonably appear to be genuine and ask employees who present questionable documentation for other documentation that satisfy the I-9 requirements. Employees who are unable to present acceptable documents should be terminated. Employers who choose to retain such employees may be subject to penalties for improper completion of the form or for "knowingly continuing to employ" unauthorized workers if such workers are in fact unauthorized.

Note: Employers should be alert for signs of fraud, such as a social security card that contains more than nine digits or that begins with "000."

Signature and Date: Employers

Employers are required to sign and date the bottom of Section 2 and provide all requested information in the **CERTIFICATION** portion.

Note: *The personal attestation and signature of the employer are extremely important.* The person who actually reviews original documents -- whether that person is the employer, or an agent of the employer, such as a provider of contract services to the employer-- must sign and date the I-9 form.

SECTION 3: UPDATING AND REVERIFICATION[12]

Reverification requirement: Employers are required to reverify employment eligibility. When an employee's employment authorization (indicated in Section 1) or evidence of employment authorization recorded in Section 2 has expired. An employer may also reverify employment authorization, in lieu of completing a new I-9, when an employee is rehired within three years of the date that the I-9 was originally completed and the employee's work authorization or evidence of work authorization has expired. The reverification requirement does not apply to the U.S. passport or "green card" (Form I-551). Note that temporary evidence of permanent resident status in the form of an unexpired foreign passport containing a temporary I-551 ADIT stamp is subject to the reverification requirement.

IMPORTANT: Most employers find it useful to institute a system that reminds them automatically, in advance, that a given employee's authorization document will expire. Advance warning assists both employees and employers, since early notice will usually allow employees time to renew the authorization prior to the expiration date and avoid penalties to employers for continuing to employ unauthorized workers. Enough advance warning is important so the employee can apply for and receive replacement documents in time to maintain uninterrupted employment.

Reverification Process

No later than the date that employment authorization or employment authorization documentation expires, employers must reverify employment authorization on Section 3 of the I-9, or by completing a new I-9 form to be attached to the original I-9. To reverify expired status (Section 1) and/or expired work authorization document(s) (Section 2), an employee may present any currently valid List A or List C document. **Remember:** Receipts showing that the employee has applied for an extension of an expired employment authorization document is not an acceptable. (See Receipt Rule.)

Note: Employees are not required to present, for reverification purposes, a new version of the same document that was presented to satisfy Section 2 but subsequently expired. Any document or combination of documents that would be acceptable to demonstrate work eligibility/authorization under Section 2 may be presented for reverification purposes. It is the employee's choice as to which document to present.

---

[11] See Employer Information Bulletin 103.
[12] See Employer Information Bulletin 107.

The I-9 Process in a Nutshell (continued)

Where Reverification is *not* Required

Permanent Resident Cards (also known as Alien Registration Receipt cards, Forms I-551, Resident Alien Cards, Permanent Resident Cards, or "Green Cards") are issued to lawful permanent residents[13] and conditional resident and should not be reverified when the cards expire. Temporary evidence of permanent resident status in the form of a temporary I-551 stamp in an unexpired foreign passport is subject to reverification. This is because of the temporary nature of this document. Likewise, List B documents need not be reverified when they expire. In fact, List B documents are acceptable when initially shown, even when expired.

Rehires

Employers may reverify information of an employee rehired within 3 years of the date of the initial execution of the Form I-9 as an alternative to completing a new Form I-9.   If the rehire's basis of employment eligibility, as listed on the retained I-9, remains the same, the employer must update the previously completed I-9. If the basis of work eligibility has expired, the employer must reverify. To update or reverify on the previously completed I-9, employers must complete Section 3 items A (name), B (date of rehire), and C (new documentation) in full, as applicable. In this section, as in Section 2, it is important that the person who actually examines the documents on behalf of the employer personally sign and date the attestation provision at the bottom of the form.

To update: Employers should record the date of rehire, sign and date Section 3 of the previously completed I-9 or complete a new I-9.

To reverify: Employers should record the date of rehire, record the document title, number, and expiration date (if any) of documentation presented to reverify expired work authorization or work authorization documentation, sign, and date Section 3 of the previously completed I-9. A new Form I-9 may be chosen to be completed instead.

Note: Documentation for reverification purposes may be the renewed version of the originally presented document or any other acceptable document from List A or List C that demonstrates current work eligibility/authorization. List B documents do not need to be updated or reverified, even if expired.

Other Issues

Copying of Documentation

- An employer may, but is not required to, copy a document (front and back) presented by an individual solely for the purpose of complying with the I-9 verification requirements. If such a copy is made, it must be retained with the Form I-9. The copying of any such document and retention of the copy does not relieve the employer from the requirement to fully complete Section 2 of the Form I-9. If employers choose to keep copies of I-9 documentation, then it should be done for all employees, and the copies should be attached to the related I-9. Employers should not copy the documents only of individuals of certain national origin or citizenship status. To do so may constitute unlawful discrimination under section 274B of the Immigration and Nationality Act.

Interim Employment Authorization

- Also note, except in the case of an initial application for employment authorization in the case of an applicant for asylum and certain applicants for adjustment of status, the Department of Homeland Security is required to adjudicate applications for employment authorization on Form I-765 within 90 days from the date of receipt of the application by the U.S. Citizenship and Immigration Services.   Failure to complete the adjudication within 90 days will result in the grant of an employment authorization document for a period not to exceed 240 days. Such authorization shall be subject to any conditions noted on the employment authorization document. However, if the application is denied prior to the expiration date of the interim employment authorization, the interim employment authorization document granted under this section shall automatically terminate as of the date of the adjudication and denial. See 8 C.F.R. 274a.13(d) at www.uscis.gov. In order to receive this interim employment authorization document, the individual needs to go to a local U.S. Citizenship and Immigration Services office. If the local office refuses to issue an interim employment authorization document, please contact the Office of Business Liaison.

How to Document Extensions of Stay for Certain Nonimmigrants Continuing Employment with the Same Employer

- The following nonimmigrants with pending applications to extend their stay are automatically authorized to continue employment with the same employer for a period not to exceed 240 days beginning on the date of the expiration of the authorized period of stay: A-3s, E-1s, E-2s, G-5s, H-1s, H-2As, H-2Bs, H-3s, Is, J-1s, L-1s, O-1s, O-2s, P-1s, P-2s, P-3s, aliens having a religious occupation pursuant to 8 C.F.R. 214.2(r), and TNs. To document this extension of employment authorization on the Form I-9, any occupation pursuant to 8 C.F.R. 214.2(r), and TNs. To document this extension of employment authorization on the Form I-9, any expiration date noted in Sections 1 and 2 should be updated to clearly reflect this extension. The update should be initialed and dated.

---

[13] Expired cards must be renewed sot that cardholders will have valid evidence of their status and registration for new employment, for travel outside the US, and to obtain certain other benefits.

Employment Eligibility Verification and Form I-9

U.S. Department of Justice
Immigration and Naturalization Service

OMB No. 1115-0136

Employment Eligibility Verification

INSTRUCTIONS
PLEASE READ ALL INSTRUCTIONS CAREFULLY BEFORE COMPLETING THIS FORM.

Anti-Discrimination Notice. It is illegal to discriminate against any individual (other than an alien not authorized to work in the U.S.) in hiring, discharging, or recruiting or referring for a fee because of that individual's national origin or citizenship status. It is illegal to discriminate against work eligible individuals. Employers **CANNOT** specify which document(s) they will accept from an employee. The refusal to hire an individual because of a future expiration date may also constitute illegal discrimination.

Section 1 - Employee.
All employees, citizens and noncitizens, hired after November 6, 1986, must complete Section 1 of this form at the time of hire, which is the actual beginning of employment.**The employer is responsible for ensuring that Section 1 is timely and properly completed.**

Preparer/Translator Certification. The Preparer/Translator Certification must be completed if Section 1 is prepared by a person other than the employee. A preparer/translator may be used only when the employee is unable to complete Section 1 on his/her own. However, the employee must still sign Section 1.

Section 2 - Employer.
For the purpose of completing this form, the term "employer" includes those recruiters and referrers for a fee who are agricultural associations, agricultural employers or farm labor contractors.

Employers must complete Section 2 by examining evidence of identity and employment eligibility within three (3) business days of the date employment begins. If employees are authorized to work, but are unable to present the required document(s) within three business days, they must present a receipt for the application of the document(s) within three business days and the actual document(s) within ninety (90) days. However, if employers hire individuals for a duration of less than three business days, Section 2 must be completed at the time employment begins. **Employers must record: 1)** document title; **2)** issuing authority; **3)** document number,**4)** expiration date, if any; and **5)** the date employment begins. Employers must sign and date the certification. Employees must present original documents. Employers may, but are not required to, photocopy the document(s) presented. These photocopies may only be used for the verification process and must be retained with the I-9. **However, employers are still responsible for completing the I-9.**

Section 3 - Updating and Reverification.
Employers must complete Section 3 when updating and/or reverifying the I-9. Employers must reverify employment eligibility of their employees on or before the expiration date recorded in Section 1. Employers **CANNOT** specify which document(s) they will accept from an employee.

- If an employee's name has changed at the time this form is being updated/ reverified, complete Block A.

- If an employee is rehired within three (3) years of the date this form was originally completed and the employee is still eligible to be employed on the same basis as previously indicated on this form (updating), complete Block B and the signature block.

- If an employee is rehired within three (3) years of the date this form was originally completed and the employee's work authorization has expired **or** if a current employee's work authorization is about to expire (reverification), complete Block B and:
  - examine any document that reflects that the employee is authorized to work in the U.S. (see List A **or** C),
  - record the document title, document number and expiration date (if any) in Block C, and complete the signature block.

Photocopying and Retaining Form I-9. A blank I-9 may be reproduced, provided both sides are copied. The Instructions must be available to all employees completing this form. Employers must retain completed I-9s for three (3) years after the date of hire or one (1) year after the date employment ends, whichever is later.

For more detailed information, you may refer to the INS Handbook for Employers, (Form M-274). You may obtain the handbook at your local INS office.

Privacy Act Notice. The authority for collecting this information is the Immigration Reform and Control Act of 1986, Pub. L. 99-603 (8 USC 1324a).

This information is for employers to verify the eligibility of individuals for employment to preclude the unlawful hiring, or recruiting or referring for a fee, of aliens who are not authorized to work in the United States.

This information will be used by employers as a record of their basis for determining eligibility of an employee to work in the United States. The form will be kept by the employer and made available for inspection by officials of the U.S. Immigration and Naturalization Service, the Department of Labor and the Office of Special Counsel for Immigration Related Unfair Employment Practices.

Submission of the information required in this form is voluntary. However, an individual may not begin employment unless this form is completed, since employers are subject to civil or criminal penalties if they do not comply with the Immigration Reform and Control Act of 1986.

Reporting Burden. We try to create forms and instructions that are accurate, can be easily understood and which impose the least possible burden on you to provide us with information. Often this is difficult because some immigration laws are very complex. Accordingly, the reporting burden for this collection of information is computed as follows:**1)** learning about this form, 5 minutes; **2)** completing the form, 5 minutes; and **3)** assembling and filing (recordkeeping) the form, 5 minutes, for an average of 15 minutes per response. If you have comments regarding the accuracy of this burden estimate, or suggestions for making this form simpler, you can write to the Immigration and Naturalization Service, HQPDI, 425 I Street, N.W., Room 4034, Washington, DC 20536. OMB No. 1115-0136.

EMPLOYERS MUST RETAIN COMPLETED FORM I-9
PLEASE DO NOT MAIL COMPLETED FORM I-9 TO INS

Form I-9 (Rev. 11-21-91)N

Employment Eligibility Verification and Form I-9 (continued)

U.S. Department of Justice
Immigration and Naturalization Service

OMB No. 1115-0136

Employment Eligibility Verification

Please read instructions carefully before completing this form. The instructions must be available during completion of this form. **ANTI-DISCRIMINATION NOTICE:** It is illegal to discriminate against work eligible individuals. Employers **CANNOT** specify which document(s) they will accept from an employee. The refusal to hire an individual because of a future expiration date may also constitute illegal discrimination.

Section 1. Employee Information and Verification. To be completed and signed by employee at the time employment begins.

Print Name: Last	First	Middle Initial	Maiden Name

Address (Street Name and Number) | Apt. # | Date of Birth (month/day/year)

City | State | Zip Code | Social Security #

I am aware that federal law provides for imprisonment and/or fines for false statements or use of false documents in connection with the completion of this form.

I attest, under penalty of perjury, that I am (check one of the following):
- ☐ A citizen or national of the United States
- ☐ A Lawful Permanent Resident (Alien # A_____)
- ☐ An alien authorized to work until ___/___/___
(Alien # or Admission #)_____

Employee's Signature | Date (month/day/year)

Preparer and/or Translator Certification. (To be completed and signed if Section 1 is prepared by a person other than the employee.) I attest, under penalty of perjury, that I have assisted in the completion of this form and that to the best of my knowledge the information is true and correct.

Preparer's/Translator's Signature | Print Name

Address (Street Name and Number, City, State, Zip Code) | Date (month/day/year)

Section 2. Employer Review and Verification. To be completed and signed by employer. Examine one document from List A OR examine one document from List B and one from List C, as listed on the reverse of this form, and record the title, number and expiration date, if any, of the document(s)

List A	OR	List B	AND	List C
Document title:_____		_____		_____
Issuing authority:_____		_____		_____
Document #: _____		_____		_____
Expiration Date (if any): __/__/__		__/__/__		__/__/__
Document #: _____				
Expiration Date (if any): __/__/__				

CERTIFICATION - I attest, under penalty of perjury, that I have examined the document(s) presented by the above-named employee, that the above-listed document(s) appear to be genuine and to relate to the employee named, that the employee began employment on (month/day/year) ___/___/___ and that to the best of my knowledge the employee is eligible to work in the United States. (State employment agencies may omit the date the employee began employment.)

Signature of Employer or Authorized Representative | Print Name | Title

Business or Organization Name | Address (Street Name and Number, City, State, Zip Code) | Date (month/day/year)

Section 3. Updating and Reverification. To be completed and signed by employer.

A. New Name (if applicable) | B. Date of rehire (month/day/year) (if applicable)

C. If employee's previous grant of work authorization has expired, provide the information below for the document that establishes current employment eligibility.

Document Title:_____ | Document #: _____ | Expiration Date (if any):___/___/___

I attest, under penalty of perjury, that to the best of my knowledge, this employee is eligible to work in the United States, and if the employee presented document(s), the document(s) I have examined appear to be genuine and to relate to the individual.

Signature of Employer or Authorized Representative | Date (month/day/year)

Employment Eligibility Verification and Form I-9 (continued)

LISTS OF ACCEPTABLE DOCUMENTS

LIST A		LIST B		LIST C
Documents that Establish Both Identity and Employment Eligibility	**OR**	**Documents that Establish Identity**	**AND**	**Documents that Establish Employment Eligibility**

LIST A — Documents that Establish Both Identity and Employment Eligibility

1. U.S. Passport (unexpired or expired)

2. Certificate of U.S. Citizenship *(INS Form N-560 or N-561)*

3. Certificate of Naturalization *(INS Form N-550 or N-570)*

4. Unexpired foreign passport, with *I-551 stamp or* attached *INS Form I-94* indicating unexpired employment authorization

5. Permanent Resident Card or Alien Registration Receipt Card with photograph *(INS Form I-151 or I-551)*

6. Unexpired Temporary Resident Card *(INS Form I-688)*

7. Unexpired Employment Authorization Card *(INS Form I-688A)*

8. Unexpired Reentry Permit *(INS Form I-327)*

9. Unexpired Refugee Travel Document *(INS Form I-571)*

10. Unexpired Employment Authorization Document issued by the INS which contains a photograph *(INS Form I-688B)*

LIST B — Documents that Establish Identity

1. Driver's license or ID card issued by a state or outlying possession of the United States provided it contains a photograph or information such as name, date of birth, gender, height, eye color and address

2. ID card issued by federal, state or local government agencies or entities, provided it contains a photograph or information such as name, date of birth, gender, height, eye color and address

3. School ID card with a photograph

4. Voter's registration card

5. U.S. Military card or draft record

6. Military dependent's ID card

7. U.S. Coast Guard Merchant Mariner Card

8. Native American tribal document

9. Driver's license issued by a Canadian government authority

For persons under age 18 who are unable to present a document listed above:

10. School record or report card

11. Clinic, doctor or hospital record

12. Day-care or nursery school record

LIST C — Documents that Establish Employment Eligibility

1. U.S. social security card issued by the Social Security Administration *(other than a card stating it is not valid for employment)*

2. Certification of Birth Abroad issued by the Department of State *(Form FS-545 or Form DS-1350)*

3. Original or certified copy of a birth certificate issued by a state, county, municipal authority or outlying possession of the United States bearing an official seal

4. Native American tribal document

5. U.S. Citizen ID Card *(INS Form I-197)*

6. ID Card for use of Resident Citizen in the United States *(INS Form I-179)*

7. Unexpired employment authorization document issued by the INS *(other than those listed under List A)*

Illustrations of many of these documents appear in Part 8 of the Handbook for Employers (M-274)

APPENDIX E

OSHA

29 CFR OSHA 1904

29 CFR OSHA 1904 -- Recording and Reporting Occupational Injuries and Illnesses

Subpart A -- Purpose
§ 1904.0 Purpose.
The purpose of this rule (Part 1904) is to require employers to record and report work-related fatalities, injuries and illnesses.

Note to § 1904.0: Recording or reporting a work-related injury, illness, or fatality does not mean that the employer or employee was at fault, that an OSHA rule has been violated, or that the employee is eligible for workers' compensation or other benefits.

Non-Mandatory Appendix A to Subpart B -- Partially Exempt Industries
Employers are not required to keep OSHA injury and illness records for any establishment classified in the following Standard Industrial Classification (SIC) codes, unless they are asked in writing to do so by OSHA, the Bureau of Labor Statistics (BLS), or a state agency operating under the authority of OSHA or the BLS. All employers, including those partially exempted by reason of company size or industry classification, must report to OSHA any workplace incident that results in a fatality or the hospitalization of three or more employees (see § 1904.39).

SIC code	Industry description	SIC code	Industry description
525	Hardware Stores	725	Shoe Repair and Shoeshine Parlors
542	Meat and Fish Markets	726	Funeral Service and Crematories
544	Candy, Nut, and Confectionery Stores	729	Miscellaneous Personal Services
545	Dairy Products Stores	731	Advertising Services
546	Retail Bakeries	732	Credit Reporting and Collection Services
549	Miscellaneous Food Stores	733	Mailing, Reproduction, & Stenographic Services
551	New and Used Car Dealers	737	Computer and Data Processing Services
552	Used Car Dealers	738	Miscellaneous Business Services
554	Gasoline Service Stations	764	Reupholstery and Furniture Repair
557	Motorcycle Dealers	78	Motion Picture
56	Apparel and Accessory Stores	791	Dance Studios, Schools, and Halls
573	Radio, Television, & Computer Stores	792	Producers, Orchestras, Entertainers
58	Eating and Drinking Places	793	Bowling Centers
591	Drug Stores and Proprietary Stores	801	Offices & Clinics Of Medical Doctors
592	Liquor Stores	802	Offices and Clinics Of Dentists
594	Miscellaneous Shopping Goods Stores	803	Offices Of Osteopathic
599	Retail Stores, Not Elsewhere Classified	804	Offices Of Other Health Practitioners
60	Depository Institutions (banks & savings institutions)	807	Medical and Dental Laboratories
61	Nondepository	809	Health and Allied Services, Not Elsewhere Classified
62	Security and Commodity Brokers	81	Legal Services
63	Insurance Carriers	82	Educational Services (schools, colleges, universities and libraries)
64	Insurance Agents, Brokers & Services	832	Individual and Family Services
653	Real Estate Agents and Managers	835	Child Day Care Services
654	Title Abstract Offices	839	Social Services, Not Elsewhere Classified
67	Holding and Other Investment Offices	841	Museums and Art Galleries

29 CFR OSHA 1904 (continued)

722	Photographic Studios, Portrait	86	Membership Organizations
723	Beauty Shops	87	Engineering, Accounting, Research, Management, and Related Services
724	Barber Shops	899	Services, not elsewhere classified

Note to Subpart B: All employers covered by the Occupational Safety and Health Act (OSH Act) are covered by these Part 1904 regulations. However, most employers do not have to keep OSHA injury and illness records unless OSHA or the Bureau of Labor Statistics (BLS) informs them in writing that they must keep records. For example, employers with 10 or fewer employees and business establishments in certain industry classifications are partially exempt from keeping OSHA injury and illness records.

1904.1(a)
Basic requirement.

1904.1(a)(1)
If your company had ten (10) or fewer employees at all times during the last calendar year, you do not need to keep OSHA injury and illness records unless OSHA or the BLS informs you in writing that you must keep records under § 1904.41 or § 1904.42. However, as required by § 1904.39, all employers covered by the OSH Act must report to OSHA any workplace incident that results in a fatality or the hospitalization of three or more employees.

1904.1(a)(2)
If your company had more than ten (10) employees at any time during the last calendar year, you must keep OSHA injury and illness records unless your establishment is classified as a partially exempt industry under § 1904.2.

1904.1(b)
Implementation.

1904.1(b)(1)
Is the partial exemption for size based on the size of my entire company or on the size of an individual business establishment? The partial exemption for size is based on the number of employees in the entire company.

1904.1(b)(2)
How do I determine the size of my company to find out if I qualify for the partial exemption for size? To determine if you are exempt because of size, you need to determine your company's peak employment during the last calendar year. If you had no more than 10 employees at any time in the last calendar year, your company qualifies for the partial exemption for size.

1904.2(a)
Basic requirement.

1904.2(a)(1)
If your business establishment is classified in a specific low hazard retail, service, finance, insurance or real estate industry listed in Appendix A to this Subpart B, you do not need to keep OSHA injury and illness records unless the government asks you to keep the records under § 1904.41 or § 1904.42. However, all employers must report to OSHA any workplace incident that results in a fatality or the hospitalization of three or more employees (see § 1904.39).

1904.2(a)(2)
If one or more of your company's establishments are classified in a non-exempt industry, you must keep OSHA injury and illness records for all of such establishments unless your company is partially exempted because of size under § 1904.1.

1904.2(b)
Implementation.

29 CFR OSHA 1904 (continued)

1904.2(b)(1)

Does the partial industry classification exemption apply only to business** establishments **in the retail, services, finance, insurance or real estate industries (SICs 52-89)? Yes, business establishments classified in agriculture; mining; construction; manufacturing; transportation; communication, electric, gas and sanitary services; or wholesale trade are not eligible for the partial industry classification exemption.

1904.2(b)(2)

Is the partial industry classification exemption based on the industry classification of my entire company or on the classification of individual business establishments operated by my company? The partial industry classification exemption applies to individual business establishments. If a company has several business establishments engaged in different classes of business activities, some of the company's establishments may be required to keep records, while others may be exempt.

1904.2(b)(3)

How do I determine the Standard Industrial Classification code for my company or for individual establishments? You determine your Standard Industrial Classification (SIC) code by using the Standard Industrial Classification Manual, Executive Office of the President, Office of Management and Budget. You may contact your nearest OSHA office or State agency for help in determining your SIC.

1904.3

If you create records to comply with another government agency's injury and illness recordkeeping requirements, OSHA will consider those records as meeting OSHA's Part 1904 recordkeeping requirements if OSHA accepts the other agency's records under a memorandum of understanding with that agency, or if the other agency's records contain the same information as this Part 1904 requires you to record. You may contact your nearest OSHA office or State agency for help in determining whether your records meet OSHA's requirements.

1904.4

Note to Subpart C: This Subpart describes the work-related injuries and illnesses that an employer must enter into the OSHA records and explains the OSHA forms that employers must use to record work-related fatalities, injuries, and illnesses.

1904.4(a)

Basic requirement. Each employer required by this Part to keep records of fatalities, injuries, and illnesses must record each fatality, injury and illness that:

1904.4(a)(1)

Is work-related; and

1904.4(a)(2)

Is a new case; and

1904.4(a)(3)

Meets one or more of the general recording criteria of § 1904.7 or the application to specific cases of § 1904.8 through § 1904.12.

1904.4(b)

Implementation.

1904.4(b)(1)

What sections of this rule describe recording criteria for recording work-related injuries and illnesses? The table below indicates which sections of the rule address each topic.

1904.4(b)(1)(i)

Determination of work-relatedness. See § 1904.5.

1904.4(b)(1)(ii)

Determination of a new case. See § 1904.6.

29 CFR OSHA 1904 (continued)

1904.4(b)(1)(iii)
General recording criteria. See § 1904.7.

1904.4(b)(1)(iv)
Additional criteria. (Needlestick and sharps injury cases, tuberculosis cases, hearing loss cases, medical removal cases, and musculoskeletal disorder cases). See § 1904.8 through § 1904.12.

1904.4(b)(2)
How do I decide whether a particular injury or illness is recordable? The decision tree for recording work-related injuries and illnesses below shows the steps involved in making this determination.

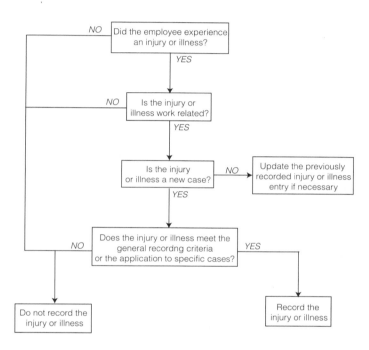

1904.5(a)
Basic requirement. You must consider an injury or illness to be work-related if an event or exposure in the work environment either caused or contributed to the resulting condition or significantly aggravated a pre-existing injury or illness. Work-relatedness is presumed for injuries and illnesses resulting from events or exposures occurring in the work environment, unless an exception in § 1904.5(b)(2) specifically applies.

1904.5(b)
Implementation.

1904.5(b)(1)
What is the "work environment"? OSHA defines the work environment as "the establishment and other locations where one or more employees are working or are present as a condition of their employment. The work environment includes not only physical locations, but also the equipment or materials used by the employee during the course of his or her work."

1904.5(b)(2)
Are there situations where an injury or illness occurs in the work environment and is not considered work-related? Yes, an injury or illness occurring in the work environment that falls under one of the following exceptions is not work-related, and therefore is not recordable.

29 CFR OSHA 1904 (continued)

1904.5(b)(2)	You are not required to record injuries and illnesses if . . .
(i)	At the time of the injury or illness, the employee was present in the work environment as a member of the general public rather than as an employee.
(ii)	The injury or illness involves signs or symptoms that surface at work but result solely from a non-work-related event or exposure that occurs outside the work environment.
(iii)	The injury or illness results solely from voluntary participation in a wellness program or in a medical, fitness, or recreational activity such as blood donation, physical examination, flu shot, exercise class, racquetball, or baseball.
(iv)	The injury or illness is solely the result of an employee eating, drinking, or preparing food or drink for personal consumption (whether bought on the employer's premises or brought in). For example, if the employee is injured by choking on a sandwich while in the employer's establishment, the case would not be considered work-related. **Note:** If the employee is made ill by ingesting food contaminated by workplace contaminants (such as lead), or gets food poisoning from food supplied by the employer, the case would be considered work-related.
(v)	The injury or illness is solely the result of an employee doing personal tasks (unrelated to their employment) at the establishment outside of the employee's assigned working hours.
(vi)	The injury or illness is solely the result of personal grooming, self medication for a non-work-related condition, or is intentionally self-inflicted.
(vii)	The injury or illness is caused by a motor vehicle accident and occurs on a company parking lot or company access road while the employee is commuting to or from work.
(viii)	The illness is the common cold or flu (Note: contagious diseases such as tuberculosis, brucellosis, hepatitis A, or plague are considered work-related if the employee is infected at work).
(ix)	The illness is a mental illness. Mental illness will not be considered work-related unless the employee voluntarily provides the employer with an opinion from a physician or other licensed health care professional with appropriate training and experience (psychiatrist, psychologist, psychiatric nurse practitioner, etc.) stating that the employee has a mental illness that is work-related.

1904.5(b)(3)
How do I handle a case if it is not obvious whether the precipitating event or exposure occurred in the work environment or occurred away from work? In these situations, you must evaluate the employee's work duties and environment to decide whether or not one or more events or exposures in the work environment either caused or contributed to the resulting condition or significantly aggravated a pre-existing condition.

1904.5(b)(4)
How do I know if an event or exposure in the work environment "significantly aggravated" a preexisting injury or illness? A preexisting injury or illness has been significantly aggravated, for purposes of OSHA injury and illness recordkeeping, when an event or exposure in the work environment results in any of the following:

1904.5(b)(4)(i)
Death, provided that the preexisting injury or illness would likely not have resulted in death but for the occupational event or exposure.

29 CFR OSHA 1904 (continued)

1904.5(b)(4)(ii)
Loss of consciousness, provided that the preexisting injury or illness would likely not have resulted in loss of consciousness but for the occupational event or exposure.

1904.5(b)(4)(iii)
One or more days away from work, or days of restricted work, or days of job transfer that otherwise would not have occurred but for the occupational event or exposure.

1904.5(b)(4)(iv)
Medical treatment in a case where no medical treatment was needed for the injury or illness before the workplace event or exposure, or a change in medical treatment was necessitated by the workplace event or exposure.

1904.5(b)(5)
Which injuries and illnesses are considered pre-existing conditions? An injury or illness is a preexisting condition if it resulted solely from a non-work-related event or exposure that occured outside the work environment.

1904.5(b)(6)
How do I decide whether an injury or illness is work-related if the employee is on travel status at the time the injury or illness occurs? Injuries and illnesses that occur while an employee is on travel status are work-related if, at the time of the injury or illness, the employee was engaged in work activities "in the interest of the employer." Examples of such activities include travel to and from customer contacts, conducting job tasks, and entertaining or being entertained to transact, discuss, or promote business (work-related entertainment includes only entertainment activities being engaged in at the direction of the employer).

Injuries or illnesses that occur when the employee is on travel status do not have to be recorded if they meet one of the exceptions listed below.

1904.5(b)(6)	If the employee has . . .	You may use the following to determine if an injury or illness is work-related
(i)	checked into a hotel or motel for one or more days.	When a traveling employee checks into a hotel, motel, or into a other temporary residence, he or she establishes a "home away from home." You must evaluate the employee's activities after he or she checks into the hotel, motel, or other temporary residence for their work-relatedness in the same manner as you evaluate the activities of a non-traveling employee. When the employee checks into the temporary residence, he or she is considered to have left the work environment. When the employee begins work each day, he or she re-enters the work environment. If the employee has established a "home away from home" and is reporting to a fixed worksite each day, you also do not consider injuries or illnesses work-related if they occur while the employee is commuting between the temporary residence and the job location.
(ii)	taken a detour for personal reasons.	Injuries or illnesses are not considered work-related if they occur while the employee is on a personal detour from a reasonably direct route of travel (**e.g**, has taken a side trip for personal reasons).

1904.5(b)(7)
How do I decide if a case is work-related when the employee is working at home? Injuries and illnesses that occur while an employee is working at home, including work in a home office, will be considered work-related if the injury or illness occurs while the employee is performing work for pay or compensation in the home, and the injury or illness is directly related to the performance of work rather than

29 CFR OSHA 1904 (continued)

to the general home environment or setting. For example, if an employee drops a box of work documents and injures his or her foot, the case is considered work-related. If an employee's fingernail is punctured by a needle from a sewing machine used to perform garment work at home, becomes infected and requires medical treatment, the injury is considered work-related. If an employee is injured because he or she trips on the family dog while rushing to answer a work phone call, the case is not considered work-related. If an employee working at home is electrocuted because of faulty home wiring, the injury is not considered work-related.

1904.6(a)
Basic requirement. You must consider an injury or illness to be a "new case" if:

1904.6(a)(1)
The employee has not previously experienced a recorded injury or illness of the same type that affects the same part of the body, or

1904.6(a)(2)
The employee previously experienced a recorded injury or illness of the same type that affected the same part of the body but had recovered completely (all signs and symptoms had disappeared) from the previous injury or illness and an event or exposure in the work environment caused the signs or symptoms to reappear.

1904.6(b)
Implementation.

1904.6(b)(1)
When an employee experiences the signs or symptoms of a chronic work-related illness, do I need to consider each recurrence of signs or symptoms to be a new case? No, for occupational illnesses where the signs or symptoms may recur or continue in the absence of an exposure in the workplace, the case must only be recorded once. Examples may include occupational cancer, asbestosis, byssinosis and silicosis.

1904.6(b)(2)
When an employee experiences the signs or symptoms of an injury or illness as a result of an event or exposure in the workplace, such as an episode of occupational asthma, must I treat the episode as a new case? Yes, because the episode or recurrence was caused by an event or exposure in the workplace, the incident must be treated as a new case.

1904.6(b)(3)
May I rely on a physician or other licensed health care professional to determine whether a case is a new case or a recurrence of an old case? You are not required to seek the advice of a physician or other licensed health care professional. However, if you do seek such advice, you must follow the physician or other licensed health care professional's recommendation about whether the case is a new case or a recurrence. If you receive recommendations from two or more physicians or other licensed health care professionals, you must make a decision as to which recommendation is the most authoritative (best documented, best reasoned, or most authoritative), and record the case based upon that recommendation.

1904.7(a)
Basic requirement. You must consider an injury or illness to meet the general recording criteria, and therefore to be recordable, if it results in any of the following: death, days away from work, restricted work or transfer to another job, medical treatment beyond first aid, or loss of consciousness. You must also consider a case to meet the general recording criteria if it involves a significant injury or illness diagnosed by a physician or other licensed health care professional, even if it does not result in death, days away from work, restricted work or job transfer, medical treatment beyond first aid, or loss of consciousness.

1904.7(b)
Implementation.

1904.7(b)(1)
How do I decide if a case meets one or more of the general recording criteria? A work-related injury or illness must be recorded if it results in one or more of the following:

29 CFR OSHA 1904 (continued)

1904.7(b)(1)(i)
Death. See § 1904.7(b)(2).

1904.7(b)(1)(ii)
Days away from work. See § 1904.7(b)(3).

1904.7(b)(1)(iii)
Restricted work or transfer to another job. See § 1904.7(b)(4).

1904.7(b)(1)(iv)
Medical treatment beyond first aid. See § 1904.7(b)(5).

1904.7(b)(1)(v)
Loss of consciousness. See § 1904.7(b)(6).

1904.7(b)(1)(vi)
A significant injury or illness diagnosed by a physician or other licensed health care professional. See § 1904.7(b)(7).

1904.7(b)(2)
How do I record a work-related injury or illness that results in the employee's death? You must record an injury or illness that results in death by entering a check mark on the OSHA 300 Log in the space for cases resulting in death. You must also report any work-related fatality to OSHA within eight (8) hours, as required by § 1904.39.

1904.7(b)(3)
How do I record a work-related injury or illness that results in days away from work? When an injury or illness involves one or more days away from work, you must record the injury or illness on the OSHA 300 Log with a check mark in the space for cases involving days away and an entry of the number of calendar days away from work in the number of days column. If the employee is out for an extended period of time, you must enter an estimate of the days that the employee will be away, and update the day count when the actual number of days is known.

1904.7(b)(3)(i)
Do I count the day on which the injury occurred or the illness began? No, you begin counting days away on the day after the injury occurred or the illness began.

1904.7(b)(3)(ii)
How do I record an injury or illness when a physician or other licensed health care professional recommends that the worker stay at home but the employee comes to work anyway? You must record these injuries and illnesses on the OSHA 300 Log using the check box for cases with days away from work and enter the number of calendar days away recommended by the physician or other licensed health care professional. If a physician or other licensed health care professional recommends days away, you should encourage your employee to follow that recommendation. However, the days away must be recorded whether the injured or ill employee follows the physician or licensed health care professional's recommendation or not. If you receive recommendations from two or more physicians or other licensed health care professionals, you may make a decision as to which recommendation is the most authoritative, and record the case based upon that recommendation.

1904.7(b)(3)(iii)
How do I handle a case when a physician or other licensed health care professional recommends that the worker return to work but the employee stays at home anyway? In this situation, you must end the count of days away from work on the date the physician or other licensed health care professional recommends that the employee return to work.

1904.7(b)(3)(iv)
How do I count weekends, holidays, or other days the employee would not have worked anyway? You must count the number of calendar days the employee was unable to work as a result of the injury or illness, regardless of whether or not the employee was scheduled to work on those day(s). Weekend days,

29 CFR OSHA 1904 (continued)

holidays, vacation days or other days off are included in the total number of days recorded if the employee would not have been able to work on those days because of a work-related injury or illness.

1904.7(b)(3)(v)

How do I record a case in which a worker is injured or becomes ill on a Friday and reports to work on a Monday, and was not scheduled to work on the weekend? You need to record this case only if you receive information from a physician or other licensed health care professional indicating that the employee should not have worked, or should have performed only restricted work, during the weekend. If so, you must record the injury or illness as a case with days away from work or restricted work, and enter the day counts, as appropriate.

1904.7(b)(3)(vi)

How do I record a case in which a worker is injured or becomes ill on the day before scheduled time off such as a holiday, a planned vacation, or a temporary plant closing? You need to record a case of this type only if you receive information from a physician or other licensed health care professional indicating that the employee should not have worked, or should have performed only restricted work, during the scheduled time off. If so, you must record the injury or illness as a case with days away from work or restricted work, and enter the day counts, as appropriate.

1904.7(b)(3)(vii)

Is there a limit to the number of days away from work I must count? Yes, you may "cap" the total days away at 180 calendar days. You are not required to keep track of the number of calendar days away from work if the injury or illness resulted in more than 180 calendar days away from work and/or days of job transfer or restriction. In such a case, entering 180 in the total days away column will be considered adequate.

1904.7(b)(3)(viii)

May I stop counting days if an employee who is away from work because of an injury or illness retires or leaves my company? Yes, if the employee leaves your company for some reason unrelated to the injury or illness, such as retirement, a plant closing, or to take another job, you may stop counting days away from work or days of restriction/job transfer. If the employee leaves your company because of the injury or illness, you must estimate the total number of days away or days of restriction/job transfer and enter the day count on the 300 Log.

1904.7(b)(3)(ix)

If a case occurs in one year but results in days away during the next calendar year, do I record the case in both years? No, you only record the injury or illness once. You must enter the number of calendar days away for the injury or illness on the OSHA 300 Log for the year in which the injury or illness occurred. If the employee is still away from work because of the injury or illness when you prepare the annual summary, estimate the total number of calendar days you expect the employee to be away from work, use this number to calculate the total for the annual summary, and then update the initial log entry later when the day count is known or reaches the 180-day cap.

1904.7(b)(4)

How do I record a work-related injury or illness that results in restricted work or job transfer? When an injury or illness involves restricted work or job transfer but does not involve death or days away from work, you must record the injury or illness on the OSHA 300 Log by placing a check mark in the space for job transfer or restriction and an entry of the number of restricted or transferred days in the restricted workdays column.

1904.7(b)(4)(i)

How do I decide if the injury or illness resulted in restricted work? Restricted work occurs when, as the result of a work-related injury or illness:

1904.7(b)(4)(i)(A)

You keep the employee from performing one or more of the routine functions of his or her job, or from working the full workday that he or she would otherwise have been scheduled to work; or

29 CFR OSHA 1904 (continued)

1904.7(b)(4)(i)(B)
A physician or other licensed health care professional recommends that the employee not perform one or more of the routine functions of his or her job, or not work the full workday that he or she would otherwise have been scheduled to work.

1904.7(b)(4)(ii)
What is meant by "routine functions"? For recordkeeping purposes, an employee's routine functions are those work activities the employee regularly performs at least once per week.

1904.7(b)(4)(iii)
Do I have to record restricted work or job transfer if it applies only to the day on which the injury occurred or the illness began? No, you do not have to record restricted work or job transfers if you, or the physician or other licensed health care professional, impose the restriction or transfer only for the day on which the injury occurred or the illness began.

1904.7(b)(4)(iv)
If you or a physician or other licensed health care professional recommends a work restriction, is the injury or illness automatically recordable as a "restricted work" case? No, a recommended work restriction is recordable only if it affects one or more of the employee's routine job functions. To determine whether this is the case, you must evaluate the restriction in light of the routine functions of the injured or ill employee's job. If the restriction from you or the physician or other licensed health care professional keeps the employee from performing one or more of his or her routine job functions, or from working the full workday the injured or ill employee would otherwise have worked, the employee's work has been restricted and you must record the case.

1904.7(b)(4)(v)
How do I record a case where the worker works only for a partial work shift because of a work-related injury or illness? A partial day of work is recorded as a day of job transfer or restriction for recordkeeping purposes, except for the day on which the injury occurred or the illness began.

1904.7(b)(4)(vi)
If the injured or ill worker produces fewer goods or services than he or she would have produced prior to the injury or illness but otherwise performs all of the routine functions of his or her work, is the case considered a restricted work case? No, the case is considered restricted work only if the worker does not perform all of the routine functions of his or her job or does not work the full shift that he or she would otherwise have worked.

1904.7(b)(4)(vii)
How do I handle vague restrictions from a physician or other licensed health care professional, such as that the employee engage only in "light duty" or "take it easy for a week"? If you are not clear about the physician or other licensed health care professional's recommendation, you may ask that person whether the employee can do all of his or her routine job functions and work all of his or her normally assigned work shift. If the answer to both of these questions is "Yes," then the case does not involve a work restriction and does not have to be recorded as such. If the answer to one or both of these questions is "No," the case involves restricted work and must be recorded as a restricted work case. If you are unable to obtain this additional information from the physician or other licensed health care professional who recommended the restriction, record the injury or illness as a case involving restricted work.

1904.7(b)(4)(viii)
What do I do if a physician or other licensed health care professional recommends a job restriction meeting OSHA's definition, but the employee does all of his or her routine job functions anyway? You must record the injury or illness on the OSHA 300 Log as a restricted work case. If a physician or other licensed health care professional recommends a job restriction, you should ensure that the employee complies with that restriction. If you receive recommendations from two or more physicians or other licensed health care professionals, you may make a decision as to which recommendation is the most authoritative, and record the case based upon that recommendation.

1904.7(b)(4)(ix)
How do I decide if an injury or illness involved a transfer to another job? If you assign an injured or ill employee to a job other than his or her regular job for part of the day, the case involves transfer to another job. Note: This does not include the day on which the injury or illness occurred.

29 CFR OSHA 1904 (continued)

1904.7(b)(4)(x)

Are transfers to another job recorded in the same way as restricted work cases? Yes, both job transfer and restricted work cases are recorded in the same box on the OSHA 300 Log. For example, if you assign, or a physician or other licensed health care professional recommends that you assign, an injured or ill worker to his or her routine job duties for part of the day and to another job for the rest of the day, the injury or illness involves a job transfer. You must record an injury or illness that involves a job transfer by placing a check in the box for job transfer.

1904.7(b)(4)(xi)

How do I count days of job transfer or restriction? You count days of job transfer or restriction in the same way you count days away from work, using § 1904.7(b)(3)(i) to (viii), above. The only difference is that, if you permanently assign the injured or ill employee to a job that has been modified or permanently changed in a manner that eliminates the routine functions the employee was restricted from performing, you may stop the day count when the modification or change is made permanent. You must count at least one day of restricted work or job transfer for such cases.

1904.7(b)(5)

How do I record an injury or illness that involves medical treatment beyond first aid? If a work-related injury or illness results in medical treatment beyond first aid, you must record it on the OSHA 300 Log. If the injury or illness did not involve death, one or more days away from work, one or more days of restricted work, or one or more days of job transfer, you enter a check mark in the box for cases where the employee received medical treatment but remained at work and was not transferred or restricted.

1904.7(b)(5)(i)

What is the definition of medical treatment? "Medical treatment" means the management and care of a patient to combat disease or disorder. For the purposes of Part 1904, medical treatment does not include:

1904.7(b)(5)(i)(A)

Visits to a physician or other licensed health care professional solely for observation or counseling;

1904.7(b)(5)(i)(B)

The conduct of diagnostic procedures, such as x-rays and blood tests, including the administration of prescription medications used solely for diagnostic purposes (***e.g.***, eye drops to dilate pupils); or

1904.7(b)(5)(i)(C)

"First aid" as defined in paragraph (b)(5)(ii) of this section.

1904.7(b)(5)(ii)

What is "first aid"? For the purposes of Part 1904, "first aid" means the following:

1904.7(b)(5)(ii)(A)

Using a non-prescription medication at nonprescription strength (for medications available in both prescription and non-prescription form, a recommendation by a physician or other licensed health care professional to use a non-prescription medication at prescription strength is considered medical treatment for recordkeeping purposes);

1904.7(b)(5)(ii)(B)

Administering tetanus immunizations (other immunizations, such as Hepatitis B vaccine or rabies vaccine, are considered medical treatment);

1904.7(b)(5)(ii)(C)

Cleaning, flushing or soaking wounds on the surface of the skin;

1904.7(b)(5)(ii)(D)

Using wound coverings such as bandages, Band-Aids™, gauze pads, etc.; or using butterfly bandages or Steri-Strips™ (other wound closing devices such as sutures, staples, etc., are considered medical treatment);

1904.7(b)(5)(ii)(E)

Using hot or cold therapy;

29 CFR OSHA 1904 (continued)

1904.7(b)(5)(ii)(F)
Using any non-rigid means of support, such as elastic bandages, wraps, non-rigid back belts, etc. (devices with rigid stays or other systems designed to immobilize parts of the body are considered medical treatment for recordkeeping purposes);

1904.7(b)(5)(ii)(G)
Using temporary immobilization devices while transporting an accident victim (*e.g.*, splints, slings, neck collars, back boards, etc.).

1904.7(b)(5)(ii)(H)
Drilling of a fingernail or toenail to relieve pressure, or draining fluid from a blister;

1904.7(b)(5)(ii)(I)
Using eye patches;

1904.7(b)(5)(ii)(J)
Removing foreign bodies from the eye using only irrigation or a cotton swab;

1904.7(b)(5)(ii)(K)
Removing splinters or foreign material from areas other than the eye by irrigation, tweezers, cotton swabs or other simple means;

1904.7(b)(5)(ii)(L)
Using finger guards;

1904.7(b)(5)(ii)(M)
Using massages (physical therapy or chiropractic treatment are considered medical treatment for recordkeeping purposes); or

1904.7(b)(5)(ii)(N)
Drinking fluids for relief of heat stress.

1904.7(b)(5)(iii)
Are any other procedures included in first aid? No, this is a complete list of all treatments considered first aid for Part 1904 purposes.

1904.7(b)(5)(iv)
Does the professional status of the person providing the treatment have any effect on what is considered first aid or medical treatment? No, OSHA considers the treatments listed in § 1904.7(b)(5)(ii) of this Part to be first aid regardless of the professional status of the person providing the treatment. Even when these treatments are provided by a physician or other licensed health care professional, they are considered first aid for the purposes of Part 1904. Similarly, OSHA considers treatment beyond first aid to be medical treatment even when it is provided by someone other than a physician or other licensed health care professional.

1904.7(b)(5)(v)
What if a physician or other licensed health care professional recommends medical treatment but the employee does not follow the recommendation? If a physician or other licensed health care professional recommends medical treatment, you should encourage the injured or ill employee to follow that recommendation. However, you must record the case even if the injured or ill employee does not follow the physician or other licensed health care professional's recommendation.

1904.7(b)(6)
Is every work-related injury or illness case involving a loss of consciousness recordable? Yes, you must record a work-related injury or illness if the worker becomes unconscious, regardless of the length of time the employee remains unconscious.

29 CFR OSHA 1904 (continued)

1904.7(b)(7)
What is a "significant" diagnosed injury or illness that is recordable under the general criteria even if it does not result in death, days away from work, restricted work or job transfer, medical treatment beyond first aid, or loss of consciousness? Work-related cases involving cancer, chronic irreversible disease, a fractured or cracked bone, or a punctured eardrum must always be recorded under the general criteria at the time of diagnosis by a physician or other licensed health care professional.

Note to § 1904.7: OSHA believes that most significant injuries and illnesses will result in one of the criteria listed in § 1904.7(a): death, days away from work, restricted work or job transfer, medical treatment beyond first aid, or loss of consciousness. However, there are some significant injuries, such as a punctured eardrum or a fractured toe or rib, for which neither medical treatment nor work restrictions may be recommended. In addition, there are some significant progressive diseases, such as byssinosis, silicosis, and some types of cancer, for which medical treatment or work restrictions may not be recommended at the time of diagnosis but are likely to be recommended as the disease progresses. OSHA believes that cancer, chronic irreversible diseases, fractured or cracked bones, and punctured eardrums are generally considered significant injuries and illnesses, and must be recorded at the initial diagnosis even if medical treatment or work restrictions are not recommended, or are postponed, in a particular case.

1904.8(a)
Basic requirement. You must record all work-related needlestick injuries and cuts from sharp objects that are contaminated with another person's blood or other potentially infectious material (as defined by 29 CFR 1910.1030). You must enter the case on the OSHA 300 Log as an injury. To protect the employee's privacy, you may not enter the employee's name on the OSHA 300 Log (see the requirements for privacy cases in paragraphs 1904.29(b)(6) through 1904.29(b)(9)).

1904.8(b)
Implementation.

1904.8(b)(1)
What does "other potentially infectious material" mean? The term "other potentially infectious materials" is defined in the OSHA Bloodborne Pathogens standard at § 1910.1030(b). These materials include:

1904.8(b)(1)(i)
Human bodily fluids, tissues and organs, and

1904.8(b)(1)(ii)
Other materials infected with the HIV or hepatitis B (HBV) virus such as laboratory cultures or tissues from experimental animals.

1904.8(b)(2)
Does this mean that I must record all cuts, lacerations, punctures, and scratches? No, you need to record cuts, lacerations, punctures, and scratches only if they are work-related and involve contamination with another person's blood or other potentially infectious material. If the cut, laceration, or scratch involves a clean object, or a contaminant other than blood or other potentially infectious material, you need to record the case only if it meets one or more of the recording criteria in § 1904.7.

1904.8(b)(3)
If I record an injury and the employee is later diagnosed with an infectious bloodborne disease, do I need to update the OSHA 300 Log? Yes, you must update the classification of the case on the OSHA 300 Log if the case results in death, days away from work, restricted work, or job transfer. You must also update the description to identify the infectious disease and change the classification of the case from an injury to an illness.

1904.8(b)(4)
What if one of my employees is splashed or exposed to blood or other potentially infectious material without being cut or scratched? Do I need to record this incident? You need to record such an incident on the OSHA 300 Log as an illness if:

1904.8(b)(4)(i)
It results in the diagnosis of a bloodborne illness, such as HIV, hepatitis B, or hepatitis C; or
1904.8(b)(4)(ii)

It meets one or more of the recording criteria in § 1904.7.

29 CFR OSHA 1904 (continued)

1904.9(a)
Basic requirement. If an employee is medically removed under the medical surveillance requirements of an OSHA standard, you must record the case on the OSHA 300 Log.

1904.9(b)
Implementation.

1904.9(b)(1)
How do I classify medical removal cases on the OSHA 300 Log? You must enter each medical removal case on the OSHA 300 Log as either a case involving days away from work or a case involving restricted work activity, depending on how you decide to comply with the medical removal requirement. If the medical removal is the result of a chemical exposure, you must enter the case on the OSHA 300 Log by checking the "poisoning" column.

1904.9(b)(2)
Do all of OSHA's standards have medical removal provisions? No, some OSHA standards, such as the standards covering bloodborne pathogens and noise, do not have medical removal provisions. Many OSHA standards that cover specific chemical substances have medical removal provisions. These standards include, but are not limited to, lead, cadmium, methylene chloride, formaldehyde, and benzene.

1904.9(b)(3)
Do I have to record a case where I voluntarily removed the employee from exposure before the medical removal criteria in an OSHA standard are met? No, if the case involves voluntary medical removal before the medical removal levels required by an OSHA standard, you do not need to record the case on the OSHA 300 Log.

1904.10(a)
Basic requirement. If an employee's hearing test (audiogram) reveals that the employee has experienced a work-related Standard Threshold Shift (STS) in hearing in one or both ears, and the employee's total hearing level is 25 decibels (dB) or more above audiometric zero (averaged at 2000, 3000, and 4000 Hz) in the same ear(s) as the STS, you must record the case on the OSHA 300 Log.

1904.10(b)
Implementation.

1904.10(b)(1)
What is a Standard Threshold Shift? A Standard Threshold Shift, or STS, is defined in the occupational noise exposure standard at 29 CFR 1910.95(g)(10)(i) as a change in hearing threshold, relative to the baseline audiogram for that employee, of an average of 10 decibels (dB) or more at 2000, 3000, and 4000 hertz (Hz) in one or both ears.

1904.10(b)(2)
How do I evaluate the current audiogram to determine whether an employee has an STS and a 25-dB hearing level?

1904.10(b)(2)(i)
STS. If the employee has never previously experienced a recordable hearing loss, you must compare the employee's current audiogram with that employee's baseline audiogram. If the employee has previously experienced a recordable hearing loss, you must compare the employee's current audiogram with the employee's revised baseline audiogram (the audiogram reflecting the employee's previous recordable hearing loss case).

1904.10(b)(2)(ii)
25-dB loss. Audiometric test results reflect the employee's overall hearing ability in comparison to audiometric zero. Therefore, using the employee's current audiogram, you must use the average hearing level at 2000, 3000, and 4000 Hz to determine whether or not the employee's total hearing level is 25 dB or more.

29 CFR OSHA 1904 (continued)

1904.10(b)(3)

May I adjust the current audiogram to reflect the effects of aging on hearing? Yes. When you are determining whether an STS has occurred, you may age adjust the employee's current audiogram results by using Tables F-1 or F-2, as appropriate, in Appendix F of 29 CFR 1910.95. You may not use an age adjustment when determining whether the employee's total hearing level is 25 dB or more above audiometric zero.

1904.10(b)(4)

Do I have to record the hearing loss if I am going to retest the employee's hearing? No, if you retest the employee's hearing within 30 days of the first test, and the retest does not confirm the recordable STS, you are not required to record the hearing loss case on the OSHA 300 Log. If the retest confirms the recordable STS, you must record the hearing loss illness within seven (7) calendar days of the retest. If subsequent audiometric testing performed under the testing requirements of the § 1910.95 noise standard indicates that an STS is not persistent, you may erase or line-out the recorded entry.

1904.10(b)(5)

Are there any special rules for determining whether a hearing loss case is work-related? No. You must use the rules in § 1904.5 to determine if the hearing loss is work-related. If an event or exposure in the work environment either caused or contributed to the hearing loss, or significantly aggravated a pre-existing hearing loss, you must consider the case to be work related.

1904.10(b)(6)

If a physician or other licensed health care professional determines the hearing loss is not work-related, do I still need to record the case? If a physician or other licensed health care professional determines that the hearing loss is not work-related or has not been significantly aggravated by occupational noise exposure, you are not required to consider the case work-related or to record the case on the OSHA 300 Log.

1904.10(b)(7)

How do I complete the 300 Log for a hearing loss case? When you enter a recordable hearing loss case on the OSHA 300 Log, you must check the 300 Log column for hearing loss. (Note: § 1904.10(b)(7) is effective beginning January 1, 2004.)

1904.11(a)

Basic requirement. If any of your employees has been occupationally exposed to anyone with a known case of active tuberculosis (TB), and that employee subsequently develops a tuberculosis infection, as evidenced by a positive skin test or diagnosis by a physician or other licensed health care professional, you must record the case on the OSHA 300 Log by checking the "respiratory condition" column.

1904.11(b)

Implementation.

1904.11(b)(1)

Do I have to record, on the Log, a positive TB skin test result obtained at a pre-employment physical? No, you do not have to record it because the employee was not occupationally exposed to a known case of active tuberculosis in your workplace.

1904.11(b)(2)

(May I line-out or erase a recorded TB case if I obtain evidence that the case was not caused by occupational exposure?) Yes, you may line-out or erase the case from the Log under the following circumstances:

1904.11(b)(2)(i)

The worker is living in a household with a person who has been diagnosed with active TB;

1904.11(b)(2)(ii)

The Public Health Department has identified the worker as a contact of an individual with a case of active TB unrelated to the workplace; or

29 CFR OSHA 1904 (continued)

1904.11(b)(2)(iii)
A medical investigation shows that the employee's infection was caused by exposure to TB away from work, or proves that the case was not related to the workplace TB exposure.

1904.29(a)
Basic requirement. You must use OSHA 300, 300-A, and 301 forms, or equivalent forms, for recordable injuries and illnesses. The OSHA 300 form is called the Log of Work-Related Injuries and Illnesses, the 300-A is the Summary of Work-Related Injuries and Illnesses, and the OSHA 301 form is called the Injury and Illness Incident Report.

1904.29(b)
Implementation.

1904.29(b)(1)
What do I need to do to complete the OSHA 300 Log? You must enter information about your business at the top of the OSHA 300 Log, enter a one or two line description for each recordable injury or illness, and summarize this information on the OSHA 300-A at the end of the year.

1904.29(b)(2)
What do I need to do to complete the OSHA 301 Incident Report? You must complete an OSHA 301 Incident Report form, or an equivalent form, for each recordable injury or illness entered on the OSHA 300 Log.

1904.29(b)(3)
How quickly must each injury or illness be recorded? You must enter each recordable injury or illness on the OSHA 300 Log and 301 Incident Report within seven (7) calendar days of receiving information that a recordable injury or illness has occurred.

1904.29(b)(4)
What is an equivalent form? An equivalent form is one that has the same information, is as readable and understandable, and is completed using the same instructions as the OSHA form it replaces. Many employers use an insurance form instead of the OSHA 301 Incident Report, or supplement an insurance form by adding any additional information required by OSHA.

1904.29(b)(5)
May I keep my records on a computer? Yes, if the computer can produce equivalent forms when they are needed, as described under §§ 1904.35 and 1904.40, you may keep your records using the computer system.

1904.29(b)(6)
Are there situations where I do not put the employee's name on the forms for privacy reasons? Yes, if you have a "privacy concern case," you may not enter the employee's name on the OSHA 300 Log. Instead, enter "privacy case" in the space normally used for the employee's name. This will protect the privacy of the injured or ill employee when another employee, a former employee, or an authorized employee representative is provided access to the OSHA 300 Log under § 1904.35(b)(2). You must keep a separate, confidential list of the case numbers and employee names for your privacy concern cases so you can update the cases and provide the information to the government if asked to do so.

1904.29(b)(7)
How do I determine if an injury or illness is a privacy concern case? You must consider the following injuries or illnesses to be privacy concern cases:

1904.29(b)(7)(i)
An injury or illness to an intimate body part or the reproductive system;

1904.29(b)(7)(ii)
An injury or illness resulting from a sexual assault;

1904.29(b)(7)(iii)
Mental illnesses;

29 CFR OSHA 1904 (continued)

1904.29(b)(7)(iv)
HIV infection, hepatitis, or tuberculosis;

1904.29(b)(7)(v)
Needlestick injuries and cuts from sharp objects that are contaminated with another person's blood or other potentially infectious material (see § 1904.8 for definitions); and

1904.29(b)(7)(vi)
Other illnesses, if the employee voluntarily requests that his or her name not be entered on the log.

1904.29(b)(8)
May I classify any other types of injuries and illnesses as privacy concern cases? No, this is a complete list of all injuries and illnesses considered privacy concern cases for Part 1904 purposes.

1904.29(b)(9)
If I have removed the employee's name, but still believe that the employee may be identified from the information on the forms, is there anything else that I can do to further protect the employee's privacy? Yes, if you have a reasonable basis to believe that information describing the privacy concern case may be personally identifiable even though the employee's name has been omitted, you may use discretion in describing the injury or illness on both the OSHA 300 and 301 forms. You must enter enough information to identify the cause of the incident and the general severity of the injury or illness, but you do not need to include details of an intimate or private nature. For example, a sexual assault case could be described as "injury from assault," or an injury to a reproductive organ could be described as "lower abdominal injury."

1904.29(b)(10)
What must I do to protect employee privacy if I wish to provide access to the OSHA Forms 300 and 301 to persons other than government representatives, employees, former employees or authorized representatives? If you decide to voluntarily disclose the Forms to persons other than government representatives, employees, former employees or authorized representatives (as required by §§ 1904.35 and 1904.40), you must remove or hide the employees' names and other personally identifying information, except for the following cases. You may disclose the Forms with personally identifying information only:

1904.29(b)(10)(i)
to an auditor or consultant hired by the employer to evaluate the safety and health program;

1904.29(b)(10)(ii)
to the extent necessary for processing a claim for workers' compensation or other insurance benefits; or

1904.29(b)(10)(iii)
to a public health authority or law enforcement agency for uses and disclosures for which consent, an authorization, or opportunity to agree or object is not required under Department of Health and Human Services Standards for Privacy of Individually Identifiable Health Information, 45 CFR 164.512.

1904.30(a)
Basic requirement. You must keep a separate OSHA 300 Log for each establishment that is expected to be in operation for one year or longer.

1904.30(b)
Implementation.

1904.30(b)(1)
Do I need to keep OSHA injury and illness records for short-term establishments (i.e., establishments that will exist for less than a year)? Yes, however, you do not have to keep a separate OSHA 300 Log for each such establishment. You may keep one OSHA 300 Log that covers all of your short-term establishments. You may also include the short-term establishments' recordable injuries and illnesses on an OSHA 300 Log that covers short-term establishments for individual company divisions or geographic regions.

29 CFR OSHA 1904 (continued)

1904.30(b)(2)
May I keep the records for all of my establishments at my headquarters location or at some other central location? Yes, you may keep the records for an establishment at your headquarters or other central location if you can:

1904.30(b)(2)(i)
Transmit information about the injuries and illnesses from the establishment to the central location within seven (7) calendar days of receiving information that a recordable injury or illness has occurred; and

1904.30(b)(2)(ii)
Produce and send the records from the central location to the establishment within the time frames required by § 1904.35 and § 1904.40 when you are required to provide records to a government representative, employees, former employees or employee representatives.

1904.30(b)(3)
Some of my employees work at several different locations or do not work at any of my establishments at all. How do I record cases for these employees? You must link each of your employees with one of your establishments, for recordkeeping purposes. You must record the injury and illness on the OSHA 300 Log of the injured or ill employee's establishment, or on an OSHA 300 Log that covers that employee's short-term establishment.

1904.30(b)(4)
How do I record an injury or illness when an employee of one of my establishments is injured or becomes ill while visiting or working at another of my establishments, or while working away from any of my establishments? If the injury or illness occurs at one of your establishments, you must record the injury or illness on the OSHA 300 Log of the establishment at which the injury or illness occurred. If the employee is injured or becomes ill and is not at one of your establishments, you must record the case on the OSHA 300 Log at the establishment at which the employee normally works.

1904.31(a)
Basic requirement. You must record on the OSHA 300 Log the recordable injuries and illnesses of all employees on your payroll, whether they are labor, executive, hourly, salary, part-time, seasonal, or migrant workers. You also must record the recordable injuries and illnesses that occur to employees who are not on your payroll if you supervise these employees on a day-to-day basis. If your business is organized as a sole proprietorship or partnership, the owner or partners are not considered employees for recordkeeping purposes.

1904.31(b)
Implementation.

1904.31(b)(1)
If a self-employed person is injured or becomes ill while doing work at my business, do I need to record the injury or illness? No, self-employed individuals are not covered by the OSH Act or this regulation.

1904.31(b)(2)
If I obtain employees from a temporary help service, employee leasing service, or personnel supply service, do I have to record an injury or illness occurring to one of those employees? You must record these injuries and illnesses if you supervise these employees on a day-to-day basis.

1904.31(b)(3)
If an employee in my establishment is a contractor's employee, must I record an injury or illness occurring to that employee? If the contractor's employee is under the day-to-day supervision of the contractor, the contractor is responsible for recording the injury or illness. If you supervise the contractor employee's work on a day-to-day basis, you must record the injury or illness.

1904.31(b)(4)
Must the personnel supply service, temporary help service, employee leasing service, or contractor also record the injuries or illnesses occurring to temporary, leased or contract employees that I supervise on a day-to-day basis? No, you and the temporary help service, employee leasing service, personnel supply service, or contractor should coordinate your efforts to make sure that each injury and

29 CFR OSHA 1904 (continued)

illness is recorded only once: either on your OSHA 300 Log (if you provide day-to-day supervision) or on the other employer's OSHA 300 Log (if that company provides day-to-day supervision).

1904.32(a)
Basic requirement. At the end of each calendar year, you must:

1904.32(a)(1)
Review the OSHA 300 Log to verify that the entries are complete and accurate, and correct any deficiencies identified;

1904.32(a)(2)
Create an annual summary of injuries and illnesses recorded on the OSHA 300 Log;

1904.32(a)(3)
Certify the summary; and

1904.32(a)(4)
Post the annual summary.

1904.32(b)
Implementation.

1904.32(b)(1)
How extensively do I have to review the OSHA 300 Log entries at the end of the year? You must review the entries as extensively as necessary to make sure that they are complete and correct.

1904.32(b)(2)
How do I complete the annual summary? You must:

1904.32(b)(2)(i)
Total the columns on the OSHA 300 Log (if you had no recordable cases, enter zeros for each column total); and

1904.32(b)(2)(ii)
Enter the calendar year covered, the company's name, establishment name, establishment address, annual average number of employees covered by the OSHA 300 Log, and the total hours worked by all employees covered by the OSHA 300 Log.

1904.32(b)(2)(iii)
If you are using an equivalent form other than the OSHA 300-A summary form, as permitted under § 1904.6(b)(4), the summary you use must also include the employee access and employer penalty statements found on the OSHA 300-A Summary form.

1904.32(b)(3)
How do I certify the annual summary? A company executive must certify that he or she has examined the OSHA 300 Log and that he or she reasonably believes, based on his or her knowledge of the process by which the information was recorded, that the annual summary is correct and complete.

1904.32(b)(4)
Who is considered a company executive? The company executive who certifies the log must be one of the following persons:

1904.32(b)(4)(i)
An owner of the company (only if the company is a sole proprietorship or partnership);

1904.32(b)(4)(ii)
An officer of the corporation;

1904.32(b)(4)(iii)
The highest ranking company official working at the establishment; or

29 CFR OSHA 1904 (continued)

1904.32(b)(4)(iv)
The immediate supervisor of the highest ranking company official working at the establishment.

1904.32(b)(5)
How do I post the annual summary? You must post a copy of the annual summary in each establishment in a conspicuous place or places where notices to employees are customarily posted. You must ensure that the posted annual summary is not altered, defaced or covered by other material.

1904.32(b)(6)
When do I have to post the annual summary? You must post the summary no later than February 1 of the year following the year covered by the records and keep the posting in place until April 30.

1904.33(a)
Basic requirement. You must save the OSHA 300 Log, the privacy case list (if one exists), the annual summary, and the OSHA 301 Incident Report forms for five (5) years following the end of the calendar year that these records cover.

1904.33(b)
Implementation.

1904.33(b)(1)
Do I have to update the OSHA 300 Log during the five-year storage period? Yes, during the storage period, you must update your stored OSHA 300 Logs to include newly discovered recordable injuries or illnesses and to show any changes that have occurred in the classification of previously recorded injuries and illnesses. If the description or outcome of a case changes, you must remove or line out the original entry and enter the new information.

1904.33(b)(2)
Do I have to update the annual summary? No, you are not required to update the annual summary, but you may do so if you wish.

1904.33(b)(3)
Do I have to update the OSHA 301 Incident Reports? No, you are not required to update the OSHA 301 Incident Reports, but you may do so if you wish.

1904.34
If your business changes ownership, you are responsible for recording and reporting work-related injuries and il only for that period of the year during which you owned the establishment. You must transfer the Part 1904 rec the new owner. The new owner must save all records of the establishment kept by the prior owner, as required 1904.33 of this Part, but need not update or correct the records of the prior owner.

1904.35(a)
Basic requirement. Your employees and their representatives must be involved in the recordkeeping system in several ways.

1904.35(a)(1)
You must inform each employee of how he or she is to report an injury or illness to you.

1904.35(a)(2)
You must provide limited access to your injury and illness records for your employees and their representatives.

1904.35(b)
Implementation.

1904.35(b)(1)
What must I do to make sure that employees report work-related injuries and illnesses to me?

29 CFR OSHA 1904 (continued)

1904.35(b)(1)(i)

You must set up a way for employees to report work-related injuries and illnesses promptly; and

1904.35(b)(1)(ii)

You must tell each employee how to report work-related injuries and illnesses to you.

1904.35(b)(2)

Do I have to give my employees and their representatives access to the OSHA injury and illness records? Yes, your employees, former employees, their personal representatives, and their authorized employee representatives have the right to access the OSHA injury and illness records, with some limitations, as discussed below.

1904.35(b)(2)(i)

Who is an authorized employee representative? An authorized employee representative is an authorized collective bargaining agent of employees.

1904.35(b)(2)(ii)

Who is a "personal representative" of an employee or former employee? A personal representative is:

1904.35(b)(2)(ii)(A)

Any person that the employee or former employee designates as such, in writing; or

1904.35(b)(2)(ii)(B)

The legal representative of a deceased or legally incapacitated employee or former employee.

1904.35(b)(2)(iii)

If an employee or representative asks for access to the OSHA 300 Log, when do I have to provide it? When an employee, former employee, personal representative, or authorized employee representative asks for copies of your current or stored OSHA 300 Log(s) for an establishment the employee or former employee has worked in, you must give the requester a copy of the relevant OSHA 300 Log(s) by the end of the next business day.

1904.35(b)(2)(iv)

May I remove the names of the employees or any other information from the OSHA 300 Log before I give copies to an employee, former employee, or employee representative? No, you must leave the names on the 300 Log. However, to protect the privacy of injured and ill employees, you may not record the employee's name on the OSHA 300 Log for certain "privacy concern cases," as specified in paragraphs 1904.29(b)(6) through 1904.29(b)(9).

1904.35(b)(2)(v)

If an employee or representative asks for access to the OSHA 301 Incident Report, when do I have to provide it?

1904.35(b)(2)(v)(A)

When an employee, former employee, or personal representative asks for a copy of the OSHA 301 Incident Report describing an injury or illness to that employee or former employee, you must give the requester a copy of the OSHA 301 Incident Report containing that information by the end of the next business day.

1904.35(b)(2)(v)(B)

When an authorized employee representative asks for a copies of the OSHA 301 Incident Reports for an establishment where the agent represents employees under a collective bargaining agreement, you must give copies of those forms to the authorized employee representative within 7 calendar days. You are only required to give the authorized employee representative information from the OSHA 301 Incident Report section titled "Tell us about the case." You must remove all other information from the copy of the OSHA 301 Incident Report or the equivalent substitute form that you give to the authorized employee representative.

1904.35(b)(2)(vi)

May I charge for the copies? No, you may not charge for these copies the first time they are provided. However, if one of the designated persons asks for additional copies, you may assess a reasonable charge for retrieving and copying the records.

29 CFR OSHA 1904 (continued)

1904.36

Section 11(c) of the Act prohibits you from discriminating against an employee for reporting a work-related fatality, injury or illness. That provision of the Act also protects the employee who files a safety and health complaint, asks for access to the Part 1904 records, or otherwise exercises any rights afforded by the OSH Act.

1904.37(a)

Basic requirement. Some States operate their own OSHA programs, under the authority of a State Plan approved by OSHA. States operating OSHA-approved State Plans must have occupational injury and illness recording and reporting requirements that are substantially identical to the requirements in this Part (see 29 CFR 1902.3(k), 29 CFR 1952.4 and 29 CFR 1956.10(i)).

1904.37(b)

Implementation.

1904.37(b)(1)

State-Plan States must have the same requirements as Federal OSHA for determining which injuries and illnesses are recordable and how they are recorded.

1904.37(b)(2)

For other Part 1904 provisions (for example, industry exemptions, reporting of fatalities and hospitalizations, record retention, or employee involvement), State-Plan State requirements may be more stringent than or supplemental to the Federal requirements, but because of the unique nature of the national recordkeeping program, States must consult with and obtain approval of any such requirements.

1904.37(b)(3)

Although State and local government employees are not covered Federally, all State-Plan States must provide coverage, and must develop injury and illness statistics, for these workers. State Plan recording and reporting requirements for State and local government entities may differ from those for the private sector but must meet the requirements of paragraphs 1904.37(b)(1) and (b)(2).

1904.37(b)(4)

A State-Plan State may not issue a variance to a private sector employer and must recognize all variances issued by Federal OSHA.

1904.37(b)(5)

A State Plan State may only grant an injury and illness recording and reporting variance to a State or local government employer within the State after obtaining approval to grant the variance from Federal OSHA.

1904.38(a)

Basic requirement. If you wish to keep records in a different manner from the manner prescribed by the Part 1904 regulations, you may submit a variance petition to the Assistant Secretary of Labor for Occupational Safety and Health, U.S. Department of Labor, Washington, DC 20210. You can obtain a variance only if you can show that your alternative recordkeeping system:

1904.38(a)(1)

Collects the same information as this Part requires;

1904.38(a)(2)

Meets the purposes of the Act; and

1904.38(a)(3)

Does not interfere with the administration of the Act.

1904.38(b)

Implementation.

1904.38(b)(1)

What do I need to include in my variance petition? You must include the following items in your petition:

29 CFR OSHA 1904 (continued)

1904.38(b)(1)(i)
Your name and address;

1904.38(b)(1)(ii)
A list of the State(s) where the variance would be used;

1904.38(b)(1)(iii)
The address(es) of the business establishment(s) involved;

1904.38(b)(1)(iv)
A description of why you are seeking a variance;

1904.38(b)(1)(v)
A description of the different recordkeeping procedures you propose to use;

1904.38(b)(1)(vi)
A description of how your proposed procedures will collect the same information as would be collected by this Part and achieve the purpose of the Act; and

1904.38(b)(1)(vii)
A statement that you have informed your employees of the petition by giving them or their authorized representative a copy of the petition and by posting a statement summarizing the petition in the same way as notices are posted under § 1903.2(a).

1904.38(b)(2)
How will the Assistant Secretary handle my variance petition? The Assistant Secretary will take the following steps to process your variance petition.

1904.38(b)(2)(i)
The Assistant Secretary will offer your employees and their authorized representatives an opportunity to submit written data, views, and arguments about your variance petition.

1904.38(b)(2)(ii)
The Assistant Secretary may allow the public to comment on your variance petition by publishing the petition in the **Federal Register**. If the petition is published, the notice will establish a public comment period and may include a schedule for a public meeting on the petition.

1904.38(b)(2)(iii)
After reviewing your variance petition and any comments from your employees and the public, the Assistant Secretary will decide whether or not your proposed recordkeeping procedures will meet the purposes of the Act, will not otherwise interfere with the Act, and will provide the same information as the Part 1904 regulations provide. If your procedures meet these criteria, the Assistant Secretary may grant the variance subject to such conditions as he or she finds appropriate.

1904.38(b)(2)(iv)
If the Assistant Secretary grants your variance petition, OSHA will publish a notice in the **Federal Register** to announce the variance. The notice will include the practices the variance allows you to use, any conditions that apply, and the reasons for allowing the variance.

1904.38(b)(3)
If I apply for a variance, may I use my proposed recordkeeping procedures while the Assistant Secretary is processing the variance petition? No, alternative recordkeeping practices are only allowed after the variance is approved. You must comply with the Part 1904 regulations while the Assistant Secretary is reviewing your variance petition.

1904.38(b)(4)
If I have already been cited by OSHA for not following the Part 1904 regulations, will my variance petition have any effect on the citation and penalty? No, in addition, the Assistant Secretary may elect not to review your variance petition if it includes an element for which you have been cited and the citation is still under review by a court, an Administrative Law Judge (ALJ), or the OSH Review Commission.

29 CFR OSHA 1904 (continued)

1904.38(b)(5)
If I receive a variance, may the Assistant Secretary revoke the variance at a later date? Yes, the Assistant Secretary may revoke your variance if he or she has good cause. The procedures revoking a variance will follow the same process as OSHA uses for reviewing variance petitions, as outlined in paragraph 1904.38(b)(2). Except in cases of willfulness or where necessary for public safety, the Assistant Secretary will:

1904.38(b)(5)(i)
Notify you in writing of the facts or conduct that may warrant revocation of your variance; and

1904.38(b)(5)(ii)
Provide you, your employees, and authorized employee representatives with an opportunity to participate in the revocation procedures.

1904.39(a)
Basic requirement. Within eight (8) hours after the death of any employee from a work-related incident or the in-patient hospitalization of three or more employees as a result of a work-related incident, you must orally report the fatality/multiple hospitalization by telephone or in person to the Area Office of the Occupational Safety and Health Administration (OSHA), U.S. Department of Labor, that is nearest to the site of the incident. You may also use the OSHA toll-free central telephone number, 1-800-321-OSHA (1-800-321-6742).

1904.39(b)
Implementation.

1904.39(b)(1)
If the Area Office is closed, may I report the incident by leaving a message on OSHA's answering machine, faxing the area office, or sending an e-mail? No, if you can't talk to a person at the Area Office, you must report the fatality or multiple hospitalization incident using the 800 number.

1904.39(b)(2)
What information do I need to give to OSHA about the incident? You must give OSHA the following information for each fatality or multiple hospitalization incident:

1904.39(b)(2)(i)
The establishment name;

1904.39(b)(2)(ii)
The location of the incident;

1904.39(b)(2)(iii)
The time of the incident;

1904.39(b)(2)(iv)
The number of fatalities or hospitalized employees;

1904.39(b)(2)(v)
The names of any injured employees;

1904.39(b)(2)(vi)
Your contact person and his or her phone number; and

1904.39(b)(2)(vii)
A brief description of the incident.

1904.39(b)(3)
Do I have to report every fatality or multiple hospitalization incident resulting from a motor vehicle accident? No, you do not have to report all of these incidents. If the motor vehicle accident occurs on a public street or highway, and does not occur in a construction work zone, you do not have to report the

29 CFR OSHA 1904 (continued)

incident to OSHA. However, these injuries must be recorded on your OSHA injury and illness records, if you are required to keep such records.

1904.39(b)(4)
Do I have to report a fatality or multiple hospitalization incident that occurs on a commercial or public transportation system? No, you do not have to call OSHA to report a fatality or multiple hospitalization incident if it involves a commercial airplane, train, subway or bus accident. However, these injuries must be recorded on your OSHA injury and illness records, if you are required to keep such records.

1904.39(b)(5)
Do I have to report a fatality caused by a heart attack at work? Yes, your local OSHA Area Office director will decide whether to investigate the incident, depending on the circumstances of the heart attack.

1904.39(b)(6)
Do I have to report a fatality or hospitalization that occurs long after the incident? No, you must only report each fatality or multiple hospitalization incident that occurs within thirty (30) days of an incident.

1904.39(b)(7)
What if I don't learn about an incident right away? If you do not learn of a reportable incident at the time it occurs and the incident would otherwise be reportable under paragraphs (a) and (b) of this section, you must make the report within eight (8) hours of the time the incident is reported to you or to any of your agent(s) or employee(s).

1904.40(a)
Basic requirement. When an authorized government representative asks for the records you keep under Part 1904, you must provide copies of the records within four (4) business hours.

1904.40(b)
Implementation.

1904.40(b)(1)
What government representatives have the right to get copies of my Part 1904 records? The government representatives authorized to receive the records are:

1904.40(b)(1)(i)
A representative of the Secretary of Labor conducting an inspection or investigation under the Act;

1904.40(b)(1)(ii)
A representative of the Secretary of Health and Human Services (including the National Institute for Occupational Safety and Health -- NIOSH) conducting an investigation under section 20(b) of the Act, or

1904.40(b)(1)(iii)
A representative of a State agency responsible for administering a State plan approved under section 18 of the Act.

1904.40(b)(2)
Do I have to produce the records within four (4) hours if my records are kept at a location in a different time zone? OSHA will consider your response to be timely if you give the records to the government representative within four (4) business hours of the request. If you maintain the records at a location in a different time zone, you may use the business hours of the establishment at which the records are located when calculating the deadline.

1904.41(a)
Basic requirement. If you receive OSHA's annual survey form, you must fill it out and send it to OSHA or OSHA's designee, as stated on the survey form. You must report the following information for the year described on the form:

1904.41(a)(1)
the number of workers you employed;

29 CFR OSHA 1904 (continued)

1904.41(a)(2)
the number of hours worked by your employees; and

1904.41(a)(3)
the requested information from the records that you keep under Part 1904.

1904.41(b)
Implementation.

1904.41(b)(1)
Does every employer have to send data to OSHA? *No, each year, OSHA sends injury and illness survey forms to employers in certain industries. In any year, some employers will receive an OSHA survey form and others will not. You do not have to send injury and illness data to OSHA unless you receive a survey form.*

1904.41(b)(2)
How quickly do I need to respond to an OSHA survey form? *You must send the survey reports to OSHA, or OSHA's designee, by mail or other means described in the survey form, within 30 calendar days, or by the date stated in the survey form, whichever is later.*

1904.41(b)(3)
Do I have to respond to an OSHA survey form if I am normally exempt from keeping OSHA injury and illness records? *Yes, even if you are exempt from keeping injury and illness records under § 1904.1 to § 1904.3, OSHA may inform you in writing that it will be collecting injury and illness information from you in the following year. If you receive such a letter, you must keep the injury and illness records required by § 1904.5 to § 1904.15 and make a survey report for the year covered by the survey.*

1904.41(b)(4)
Do I have to answer the OSHA survey form if I am located in a State-Plan State? *Yes, all employers who receive survey forms must respond to the survey, even those in State-Plan States.*

1904.41(b)(5)
Does this section affect OSHA's authority to inspect my workplace? *No, nothing in this section affects OSHA's statutory authority to investigate conditions related to occupational safety and health.*

1904.42(a)
Basic requirement. If you receive a Survey of Occupational Injuries and Illnesses Form from the Bureau of Labor Statistics (BLS), or a BLS designee, you must promptly complete the form and return it following the instructions contained on the survey form.

1904.42(b)
Implementation.

1904.42(b)(1)
Does every employer have to send data to the BLS? *No, each year, the BLS sends injury and illness survey forms to randomly selected employers and uses the information to create the Nation's occupational injury and illness statistics. In any year, some employers will receive a BLS survey form and others will not. You do not have to send injury and illness data to the BLS unless you receive a survey form.*

1904.42(b)(2)
If I get a survey form from the BLS, what do I have to do? *If you receive a Survey of Occupational Injuries and Illnesses Form from the Bureau of Labor Statistics (BLS), or a BLS designee, you must promptly complete the form and return it, following the instructions contained on the survey form.*

1904.42(b)(3)
Do I have to respond to a BLS survey form if I am normally exempt from keeping OSHA injury and illness records? *Yes, even if you are exempt from keeping injury and illness records under § 1904.1 to § 1904.3, the BLS may inform you in writing that it will be collecting injury and illness information from you in the coming year. If you receive such a letter, you must keep the injury and illness records required by § 1904.5 to § 1904.15 and make a survey report for the year covered by the survey.*

29 CFR OSHA 1904 (continued)

1904.42(b)(4)

Do I have to answer the BLS survey form if I am located in a State-Plan State? *Yes, all employers who receive a survey form must respond to the survey, even those in State-Plan States.*

1904.44

You must save your copies of the OSHA 200 and 101 forms for five years following the year to which they relate ar continue to provide access to the data as though these forms were the OSHA 300 and 301 forms. You are not requ to update your old 200 and 101 forms.

1904.45

The following sections each contain a collection of information requirement which has been approved by the Office of Management and Budget under the control number listed

29 CFR citation	OMB Control No.
1904.4-35	1218-0176
1904.39-41	1218-0176
1904.42	1220-0045
1904.43-44	1218-0176

1904.46

Definitions

The Act. The Act means the Occupational Safety and Health Act of 1970 (29 U.S.C. 651 et seq.). The definitions contained in section 3 of the Act (29 U.S.C. 652) and related interpretations apply to such terms when used in this Part 1904.

Establishment. An establishment is a single physical location where business is conducted or where services or industrial operations are performed. For activities where employees do not work at a single physical location, such as construction; transportation; communications, electric, gas and sanitary services; and similar operations, the establishment is represented by main or branch offices, terminals, stations, etc. that either supervise such activities or are the base from which personnel carry out these activities.

1904.46(1)

Can one business location include two or more establishments? Normally, one business location has only one establishment. Under limited conditions, the employer may consider two or more separate businesses that share a single location to be separate establishments. An employer may divide one location into two or more establishments only when:

1904.46(1)(i)

Each of the establishments represents a distinctly separate business;

1904.46(1)(ii)

Each business is engaged in a different economic activity;

1904.46(1)(iii)

No one industry description in the Standard Industrial Classification Manual (1987) applies to the joint activities of the establishments; and

1904.46(1)(iv)

Separate reports are routinely prepared for each establishment on the number of employees, their wages and salaries, sales or receipts, and other business information. For example, if an employer operates a construction company at the same location as a lumber yard, the employer may consider each business to be a separate establishment.

1904.46(2)

Can an establishment include more than one physical location? Yes, but only under certain conditions. An employer may combine two or more physical locations into a single establishment only when:

29 CFR OSHA 1904 (continued)

1904.46(2)(i)
The employer operates the locations as a single business operation under common management;

1904.46(2)(ii)
The locations are all located in close proximity to each other; and

1904.46(2)(iii)
The employer keeps one set of business records for the locations, such as records on the number of employees, their wages and salaries, sales or receipts, and other kinds of business information. For example, one manufacturing establishment might include the main plant, a warehouse a few blocks away, and an administrative services building across the street.

1904.46(3)
If an employee telecommutes from home, is his or her home considered a separate establishment?
No, for employees who telecommute from home, the employee's home is not a business establishment and a separate 300 Log is not required. Employees who telecommute must be linked to one of your establishments under § 1904.30(b)(3).

Injury or illness. An injury or illness is an abnormal condition or disorder. Injuries include cases such as, but not limited to, a cut, fracture, sprain, or amputation. Illnesses include both acute and chronic illnesses, such as, but not limited to, a skin disease, respiratory disorder, or poisoning. (Note: Injuries and illnesses are recordable only if they are new, work-related cases that meet one or more of the Part 1904 recording criteria.)

Physician or Other Licensed Health Care Professional. A physician or other licensed health care professional is an individual whose legally permitted scope of practice (i.e., license, registration, or certification) allows him or her to independently perform, or be delegated the responsibility to perform, the activities described by this regulation.

You. "You" means an employer as defined in Section 3 of the Occupational Safety and Health Act of 1970 (29 U.S.C. 652).

GLOSSARY

A

accelerated depreciation Depreciation method in which a greater amount of depreciation or expense is taken in the early years and less in the later years.

accounts payable Money owed by the business.

accounts receivable Money owed to the business.

accrual method Accounting method that records income and expenses when they are earned or incurred, even though no payment is made.

accumulated depreciation The total amount of depreciation accumulated over several years and charged against appropriate fixed assets.

acid-test ratio Similar to the current ratio, but is a more severe test for businesses that carry a large amount of inventory.

action level The limit of employee exposure, without regard to the use of respirators, to an airborne concentration of lead of 30 micrograms per cubic meter of air (30 μg/m^3) calculated as an 8-hour time-weighted average (TWA).

addenda Changes, additions, or clarifications developed after the project has been released for bid.

agent authority An agent representing an LLC who signs contracts for the LLC.

agent of the principal The person signing for the company; must be identified as acting as an agent of the company (agent of the principal) and must be acting solely in the interests of the company.

allowances Funds for unique items or skilled work in the project.

Americans with Disabilities Act (ADA) Prohibits job discrimination based on disability. The Americans with Disabilities Act applies to all employers with 15 or more employees.

Articles of Incorporation The corporate bylaws that control what a corporation does, how it is organized, and its financial activities.

asbestos A fibrous mineral with thin fibers.

asset Anything of value belonging to the business. Assets include accounts receivable, cash, land, prepaid bills, equipment, buildings, furniture, and fixtures.

asset management ratio A measure of how well a company is managing its assets.

at-will employment When an employee is hired for an indefinite period of time without an employment contract.

automobile (vehicle) insurance Insurance that covers cars, trucks, trailers, or other self-propelled or towed vehicles used for the business.

average collection period (ACP) An indication of the average number of days required to collect receivables. It is a measure of the company's ability to collect debts (receivables).

B

balance sheet Form that shows the financial condition of the company on a given day.

bid An offer to furnish labor, equipment, and materials in a specified manner and time and for a certain price.

bid bond A guarantee that the successful bidder will enter into a project contract for the agreed-upon price.

bid rigging When a contractor conspires with other bidders to ensure the award of a bid, with the result of a certain bid.

bid sheet A form that must be used to submit a formal bid proposal.

bid shopping Revealing a subcontractor's bid information to a competitor.

board of directors Act as the representatives of the corporation in overseeing the operation of the corporation.

bond A surety that guarantees completion of a project or recovery of a loss.

bond rating The measure of risk of a bond going into default.

builder's risk insurance Insurance that protects the contractor against any loss or damage to the project structure and materials or equipment purchased for the project while it is under construction.

burglary insurance Insurance against burglary, robbery, and theft by persons other than employees.

business plan An organized summary of a business.

C

capacity The bonding agency's statement of the maximum amount of bonds they will carry for the contractor.

cash budget A comparison of expected receipts and planned expenses, disregarding all non-cash assets. A cash budget is intended to ensure that there is enough money for payroll, accounts payable, and other short-term obligations.

cash discount A discount in the purchase price of supplies or a deduction off the invoice in exchange for prompt payment.

cash flow Money that has been received and spent. Cash flow is based on cash receipts minus cash disbursements from a given operation over a given period.

cash flow schedule Reflects the costs of each portion of the project and the anticipated revenues from each progress payment.

cash flow statement Statement that shows revenue receipts and expenses for a particular reporting period.

cash method Accounting method that records transactions only when money exchanges hands, that is, when a check is written or a deposit is made.

Circular E An IRS publication that explains the federal tax responsibilities of an employer.

Civil Rights Act of 1964 Act that prohibits employment discrimination based on race, color, religion, sex, or national origin.

claim   A written statement of disagreement with the purpose of putting a disagreement in writing.

completed contract method   Accounting method that recognizes profit only when the job is completed.

completion-capitalized cost method   Accounting method in which a certain percentage of the project cost and revenue is identified and income and expenses are calculated by that percentage in the current year. The balance is deferred until the project is completed in the next year.

comprehensive general liability (CGL)   A blanket insurance policy that provides broad coverage for personal injuries or property damage caused to others who are not employed by the contractor.

Consolidated Omnibus Reconciliation Act (COBRA)   Act that provides for continuing health care benefits for individuals who have lost coverage because of termination of employment or death or divorce of a spouse who had the coverage.

contingency   A percentage added to an estimate to cover any unexpected costs.

contract   A binding agreement between two or more persons.

contract bond (performance bond)   A guarantee that the successful bidder will complete the project in accordance with the plans and specifications and in a timely manner.

contractual employment   A contract is signed for a specified period and the employment can be terminated only for cause.

Contract Work Hours and Safety Standards Act   Act that applies to contractors or subcontractors who have service or construction contracts with the federal government for over $100,000.

corporation   A legally unique entity, separate from its partners (called shareholders). The main benefit to the shareholders is limited liability.

cost control   Monitoring costs as the project progresses.

cost of goods sold   The sum of the costs of materials sold to a customer.

cost plus contract   A contract that charges for materials plus a fee for the contractor.

cost plus fee contract   A contract in which a fixed dollar amount is paid to the contractor for his or her services.

cost plus percentage contract   A contract similar to a cost plus fee contract, except that the fee is a percentage of the costs.

critical task   A task that must be completed before another is started.

critical task analysis   The process of looking at an entire project, identifying each task, and determining how long each task will take.

current asset   Cash or any asset that can be converted to cash within one year or one operating cycle. Such assets may include accounts receivable, inventory, and prepaid expenses.

current liability   Any money owed by the contracting company that must be paid within one year. Current liabilities may include loan payments due, accounts payable, wages, and taxes.

current ratio   A measure of the ability of a company to pay bills promptly.

D

daily log   Log completed every day to create a complete record of everything that happens at the construction site.

Davis-Bacon Act   Act that requires that prevailing wage rates and fringe benefits be paid to all employees involved with federal construction projects valued in excess of $2,000.

debt to equity ratio   A measure of the investment of creditors and contractors.

depreciation   A method of spreading out the cost of equipment or property (asset) over its life span rather than entering the full cost in the first year.

design/build contract   A contract in which a prime (or general) contractor takes responsibility for the architectural, engineering, bidding, contracting, construction (building) inspection, and final approval of the project.

detailed survey estimate   Estimate that is based on a take-off from the drawings and specifications and applies unit costs to all required materials and labor.

direct costs   Costs that relate to the actual productive activities of the business.

direct labor cost   The basic hourly rate for building, installing, or modifying a work item (unit).

director's and officer's (D&O) liability insurance   A type of professional liability insurance that protects the company's senior management for reasonable, proper, and legal acts that they perform in carrying out their role as officers of the company.

disbursements journal   A journal that tracks how monies are paid out and in what amounts.

doing business as (DBA)   A term used to describe a company that uses a name other than the owner's birth name.

drawings   Illustrations that detail the architectural, electrical, mechanical, and plumbing portions of the project.

duration   1. The legal life or existence of the company. 2. The time required to complete each task expressed in hours, shifts, or days.

E

emergency action plan   A plan that details what to do in case of an emergency, such as a fire, and what the responsibilities of employees and the employer are, for example, who is responsible for calling 911.

Employee Polygraph Protection Act   Act that prohibits most private employers from using any type of lie detector test either for pre-employment screening of job applicants or for testing current employees during the course of employment.

Employee Retirement Income Security Act (ERISA)   Act that regulates the minimum standards for employers who maintain pension plans; however, ERISA does not require that employers have pension plans.

Equal Pay Act   Act that requires that men and women be paid equal pay for equal work in an establishment.

equipment costs   All expenses associated with any equipment used for the job.

equipment leasing   Rental of equipment using long-term contracts lasting one year or more.

equipment rental   Rental of equipment to meet short-term equipment needs.

estimate   A projection of job costs.

ethics   Practicing a standard of honesty in all business dealings.

executive summary   A description of the business.

exempt employees   Employees, administrators, and professionals who are exempt from overtime pay requirements and minimum wage provisions because they are salaried employees.

expediter   Orders materials, sets delivery schedules, monitors the ordering process, and reports the delivery status to the site superintendent.

F

Fair Labor Standards Act (FLSA)   Act that sets minimum wage and overtime requirements, including child labor standards.

Family and Medical Leave Act (FMLA)   Act that entitles eligible employees to take up to 12 weeks of unpaid job-protected leave each year, with maintenance of group health insurance, for the birth and care of a child, for the placement of a child for adoption or foster care, for the care of a child, spouse, or parent with a serious health condition, or for the employee's serious health condition.

fast track contract   A contract that provides for starting construction before all the plans and drawings are complete.

federal unemployment tax (FUTA)   Taxes that are paid by the employer and not deducted from the employee's paycheck. Federal unemployment tax is 6.2 percent of the first $7,000 earned by each employee during the year.

financials   An outline of the funds that are needed to achieve the goals established in the business plan.

first aid   Any one-time treatment and any follow-up visit for the purpose of observation for minor scratches, cuts, burns, splinters, and so forth, which do not ordinarily require medical care.

fixed asset   Property owned by the business that will not be converted to cash within one year. Fixed assets include land, buildings, equipment, furniture, and fixtures.

float time   Excess time on a project that results when a task is completed in less than the scheduled time.

foreman   Provides support to the site superintendent.

formal bid   A statement that the contractor agrees to build the project in accordance with the bid documents for the stated price.

Form W-2   *Wage and Tax Statement*; the only document used to transmit information on employees' Social Security and Medicare wages for the year.

Form W-3   A summary of all W-2s issued to employees.

Form W-4   *Employee's Withholding Allowance Certificate*; tells the employer how many withholding allowances to use when deducting federal income tax from a newly hired employee's pay.

G

general and administrative costs   Costs incurred in the daily operation of a business.

general conditions   Outline the roles of the owner, contractor, architect, and engineer.

general journal   A record of non-cash transactions, such as depreciation of assets and corrections.

general ledger   A form that contains a monthly summary of information by numerical number, by entering the data from the journals.

general overhead   Represents all the operating costs of the company that are not related to any project.

general partnership   Business formed by two or more persons. Partners may share equally in the business or they may invest different amounts, have different responsibilities, and share different percentages of the profits.

goals   What the company hopes to achieve.

gross profit   The amount remaining after deducting direct and indirect costs from revenues.

H

hours worked   All time an employee must be on duty or at the place of business.

I

immaterial breach   Although technically a violation of the contract, a minor or inconsequential violation.

Immigration and Nationality Act   Act that requires every employer to verify the nationality and employability of every candidate for employment.

income statement   Form that shows the financial position of a company for the year.

indemnification clause   A contractual obligation in which one person agrees to secure another person in cases of loss or damage from certain liabilities.

independent contractor (IC)   A person who does work for the company but is not considered an employee. The company is not required to pay the IC's payroll taxes and benefits.

indirect costs   Costs that are not related to any specific job, such as the cost of company vehicles and their operation.

indirect labor costs   Unemployment insurance, workers' compensation insurance, health insurance, and so on; costs that are not a part of hourly wages.

installation floater policy   An insurance policy purchased to protect against loss or damage to equipment or goods, whether owned or rented at the building site.

inventory control   The art of keeping inventory costs as low as possible.

invitation to bid   A document that describes the proposed project and states the manner in which the bid must be prepared.

J

job cost analysis   Facilitates financial management of existing projects and provides information necessary for preparing bids for future projects.

job costs   All costs related to any single project.

joint entirety   Gives a spouse ownership in a portion of the property so it can not be considered a company asset.

joint venture   A partnership of two or more individual companies joining together to work on a particular project.

journal   A blank book with lines and columns in which all the source documents are recorded by type.

K

key man insurance   A type of life insurance that provides monetary assistance to the company in the event of the death of essential staff.

L

lead   A lustrous metal that is very soft, highly malleable, ductile, and a poor conductor of electricity.

lead pre-renovation education rule   Rule that requires distribution of the EPA pamphlet *Protect Your Family from Lead in Your Home* before starting renovation work.

liability   Any claim against the business's assets. Liabilities can be short-term (current) or long-term.

lien   A claim on the property of another as security against the payment of a just debt.

limited liability company (LLC)   Neither a strict partnership nor a corporation. An LLC has the same structure as a partnership if the company is set up without a manager; otherwise it is like a corporation with the partners as shareholders.

limited partnership   A partnership in which at least one person is considered a general partner and has the responsibility and liability for the day-to-day operation and financial decisions.

liquidity ratio   A measure of the ability of a company to pay its current liabilities.

long-term liability   Any debt or obligation normally due over a period longer than one year that is not a current liability.

lost workdays   The number of days, including the day of injury or illness during which the employee would have worked but could not, lost because of occupational injury or illness.

lump sum contract   A contract that reflects the contractor's guarantee to the owner that the project will be completed for a fixed (contract) price.

M

market analysis   An evaluation of market research that describes how the company is going to enter the market through identified goals.

marketing   Identifying customers and attracting them to the company's products and services.

material breach   A significant violation of the contract that gives the other party a right to stop further performance and sue for damages.

material costs   The total of all costs for materials used by the contractor, including the price of the materials, the cost of delivery, and any storage charges.

medical treatment   Treatment administered by a physician or by registered professional personnel under the standing orders of a physician.

mission   The foundation on which the business is built and the company's primary reason for existing.

mission statement   Identifies what the company is about.

monitoring   The process of overseeing the work and overcoming any obstacles to timely completion.

N

negotiation   When both parties discuss or bargain to reach an agreement.

net income   The amount resulting after taxes are deducted from net income before taxes.

net income before taxes (NIBT)   The amount left after subtracting general and administrative costs from gross profit. NIBT is shown on the bottom of the income statement.

net worth   The value of all assets after deducting all liabilities.

nonexempt employees   Employees who are typically paid hourly.

O

overhead costs   Expenses that are not related to any project. These include building rent, utilities, office equipment, and salaries for management, supervisors, and full-time staff.

overtime pay   Wages due an employee for hours over 40 worked in a workweek.

owner's representative   Representative that acts on the owner's behalf when any questions or issues arise about the project.

P

partnership   A for-profit business operated by two or more people.

pass-through taxation   When no tax is assessed on the profits of the company but only on the amount of income distributed to the partners.

payroll journal   A logbook that tracks employee wages and provides the records necessary for state and federal reports.

percentage of completion   Accounting method that recognizes and records expenses and revenues as the project progresses.

permissible exposure limit   The limit to the concentration of lead that an employee is exposed to, averaged over an 8-hour period.

personal representative   A person that an employee has designated in writing as representing the employee's interests.

plans (blueprints)   The drawings that detail the job.

prepaid expenses   An expense that is paid before the material is actually used.

professional liability insurance   Insurance that covers errors or negligence in performing the normal duties of a contractor.

profit (markup)   Represents the money left over after all expenses are paid.

project documents   The plans and specifications prepared for the owner by an architect and/or engineer.

project manager   Person responsible for everything relating to the project.

project overhead   The costs, except labor, associated with a particular project.

project planning   The process of carefully looking at a project to determine the time sequence of the work schedule and the relationship of job tasks to each other.

project scheduling   The process of designating where each task or work unit fits into the project plan and when it will be completed.

property insurance   Insurance that covers fire, smoke, theft, vandalism, and so on, and provides coverage on structures and their contents.

punch list   A list of deficiencies on a project, usually minor, that need to be corrected.

purchased equipment   Equipment bought as a long-term investment.

R

registered agent   The person designated by the company and named on papers filed with a state agency as acting as a public contact.

Resource Conservation and Recovery Act (RCRA) of 1976 Act intended to protect people and the environment from potential hazards due to waste disposal, and to conserve energy and natural resources.

retainage A certain percentage of the payment retained by the customer to ensure satisfactory completion of the project.

return on investment (ROI) Earnings of an investment determined by net income divided by the investment or assets; reported as a percentage.

revenue The operating income or income due to the normal activities of the business.

risk management Identifying potential risks and taking action to protect the contracting company from those risks.

S

sales and cash receipts journal A record of all income.

Service Contract Act Act that requires payment of prevailing wage rates and fringe benefits; however, this act refers specifically to contracts over $2,500 that will be using service personnel to provide services to the federal government and does not cover construction of buildings.

shop drawings Drawings prepared to clarify the architect's drawings and specifications.

site superintendent Person responsible for all the activities at the job site.

soil erosion The removal of material from a site by water, wind, or gravity.

sole proprietorship A business that is owned solely by the proprietor with no partners in the business.

source documents All documents relating to income or expenses. Source documents may include check stubs, invoices received and sent, cash receipts, and time cards.

specifications Describe the materials to be used and the quality of the construction required.

standard form of agreement A summary of all the documents related to the contract agreement that confirms the scope of the project, assigns responsibility for the project, lists bonding and insurance requirements, and sets the price and payment details.

statutory bond A bond, usually required for public projects, that has been required by law.

straight-line depreciation The cost of the asset is divided by a certain number of years and each year this cost is charged as an expense.

strategies How a goal is to be achieved.

subchapter S corporation A business form for small businesses with less than 75 shareholders and modest revenues. It has the limited liability of a corporation while avoiding the double taxation of profits characteristic of a standard corporation.

supplementary conditions Additions or modifications to the "boilerplate" general conditions that apply to the specific project.

surety bond A legal document under which one party agrees to answer to another party for the debt, default, or failure to perform for a third party.

T

taxable income Money received for work that is taxable.

time cards Form that records hours worked.

time contingency A time buffer incorporated into the schedule to provide allowances for unexpected delays.

timetable When a goal is to be achieved.

total asset utilization (TAU) Asset utilization method that measures how well a company uses or turns over its assets.

turnkey contract A contract that gives the prime contractor responsibility for developing the entire project.

U

underground utility A public service or utility that is buried below ground to prevent damage to the utility.

unemployment insurance Insurance, usually paid for by an employer, that is offered for individuals who have lost their job for reasons other than poor performance.

unit price contract A contract in which the job is priced by each unit that is required for the project.

unit price method Relies on job costs from previous projects, with labor, materials, and overhead for similar items or subassemblies combined into unit costs for those items.

V

value engineering A term applied to a contractor discovering and disclosing to the owner ways to save money on a project.

W

wage garnishment The act of withholding money from an employee's paycheck when required by a court order.

Walsh-Healey Public Contracts Act Act that requires payment of minimum wage rates and overtime pay on contracts in excess of $10,000 that provide materials, supplies, or equipment to the federal government.

wetlands Generally include swamps, marshes, bogs, and similar areas.

workers' compensation insurance Insurance, usually paid for by an employer, that offers income to employees who have become injured through an on-the-job accident or illness.

working capital Cash or equivalent assets available to pay bills.

workweek A period of 168 hours during 7 consecutive 24-hour periods. It can begin on any day of the week and at any hour of the day.

Z

zero profit method Accounting method used when the project is such that the profit is difficult to estimate, so it is determined to be zero until such time that the project has progressed sufficiently to make a determination.

INDEX

A

Accelerated completion, 50
Accelerated depreciation, 90, 93
Acceptance, 42
Access to records, 127
Accounting
    methods, 95–98
    terms, 90–92
Accounts payable, 90
Accounts receivable, 90
Accrual method, 96–97
Accumulated depreciation, 90
Acid-test ratio, 103
ACP. *See* Average collection period
Activity ratio, 104
ADA. *See* Americans with Disabilities Act
Addenda, 36, 46
Adjustment factors, 129
Aesthetic changes, 50
Agent authority, 5
Agent of the principal, 8
Allowances, 35
Americans with Disabilities Act (ADA),
    79–80
Architect's estimate, 37
Articles of incorporation, 6
Asbestos, 133–34
    exposure, 119–21
Asset management ratio, 103
Assets, 90, 99
At-will employment, 11
Automobile insurance, 62
Average collection period (ACP), 103–4

B

Bad faith, 63
Balance sheet, 99, 100
Banking, 10
Bid, 25, 41
    bond, 64
    calculation, 39
    rigging, 23, 40
    sample, 38–40
    shopping, 23
Bidding process, 25–28
Bid sheet, 25
CPM, 69–70
Blueprints, 29
Board of directors, 6–7
Bond rating, 64–65
Bonds, 63–65
Brand X allowance, 50
Breach of contract, 56
Builder's risk insurance, 62
Burglary insurance, 62
Business income taxes, 112–14
Business organization
    decision making, 9–11
    types of, 1–9
Business plan, 17, 19

C

Capability, 27
Capacity, 65
Cash budget, 90
Cash discount, 90
Cash flow, 90
Cash flow schedule, 69
Cash flow statement, 102
    partial, 71
Cash method, 96
Caution labels, 120
Certificate of occupancy (CO), 52
Certificate of substantial completion, 52
CGL. *See* Comprehensive general liability
Change orders, 50
Change of ownership, 127
Change rooms, 120
Child labor laws, 84
Circular E, 112
Civil Rights Act of 1964, 80
Claims, 56, 63
Cleanup, 51
CO. *See* Certificate of occupancy
COBRA. *See* Consolidated Omnibus Rec-
    onciliation Act
Code
    compliance, 51
    violations, 24
Competent parties, 42
Competitive bidding, 39–40
Complaints, 130
Completed contract method, 90, 97
Completion-capitalized cost method, 90, 98
Components estimating, 36–37
Comprehensive general liability (CGL), 60–61
Consideration, 42
Consolidated Omnibus Reconciliation Act
    (COBRA), 86–87
Construction equipment, 76–77
Construction Specifications Institute (CSI),
    28, 36
MasterFormat Divisions, 29, 30–32
Consumer Product Safety Commission, 121
Consumer Protection Act, 87
Contingency, 35
Contract, 41, 58
    accounting, 97–98
    additional categories, 47–48
    assignment, 57
    bond, 64
    construction types, 52–53
    federal government, 85–86
    legal guidelines, 42
    miscellaneous considerations, 48–52
    payments, 54–55
    rights, responsibilities, 46–47
    signing, 43–44
    standard form of agreement, 42–43
    standard forms, 44
    termination, 57
    validity, 42–44, 46
Contractor
    responsibilities, 47
    rights, 47
Contract Work Hours and Safety Standards
    Act, 86
Contractual employment, 11
Corporate debts, 7
Corporations, 5–8, 12, 114
Cost control, 76
Cost determination, 27
Cost plus contract, 53
Cost plus fee contract, 53
Cost plus percentage contract, 53
Counsel, right to, 7
CPM. *See* Critical path method
Critical path, 70
Critical path method (CPM), 68–70, 72
Critical task analysis, 68
CSI. *See* Construction Specifications Institute
Cubic-foot estimate, 37
Current asset, 90
Current liability, 91
Current ratio, 103
Customer
    interests, 15
    relations, 22–23

D

D&O liability insurance. *See* Director's and
    officer's liability insurance
Daily log, 76
Daily reports, 77
Davis-Bacon Act, 85
DBA. *See* Doing business as
Debt to equity ratio, 104
Debt management ratios, 104
Decision making, 28
Delays, 49–50
Depreciation, 91, 93
Design/build contract, 48
Detailed survey estimate, 36
Direct cost estimate, 38
Direct costs, 35, 91, 99
Direct labor cost, 33
Director's and officer's (D&O) liability
    insurance, 61
Disbursements journal, 94
Doing business as (DBA), 1, 2, 10
Double jeopardy, 7
Drawings, 29, 46
Due process, 7
Duration, 2, 7, 70

E

E&S. *See* Erosion and sediment control
EFTPS. *See* Electronic Federal Tax Payment
    System
EIN. *See* Employer identification number

Electronic Federal Tax Payment System (EFTPS), 111
Emergency action plan, 129–30
Employee
    benefits, 86–87
    not in fixed establishments, 129
Employee Polygraph Protection Act, 79, 80
Employee Retirement Income Security Act (ERISA), 86
Employees, 11, 108
Employer identification number (EIN), 5, 107, 109, 114
Employment law Web sites, 88
Endorsements, 61
Environmental Protection Agency (EPA), 134–36
EPA. *See* Environmental Protection Agency
Equal employment opportunity, 79
Equal Employment Opportunity Commission, 79–80
Equal Pay Act, 80
Equal protection, 7
Equipment
    costs, 33
    floater policy, 62
    leasing, 77
    rental, 77
Equipment rooms, 120
ERISA. *See* Employee Retirement Income Security Act
Erosion and sediment (E&S) control, 135
Estimate, 25
    sample, 38–40
Estimating, 28–29, 33–36
    methods, 36–37
Ethics, 23–24
Executive summary, 17
Exempt employees, 83
Expediter, 74
Expenses worksheet, 20
Eye protection, 118

F

Face protection, 118
Fair Labor Standards Act (FLSA), 80, 82–85
Falsification of report, 127
Family and Medical Leave Act (FMLA), 86
Fast track contract, 48
Fatality reporting, 123
Federal government contract, 85–86
Federal Tax Deposit Form 8109, 109
Federal tax late payment penalties, 112
Federal Unemployment Tax (FUTA), 109, 110–12
Fees, 51
FICA. *See* Social Security
Field orders, 50
FIFO, 96
Fifth Amendment, 7
Final payment, 54–55
Financial ratios, 103–5
Financials, 19, 20–21
Financial statements, 98–102
First aid, 122
Fixed asset, 91
Fixed price contract, 53
Float time, 72
Flowdown clause, 51–52

FLSA. *See* Fair Labor Standards Act
FMLA. *See* Family and Medical Leave Act
FOB. *See* Free on board
Foreman, 74
Form 300, *Log of Work-Related Injuries and Illnesses*, 123, 124, 125
Form 301, *Injury and Illness Incident Report*, 123, 126
Form 940, *Employer's Federal Unemployment Tax Return*, 111
Form 941, *Employer's Quarterly Federal Tax Return*, 110, 112
Form 1099, *Miscellaneous Income*, 108
Form 1120, 114
Form 1120-S, 114
Form 8109, *Federal Tax Deposit Coupon*, 111
Form 8804, *Annual Return for Partnership Withholding Tax*, 113
Form 8805, *Foreign Partner's Information Statement of Withholding Tax*, 113
Form 8813, *Partnership Withholding Tax Payment Voucher*, 113
Form W-2, *Wage and Tax Statement*, 110
Form W-3, 110
Form W-4, *Employee's Withholding Allowance Certificate*, 110
Formal bid, 37–38
Fourteenth Amendment, 7
Free on board (FOB), 76
Fringe benefits, 7
FUTA. *See* Federal Unemployment Tax

G

G&A costs. *See* General and administrative costs
Gantt chart, 72, 73
General and administrative (G&A) costs, 91, 99
General conditions, 29, 44
General journal, 94
General ledger, 95
General overhead, 34, 35
General partnership, 3–4
Goals, 19
Gross profit, 91, 99
Guidance for Controlling Asbestos-Containing Materials in Buildings, 134

H

Hazardous materials, 135
Head protection, 117–18
Hearing protection, 118
Hiring, 84–85
Hold harmless clause, 48–49
Hygiene facilities, practices, 120–21

I

IC. *See* Independent contractor
Immaterial breach, 56
Immigration and Nationality Act, 79, 80
    acceptable documents list, 81
Income statement, 99, 101–2
Income worksheet, 21
Indemnification clause, 48–49
Independent contractor (IC), 107–8
Indirect costs, 91, 99
Indirect labor cost, 33

Injury decision-making tree, 123, 127
Inspections, 74–75
Installation floater policy, 62
Insurance policy, 66
    buying, 62–63
    types, 60–63
Internal Revenue Service (IRS), 109
    Circular E, 112
    Form 1065, 113
    Form 1120, 7, 114
    Web site, 2
Inventory control, 77
Invitation to bid, 25–26
IRS. *See* Internal Revenue Service

J

Job cost analysis, 105–6
Job costs, 29, 33–34, 91
Job logic, 68
Job Service, 87
Job site inspection, 28
Joint venture, 9
Journal, 94

K–L

Key man insurance, 62
Labor costs, 29, 33
Labor Department, 80, 83–85, 87
Lead, 134–35
    exposure, 121–22
    pre-renovation education rule, 134–35
Leasing assets, 7–8
Liabilities, 2, 91, 99
Lien bond, 64
Liens, 56–57
LIFO, 96
Limited liability company (LLC), 4–5, 6, 12
Limited partnership, 4
Liquidity ratios, 103
LLC. *See* Limited liability company
Location, 27
Long-term liability, 91
Loss prevention, 59–60
Lost workdays, 122
Lump sum contract, 53
Lunchroom facilities, 120–21

M

Management, 22–23
Market
    analysis, 19
    research, 13–14, 17
Marketing, 19, 22
Markup, 35–36
Material breach, 56
Material costs, 33, 34
Material safety data sheet (MSDS), 135
Medical exams, 121
Medical treatment, 122
Medicare, 109, 113
    taxes, 2
Miller Act, 64, 65–66
Mission statement, 17
Modifications, 46
Monitoring, 74–77
MSDS. *See* Material safety data sheet
Multiple hospitalizations reporting, 123

N

Negotiation, 41
Net income, 91, 102
Net income before taxes (NIBT), 91, 102
Net worth, 92
NIBT. *See* Net income before taxes
Nonexempt employees, 83
Notice to Employees Working on Government Contracts, 86

O

Occupational injury and illness log, 123, 124, 125
Occupational Safety and Health Administration (OSHA), 51, 83, 117
   asbestos exposure, 119–21
   hazardous materials, 135
   lead exposure, 121–22
   penalties, 128–30
   personal protective equipment, 117–19
   poster, 131
   record keeping, 122–23, 127–28
Occupational Safety and Health Review Commission, 129
Offer, 41, 42, 45
On-site visit, 26
OSHA. *See* Occupational Safety and Health Administration
Other income/expenses, 102
Overhead, 92
   costs, 34–36
Overtime pay, 83
Owner
   responsibilities, 47
   rights, 46–47
Owner's representative, 74

P

Partial cash flow statement, 71
Partnering, 48
Partnerships, 2–5, 113
Pass-through taxation, 4–5
Payment bond, 64
Payroll
   journal, 94
   taxes, 108–12
Peachtree Accounting, 89
PEL. *See* Permissible exposure limit
Percentage of completion method, 92, 97, 98
Performance bond, 64
Permissible exposure limit (PEL), 119
Permits, 51
Personal protective equipment (PPE), 117–19
Personal representative, 127
Phased contract, 48
Planning, 67–70, 72
Plans, 29
Poor construction practices, 24
Posting, 130
PPE. *See* Personal protective equipment
Pre-bid meeting, 26
Pre-employment actions, 84
Pre-solicitation notices, 26
Prepared expenses, 92
Pricing, 17, 18
Prime contractor, 48, 57
Products determination, 16
Professional liability insurance, 61

Profit, 35–36
Progress payments, 54, 55
Project
   closeout, 78
   documents, 29
   overhead, 34–35
   planning, 67–68
   scheduling, 70, 72
   supervision, 72–78
Project manager, 72–73
Project superintendent, 74
Property insurance, 62
Protect Your Family from Lead in Your Home, 134
Protective clothing, 119, 120, 122
Public projects, 26
Publication requirement, 5
Punch-list, 54, 75
Purchased equipment, 77

Q

Quality control, 74–75
Quantity takeoff, 28
QuickBooks, 89
Quick ratio, 103

R

RCRA. *See* Resource Conservation and Recovery Act of 1976
Record keeping, 84–85, 93–95, 114, 120
Record retention, 128
Registered agent, 8
Resource Conservation and Recovery Act of 1976 (RCRA), 135
Respirators, 119, 121
Retainage, 54, 55, 92
Return on investment (ROI), 104–5
Revenue, 92, 99
Risk management, 59
ROI. *See* Return on investment

S

Safety nets, 118
Sales and cash receipts journal, 94
Sales tax, 11
Sales and use taxes, 114
Schedule, 27
   adjustments, 76
   major activity, 70
Schedule C, 113
Scheduling, 35, 67–70, 72
Scope of work, 26
Section 1446 withholding tax, 113
Self-incrimination, 7
Service Contract Act, 85–86
Services determination, 16
Shareholder liability, 7
Shop drawings, 75
Signature, 43–44
Site access, 51
Site conditions, 50–51
Site superintendent, 74
Site visit, 27–28
Sixth Amendment, 7
Skilled labor, 35
Social Security (FICA), 109, 113
   benefits, 2
Soil erosion, 135

Sole proprietorships, 1–2, 3, 12, 113
Source documents, 92, 93–94
Special conditions, 44
Specifications, 29, 46
Square-foot estimate, 37
Standard form of agreement, 42–43
State unemployment tax, 109
Statutory bond, 64
Stockholders' equity, 99
Straight-line depreciation, 92, 93
Subchapter S corporation, 9, 114
Subcontractor bids, 40
Subcontractors, 33, 51–52
Subject matter, 42
Supplementary conditions, 29, 44
Surety bond, 44
Surety companies, 64

T

TAA. *See* Trade Adjustment Assistance
TAU. *See* Total asset utilization
Taxable income, 112–13
Taxation
   corporation, 7
   sole proprietorship, 2
Tax deductions, 11
Taxes, depositing, 109
Tax law information Web sites, 113
Time cards, 77
Time contingencies, 72
Time extensions, 49
Time schedules, 49
Timetables, 19
Time-weighted average (TWA), 119–20
Total asset utilization (TAU), 103, 104
Trade Adjustment Assistance (TAA), 86, 87
Turnkey contract, 48
TWA. *See* Time-weighted average

U

Underground utilities, 135–36
Unemployment insurance, 87
U.S. Government Small Business Administration Web site, 19
Unit price contract, 53
Unit-price estimate, 36–37

V–Z

Value engineering, 52
Vehicle insurance, 62
Wage garnishment, 87
Wages, 80, 82–84
Walsh-Healey Public Contracts Act, 85
Warranties, 52
Waste disposal, 135
Web site, 22
Wetlands, 136
Workers compensation insurance, 87
Work hours, 80, 82–84
Working capital, 92
Work records, 75
Youth employment, 84
Zero profit method, 92, 97